Constituting Democracy
*Law, Globalism and South Africa's Political Reconstruction*
Heinz Klug

The New World Trade Organization Agreements
*Globalizing Law through Services and Intellectual Property*
Christopher Arup

The Ritual of Rights in Japan
*Law, Society, and Health Policy*
Eric A. Feldman

The Invention of the Passport
*Surveillance, Citizenship and the State*
John Torpey

Governing Morals
*A Social History of Moral Regulation*
Alan Hunt

The Colonies of Law
*Colonialism, Zionism and Law in Early Mandate Palestine*
Ronen Shamir

Law and Nature
David Delaney

Social Citizenship and Workfare in the United States and Western Europe
*The Paradox of Inclusion*
Joel F. Handler

Law, Anthropology and the Constitution of the Social
*Making Persons and Things*
Edited by Alain Pottage and Martha Mundy

Judicial Review and Bureaucratic Impact
*International and Interdisciplinary Perspectives*
Edited by Marc Hertogh and Simon Halliday

Immigrants at the Margins
*Law, Race, and Exclusion in Southern Europe*
Kitty Calavita

Lawyers and Regulation
*The Politics of the Administrative Process*
Patrick Schmidt

Law and Globalization from Below
*Toward a Cosmopolitan Legality*
Edited by Boaventura de Sousa Santos and Cesar A. Rodriguez-Garavito

# CONSTITUTIONALIZING ECONOMIC GLOBALIZATION

Are foreign investors the privileged citizens of a new constitutional order that guarantees rates of return on investment interests? David Schneiderman explores the linkages between a new investment rules regime and state constitutions – between a constitution-like regime for the protection of foreign investment and the constitutional projects of national states. The investment rules regime, as in classical accounts of constitutionalism, considers democratically authorized state action as inherently suspect. Despite the myriad purposes served by constitutionalism, the investment rules regime aims solely to enforce limits, both inside and outside of national constitutional systems, beyond which citizen-driven politics will be disabled. Drawing on contemporary and historical case studies, the author argues that any transnational regime should encourage innovation, experimentation, and the capacity to imagine alternative futures for managing the relationship between politics and markets. These objectives have been best accomplished via democratic institutions operating at national, sub-national, and local levels.

DAVID SCHNEIDERMAN is professor of law and political science at the University of Toronto.

# CAMBRIDGE STUDIES IN LAW AND SOCIETY

*Cambridge Studies in Law and Society* aims to publish the best scholarly work on legal discourse and practice in its social and institutional contexts, combining theoretical insights and empirical research.

The fields that it covers are: studies of law in action; the sociology of law; the anthropology of law; cultural studies of law, including the role of legal discourses in social formations; law and economics; law and politics; and studies of governance. The books consider all forms of legal discourse across societies, rather than being limited to lawyers' discourses alone.

The series editors come from a range of disciplines: academic law, sociolegal studies, sociology, and anthropology. All have been actively involved in teaching and writing about law in context.

*Series editors*

Chris Arup
*Victoria University, Melbourne*
Martin Chanock
*La Trobe University, Melbourne*
Pat O'Malley
*University of Sydney, Australia*
Sally Engle Merry
*New York University*
Susan Silbey
*Massachusetts Institute of Technology*

*Books in the series*

The Politics of Truth and Reconciliation in South Africa
*Legitimizing the Post-Apartheid State*
Richard A. Wilson

Modernism and the Grounds of Law
Peter Fitzpatrick

Unemployment and Government
*Genealogies of the Social*
William Walters

Autonomy and Ethnicity
*Negotiating Competing Claims in Multi-Ethnic States*
Yash Ghai

# CONSTITUTIONALIZING ECONOMIC GLOBALIZATION

Investment Rules and
Democracy's Promise

*David Schneiderman*

CAMBRIDGE
UNIVERSITY PRESS

CAMBRIDGE UNIVERSITY PRESS
Cambridge, New York, Melbourne, Madrid, Cape Town, Singapore, São Paulo, Delhi

Cambridge University Press
The Edinburgh Building, Cambridge CB2 8RU, UK

Published in the United States of America by Cambridge University Press, New York

www.cambridge.org
Information on this title: www.cambridge.org/9780521871471

First published 2008

Printed in the United Kingdom at the University Press, Cambridge

*A catalogue record for this publication is available from the British Library*

*Library of Congress Cataloguing in Publication Data*

Schneiderman, David, 1958–
    Constitutionalizing economic globalization: investment rules and democracys promise / David
Schneiderman.
        p.   cm.
    Includes bibliographical references and index.
    ISBN 978-0-521-87147-1 (hardback: alk. paper) – ISBN 978-0-521-69203-8 (pbk.: alk. paper)
    1.   Investments, Foreign–Law and legislation. 2.   Constitutional law. 3.   Globalization.
4.   Democracy. I.   Title.
    K3830.S36 2008
    346'.092–dc22
    2007038850

ISBN 978-0-521-87147-1 hardback
ISBN 978-0-521-69203-8 paperback

*To my mother, Rose Schneiderman, and to the memory of my father, Joshua Schneiderman, who experienced both the peril and promise of constitutional democracy*

# CONTENTS

# ACKNOWLEDGMENTS

In the course of toiling over this book over a number of years, I have accumulated many debts. My initial interest in the intersection between constitutionalism, markets, and economic globalization was prompted in the early 1990s while undertaking graduate work at Queen's University under the supervision of John Whyte. Returning to my post as executive director of the Centre for Constitutional Studies at the University of Alberta provided me with the institutional space to pursue further my interest in the topic. I am grateful to my colleagues at the centre, particularly Bruce Elman (now dean of law at the University of Windsor), for supporting me in these endeavors. A large measure of thanks is owed to Ron Daniels, who welcomed me into the community of scholars that is the Faculty of Law at the University of Toronto. Though he has since left the deanship, Ron built at the law school an intellectual hothouse of teaching and research. It is a delight and a privilege to be a part of this community of higher learning. I was able to make great strides in my research and writing during two terms of teaching relief that the Faculty of Law provided to me. A Canada–U.S. Fulbright Visiting Scholar Award assisted greatly during one of those terms, in the spring of 2001, enabling me to bring previously written parts of the book together as well as to wholly revise and write new chapters. The Fulbright Award also facilitated my association with two venerable New York institutions: The New School for Social Research and Columbia University. I am grateful to Sondra Farganis at the New School and to Michael Dorf at Columbia Law School for providing the institutional support which allowed me to substantially complete the book. In the book's later stages, I was fortunate to be Visiting Sabbatical Scholar and then Visiting Professor at Georgetown University Law Center. I am grateful to Dean Alex Aleinikoff and his colleagues for the congenial environment within which I was able to put the finishing touches to the book. Funding for the project also was provided by the Social Sciences and Humanities Research Council of

Canada under an MCRI grant to the Globalism Project. I am indebted to SSHRC for funding this and other of my research endeavors.

Working on globalization and investment rules from a critical angle within the legal academy is often a lonely enterprise. I am grateful, therefore, for having had the opportunity to present some of this work early on to different audiences, including associates in the Globalism Project and to researchers involved in the Consortium on Globalization, Law and Society (CONGLAS). Some of the work was also presented at seminars and conferences at Brock University, Carleton University, Georgetown University Law Center, Harvard University, New York University, Strathclyde University, the University of British Columbia, University of Toronto, and a joint Duke University-University of Geneva-University of Alberta conference on privatization.

This is a book which ranges over different disciplines and constitutional systems. I make no apologies for the fact that, methodologically, the book is eclectic in its sources and style, ranging from political theory and history to social theory and international political economy. This eclecticism is largely driven by the book's subject matter. Mapping linkages between economic globalization and constitutionalism demands a measure of interdisciplinarity that exceeds, admittedly, the bounds of any one person's expertise. The book's comparative dimension adds further layers of complexity. In my view, too much current work on economic globalization draws conclusions from impressionistic accounts of the world situation. By contrast, I endeavor here to move beyond conventional understandings and to locate how economic globalization is being made through constitution-like rules over time and in very specific locales. This requires that various constitutional systems get taken up for discussion. To the extent that this comparative endeavour is successful, it is because I have benefited from the advice of some local informants, such as Heinz Klug, Diego López-Medina, and Luz Nagle, though none should be held responsible for what appears in print. I am also pleased to acknowledge the able students who assisted with the translation of texts or otherwise with various dimensions of this research project: Rodrigo Garcia Golindo, Kyle Gooch, Moira Gracey, Mark Grzeskowiak, Ian Richler, and Mauricio Salcedo. Deborah Bays of Georgetown University Law Center provided superb secretarial assistance in the final stages.

As this is no defense of the current legal order of economic globalization, the book likely will attract the ire of economic globalization's defenders. This is because work in this area is inevitably assimilated into the political contest which currently is being played out on a global scale. It is fair to say that the investment rules regime has proved to be a flash point for some of the debate around economic globalization. As I have developed and presented the arguments in the book, I have heard supporters of the regime argue that it is continually improving and that, usually, its most recent iteration solves many of the problems critics have noted. It is true that there are continual developments in this area, such as new treaty language and recent arbitral jurisprudence. I have tried to attend to these developments in the course of my argument, though I make no claim of having reviewed all of the issues and cases that arise within the field. Readers seeking out more definitive statements of the law are advised to seek out publications by the United Nations Commission on Trade and Development as well as recent volumes on the topic (too often, regrettably, in a format which speaks only to specialists) (Bishop *et al.* 2005; Rubins and Kinsella 2005; Weiler 2004; 2005).

It remains to thank those who have read all or parts of the book. They include Richard Bauman, Stephen Clarkson, Kevin Davis, Andrew Green, Donna Greschner, Robert Howse, Heinz Klug, Patrick Macklem, Luke Eric Peterson, Pratima Rao, William Scheuerman, Vicki Jackson, and Bruce Ziff in addition to anonymous reviewers who provided their insights and made a number of helpful suggestions. A special note of thanks is due to colleagues who are working on somewhat similar terrain and from whom I have learned a great deal: Harry Arthurs, Stephen Clarkson, Stephen Gill, and M. Sornarajah.

Though the chapters have been substantially revised, earlier versions of some of the chapters appeared in the journals *Law and Social Inquiry, Constellations, Law and Contemporary Problems, Citizenship Studies,* and the *University of Toronto Law Journal,* and in the books *Governance on the Edge: Semi-Peripheral States and the Challenge of Globalization* edited by Marjorie Cohen and Stephen Clarkson and *The Migration of Constitutional Ideas* edited by Sujit Choudhry. I am very grateful to Finola O'Sullivan at Cambridge University Press and to the editors of the series for their expressions of enthusiasm and also to the able staff at Cambridge who helped to facilitate production of the book.

It would be an understatement to say that Pratima Rao has been a constant source of support and guidance, both intellectual and emotional. In addition to encouraging me to enter this field early on, she has helped me along at every step. The arrival of Joshua Kiran as I was about to submit the final version of the book may have delayed matters a little, but Kiku has provided his share of support at home with his laughter and love.

The book is dedicated to my parents, Rose and the late Joshua Schneiderman. They experienced more than their fair share of adversity in mid-twentieth century Europe. Though this book does not bear directly on that experience, the currents of their travails run deep throughout. It is my modest hope that the book will hold out some promise today for those experiencing hardship in other parts of the world.

March 2007<br>
Washington, DC

# INTRODUCTION: THE NEW
# CONSTITUTIONAL ORDER

The contemporary world appears unsettled, coming together and falling apart in a state of continual convulsion. The fall of the wall in 1989 and the subsequent collapse of the Soviet empire kicked into gear processes of seemingly interminable change. Events precipitated by 9/11 have hastened this changing global landscape. Distances contracted, time compressed, and world-interconnectedness ever widening are the characteristics often associated with the term "globalization." Much contemporary thinking about globalization is preoccupied with this sense of newness, heterogeneity, and fluidity. The mantra is that the "old word has fallen apart" (Ohmae 1995: 7) and it is being replaced by a newer and faster one where geography is immaterial, global actors improvise, and economic, political, and cultural forces are capable of being unleashed from the yoke of parochialism. Borders, Beck maintains, "have long since ceased to exist ... they are zombie categories" (2005: xi). This has unleashed a world of possibilities, it is said. Robertson and Lechner argue that the global scene is "highly pluralistic" so that, rather than one version of globalization being predominant, there is "a proliferation of ... competing definitions" of the global situation (1985: 111). In a similar vein, Albrow claims that there is "no axial principle underlying global institutions"; rather, there is a pluralism reflecting "no theory of the greater good, simply the historic accumulation and interplay of national experiences and expertise coming to terms with each other" (1997: 125).

This preoccupation with newness, mobility, and improvisation draws attention away from a transnational regime concerned with fixity and security. There has emerged out of this convulsion an ensemble of laws and institutions that governs international economic relations in the realm of foreign investment. These are rules and structures ordinarily associated, though not exclusively, with the term "economic globalization." The emergence of a transnational regime for the protection and promotion of foreign investment challenges directly the proposition that global capital has no tangible, institutional fabric. This rules regime cumulatively attempts to fashion a global tapestry of economic policy, property rights, and constitutionalism that institutionalizes the political project called neo-liberalism. This project advances the idea that the state should recede from the market, restrict its economic functions, and limit its redistributionist capacity (Harvey 2005; Przeworski 1999). The paradox is that at a time when the institutions of democracy are being reproduced globally, democracy is not to be trusted in economic matters.

Neo-liberalism and its institutional partner, the investment rules regime, aim to institutionalize a model of constitutional government intended primarily to facilitate the free flow of goods, services, capital, and persons unimpeded across the borders of national states. This is a model long promoted by the leading countries of the Organization for Economic Cooperation and Development (OECD) and by affluent minorities within developing and less-developed countries. The model takes material shape by means of the instruments intended to promote and protect foreign direct investment, such as aspects of the Uruguay Round General Agreement on Tariffs and Trade (GATT) enforced by the World Trade Organization (WTO), the investment chapter of the North American Free Trade Agreement (NAFTA), and some 2,500 bilateral investment treaties (BITs) and numbers of bilateral free trade agreements. The model was promoted in the now-stalled talks leading toward a Free Trade Agreement of the Americas (FTAA) and the failed draft Multilateral Agreement on Investment (MAI). These bilateral, regional, and sought-after multilateral instruments are intended to generate an interlocking network of rules and rule-making structures – an "investment rules regime" – that place substantive limits on state capacity in matters related to markets.

The objective of this book is to explore the implications of this new institutional fabric for democratic self-government. It aims to map the role of law – constitutional law in particular – in the formation of the rules and structures associated with economic globalization. By elucidating the linkages between the investment rules regime and constitutionalism – between the constitution-like regime for the protection of foreign investment and the projects pursued by national states – we will comprehend better some of the legal forms by which economic globalization is being made tangible.

## WHY CONSTITUTIONALISM?

Constitutionalism is not ordinarily associated with the global diffusion of the forces of production and the compression of the time-space continuum, attributes usually associated with globalization. A constitutional lens is helpful analytically as the regime of investment rules can be understood as an emerging form of supraconstitution that can supersede domestic constitutional norms. From this external perspective, investment rules can be viewed as a set of binding constraints designed to insulate economic policy from majoritarian politics. The rules and values of the regime are also being internalized and made material within national constitutional regimes. This is being accomplished through constitutional reform and, oftentimes, judicial interpretation. From this internal perspective, the investment rules regime can be seen as disciplining and reshaping the constitutional law of various states across the globe. Constitutionalism, then, is a useful heuristic device with which to examine the structuration of economic globalization in the modern world (Giddens 1993) so as to contribute to an "understanding of how the global 'system' has been and continues to be *made*" (Robertson 1992: 53).

Likening aspects of economic globalization to constitutionalism might appear unsatisfactory to some readers. Constitutions, after all, are considered to be profound expressions of national commitment – they are about the "highest of all political stakes" (Wolin 1989: 3–4). Constitutional designs institutionalize metarules and procedures that standardize the enduring rules of game, those rules that lie above the fray of ordinary politics (Rawls 1993: 161). Constitutions are intended to serve certain and predictable functions – what Elster (1984) calls a form of "precommitment strategy"[1] – and should not be too easily modified. Liberal constitutional design traditionally has offered a variety of precommitment devices "to reduce the power of the people" (Elster 1992: 40) at national political levels so as to resolve the problem of their "weakness of the will" (Elster 1984: 37) and these have been anchored within national political systems. There are, then, problems of translation inherent in attempting this kind of "stretching"

3

of the state-centered model to the domain of the transnational (Schneiderman 2007; Walker 2001: 34, 2002: 342) – with its resulting "description of oranges with a botanical vocabulary developed for apples" (Weiler 1999: 268).

The investment rules regime is constitution-like, however, in many of these ways. It has as its object the placing of legal limits on the authority of government, isolating economic from political power, and assigning to investment interests the highest possible protection – characteristics that Polanyi more than fifty years ago associated with constitutionalism as a device for securing uniformity and homogeneity in state practices (1957: 205, 225). The ensemble of rules and institutions is a form of precommitment strategy that binds future generations, through the instrumentality of national states, to certain institutional forms and substantive norms through which politics is practiced. Like constitutions, they are difficult to amend, include binding enforcement mechanisms together with judicial review, and oftentimes are drawn from the language of national constitutions.

The linkages between constitutionalism and economic globalization have been obvious to others. Former US President Ronald Reagan in 1987, at the inception of NAFTA's predecessor, the US-Canada Free Trade Agreement, characterized that agreement as a "new economic constitution for North America" (Lamont 1988). Others have noted the constitution-like features of the new institutions of the European Union (Weiler 1996) and the WTO (Jackson 1997). Advocates of the emergent global trading and investment regime describe the institutions of economic globalization precisely in this way: as serving "constitutional functions." They protect and promote freedom, non-discrimination, the rule of law, and the judicial protection of individual rights across national frontiers (Petersmann 1996–7: 405). This is in accord with the views of dominant economic actors, those whom Sklair designates the "transnational capitalist class" (Sklair 2001). Templeton investment-fund manager Mark Mobius, for instance, describes his work as crusading for "human rights," a fight for "transparency, fairness and equality before the law" (*Economist* 1999a: 67). As Mobius intimates, the language of rights and constitutional limitations permeates the promotional literature on economic globalization (Baxi 1998: 147, 2006: ch. 8). In the wake of the protest against the WTO at Seattle, editors at *The Economist* insisted, similarly, that protesters should be told that trade is "first and foremost a matter of freedom" and "liberty" (*Economist* 1999b: 17) – principles foundational to most

4

versions of liberal constitutionalism. Political and administrative operatives associated with departments of finance, trade, and treasury, which Bourdieu likened to the "right hand of the state" (1998: 2), also understand the foundational nature of these sorts of commitments. According to Egyptian finance minister, Yousef Boutros-Ghali, a free trade and investment deal with the United States would render irreversible the economic and political liberalization in his country: "if anybody in the future wants to go backwards, they cannot" (Alden 2005).

Drawing parallels between economic globalization and constitutionalism might appear dangerous to other readers. Equating the project of neoliberalism with those normative principles around which political communities are organized treacherously inflates the societal account of the former – premised upon the self-maximizing individual – while devaluing the moral significance of the latter. If everything is considered constitutional, then nothing is. Invoking the language of constitutionalism also might appear to establish economic globalization as an irreversible "fact," furnishing the convenient alibi to political and other global actors that there are no alternatives in sight (Hay and Watson 1999: 421). Yet there are appreciable benefits to scrutinizing economic globalization through the lens of constitutionalism. The discourse of constitutionalism is a powerful one and can equally rouse citizens into action as it can immobilize them. It has the advantage of assessing the new terrain of economic globalization from a perspective different from that in which it was conceived and so can engage critically with the dominant discourse of neoliberalism. A focus on the constitutional aspects of the investment rules regime positions politics and democracy in an institutional space that aims primarily to secure optimal economic returns for foreign investors. It furnishes a normative frame with which to then critique the current regime (in both its external and internal manifestations). Constitutionalism, in this way, performs a double role: both as descriptor and as normative guide to the current scene.

Nor is it anachronistic, in light of the events of 9/11, to underscore the centrality of the constitutional project of free trade and investment to developments worldwide. United States Trade Representative (USTR) Robert Zoellick signaled that, in the wake of 9/11, US leadership in the promotion of international economic architecture was now "vital." Congress, he wrote, "needs to send an unmistakable signal to the world that the United States is committed to global leadership of openness and understands that the staying power of our new coalition depends on economic growth and hope" (Zoellick 2001). Alan Greenspan, then like-minded chairman of the Federal Reserve, announced that the terrorist attacks rendered successful trade negotiations at the WTO imperative (Wayne 2001). Congressional findings in 2002 were in accord that "[t]rade agreements today serve the same purpose that security pacts played during the Cold War" – that the "national security of the United States depends on its economic security" (National Security Council 2002: 17). When President George W. Bush secured trade promotion authority that year to expand NAFTA and to conclude free trade negotiations with Chile and others, it was wrapped up in the president's strategy of responding to the threat of international terrorism. Open markets were critical to broadening America's influence and softening hostility to the means by which the United States was advancing its "war on terror." To this end, the USTR has set its sights on completing bilateral trade and investment treaties with a number of states in the Middle East, beyond extant treaties with Israel and Jordan, including Bahrain, Oman, the United Arab Emirates, and Egypt (Alden 2005).

A series of setbacks in advancing the legal regime of economic globalization – the failure of the Doha round to open up agricultural markets, for instance, or the stalling of the FTAA – may suggest that this discussion may now be anachronistic. Together with the election of a series of governments in Latin America on a program of pushing back against economic globalization's strictures – as in President Evo Morales's Bolivia – it may be that the advocates and institutions of neoliberal globalism will begin to experience a crisis of confidence. The investment rules regime, however, is intended precisely to forestall reversal of the imperatives associated with economic globalization: the openness of markets and the irrelevance of borders for global entrepreneurs. The constitution-like constraints of the regime are designed to bind states far into the future, whatever political combinations develop at home to counteract it, by imposing punishing monetary disciplines that make resistance difficult to sustain, if not futile.

It would be useful at this stage to move to a fuller explanation of what we should understand constitutionalism to mean. Before doing so, one further observation should be made regarding the advantages of exploring economic globalization through constitutionalism, and this concerns containing the role of the national state.

Economic globalization is usually thought of as happening "out there," beyond the capacity of states to control. At the very same time the modern state is being "decentred," rendered "defective," or "hollowed out" (Strange 1994: 56–7), it is also deeply implicated in the process of its presumed marginalization by establishing, through law, the permissible bounds of state action. In this process, states are important agents in the structuration of economic globalization. Careful attention needs to be paid, then, to the role of globalizing actors, such as states, in the sociolegal outcomes we associate with economic globalization, such as the investment rules regime. Building on insights regarding politics and markets developed most famously in late nineteenth- and early twentieth-century political thought, a focus on constitutionalism brings states back into the picture. Figures such as Green (1881), Hobhouse (1911), Hale (1943), and Polanyi (1957) stressed at various times the ubiquitous role of the state in the construction of markets. According to Green, it was the business of the state to maintain the conditions, through social legislation, for individuals to contribute to the common good (1881: 202). Hobhouse argued that the growth of the industrial system "rests on conditions prescribed by the State" (1911: 87) while Hale observed that "absolute freedom in economic affairs" was out of the question (1943: 626). "We shall have governmental intervention anyway, even if unplanned," he wrote, "in the form of the enforcement of property rights assigned to different individuals according to legal rules laid down by the government" (1943: 628). Polanyi's contribution to economic history in *The Great Transformation* underscores the role of states in the seemingly spontaneous emancipation of markets. "The market," Polanyi wrote, "has been the outcome of a conscious and often violent intervention on the part of government which imposed the market organization on society for noneconomic ends" (1957: 250). This intellectual past understood the state as "deeply implicated" in the operation of the market (Przeworski 1999). With some exceptions (Beck 2005; Panitch 1996b; Santos 2002; Sassen 2006), this is an insight elided in much of the discussion of economic globalization and the investment rules regime. This absence is despite the fact that the current global scene is heavily managed and regulated by states and their transnational delegates. This is not to say that management of the international economy will forever be lodged in the interstate system or primarily in institutions such as the WTO. The book remains agnostic about the possibility of transnational regulation as a valid expression of self-legislation by an engaged citizenry (Beck 2005; Held 1995). The difficulties of achieving the requisite cosmopolitan consciousness and then securing democratically legitimate transnational-legal forms for citizen participation cannot be understated, however (Maus 2006: 472).[2] In which case, it seems reasonable, at least in the medium term, to rely on those institutions that have the capacity of serving the interests of democracy promotion, namely, those associated with states – paradoxically, the very same institutional forms that have served the interests of those with powerful vested rights, including (despite the rhetoric of international investment lawyers) the interests of foreign investors.

States have made it their business to regulate the business of human activity, including its economic dimension. This relation between state and market remains one of the most significant objects of statecraft. Constitutional design concerns itself, in part, with identifying the bounds of the proper relationship between government and economic life (Hartz 1948). If constitutionalism is traditionally considered to be, "by definition," about limited government (McIlwain 1966: 21), it is also about distributing authority between public and private power (Anderson 2005). It is this balance between the public and the private, between democracy and markets, that needs readjustment within the constitution-like mechanisms of economic globalization.

## WHAT CONSTITUTIONALISM?

Let me set out, then, the presuppositions about constitutionalism that animate this project. The argument here is that the proper bounds between state and market, between public and private, should not be rigid and fixed but should aspire to be fluid and pluralistic. State capacity with regard to most subject matters, in other words, should be kept open rather than constrained by constitutional or constitution-like arrangements. Rather than instituting a transnational system for uniform economic governance, any transnational regime should encourage innovation, experimentation, and the capacity to imagine alternative futures for managing the relationship between politics and markets (Dewey 1954; Dorf and Sabel 1998; Unger 1987).[3] In the modern era, these objectives have best been accomplished through constitutional design incorporating democratic institutions operating at national, subnational, and local levels. Democratic institutions provide key resources for people to shape – both to constrain and to enable – marketplace activities. The contemporary institutions of representative democracy allow citizens to be the common authors of their own fate (de Tocqueville 2000: 9), a prerogative denied many people in their "private" work-a-day lives. The democratic institutions of public authority enable individuals to pursue collective projects, oftentimes with disappointing results, other times with surprising success. A constitution of democratic experimentalism – a constitution, as de Tocqueville would put it, of repairable mistakes (*fautes réparables*) (2000: 216) – perhaps best serves the grand object of improving both the political and the economic conditions of many people in the world. The constitutional design envisaged here would render the boundaries between majorities and markets uncertain (Przeworksi 1991: 13), confined to constitutive rules concerning such things as the political autonomy of subunits, free speech, and a pluralistic associational life. A constitutional design that promotes deliberative processes for the determination of what properly belongs within the sphere of the political I characterize as "democratizing constitutionalism." Before discussing this model further, I turn first to two complementary versions of constitutionalism, one constraining and the other enabling, both of which establish metarules that unreasonably limit the capacity of citizens to choose between continuity and change.

## The constraining version

The desire to render national economies the subject of uniform trade and investment regulation submerges the capacity to experiment politically and reduces citizenship to a single, uniform conception organized around the values of the market. This is an account of politics familiar to public choice theory and the group of scholars working under the umbrella of "constitutional political economy" (Buchanan 1991). Exercises of public power are regarded as untrustworthy. Democracy, like markets, is the locus for competition in which self-interest is paramount (Downs 1957; Schumpeter 1947). At worst, democracy is perverted by particularistic interests exploiting government and extracting "rents" or benefits in the guise of favors, loans, concessions, and contracts. As the general public is too diffuse a force to countervail the power of well-organized interest groups (Olson 1965), the state is expected to recede from the market and limits placed on its redistributive capacity. The investment rules regime aims to secure these types of advantages over democratic rule by limiting, through constitution-like edict, the capacity of self-governing communities to intervene in the market.

Constitutional theory, of course, has long been preoccupied with the fear of legislative majorities. In the *Federalist Papers*, Publius expressed much anxiety about the threat of coerced economic leveling and so advocated an institutional design for the American polity that would check legislative passions (Hamilton et al. 1961: 79). Late nineteenth-century American legal thought exhibited similar anxieties. Scholars such as Thomas M. Cooley (1868), with the judiciary in lock step, looked to the principles of the common law in order to ground their jurisprudence of state "neutrality" vis-à-vis market ordering and the redistribution of wealth (Jones 1967). *Lochner*-era courts drew on this tradition so as to check what they characterized as "partial legislation" – attempts by "competing classes," namely labor and capital, to use public power "to gain unfair or unnatural advantages" (Gillman 1993: 60). The status quo was the standard measure for all government action and deviations from this baseline presumptively were constitutionally sus-pect (Sunstein 1993). This fixation with class rule in the late nine-teenth century was not confined to constitutional law in the United States. Lawyers "on both sides of the Atlantic," observes David Sugarman, "were obsessed with the need for constitutional restraints on 'hasty and ill-conceived' change" (Sugarman 1983: 1991). This was exemplified in the work of Albert Venn Dicey, Oxford legal scholar and author of the influential *Introduction to the Study of the Law of the Constitution* (1885). Invoking common law rules and methods of judicial review, Dicey's conception of the "rule of law," it was hoped, would check democratic excesses in Britain (Schneiderman 1998). Late nineteenth-century constitutional thought was characterized, then, by a determined reluctance to incorporate oppositional protest and to imagine alternative paths to economic and political success. As we shall see, this normative nineteenth-century vision of constrained constitutionalism closely parallels the aims and objectives of the con-temporary investment rules regime.

## The enabling version

If public choice theory and constitutional political economy stress the economic model of citizenship, contemporary democratic theory – attentive to the problem of rent-seeking and collective action – endeavors to submerge the market role by generating public-regarding solutions to policy problems. The so-called republican revival (Rodgers 1992) solves the problem of the citizen-as-market actor by designing institutions that favor the cultivation of civic virtue

(Michelman 1988b). Relatedly, discourse-theoretic approaches rely on procedural models, situated within parliamentary institutions, courts, and the public sphere, that enhance political communication and rational political will formation (Habermas 1998b). In both instances, constitutionalism aspires to cultivate a responsible and active citizenry. Rather than relying on constitutional limitations to check political passions, constitutional design institutionalizes deliberative models that, it is hoped, will result in both fair play and impartial public policy.

The important contribution of these branches of contemporary constitutional theory is an insistence on constitutionalism as not being just about limitations on government action. Constitutional rules facilitate, and not only inhibit, self-government – "constitutive rules," Stephen Holmes writes, help frame and give shape to democratic discourse. They are "creative" in that they "organize new practices and generate new possibilities which would not otherwise exist" (Holmes 1988: 227). They also help to settle present controversies in accordance with rules previously laid down. By "taking for granted certain power-granting, procedure-defining, and jurisdiction-specifying decisions of the past," more pressing current-day problems become the focus of resolution (Holmes 1988: 222). This version of constitutionalism as a precommitment strategy emphasizes how binding constraints facilitate democratic decision making, exposing it to "criticism and possible revision" (Holmes 1988: 226).

But constitutive rules cannot be seen merely as neutral vis-à-vis political discourse or the balance of power within society. Rather, binding constraints tilt political discussion by preferring the resolution of political disagreement along certain predetermined paths (Offe 1996: 52). The contemporary view, in other words, underestimates the capacity for constitutional limitations to frame political possibilities. Admittedly, the rules and structures of constitutional law are not entirely determinative of political life, but neither is the subjectivity of social and political agents entirely free of these structural determinants (Giddens 1993; Jessop 1990). Constitutive rules strategically help to reproduce and advance particular understandings of state-society relations. Forbath, for instance, has shown how working-class consciousness was influenced profoundly by the possibilities and limitations offered by US constitutionalism in the *Lochner* era. Judicial review under the US constitution "shaped labor's strategic calculus" and, more subtly, labor's ideology in the late nineteenth and early twentieth centuries (1991: 7). The labor movement's more radical claims were abandoned in favor of ones that echoed the liberty of contract refrain dominant in the late nineteenth-century legal thought (1991: 130). The language of the law limited social visions, silenced aspirations, and elicited the consent of the labor movement "to the dominant groups' version of the natural and the good" (1991: 170). Forbath's work reveals that constitutional law, and legal forms in general, "set limits on what we can imagine as practical options" (Gordon 1984: 111).

Emphasizing the enabling rather than the disabling functions of constitutionalism is not entirely successful, then, in resolving the tension between democracy and constitutionalism. There is, moreover, too little mention made of constitutionalism's constraining capacity with regard to market matters. Holmes (1988), for instance, chooses to stress the structural and procedural aspects of constitutional rules, like the separation of powers or freedom of speech, rather than the ability to regulate economic subjects. The separation of powers enables self-government by disentangling jurisdictional boundaries and establishing clear lines of authority. Freedom of speech has evolved as the grievance procedure for democratic societies – a constitutional limitation that facilitates processes of self-government and encourages participation and deliberation. A discussion of other constitutional limits, such as those concerning liberty and property, conspicuously are absent in Holmes's account.[4] Elster (2000) recognizes that constitutional precommitment is less problematic when it takes the "form of delaying and stabilizing devices," like the separation of powers. It is more problematic when constitutional rules impose "substantive rights and duties combined with stringent supermajority requirements for amendment" (Elster 2000: 170). Political precommitment in these circumstances can lead to "dangerous rigidity": "the normative views of the citizens may change" or "the factual beliefs about institutional means to political ends may change" (Elster 1992: 42). Holmes also purports to prefer flexibility over rigidity. Institutional and legal frameworks, he writes, "must be devised for keeping open the widest gamut of alternatives for new and better decisions" (Holmes 1988: 240), but his account is largely silent about the regulation of economic life. Habermas's discourse theoretic account of law and democracy also elides the relationship between rights and economic power (Schneiderman 2004). For Habermas, any single regime of rights will be "fallible and revisable" but all will rest upon a regime of private autonomy rights that perform critical functions in modern economic societies (1996: 384). The primary task of citizens, according to this account, is to improve or expand upon the liberal frame of constitutional rights (1996: 386). Rights are revisable, then, but only to the extent that they reinforce and augment the regime of private rights. The worry is that this scheme of basic rights accommodates "a pact of sorts" between states and markets, whereby markets are shielded, in significant degrees, from the force of democratic power (McCarthy 1991: 153; Scheuerman 2002: 63). In which case, we might want to recalibrate the enabling version of constitutionalism so as to incorporate the possibility of more dramatic changes in both politics and markets.

### Democratizing constitutionalism

This virtue of democratic society – an openness to change of direction – was well articulated, with attendant ambivalence, by Alexis de Tocqueville in *De la Démocratie en Amérique* (2000). Open-endedness paradoxically posed one of its greatest dangers, a threat sufficiently tempered for de Tocqueville by the institutional roles played by lawyers and citizen juries in the United States. Democratic communities in America, wrote de Tocqueville, are agitated by a "permanent fever that is turned to innovation of all kinds, and innovations are almost always costly" (2000: 202). This capacity to innovate was also one of its chief advantages. This "agitation, constantly reborn," a "superabundant force, an energy," were one of the "true advantages" of democracy (2000: 233, 234). Though vested rights might be attacked, laws frequently altered, and government "costly," "the great privilege of the Americans," he wrote, "is ... to have the ability to make repairable mistakes" (2000: 202, 221, 216). Democracy in America, in other words, meant conferring on self-governing citizens the capacity to change their minds.

A principal object of democratic constitutional design – and any transcendent transnational version – should be to enable, Holmes admits, "individuals and communities to recognize their own mistakes" (Holmes 1988: 240). This conception of democratic constitutionalism is congenial to Polanyi's idea of the "double movement," namely, the ability of a political community to take measures for self-protection. Though the nineteenth century saw the spread of markets all over the world, Polanyi notes, there arose a corresponding "network of measures and policies ... integrated into powerful institutions designed to check the action of the market relative to labour, land and money"

(1944: 76). What arose, in other words, were political movements desirous of mediating the deleterious effects of rapacious capitalism. To the extent that these movements succeeded in institutionalizing social policy to "help insulate domestic groups from excessive market risks" (Rodrik 1997: 6), what the investment rules regime signals is the demise of this postwar compromise of "embedded liberalism" – the "collectivist" reaction of many states that fused legitimate political authority to a shared social purpose regarding the domestic, social, and economic role of the state (Polanyi 1944: 150; Ruggie 1998: 84). It is this capacity to take self-protective measures beyond the status quo that is threatened by the constitution-like features of the transnational investment rules regime.

Democratizing constitutionalism becomes, among other things, a means of incorporating political protest and keeping open a range of achievable political goals (Eisenstadt 1999: 67). We might characterize this kind of constitutional design as one of "rule open-endedness, or organized uncertainty" where no one societal force predetermines political outcomes (Przeworksi 1991: 13). To this end, democratizing constitutionalism institutionalizes the contingencies of political conflict (Lefort 1988: 17). De Tocqueville observed that under democratic rule there was an element of self-interest in personally obeying the law, "for whoever does not make up a part of the majority today will perhaps be in its ranks tomorrow; and the respect he professes now for the will of the legislator he will soon have occasion to require for his" (2000: 230). Przeworski builds on this insight by maintaining that democracies that precommit to a set of procedural (or constitutive) rules will evoke general compliance as all political forces "have specific minimum probability of doing well under the particular system of institutions" (1991: 30–1; Rawls 1993: 161). This openness to political possibility makes electoral competition meaningful for all interests – though we are losers today, we could be winners tomorrow. Under this model of pluralist contestation, power can be "symbolically represented as a physically and personally empty space." This space is continually "up for grabs, as it were, and can, in accordance with democratic-republican legitimacy, be periodically reoccupied" (Frankenberg 2000: 13; Lefort 1988: 17). The possibility of reoccupying political authority keeps open the possibilities of social and legal change. The institutional forms through which democracy is practiced, however, need not conform to any precise model beyond that guaranteeing basic legal minima for democratic will formation (Frankenberg 2000: 23) – beyond this, democracy too can be open to change. Democracy's indeterminacy need not be confined merely to identifying the placeholder of power. Rather, the indeterminacy associated with democracy can be expected to generate new institutional forms leaning in the direction of ever-greater inclusion, drawing out its contents more radically over time (Habermas 1996: 384, 2001: 73). This sort of indeterminacy invites breaks with the past, write Santos and Avritzer, and the formation of "new determinations, new norms and new laws" (2005: xliii).

While constraining state capacity by separating power and institutionalizing the enduring rules for political processes – through guarantees of freedom of speech, for instance – democratizing consti-tutionalism retains a capacity within the state to engage in energetic regulation with regard to subjects of fundamental importance to citi-zens. Democratizing constitutional design recognizes, as did de Toc-queville, that democracy does not necessarily provide citizens with the best and most skilful government, but it does allow for the expression of solidarity and coexistence through self-legislation. Democratizing constitutional design admits, then, that democracy is messy, faulty, and uncertain – the kind of organized uncertainty that the US Supreme Court found intolerable in *Bush v. Gore* (2000). The too-close-to-call Florida vote in the 2000 presidential election resulted in recounting procedures that exposed the "raw edges of democracy in action" (Tribe 2001: 219) but were too polluted by politics, in the opinion of the majority of the Supreme Court, to be constitutionally sustainable.

There are further advantages to removing constitutional limits on state regulation of the market. First, Linda Weiss has shown that economically successful states have a "transformational capacity" – the power to transform and adjust to changing international economic environments. The more that policy-making authorities within states can pursue "domestic adjustment strategies that, in cooperation with organized economic groups, upgrade or transform the industrial econ-omy" the more "competitive" the national economy (Weiss 1998: 5). So rather than disabling states from coordinating economic activity, competitiveness demands it: "by providing the infrastructure, social-izing the risks and encouraging cooperation, the state is in a position to orchestrate more nationally effective responses to technological competition" (Weiss 1998: 7). Second, and less having to do with the success of the competition state (Cerny 1997), Rodrik argues that institutional diversity helps to facilitate developmental strategies that better complement the needs of specific political communities.

"Transitions to high growth," he writes, "are typically sparked by a relatively narrow range of reforms that mix orthodoxy with domestic institutional innovations, and not by comprehensive transformations that mimic best-practice institutions from the West" (2002: 9). What the new disciplines foreclose, in particular, are development strategies better suited to states at differing stages of development, including ones that worked rather well for developed states in the past (Rodrik 1999: 107, 2001: 100). Constitutional rules that inhibit state response, or that force certain types of responses, impede this transformational or transitional capacity of states. This helps to explain the phenomenon described by the World Bank as the "East Asian Miracle" (1993). States such as Japan, Korea, and Taiwan were equipped to succeed, with attendant risks (Haggard 2000), in the global economy of the 1990s not because they followed a pattern of limited government but because they "at times intervened forcefully in markets" (World Bank 1993: 83). According to Stiglitz, if the "Washington Consensus" proscribed a limited role for government, in East Asia "governments helped shape and direct markets" (2002: 92). In fact, protectionism and state support for industry was a feature dominant not only in East Asia but also, as we see in Chapter nine, in US history (Chang 2002; Stiglitz 2002: 16).

We need not go so far as to insist that constitutions be emptied of all social content (as if this were even possible). Nor is this to say that propertied interests remain vulnerable entirely to majoritarian whims. If the constitutional state retains the capacity to identify both friend and enemy (Mouffe 1993: 114; Schmitt 1932), we might look to alternative mechanisms – such as national human rights instruments, discussed in Chapter nine – that safeguard investment and others interests from forms of discriminatory state action. For the purposes of this argument, however, constitutional design is sufficiently compatible with democratic principle if it is open to incorporating political protest, particularly with regard to redistributive conflicts. If democracy, Przeworski warns, "does not improve the material conditions of losers, those who expect to suffer continued deprivation under democratic institutions will turn against them." In order to enhance their legitimacy and durability, democratic institutions "must offer all the relevant political forces real opportunities to improve their material welfare" (1991: 32). Like de Tocqueville, we should embrace this paradoxical aspect of democracy in pluralistic societies: that organized uncertainty generates both volatility and regime stability and continuity (Eisenstadt 1999: 68). This precisely is the democratic project that constitutionalism should seek to frame.

## THE PLAN OF THE BOOK

Having outlined the contribution constitutional analysis can make in understanding the contemporary global scene, I take up the more detailed argument in the chapters that follow. Part one of the book comprises three chapters and provides an account of what I have called the investment rules regime. Chapter one outlines the main features of investment protection agreements and isolates the constitution-like features of this regime. I focus here on the kinds of interests these agreements are intended to protect, the rights that they generate, and their modes of dispute resolution. Investment agreements commit citizens to certain forms through which politics is practiced and institutionalize a legal incapacity to act in a variety of economic matters. These features, I argue, are premised on a distrust of democratic institutions familiar to students of constitutional theory.

Chapter two is mostly concerned with a single feature of this regime: the rule prohibiting expropriations and measures tantamount to expropriation. This "takings rule" is a feature common to most investment treaties. The takings rule can have the effect of constraining state action with regard to a variety of regulatory initiatives, such as environmental measures or municipal by-laws, as suggested by the US experience under the Fifth and Fourteenth Amendments of the Bill of Rights. Tracing early twentieth-century debates around the minimum standard of treatment required by civilized justice, I argue that the takings rule is best understood as an instance of a local rule – the US one – having gone global. The transnational rules go much further, however, by catching a wider variety of regulatory activity. A stricter approach with regard to regulatory takings fits well with the developments in international law traced in the last part of this chapter.

The objective of Chapter three is to test the constitution-like effects of the investment rules regime by reviewing some of the rulings issued by international investment tribunals, particularly those established under NAFTA. A review of this jurisprudence suggests that, though moving cautiously on occasion, the fears about NAFTA's takings rule and associated provisions have not been unfounded. The scope of compensable takings remains quite broad, whereas the categorical distinction between compensable and noncompensable regulations, as under US constitutional law, remains opaque. If investors have not systematically prevailed in their takings rule claims, they have had more success invoking the kindred standard of "fair and equitable treatment," which increasingly serves disciplinary functions similar to the takings rule. Taken as a whole, the tribunal decisions confirm that NAFTA and the investment rules regime generate a legal architecture that institutionalizes a regime of constitution-like disciplines on state regulatory capacity.

Part two concerns the projects of national states and their linkages to the investment rules regime. Here, I analyze the potential impacts of the regime on state projects with their origins in national constitutional systems that, in varying degrees, lean in the direction of (though they may not fully embrace) the democratizing constitutionalism model. Many of the state projects considered here sit uneasily with the imperatives of investment rules, though this is not inevitable (Jessop 2002: 42).[5] In each instance, I explore developments of a kind seemingly external to national states, in the realm of transnational investment law, and those clearly internal to states, in the realm of constitutional interpretation, constitutional reform, or national legislation giving expression to seemingly important social objectives. Chapter five examines an instance where large US tobacco manufacturers threatened to sue the government of Canada under NAFTA were the government to proceed with a plan for the mandatory "plain packaging" of cigarettes. Domestic Canadian law secured similar objectives in a second instance, where the Ethyl Corporation, threatened to sue Canada for banning the use of its gasoline additive, MMT, in automotive fuel sold in Canada. In both cases, US companies and their allies successfully put a halt to regulatory measures that threatened unduly their future profitability.

Chapter six explores linkages between the investment rules regime and the new South African Constitution. The South African Constitution's property clause envisages a relationship between state and market seemingly at odds with transnational investment rules. In the chapter's first part, I detail the linkages and potential disciplinary effects of investment rules on constitutionalism in South Africa, suggesting that conflicts between the national and the transnational in this realm threaten to undermine the South African constitutional project. Despite constitutional commitments to equality and wealth redistribution, the South African government's response to economic inequality largely has been shaped by a disposition toward market-based solutions and a fear of capital flight. The program of broad-based black economic empowerment aims to generate an indigenous black middle class as a salve to the grim reality of apartheid's legacy of inequality, and this provides a second focal point for discussion. Though intended to avoid direct conflict with investment rules, by invoking the discourse of voluntarism and good governance, the program has generated points of abrasion resulting in push-back from some investors. This suggests that the ANC government has reached the outer limits of permissible state conduct under investment rules. Without further modification of the investment treaty regime, modest state-led programs with the objective of sparking indigenous entrepreneurial initiative may not survive investment rules disciplines.

A final national constitutional project is examined in Chapter seven. Latin American constitutional systems traditionally have been at odds with the approach to the protection of foreign investment promoted by countries such as the United States. Reforms to the Constitution of Colombia in 1992, in which remnants of old-style Latin American constitutionalism were preserved, are instructive in this regard. Although the constitution contemplates the privatization of key resource sectors, the state is obliged to democratize property in the event of privatization of state enterprise. These domestic constitutional commitments are tested against transnational standards reflected in BITs and the failed MAI. Under pressure from the investment rules regime, the constitution continues to undergo reform. Recent changes to the constitutional property clause are discussed, providing an opportunity to map changes prompted by the disciplines of economic globalization.

Part three addresses, from a variety of angles, resources for disrupting the investment rules regime. It can be said that a particular view of citizenship flows from the institutional logic of the investment rules regime, one constructed around the values of the market. Chapter eight takes up this version of economic citizenship and considers those places where alternative futures might be explored. This is undertaken from three different perspectives: the consumer citizen, the "local" or federal citizen, and the "wired" or computer-mediated citizen. Each perspective illustrates the possibilities for citizenship in an era of economic globalization. The discussion suggests that citizenship practices that rub against dominant market values (such as local resistance to socially irresponsible transnational economic actors) are more likely to be constrained by the legal disciplines of economic globalization than those practices considered consonant with market values (like consumer activism).

The investment rules regime has been characterized as advancing the "rule of law," by laying down limits to government action. In Chapter nine, I examine the parameters of this contemporary rule-of-law project that is being pursued at a rapid pace on a global scale. Some observers of the global scene suggest that the forces propelling economic globalization could themselves be tamed by the "rule of law" idea. The chapter examines this perspective by taking up a historical case study: the debate amongst Weimar-era legal theorists regarding the "social rule of law." This social-democratic version of the rule of law was intended both to promote economic freedom for laboring classes and to check the economic power of private actors. These objectives, given expression in the Weimar constitution, ultimately were thwarted by the twin techniques of reactionary legal analysis and judicial review, both predisposed to value free enterprise over state regulation. Contemporary accounts, I argue, are unduly optimistic about the capacity to alter the thrust of rule-of-law thought in more social-democratic directions.

In the final chapter, I return to some of the themes introduced in Chapter one. The task of constitutionalism, following de Tocqueville and others, is to keep open the channels of change. So, rather than inhibiting state action with regard to economic subjects, constitutional design should accept its possibility, even desirability. In addition to identifying a number of nonconstitutional alternatives to investor protection, the closing chapter examines an alternative account of US constitutionalism: the "commonwealth" period, running roughly from 1800 to 1860. In the antebellum United States, capital was scarce and so the state played an active role, together with private partners, in the development of a new national economy. Rather than blocking options and preserving vested interests, courts and constitutional law of the period stayed out of the way, even enlarging the practical range of possibilities. Law and legal institutions in the commonwealth period generated the conditions for economic development in circumstances of capital scarcity. Those states entering into the legal strictures of the investment rules regime, I argue, deny to citizens the ability to generate national economic development along similar paths.

The work, in sum, aims to explicate, critique, and suggest openings for alternative futures to be imagined and alternative paths to be pursued. I do not assume to know what paths these futures might take, but I do consider it imperative that we institutionalize a limited set of constitutional rules that do not impede the possibility of living up to democracy's promise, that of innovation through self-government for the purposes of collective betterment.

# PART ONE

## RULES

# CHAPTER ONE

# THE INVESTMENT RULES REGIME

There are powerful forces promoting economic globalization and they probably have had no greater success in the contemporary world than in institutionalizing rules and structures to protect and promote foreign investment. A series of bilateral, regional, and multilateral agreements promoting and protecting foreign direct investment (FDI) generates together an interlocking web of rules and rule-enforcing structures that can place significant limits on state action.

The confluence of world-shaking events, the successful branding of economic liberalism as the only viable alternative, the daily deluge of new technologies together with the sense that forces have been unleashed beyond the competence of ordinary legislative power to curtail, have all contributed to this success story. The proliferation of investment rule-making structures signals that trade promotion is viewed no longer as sufficient to ensure the background conditions for freedom of movement in the global marketplace. Rather, the expansion of FDI is linked closely to the exigencies of international trade. The WTO Secretariat describes foreign investment as one of the "forces propelling" globalization (WTO 1996: 1) while the World Bank looks to increased capital flows represented by FDI as one of the defining features of globalization (2007: 35). Investment lawyers now claim that investment protection "is as central a feature in deeper integration as trade was in the past" (Alexandroff 2006: 12) and "reside[s] at the heart of the globalization debate" (Appleton 2006).

The WTO monitors market access on behalf of transnational producers of goods and services by ensuring the free flow of goods and services across state boundaries. This has not been seen as sufficient. It is argued that market *presence* – a firm foothold within states – is a constituent element of real freedom of trade (Ruggiero 1996: 2; Sauvé 1996: 26). Nor is FDI concerned merely with overcoming barriers to trade or gaining access to natural resources. Rather, FDI "brings entrepreneurship, technology, managerial skills and marketing know-how – assets that are in short supply in many countries" (Moore 2003: 155).

With the establishment of its investment, foreign capital becomes fixed within the boundaries of the national state, making the "geographical landscape of capitalism more and more sclerotic with time" (Harvey 2000: 59). This immobility renders FDI a risky venture. It is vulnerable to local instabilities, prejudices, and the vagaries of host state laws. Nor are traditional forms of investment protection – state-to-state dispute settlement mechanisms or investment insurance – deemed sufficient to protect these interests (Shihata 1993). Instead, codification of the rules for the protection and promotion of foreign investment is advanced as an appropriate means of guarding against this vulnerability. As a result, the construction of an investment rules regime has become a priority item for international economic law. All of this is occurring under the pretext that the forces of economic globalization must be unfettered so as to move freely through time and space.

I characterize this interlocking web of agreements as a "regime," following work in international relations (Lipson 1985: 11). Krasner describes regimes as sets of implicit or explicit "principles, norms, rules and decision making procedures around which actors' expectations converge" (Krasner 1983: 2). Regimes usually are constructed to solve specific policy problems, rather than provide comprehensive solutions to public order problems (Young 1999: 6). Yet, they are more than one-shot affairs: they constitute sets of rules, practices, and procedures to which actors are expected to remain faithful over time. These patterns of behavior do not remain static; rather, a regime's features will adjust with knowledge and practice. Indeed, there might be incoherence – fractures and contradictions – among the various components that make up a regime (Ruggie 1998: 99).

Regimes take a variety of forms, including legally binding rules and nonbinding soft law. According to Keohane, the former are "relatively rare and unimportant" and "do not constitute the essence of international regimes" (Keohane 1982: 153). Nevertheless, regimes increasingly are being understood in rules-based terms. From this perspective, the investment rules regime might be considered an exemplar of this "move to law" (Goldstein et al. 2001: 4). Though more narrowly focused studies of trading regimes are preferred, specific regime studies could well reveal constitutional features that regime theorists would not want to overlook. An examination of the investment rules regime, I maintain, reveals precisely these constitution-like characteristics (Stone 1994; Stone Sweet 2004: 155). Before turning to that discussion, however, I review the dominant features of a typical investment treaty, considering such things as its breadth of scope, definitions, protections, and methods of enforcement.

## THE REGIME IN OUTLINE

The protection of foreign investment has long been an issue of controversy between the countries of the global North and South. Emerging from the first wave of decolonization and distrustful of the continued economic influence of the developed world, the countries of the (commonly called) less-developed and developing world insisted on control over the admission and activity of foreign investment. This was accomplished by means of constitutional provisions (such as Mexico's Calvo Clause, discussed in Chapter four), international covenants (such as the 1974 UN Charter of Economic Rights and Duties), and domestic laws to regulate and control the inflow of investment (as in Canada, through the screening mechanism of the Foreign Investment Review Agency). Policy instruments such as performance requirements, import substitution, nationalization, and state monopolies were designed to resist the encroachment of foreign influence and distribute the gains from economic development more evenly across a broader socio-economic spectrum within the national state.

This resistance appears largely to have been abandoned. With its modest beginnings in a series of "Friendship, Commerce and Navigation" treaties negotiated by the United States, Japan, and a few West European countries in the 1950s, a transnational legal framework for the protection of foreign investment has come clearly into view. An interlocking network of rules for the protection and liberalization of FDI can be found in BITs, bilateral free trade agreements, regional free trade agreements such as NAFTA and the European Energy Charter Treaty, and at the multilateral level in the agreement on Trade-Related Investment Measures (TRIMs) (Fatouros 1996). The World Bank has

27

issued Guidelines on the Legal Treatment of Foreign Investment (Shihata 1993); a similar set of nonbinding investment principles has been agreed to amongst APEC economies, while the OECD attempted, unsuccessfully, to complete a multilateral agreement to which other states outside of the OECD would have been invited to accede (Schneiderman 1999b). The push for a multilateral framework continues (Perezcano 2003; Salacuse 2004). A new global agreement on investment "underwritten by WTO rules, surveillance and dispute settlement arrangements," writes Mike Moore, would "help to close the gap between perceived and actual policy risks in the eye of foreign investors [just] as it has done in the area of international trade" (2003: 156). To that end, the WTO ministerial at Doha, Qatar, agreed to prepare negotiations for a framework agreement on FDI. No consensus was reached on commencing those negotiations after the spectacular collapse of the WTO talks at Cancun in September 2003 (Bhagwati 2004; Jackson 2006: 242). Despite a few setbacks, these instruments of state discipline and neoliberal principle negotiated and yet to be negotiated "reflect a remarkable consensus" (Parra 1996: 31): that the world should be made as safe as possible for foreign investors.

Even Latin American states, home to the Calvo doctrine – that foreign nationals receive no better treatment than local citizens (discussed in Chapter six) – and traditional adherence to the principle of national sovereignty (Sornarajah 2000: 81–3) increasingly have become party to BITs that incorporate strict standards for the protection of FDI (UNCTAD 1997a: 76–7). As of the end of 2002, 413 BITs had been concluded by the countries of Latin America and the Caribbean (UNCTAD 2003: 55). The global pace of BIT growth is striking: the UN Commission on Trade and Development reports that at year end 2006, more than 2,573 BITs had been completed involving over 175 countries – remarkably, two-thirds of these agreements were negotiated during the 1990s (UNCTAD 2003: 88, 2007: 16). Germany leads the pack having negotiated the greatest number of BITs. China is a close second with Switzerland third; the United Kingdom, Egypt, France, and Italy have been actively pursuing investment agreement partners and follow closely behind (UNCTAD 2007: 18). The United States falls in the top thirty countries (UNCTAD 2000: 17). Not all of these agreements, however, are in force. Approximately 700 of the almost 2,500 agreements have not yet entered into force, and almost half of them for a period exceeding 5 years. UNCTAD speculates that delay may be due to the necessities of enacting implementing legislation, changes in government, unrest, and civil war, "or a deliberate policy choice of government" (UNCTAD 2005a: 24). If a delibrate policy choice, it will have been precipitated, as in the case of a Canada-South Africa BIT discussed in Chapter five, by some of the factors detailed in this book.

At the domestic level, the liberalization of national laws governing investments has kept pace with the rapid expansion of the trans-national regime: in the period 1991–2004, 2,006 of 2,156 amendments to national investment laws were in a liberalizing direction (UNCTAD 2005a: 26). The year 2005, however, saw the greatest number of changes less favorable to FDI, with a large share of these changes issuing out of Latin America (UNCTAD 2006b: 25; 2007: 14). At the regional level, NAFTA's investment chapter and its related provisions have codified a set of protections long sought after by developed countries in the international community (Daly 1994; Shihata 1994). The substantive protections of investments under NAFTA, including provision for investor-state dispute settlement, in many but not all of its features, followed the pattern of a typical US BIT (E. Murphy 1995: 93; Shihata 1994: 56). That pattern was modified following pending and feared NAFTA claims against the United States (Kantor 2004); these are discussed further in Chapter three.

Important differences remain among the investment protection instruments. Sornarajah cautions that, though the contents of BITs have a basic similarity, this gives rise to a superficial impression that they contain identical standards (Sornarajah 2004: 206). It also leads to the impression that these treaties confirm or give rise to new customary international law on foreign investment (CME 2003). The variation in treaty standards, Sornarajah warns, often reflect the bargaining strength and mutual dependencies of the various parties (2000: 219, 2004: 207). Indeed, there will be differences even among the leading OECD states – US and Canadian standards are more favorable to investors in the establishment phase than are those reflected in BITs with the states of the EU, for instance (Gugler and Tomsik 2006). Also, there will be variations even within a single country's investment treaty program, as in the case of Germany (Karl 1996). Though we should keep these cautions in mind, it cannot be denied that there are some significant similarities (Perezcano 2003: 935). It is also the case that the details of the investment rules regime are evolving – treaties are growing "more sophisticated" and encompassing a "broader range of issues," according to UNCTAD (2006a: 9). The following discussion is not intended to be exhaustive, rather, only illustrative of the main features of the regime's disciplines. For these purposes, I draw principally on the text of the model German and US BITs (UNCTAD 2002; USTR 2004b). Those familiar with the investment treaty regime can proceed to the next part of the chapter where I turn to its constitution-like features. There will be little reference here to the recent decisions of international arbitration tribunals that have been issued under NAFTA and BITs. The object is to outline the parameters of the substantive commitments made in these texts, rather than their interpretation. Chapter three is devoted to developments concerning treaty interpretation.

## Preambles

Investment agreements are framed through a certain prism. Preambles to investment treaties, as indicative of the treaty's object and purpose (Vienna Convention Art. 31[2]), indicate unequivocally that the investment rules regime is intended to establish "stable frameworks" (the 2004 US Model Treaty) generating "favorable conditions" for investment decisions (the 1994 German Model Treaty). Agreements are premised on the certainty that binding enforcement mechanisms, as an effective means of asserting claims and enforcing rights (the 2004 US Model Treaty), will "stimulate private business initiative and ... increase prosperity" (the 1994 German Model Treaty). These are the "embedded preferences" framing investment protection agreements – they indicate the interests that these agreements are intended to protect (Koskenniemi 2007: 9). The German model preamble maintains, however, that these objectives can be secured "without relaxing health, safety and environmental measures of general application."

## Definitions

The obligations concerning investment take their shape through a series of common tenets. They include a wide definition of the term "investment," usually intended to cover all varieties of economic interests – in the model German BIT, protected investments comprise "every kind of asset." Typically, covered investments include any business enterprise; ownership of shares, stocks, and bonds; rights under contract; intellectual property rights; and every kind of property right, both tangible and intangible. An investment of any size or quantity, "even a single share of stock," will qualify (Alexandrov 2005: 394). The definition section of BITs is usually meant to be illustrative, rather than exhaustive, of the list of protected investments interests. Recent changes to the Canadian model treaty, however, have narrowed the definition by closing the list of protected interests that qualify as covered investments (McIlroy 2004: 629; see, generally, UNCTAD 2004b: 77–81, c. 3). For the most part, UNCTAD advises developing countries to adhere to the broad definition as "virtually any asset can contribute to economic development . . . and that to exclude certain assets could risk undermining the purpose of the treaty" (UNCTAD 2006a: 19).

## Admission

Often, provision is made for the admission of, and the promotion of conditions favorable to, foreign investment. The German BIT requires the host state to "promote" investments by German nationals and to admit investments "in accordance with" existing legislation. Usually, BITs reserve the ability of host states to screen investments – in these instances, no standards of protection are accorded to investors in the preestablishment phase. The typical US BIT and post-NAFTA Canadian BITs calls for the more stringent standard of "non-discrimination" in the admission or establishment of investments, not merely fair treatment. This may be accompanied by a "negative list" of sectors to which the standard will not apply (UNCTAD 2006a: 27–8).

## Standards of protection

Two key measures concern "nondiscrimination" in the treatment of established investments – these lie at the core of efforts to build a liberalized transnational investment regime (Vandevelde 2000: 500). First, under provisions requiring "national treatment," investors are entitled to "treatment no less favourable" than that available to nationals within the host state. States, in other words, are not entitled to prefer local economic concerns over the interests of investors who have their home in the host state. Put another way, foreign investors are entitled to be treated as if they already were domicile within (or citizens of) the host state.[1] Second, the "most-favored nation" (MFN) status – a "central pillar of trade policy for centuries" (Jackson 1997: 157) – mandates that foreign investors are entitled to treatment no less favorable than that available to foreign investors of any other third country.[2]

Commitments to nondiscrimination are available to protect traders and investors in the field of services pursuant to the General

Agreement on Trade in Services (GATS) enforced by the WTO. First, a negative list of specific exemptions applies to the general requirement of MFN treatment in GATS. Second, a separate "positive list" of obligations, including national treatment, applies only to the sectors that member countries have elected to open up to foreign competition (UNCTAD 2004b: 72). Unlike the typical BIT, these commitments are enforceable before the WTO dispute resolution system by the party states, and not by foreign investors themselves.

As mentioned, under the US BIT treaty program these principles of "nondiscrimination" operate both prior to and after an investor has entered the host state. According to the US rule (also the NAFTA standard), nonresident foreign investors who merely wish to establish a presence in the host country are entitled to equal treatment with domestic nationals even before they make any investment. There is no possibility, then, to screen investments or attach any conditions to their entry.

Connected to these provisions may be prohibitions on "performance requirements," such as rules requiring the use of local labor or products (except those that promote health or the environment) or investment incentives. Entry and exit rights for corporations and their key personnel are guaranteed as may be transfers of income out of the country connected with an investment. Comprehensive bilateral and regional investment agreements, like NAFTA, prohibit performance requirements and this likely has the effect of barring a wide range of policy instruments including the requirement that investors achieve certain levels of domestic content, purchasing and employment preferences, technology transfers, or insisting that investors be headquartered in the investing state. Most non-US BITs are silent about performance requirements, though these sorts of measures will continue to be subject to other investment disciplines, like national treatment (UNCTAD 2006a: 41). The agreement on TRIMs, part of the Uruguay-round GATT policed by the WTO, also commits states not to impose local content or purchasing requirements or other sorts of trade-distorting performance requirements in relation to trade in goods that are "mandatory" or where compliance "is necessary to obtain an advantage" (TRIMs Annex).

As all varieties of property – tangible and intangible – are included within the definition of an investment, there is little doubt that intellectual property is protected generally, when not specifically, by investment rules. High standards for the protection of copyrights, patents, and trademarks – including nondiscrimination and lengthy periods of monopoly rights – first were articulated in NAFTA and some forty bilateral treaties negotiated by the US (Braithwaite and Drahos 2000: 198). These high standards were incorporated into the Uruguay-round Agreement on Trade-Related Intellectual Property Rights (TRIPs), now enforced by the WTO and increasingly are included in trade and investment treaties. Recent US practice goes beyond TRIPs compliance and seeks "TRIPs plus" protections for those sectors considered to be among the United States' principal exports. TRIPs-plus standards, among other things, extend the life of patents, criminalize conduct interfering with digital copyright, and tighten up the rules on parallel imports and compulsory licensing (Drahos 2002; Mayne 2005).[3]

BITs typically include general levels of protection for investments. These norms are claimed to be drawn from customary international law, though there is some dispute as to precisely what minimum level of protection is required (discussed further in Chapter three). States are mandated, for instance, to provide "fair and equitable treatment" and "full protection and security" of foreign investments. The standard of treatment is expected to be no less favorable than that required by customary international law or, perhaps, one even greater (Choudhury 2005; Dolzer 2005; Schreuer 2005). Nor may a state impair by "unreasonable," "arbitrary, or "discriminatory" measures the value of an investment. In NAFTA and other investment disputes, the "fair and equitable treatment" standard has proven to be of some importance in resolving claims in favor of foreign investors, functionally supplanting the prohibition on takings, to which I turn next.

### Takings

Most all modern investment agreements include protection from expropriation and nationalization (the "takings rule"). The rule prohibits measures that "directly or indirectly" expropriate or nationalize an investment or measures that have an "effect equivalent to" or are "tantamount to" nationalization or expropriation (2005 Germany-China BIT: Art. 4). The German model BIT establishes a broader claim to compensation in circumstances where the "economic substance" of an investment "is severely impaired" by host state action. The chapters that follow illustrate that the takings rule potentially poses a significant barrier for the ability of states to intervene in the marketplace. It is for these reasons that both the United States and Canada modified their treaty practice so as to reign in the scope of the

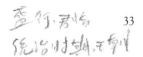

takings rule. Takings are limited to a class of regulatory expropriations which, for the most part, satisfy the multifactor balancing criteria laid down in the US Supreme Court case of *Penn Central* (1977) (discussed in Chapter two). Only in rare circumstances, the US model treaty provides, will nondiscriminatory regulatory actions intended to "protect legitimate public welfare objectives, such as public health, safety, and the environment" constitute an indirect, and thereby compensable, expropriation.

Those measures that amount to expropriation or nationalization are prohibited outright unless they are in the public interest, non-discriminatory, and in accordance with the "due process of law" (reminiscent of language found in the Fourteenth Amendment to the US Constitution). Takings are required to be accompanied by prompt, adequate, and effective compensation payable at fair market value, without delay, and fully realizable and transferable. This is the strict standard of compensation known as the "Hull Formula," advocated by former US Secretary of State Cordell Hull (Hull 1938) and long championed by the United States as the standard of compensation required by international law. It is to be contrasted with the standard of "appropriate compensation" (discussed in Chapter five) long advocated by countries from the South.

### Investor-state disputes
North Americans rightly can lay claim to having launched this innovation, initially in United States BITs and a handful of Canadian BITs (Dodge 2006), then receiving its fullest articulation in NAFTA. States and investors alike are entitled to trigger mechanisms for the settlement and conciliation of complaints that a state has breached the terms of an investment agreement. Many BITs, as do the German and US models, provide this right of standing to sue for foreign investors although it is conspicuously absent from the 2004 US-Australia free trade and investment agreement. In the event of irreconcilable difference, states and investors may seek resolution of a complaint before international tribunals who are entitled to issue declarations, orders for compensatory damages, and restitution. The awards of tribunals are entitled to be registered and enforceable within those same domestic courts. The recent China BITs permit investor-state disputes subject to certain qualifications. The 2005 Germany-China BIT, for instance, calls for the passage of 3 months time since the investor submitted the issue to a Chinese court and withdrawal of the case before a judgment is delivered.

## Exceptions and reservations

Some general exceptions to these strictures usually are available to state parties, such as those relating to the protection of "essential security interests" (Shihata 1994: 52). The 2005 Germany-China BIT is atypical for having exempted from national and MFN treatment measures "taken for reasons of public security and order, public health or morality" (2005: Prot. para. 4[á]). But for similar carve outs for bona fide public health, safety, and environmental measures in new US and Canadian investment agreements, exceptions such as these are not usually available in the case of expropriation or nationalization. Each party state, in addition, typically is entitled to list specific reservations (or non-conforming measures) to a BIT but, again, not usually in respect of takings. These are accomplished by means of a negative list, where certain investment treaty disciplines will not apply, or a positive list, as in the GATS (UNCTAD 2006c: 11). Under a negative list approach, often no further measures can be listed after the agreement comes into force, implying a "standstill" commitment (Shihata 1994: 59; UNCTAD 2006: 19). Recent Chinese BITs exploit this opening by listing existing nonconforming measures and future amendments (so long as the amendment does not increase nonconformity) as exempt from national treatment and other standards of protection. China undertakes in these agreements, however, to progressively remove all nonconforming measures. The OECD-drafted MAI similarly contemplated that reservations would be rolled back "with a view to their eventual elimination," having a "ratchet" or rollback effect (Witherell 1995: 11). The use of reservations by way of a negative list calls on states to identify "up-front" those nonconforming measures they wish to maintain (UNCTAD 2006c: 11), and this, in turn, will call for an extraordinary amount of *ex ante* knowledge about the policy options a state may wish to pursue far into the future (Cho and Dubash 2005: 149). Short of a GATS-type positive-list approach, UNCTAD suggests, alternatively, that reservations be listed quite broadly and not correspond to any existing measures. Their report cautions, however, that reservations should not be "lodged too broadly" for fear they will not enhance transparency or a "host country's investment climate" (UNCTAD 2006c: 31–2).

Save for these general exceptions and country-specific reservations, parties are not entitled to deviate from these commitments, and any changes may only further liberalize, or further protect, foreign investors. That is, once an investor has entered the geographic space of the party-state under the terms and conditions of an investment treaty, the state may not impose further or new conditions on investors and their investment interests.

## Enforcement

Enforcement of investment disputes often are assigned expressly in agreements to the International Centre for the Settlement of Investment Disputes (ICSID) at the World Bank, or may be brought before the United Nations Commission on International Trade Law (UNCITRAL), the Court of International Arbitration of the International Chamber of Commerce in Paris, the Stockholm Chamber of Commerce, or the Cairo Regional Centre for International Commercial Arbitration. In the case of some BITs, enforcement is also assigned to national courts within the host state. US practice, for instance, offers investors a variety of institutions through which they can pursue the resolution of investment disputes (Dolzer and Stevens 1995: 133, 154). Tribunal awards are also intended to be binding and enforceable within the legal system of the offending state as if, according to the ICSID Convention (1966), they "were a final judgement of a court in that State" (Art. 54).

State-to-state practice shows, according to Vandevelde, that international arbitration is "an entirely workable mechanism of dispute resolution" in the modern world (Vandevelde 1992: 190). The mechanisms for investor-state dispute settlement in BITs may prove to be faulty in some cases as ICSID cannot have jurisdiction without the written consent of the parties to a particular dispute. As investment agreements create obligations only between states, Sornarajah argues, there must be a further act of consent in order for nationals in one party state to sue another party state (Mann 1990: 244; Sornarajah 2000: 214–15). States, therefore, can evade investment-rule disciplines by refusing to provide that consent in the case of an investor-to-state dispute. Current BIT practice attempts to solve this problem by expressly providing that the agreement satisfies the requirement of written consent for the purposes of ICSID and other international arbitration conventions (Schreuer 2001: 210). In cases against Argentina, for instance, ICSID panels found the consent requirement satisfied as soon as the state, via a BIT, extended a "generic invitation" to all investors from the other contracting state (*Lanco International* 2001: para. 43). Investors are entitled to accept this offer which, when accepted, cannot be withdrawn unilaterally, nor is that consent vitiated by a clause in a concession contract entitling investors to pursue their claims in local courts (*Lanco International* 2001: para. 40).

## Termination

The extent to which state parties have committed to investment rules is underscored by the standard termination clauses. Unlike ordinary legislative measures, the investment rules regime ensures certainty in the long run by making onerous any withdrawal from investment disciplines. In many BITs, termination of the agreement is permitted only after a 10-year period of duration, after which notice of termination may be given effective in 12 months' time. Investment rule disciplines continue in force, however, for periods ranging from 10 to 20 years for those investments made during the period the BIT has been in force. In the case of the draft MAI, rules would have continued to apply for 15 years after a notice of withdrawal. In sum, termination is made not only legally onerous but also practically impossible. The less economically powerful parties to the BIT regime are not likely to want to incur the wrath of more powerful economic forces in the developed world. Structural adjustments, therefore, are set in motion under the investment rules regime that are difficult to reverse and increasingly costly to abrogate (Robinson 1993: 217).

## ITS CONSTITUTION-LIKE FEATURES

Constitutionalism encompasses, in part, those formal institutional arrangements that give binding effect to the basic norms by which a political community is organized. In so far as the investment rules regime reflects constitutional characteristics, the norms of democratizing constitutionalism – of pluralism and of self-government – make this new form of constitutionalism suspect. The regime freezes existing distributions of wealth and privileges "status quo neutrality" (Sunstein 1993). It does not merely commit citizens to predetermined institutions and rules through which political objectives are realized but also institutionalizes a legal incapacity to act in a variety of economic matters. It is not an enabling precommitment strategy; rather, it is largely a disabling one. At bottom, the investment rules regime represents a form of constitutional precommitment binding across generations that unreasonably constrains the capacity for self-government.

The constraining model of constitutionalism (as I have described in the Introduction) resolves the tension between majoritarian democracy and the protection of minority interests in favor of limits on government action. The investment rules regime similarly resolves this tension in favor of foreign investors by rendering them equivalent to vulnerable minority groups. Governments thereby are legally constrained from pursuing a range of legislative strategies that significantly impair investment interests. That is, investment agreements place binding limits on what governments can and cannot do. Stephen Gill associates this with the "new constitutionalism," the institutional manifestation of disciplinary neoliberalism (Gill 1995: 411, 2003: 131). The new constitutionalism emphasizes "market efficiency, discipline and confidence; economic policy and consistency; and limitation on democratic decision making processes." The new constitutionalism "insulates key aspects of the economy from the influence of politicians or the mass of citizens by imposing, internally and externally, 'binding constraints' on the conduct of fiscal, monetary, and trade and investment policies" (Gill 1995: 412, 2003: 132). This is an understanding of constitutionalism that is congenial to public-choice accounts. It is a view distrustful of democratic government, seen as captive of particularistic interests. The investment rules regime resolves this problem by removing from the range of public regulation certain subjects in order to achieve "stability" and "efficiency" (Posner 1987: 4; Sunstein 1991: 639) in the practice of normal, quotidian politics.

I have said that these agreements are binding across generations. This is achieved by setting a high threshold for amendment or repeal. Constitutionalism also sets high thresholds for change. In federations such as the United States and Canada, it is, on the whole, very difficult to secure formal amendment (Lutz 1995). In the case of NAFTA, unanimity is required to amend its terms while only 6 months' notice is required for a state to withdraw unilaterally. Practically, withdrawal will not easily be achieved for any of the parties to NAFTA but the United States, and this primarily has to do with the punitive economic consequences likely to befall either of the other two states were they to walk away from the agreement. As one arbitrator in a NAFTA dispute admitted, "[p]ulling out of a trade agreement [like NAFTA] may create too much risk of reverting to trade wars, and may upset settled expectations of many participants in the economy" (S. D. Myers 2001: Separate Opinion para. 34). In the case of the MAI, withdrawal would have been not only practically impossible but also legally onerous. According to the draft MAI, no state could have withdrawn until 5 years after the agreement came into force. After the initial 5-year period, a state could withdraw after 6 months' notice but the MAI would continue to apply to existing investments for a period of 15 years after a notice of withdrawal (BITs, on the other hand, typically continue in force 10 years after pullout [Siqueiros 1994: 267]). In other words, no state would have been able to withdraw completely until more than 20 years had passed since the MAI's coming into force. In addition, each of the twenty-nine state parties would have a veto over subsequent changes (no consent, however, was required for any state to accede to the strict terms of the MAI).

Constitutions often have binding enforcement mechanisms and these usually take the form of judicial review. In the case of most investment agreements, state parties are entitled to trigger dispute settlement mechanisms that can ultimately lead to binding arbitration before international trade tribunals composed of recognized experts in the field. These awards usually are registerable in the court system of the rogue state and enforceable as if they were judgments obtained in the usual way within its domestic court system. These rights of enforcement also are available to the foreign investor who has claimed abrogation of an investment agreement. Investors, in short, are entitled to trigger the dispute settlement mechanism that, in the past, was available only to the contracting states. As detailed in the subsequent chapters, this gives investors license to meddle significantly in public policy development within states party to these agreements.

Constitutional texts ordinarily establish both an institutional framework for the operation of government and a series of textual limits on what governments can and cannot do. This can take the form of structural and rights-based approaches. The Republic of South Africa, for instance, has adopted both approaches. According to federal arrangements, the constitution expressly limits government at the national and subnational levels according to a division of legislative powers. The South African Bill of Rights limits outright what governments at both levels are entitled to do. These limits take shape through vague and abstract constitutional guarantees that call for judicial review so as to give substance to these rights (Davis 1999).

Investment protection agreements similarly contain vague and abstract rights language, such as "fair and equitable treatment," standards of reasonableness, arbitrariness, and due process. These deliberately vague concepts are intended to capture or threaten to capture a wide range of state activities that impact negatively on international capital. In order to make the stronger point about the constitutional nature of the investment rules regime, much of the remaining focus of this and the next chapter is on the rule concerning prohibitions on nationalization and expropriation.

If the investment rules regime has attained hegemonic status, it might seem odd to focus on a rule prohibiting expropriation and nationalization. These kinds of prohibitions appear to pose no significant problem for state authority. After all, there is an apparent convergence across states on the dominant value system, and an apparent absence of alternatives, through which happiness and prosperity will be secured. Yet, it can be argued that the removal of this policy option from the stable of instruments for controlling investment is a serious limitation on state capacity and has the potential of disrupting significantly any proposed new regulation of the marketplace. This is not commonly acknowledged by proponents of free trade and investment rules. The brief experience under NAFTA's investment chapter (discussed in Chapter three), in addition to developments elsewhere, suggests that we should not be sanguine about these effects.

The classic candidate caught by this prohibition is outright takings of title to property by the state – the nationalization of the forces of production under socialism, for instance. Takings of this sort have diminished greatly in number, however, and are likely of less concern to contemporary investors (Wälde and Dow 2000: 4). One study, for instance, recorded eighty-three expropriations in 1975 alone and only eleven between the years 1981 and 1992 (Minor 1994: 178; Powers 1998: 132). Undoubtedly, these numbers continued to decline through the 1990s. Recent land and economic reform efforts in Latin America may give rise to new investment disputes. The Hugo Chavez-led government in Venezuela initiated land reform efforts to redistribute idle property and this precipitated a claim by a UK investor, which has since been settled (Peterson 2006a). President Evo Morales of Bolivia declared his intention to nationalize the oil and gas industry (Weitzman 2006a) and this resulted in newly negotiated contracts with foreign energy firms who agreed to dedicate over 50 percent of their revenues to the state (*New York Times* 2006). These and other measures, such as proposed land reforms (*Economist* 2006) or nationalization measures (Gunson 2006), might give rise to old-style disputes (Peterson 2006b). Some, like the plan to nationalize Bolivian mines, likely will be suspended because of the diminished fiscal capacity of the state to provide some compensation (Weitzman 2006b).

Despite the echo of old-style disputes today, what has been of concern to investors in the late twentieth and early twenty-first centuries and what the takings rule is intended to catch are not express takings but what are called "creeping" expropriations (measures that cumulatively amount to expropriation) and regulatory expropriations (measures that so impact on an investment interest that they are equivalent to expropriation). Measures that only "partially" expropriate – that take one stick out of the bundle of sticks that make up an investment interest – are prohibited (Vandevelde 1992: 121). Regulatory changes that "go too far," in Justice Holmes's famous words, (*Pennsylvania Coal* 1922), are intended to be caught by this rule. The underlying premise is that governments can be expected to perform only limited regulatory functions, all of which are inescapably subordinated to "private" markets.[4]

Regulatory measures of uncertain magnitude are prohibited entirely unless they are for a "public purpose," are "nondiscriminatory" (i.e., are general and do not target foreign investors), and are in accordance with the "due process of law" (likely necessitating access to judicial review) (Khalil 1993: 299; Vandevelde 1992: 121). If a taking meets these preliminary criteria, the expropriating state must then provide compensation according to the strictest available criteria: compensation equivalent to fair market value, paid without delay, fully realizable, and transferable. As mentioned, these disciplines are enforceable not just by states party to these agreements but also by foreign investors themselves.

These constitution-like commitments make suspect claims that the proliferation of BITs in the post-1989 environment merely are intended to be symbolic. Vandevelde, for instance, writes that these agreements are "a relatively easy way" for states to "demonstrate" and "symbolize" their commitment to economic liberalism (1998: 628). With the exception of the US BIT program, Vandevelde finds that investment protection agreements facilitate old-style interventionist tactics. This particularly is the case when it comes to the admission and establishment of investments and, in the postestablishment phase, in the area of performance requirements, which largely remain unregulated by BITs (1998: 634). Further in his argument, however, Vandevelde admits that investment protection provided by BITs is "quite strong" (1998: 632).

If investment rules merely perform a "signaling" function addressed to the investment community-at-large that there has been a change of direction in economic policy, this seems an overly extravagant response. Binding rules that are required to remain in force for a period of at least 20 years seem to be the most drastic means of communicating this intention. As Guzman shows, though BITs represent a means by which less developed countries can credibly commit to foreign investors, they may make these countries worse off by denying them the right to "unilaterally change the conditions under which the firm operates" (1998: 673). Legislative reform, increasing transparency, and privatization measures, to name a few policy options, perform similar signaling functions. Moreover, the benefits accruing to states that commit to these constitution-like rules remain in some doubt (Sornarajah 2004: 216–17). Hallward-Driemeier's empirical analysis of FDI flows from OECD to developing host states in the period 1980–2000 found a "significant negative finding on the impact of ratifying a BIT" (2003: 19). Her data suggests that domestic institutional supports are more likely to assist in attracting FDI than the mere ratification of investment commitments (2003: 21). This is confirmed by UNCTAD's earlier findings that investment protection agreements are relatively insignificant in determining amounts of FDI. Other factors such as market size and growth, exchange rates, and country risks appear to be more important determinants of FDI (UNCTAD 1997a: 37, 1998a: 117, 1998b: 118, 2003: 89). Some studies suggest that BITs do serve the purpose of attracting FDI. Salacuse and Sullivan claim that there is a positive correlation between a US BIT and FDI inflows and call, therefore, for a return to multilateral negotiations leading to a new MAI (2005: 105, 112). Tobin and Rose-Ackerman in one study find that BITs have "little impact" on the attraction of FDI, though they may have more of an impact in countries with higher political risks (2004: 19). In a second study, using new data, they find that the number of BITs a country has signed with a "high income country" the more the amount of FDI inflow (2006: 18). The marginal benefit of an extra BIT to the host country declines, however, as countries around the world increasingly take up investment rules (2006: 21). In one of the most comprehensive studies completed yet, Neumayer and Spess find that there is a positive and statistically significant effect of signing BITs on FDI flows and that the greater the number of BITs signed with capital-exporting countries, the greater the amount of FDI (2005: 1568, 1585). Replicating Neumayer's and Spess's model, Yackee finds that the relationship of BITs to FDI flows is marginal and much smaller than

Neumayer and Spess suggest (2006: 31). Their findings, "the most convincing evidence to date," Yackee writes, "rest on quite unstable ground" and "are far less robust" than a casual reading of their article would suggest (2006: 51). In sum, the scant empirical evidence available indicates some ambivalence about the relationship between BITs and FDI inflows. The case of Brazil lends some doubt about the utility of investment agreements in attracting FDI. Brazil is one of the largest magnets for inward FDI in Latin America (UNCTAD 2003: 53). Three quarters of the largest transnational corporations have affiliates in Brazil – it is, according to UNCTAD, one of the "favorite" host developing country locations (UNCTAD 2005c: 1). Yet, Brazil has not one BIT presently in force, though fourteen have been signed.

The ambivalent relationship between BITs and increased investment is consistent with the finding that the bulk of FDI continues to be directed in and out of the triad of North America, Europe, and Japan together with several associated countries (Hirst and Thompson 1999: 71; Stopford and Strange 1991: 18; UNCTAD 2003: 23, 2006b: 6).[5] UNCTAD hypothesizes that clusters of nontriad countries with strong economic links to triad members are more likely to enter into international investment agreements. In which case, FDI is more likely to flow to these countries not because of investor rights but because of membership in a triad block (UNCTAD 2003: 24–6). With the concentration of FDI in the triad and associated member states, accompanying the rise of the investment rules regime has been – though there is some dispute about the reliability of the data (Held and Kaya 2007: 11) – a growing inequality within and between rich and poor states (IMF 2007: 32), mitigated by rising economic wealth in China and India (Milanovic 2005: 87), such that "global inequality remains at extra-ordinarily high levels" (UNDP 2005: 33). Binding precommitment strategies – constitution-like rules – seem out of proportion, then, to the actual objectives of securing increased FDI. While seemingly providing some stability to investment interests, it destabilizes the capacity for self-government represented by constitutional rules that enable democratic processes to do their work.

Though I have argued that this new form of constitutionalism has old-style constitutional features, it also departs from the old forms in a number of important ways. Responding to claims that the WTO is a fully "constitutionalized" entity, Cass argues that there are six elements that comprise processes of constitutionalization (2005: 19): a set of social practices that constrain behavior, a belief in their foundational nature, authorized by a political community, with the requisite legitimacy, through processes of deliberative law making, resulting in a structural realignment between the new entity and its subparts (2005: 19). Testing constitutionalist claims against these familiar processes, Cass concludes that that the WTO has "some ground to make up before it deserves the label 'constitutional'" (2005: 23). Walker, similarly, has developed seven indices of constitutionalism that consider some of the same but also broader factors, such as the generation of an explicit constitutional discourse (2002: 343). He describes the WTO as "only a very modestly constitutionalised entity" (2001: 50).

By no means does the investment rules regime qualify as a fully constitutionalized entity along these lines. One dimension is the seeming absence of a legitimate political community – a "people," so to speak – from the scheme. On most normative scales, the transnational investment rules regime fails to satisfy most of the basic prerequisites of a liberal constitutional order. I have been suggesting, however, not that it is a fully constitutionalized order but that it strikingly has constitution-like features.[6] An examination of these features generates important insights about the rules and processes we associate with economic globalization. It might be claimed, nevertheless, that the regime satisfies some of the basic criteria that Cass sets out. Habermas gives expression to this point of view by arguing that regimes, such as WTO, are not wholly without legitimacy. These arrangements, Habermas insists, were not imposed unilaterally by the United States but were the consequence of "cumulative negotiated agreements ... coordinated in concessive negotiations between a large number of individual governments" (2002: 224). Constitutional authorship, according to this account, can be attributed to states many of which are representative democracies. In Chapter seven, I consider the role of states and citizens in authoring and resisting the investment rules regime. Though there are openings for greater citizen involvement, through coordinated social movement involvement, for instance, the traditional state, as Habermas insinuates, remains a salient locus of citizenship.

In which case, we should not understand the rules and structures of economic globalization as the product of some immanent and idealized transnational consensus. The next chapter reveals that this is far from the truth. The global regime for the promotion and protection of foreign investment, rather, is generated in specific locales and intended to replicate particular national experiences, namely, those of the United States and other dominant European powers. The regime, then, is designed to spread patterns of constitutional design that seemingly have stimulated economic success in the global North and that other states should want to replicate.

# CHAPTER TWO

# THE TAKINGS RULE

Investment agreements commonly prohibit expropriation or nationaliza-tion. Concomitant with the prohibition is an exceptional remedy for investors who make their home in states party to these agreements. Should an investment have been expropriated or nationalized directly or indirectly, or subjected to measures tantamount to expropriation, investment agreements entitle investors to seek damages before international tribunals. The tribunal's awards then are enforceable within the domestic courts of the offending state party. Expropriation provisions are unique in that most other international agreements entitle only state parties to initiate mechanisms for compliance (Lauterpacht 1997; Roth 1949: 62). The expropriation provisions are also distinctive in that they appear to be influenced heavily by US constitutional standards that prohibit the "taking" of private property.

Others characterize the global takings rule as arising, unvarnished, as a principle of customary of international law (Carbonneau 2002: 803). This chapter traces the contours of an international standard that, I argue, borrows heavily from the constitutional experience of the United States and other economically powerful countries of the North. Whatever the origins of this rule, the modern-day version has clear affinities with regulatory takings doctrine drawn from US consti-tutional experience. The transnational version, however, is the most stringent possible and so extends beyond even the outer limits of the rule acceptable within mainstream US constitutional doctrine. In this way, the transnational version enhances and multiplies the possibilities for confining and disciplining government action.

This is not to say that all legal outcomes associated with economic globalization merely reflect US global dominance. One could take the view that the outcomes associated with economic globalization are the product of a 500-year-old world historical process in which the US version currently is hegemonic (Arrighi and Silver 1999; Taylor 2000). Also it cannot be said that the transnational rule mirrors precisely its US analogue. The scope of protected interests covered by investment agreements is much broader than the property-related interests covered by the US takings rule. As Been and Beauvais have demonstrated, the NAFTA rule significantly "exceeds" US takings protections in important substantive and procedural respects (2003: 5, 26). What is argued here, instead, is that the general outline of the rules and institutions associated with economic globalization are the product of local rules that successfully have gone global – what Santos calls "globalized localism" (Santos 2002: 179). This chapter, then, aims to uncover the repressed privileging of the contours of US constitutional law – the "forgetting or deliberate concealment" of the conditions giving rise to the "universal" (Bourdieu 2000: 70) – underlying emergent transnational standards for the protection and promotion of foreign investment.

The first part of the chapter reviews the takings rule in US constitutional law. What is emphasized is the shift over time from deference to stricter scrutiny of economic regulation that has been signaled by the US Supreme Court, though shifts in the opposite direction remain viable. Following the trail from the US rule to international standards, the second part reviews the parameters of a debate predominant in the early part of the twentieth century concerning the "minimum standard of treatment" due to foreign investors under international law, which purported to include a prohibition on takings. The third part considers recent developments in international law that signal a shift toward stricter standards and which parallel trends in US constitutional law. This is not to say that the emergent standard necessarily will reproduce the strictest version of the takings rule. If many of the outcomes we associate with globalization should be understood as contingent (Hay and Marsh 2000: 6; Rosenau 1998: 28), then cautious forecasting in the realm of investment rules is appropriate. If globalization is envisaged as a field of struggle, however, the structure of the emergent investment rules regime suggests a field that is tilted decidedly in one direction.

## GOING TOO FAR?

The Fifth Amendment to the US Constitution provides that private property shall not be taken for public use without just compensation.[1] The "public use" requirement was the subject of serious consideration in the late nineteenth century (Cooley 1868: 357). The requirement was designed to prevent the use of public power for private gain or, to borrow from the language of contemporary public choice theory, rent seeking. In the period after World War I, the standard was relaxed and easily satisfied in most takings cases (Michelman 1988a: 1621; Nedelsky 1990: 231–4). Once "the legislature has spoken," the US Supreme Court famously declared in *Berman v. Parker* (1954), "the public interest has been declared in terms well nigh conclusive" (*Berman* 1954: 32). In these cases, the public use requirement was considered coterminous with the scope of the "police power" – the authority of state governments to enact measures to protect public health, welfare, and morals. The public use requirement effectively was satisfied any time the legislature, speaking on behalf of its public, chose to exercise its police power authority (*Hawaii Housing Authority* 1984: 240). This measure of deference was confirmed in *Kelo* (2005) though it generated significant controversy – *Kelo* has been called a "crushing defeat ... for ordinary people" (Epstein 2006: 134). The City of New London, Connecticut, designated an area for economic revitalization in which the property of Kelo and others fell – these included private homes together with investment properties. The city condemned these parcels of land but the petitioners resisted, arguing that the public use requirement was not satisfied when expropriated lands were being turned over to private developers for economic development. The five-justice majority of the court rejected their plea, declining to "second-guess the City's considered judgments" while acknowledging that "the government's pursuit of a public purpose will often benefit individual private parties" (*Kelo* 2005: 488, 485). The four dissenting justices concluded that under this rule "all private property" was now vulnerable to be taken "under the banner of economic development" (2005: 494). The public use requirement, they concluded, could only be satisfied where there is evidence that the condemned property is causing "social harm" of some kind (2005: 500). Without this, now there was "[n]othing to prevent the State from replacing any Motel 6 with a Ritz Carlton, any home with a shopping mall, or any farm with a factory" (2005: 503). The ruling triggered a firestorm of criticism and a range of public responses: from initiating eminent domain proceedings against Justice David Souter's house in New Hampshire to state-wide ballot initiatives restricting the use of condemnation or requiring the payment of compensation in the event of any new land use rule (Cooper 2006; Liptak 2006). Nine of the eleven state ballot initiatives of this sort were approved overwhelmingly in November 2006 (Davey 2006).

What constitutes a taking of property requiring the provision of just compensation has been subject to fluctuating legal standards. If the standard was strictest in the *Lochner* era – that period in the late nineteenth and early twentieth centuries when state and federal economic regulation was subject to the closest scrutiny – it has loosened up since the New Deal consensus when judicial scrutiny of economic legislation relaxed significantly (Ackerman 1991; *Penn Central* 1977). Outright takings of property to develop an airport or highway, for instance, usually will attract the duty of compensation. Regulatory measures, such as municipal zoning, environmental protection, or commercial regulation – even those that will have a significant detrimental impact on the economic value of property – usually will not attract compensation. These regulatory measures more often than not will be categorized as non-compensable exercises of state police power jurisdiction or an exercise of federal authority to regulate interstate commerce (Sax 1964). Regulatory measures, however, can attract the duty of compensation if a measure should go "too far." The beginnings of the regulatory takings doctrine is usually traced back to Justice Holmes in *Pennsylvania Coal* (1922: 1659). "The general rule," he wrote, "is that while property may be regulated to a certain extent, if regulation goes too far it will be recognized as a taking." So when regulation "reaches a certain magnitude, in most if not all cases" there must be the payment of compensation.[2] In the case of impugned regulatory activity, a variety of factors usually will be determinative – the character of government action, its economic impact, and the extent to which investment-backed expectations are affected (*Kaiser Aetna* 1979: 175; *Penn Central* 1977: 124) – taking into account their aggregate "interference with rights in the parcel as a whole" (*Penn Central* 1977: 130–1; *San Diego Gas* 1981: 636).[3] The weight to be attributed to these various interests is hardly an obvious one (Kelman 1999: 21) and so judicial decision making in this area has been described as unsatisfactory and haphazard (Sax 1964: 46) and "highly uncertain" (Dana and Merrill 2002: 163–4). "Takings Doctrine is not just vague," writes Poirier, "it is hugely vague" (2002: 138).

Public choice scholars, Epstein (1985) among them, have taken the court to task for relaxing the takings rule in the post-New Deal era. By what logic, asks Epstein, should the Fifth Amendment be reduced to an inferior constitutional status vis-à-vis other parts of the Constitution (Epstein 1992: 56)? The Rehnquist Court responded favorably in the mid-1980s (Alexander 2006: 77–83; Underkuffler 2004: 737–46): "We see no reason why the Takings Clause of the Fifth Amendment, as much a part of the Bill of Rights as the First Amendment or the Fourth Amendment, should be relegated to the status of a poor relation in these comparable circumstances," wrote Justice Scalia for the court (*Dolan* 1994: 321). This conception of takings doctrine, which Underkuffler associates with Scalia (2004: 733), is noted for its emphasis on losses suffered by individual claimants to the exclusion of the public interest served by the government action. Investment-backed expectations are the major consideration in this analysis – the effect on owners are the driving priority.

The easiest instance in which the rule has been applied is that where the state takes physical occupation of private property – these are instances of per se takings (Tribe 1988: 592–5). What constitutes physical occupation was expanded by the Rehnquist Court in *Loretto* (1982). There, the court found that a New York law requiring that landlords provide tenants with access to television cable services constituted a taking because it mandated that space be provided to cable operators on the roofs of city buildings. In doing so, the court expanded the scope of regulatory takings to include physical intrusions of only a *de minimis* nature. No "matter how minute the intrusion, and no matter how weighty the public purpose behind it," compensation will be required, the court declared (*Lucas* 1992: 2893).

As the notion of regulatory takings expands, measures that control property, such as zoning, land use, and environmental regulations, are threatened to be caught by the rule. In *Lucas* (1992), the court held that a South Carolina law that forbade building on vacant coastline property – a law enforced to protect all of the South Carolina sea coast – was an unconstitutional taking. The court in *Lucas* expanded the scope of per se takings to include a second categorical rule of regulations that deny "all economically beneficial or productive use of land." A court need not take heed, in these instances, of the "public interest advanced in support of the restraint" (*Lucas* 1992: 1015). To have concluded otherwise, wrote Justice Scalia for the court, would be "inconsistent with the historical compact recorded in the Takings Clause that has become part of our constitutional culture" (*Lucas* 1992: 1028). This new category of takings would not extend to regulations aimed at preventing a public or private nuisance, as nuisance represents the outer limits of a compensable property interest at common law, in which case no compensation would be forthcoming (Dana and Merrill 2002: 106).

Rather than reviving the "public use" requirement (*Kelo* 2005), the court instead has narrowed the scope of the police powers exception, requiring a close connection between the means used and the governmental objective sought to be achieved, while expanding the categories of per se takings. Recall that a taking occurs not only in the case of trivial physical occupation, but also "where regulation denies all economically beneficial and productive use" of property. Does this mean that *all* economically viable use needs to be denied in order for there to be a taking requiring compensation, or might it mean that *any* aspect of viable use that may have been contemplated originally by the owner, if denied, amounts to a regulatory taking? The legal realist insight that property consists of a "bundle of rights" helps us to understand the implications of the latter proposition.[4] The realists conceived of property as a bundle of rights in order to reallocate rights in property more broadly across the socioeconomic spectrum. Disaggregating property rights from the single-owner model to the many helped ensure that property rights were defined in ways that accommodated multiple interests beyond that of the owner (Singer 2000: 82). Public choice scholars appropriated the bundle-of-rights analogy but kept ownership in the hands of the sole owner. Limiting or denying access to the use of one of the sticks in the bundle of rights now is considered equivalent to denying access to the use of the whole bundle of rights. Epstein has argued in this vein that the eminent domain clause catches within its net each attribute of private property. "No matter how the basic entitlements contained within the bundle of ownership rights are divided," writes Epstein, "all of the pieces together, and each of them individually, fall within the scope of the eminent domain clause" (1985: 57). Radin tagged this move as "conceptual severance," where a taking consists "of just what the government action has removed from the owner, and then asserts that particular whole thing has been permanently taken" (1993: 127–8). The property interest is conceptually severed from the bundle of rights that makes up the whole – in other words, one of the incidents of ownership is equated with all of the incidents of ownership. Regulation of one of these elements that amounts to a deprivation is an unconstitutional taking mandating compensation (Singer and Beermann 1993: 222).

Though the court has denied that it employs a doctrine of conceptual severance (*Tahoe-Sierra* 2002: 27), a variety of governmental regulations concerning property use have been struck down employing its logic (Alexander 2006: 78–80; Radin 1993: 128). In *Nollan* (1986) the court held that a permit for the redevelopment of a waterfront lot along the California coast could not be conditioned on making the beach lot accessible to the public. The state interest advanced for requiring this condition was that the new residence potentially could block both the view of, and pedestrian access to, the beach from the street. The court could find no reasonable "nexus" between conditions for redevelopment and public access that could satisfy the takings rule. The requirement for stricter scrutiny of a state's exercise of police powers was heralded by this statement: "We view the Fifth Amendment's Property Clause to be more than a pleading requirement, and compliance with it to be more than an exercise in cleverness and imagination" (1986: 841).

In *Dolan* (1994), the court required not only that a nexus exist between the legitimate state interest and the condition attached to a business building permit but also that the conditions be "roughly proportional" to the impact on the proposed development. The court required that some sort of "individualized determination" be undertaken of the relationship between the public use served and the property taken (1994: 321). In this case, Florence Dolan sought a permit to build a bigger store on a lot across the street from her current location. As the proposed site was in the floodplain of the local creek, the city required that she dedicate a portion of her lot to a public greenway adjacent to the floodplain and to a bicycle and pedestrian path that would help to alleviate traffic congestion on the nearby main street. There was no evidence that either of these conditions would have any impact on the proposed redevelopment project. Nevertheless, the court held that there was no reasonable relationship between the permit conditions and the burden the conditions would have on Dolan's rights of exclusion. Justice Blackmun, in dissent, likened the court's approach to "the resurrection of a species of substantive due process analysis" associated with the *Lochner* era. The *Lochner* courts similarly refused to presume reasonable relationships between regulatory objectives and the means used to pursue those objectives – in that instance, between the health and safety of bakery workers and limiting their weekly hours of work (*Lochner* 1905). The municipality was required, then, to provide just compensation for this taking, even though no easily quantifiable use was denied by the conditions attached to the permit.[5]

Modern takings doctrine has not gone so far as to limit state capacity to redistribute wealth and equalize power relations, as in the *Lochner* era (Radin 1993: 131). Rather, what are at stake are regulations that implicate what McUsic calls fundamental or core property interests, those interests "centred around the right to control land" (1996: 608; Kelman 1999: 31). Although the court imposes few limits on well-established forms of social redistribution, novel social reform agendas are more vulnerable – what Alexander describes as "extreme property-regulating government action" will not be safe (2006: 94). What might be at risk are environmental regulations that prohibit development or development exactions, such as programs requiring low-income housing development (McUsic 1996: 660). These are the kinds of measures that "readjust property rights in the face of changing resource congestion" (Rose 2000: 23) – measures that Radin associates with the problem of "transition" (1993: 162).

Though there is a clear divide on the US Supreme Court on such matters, some justices have indicated a willingness to expand the takings rule even beyond its conventional limits, centered around land, to the protection of wealth and future profits uncoupled from specific property interests. This development portends an expansion of the takings rule in the direction of the transnational investment rule. In *Phillips* (1998), the majority of the court extended the notion of constitutional property to include interest earned on client's funds deposited in lawyer's trust accounts. Separating out interest earned from the client's principal funds amounted, writes Merrill, to an "egregious form of conceptual severance" (2000: 900). Though it may have amounted to a taking, the government action ultimately did not require the payment of compensation as the net loss to the client was *de minimus* (*Brown* 2003). At issue in *Eastern Enterprises* (1998) was whether a Congressional requirement that former employers contribute to a health-care fund for retired coal miners and their dependents was an unconstitutional taking requiring the payment of compensation. Eastern Enterprises had quit the coal industry some 30 years earlier but retained an interest in the industry through a single subsidiary. Eastern challenged the levy on the basis that it was a retroactive measure substantially interfering with the company's reasonable investment-backed expectations, amounting to an unconstitutional taking of Eastern's future profitability (1998: 518). Four justices agreed this was a taking, and this would have amounted to an unsettling expansion of traditional takings doctrine. Justice Kennedy also found for Eastern but for different reasons. He observed that regulatory takings cases always have concerned a "specific property right or interest." The congressional law at issue here, by contrast, imposed an obligation to pay benefits not tied to any specific property interest (1998: 541). Removing this "constant characteristic from takings analysis," Justice Kennedy wrote, "would expand an already difficult and uncertain rule to a vast category of cases not deemed, in our law, to implicate the takings clause" (1998: 542). Justice Kennedy preferred to undertake his analysis, instead, under the discredited due process clause. It was the Fourteenth Amendment's "due process" clause that was invoked by American state and supreme courts in the late nineteenth century to strike down a wide variety of state interventions into the marketplace, such as the one in *Lochner* (1905). Since the New Deal, however, the American Supreme Court largely has abandoned the concept that the Fourteenth Amendment protects economic rights beyond a simple threshold requirement of legislative rationality (*Williamson* 1955). Preferring to revive soiled constitutional doctrine, Justice Kennedy resolved that the wisdom and fundamental fairness of the regulation at issue was better examined under due process grounds. Here, the legislature "exceeded the limits imposed by due process." The statutory obligations visited upon Eastern Enterprises upset settled legal doctrine against retroactive obligations and bore no legitimate relation to the governmental interest being pursued (1998: 549).

The dissenting justices in *Eastern Enterprises* agreed that the regulation at issue here reduced profitability and was better tested under due process grounds – that the measure "deprived property without due process" – rather than undertaking the unseemly expansion of regulatory takings doctrine. The justices disagreed, however, that the measure was an unfair one. Eastern Enterprises had contributed to the making of a "promise" or "reasonable expectation" (1998: 559) – admittedly not a contractually binding promise (1998: 560) – that it would continue to fund health care for retired coal miners. Eastern was well aware, before it quit the industry, that it was a "serious possibility" that Congress would step in and solve the health-care funding problem (1998: 566). This also was an industry in which Eastern made substantial profits, and in which it continued to do so through a subsidiary. If it was a reasonable expectation that some solution to the funding of health care would be sought from former employers, the scheme could not be considered fundamentally unfair to Eastern.

The plurality examined the same record yet concluded otherwise: that it was not a reasonable investment-backed expectation to impose these sorts of obligations on former employers. There was, after all, no promise of "guaranteed" benefits when Eastern was an employer in the coal industry (1998: 34). The plurality, in effect, equates contractually binding promises of funding with reasonable investment-backed expectations. A promise of guaranteed benefits, however, would not have necessitated federal government intervention.

To be sure, regulatory takings doctrine has stopped just short of filling the void left by the US Supreme Court's retreat from substantive due process in economic matters. The class of interests protected by takings doctrine is narrower than that covered by the due process clause, the court has affirmed (*Lingle* 2005). But members of the court have expressed a clear willingness to expand the protection covered by the Fifth Amendment beyond core property rights to include interests uncoupled from traditional property interests, such as interest earned on deposited funds. These developments have been described as an enormous expansion of the potential reach of takings doctrine (Underkuffler 2004: 745). At the same time, members of the court have signaled a willingness to revive due process in the realm of economic regulation. At the same time, other members of the court have pushed back and succeeded in restoring some balance to takings doctrine in cases like *Tahoe-Sierra* (2002) and *Palazzolo* (2001) where the multi-factor balancing process outlined in *Penn Central* (1978), rather than solely an adverse effect on reasonable investment-backed expectations, was controlling. Justice O'Connor, for instance, admitted in *Palazzolo* that investment-backed expectations, "though important, are not talismanic" (2001: 634). Much of the tenor of the court's jurisprudence, nevertheless, is that economic regulation that deviates from some mythical status quo is constitutionally suspect. This is a fuzzy domain of excessive regulatory action that is no clearer than Holmes's formulation of measures that "go too far" (*Pennsylvania Coal* 1922: 1659) or what Alexander calls "extreme property-regulating government action" (2006: 94). This fits well the "chastened" constitutional regime described by Mark Tushnet (1999). In an era of government downsizing, the aspirations of government are attenuated but not eliminated

entirely – "the guiding principle of the new regime is not that government cannot solve problems, but that it cannot solve any more problems" (Tushnet 1999: 63, 76). To the extent that the court stands in the way of economic regulation, it can hinder or frustrate transitions to a better future, or at least a more tolerable one. The wide range of economic interests that fall within the protective scope of the investment regime's takings rule complements well the idea of a chastened constitutional regime and its mandate of "lowering of ambitions" (Gauchet 2000: 26). The extent to which an expansive version of the takings rule is embraced by the investment rules regime is taken up next.

## FOURTEENTH AMENDMENT PSYCHOLOGY

International law might be thought of as less solicitous toward private property and investment interests. Indeed, customary international law reveals no real consensus concerning many of the issues raised by regime's takings rule (Dolzer 1986; Sornorajah 2004). Yet capital-exporting countries long have attempted to shape the development of international law by transferring idealized versions of their domestic legal arrangements to the international plane. Lauterpacht argued years ago that, in international law, the "conduct of its members must to a certain extent occupy the place of a source of law" (Lauterpacht 1929: 85; Dolzer 1981: 568). I argue here that the influence of US constitutional values – its "Fourteenth Amendment psychology" (Wild 1939: 10) – has loomed large in international developments and continues to play a formidable role in the takings doctrine currently unfolding worldwide.

It should be uncontroversial to claim that capital-exporting states have sought to conscript international law to protect the interests of investors who have their base of operation in these states. This is a phenomenon traceable back, at least, to the early twentieth century (Lipson 1985: 20). In the literature of that period, which I discuss in this section, one commonly finds reference to a laundry-list of national constitutional provisions that protect property which, taken together, give rise to an international standard for the protection of foreign-owned property (Anderson 1927; International Law Association 1926). Reference also would be made to writers such as Grotius (1625) or Blackstone (1750), who expressed reverence for property rights and called for compensation in the event that a state takes private property

(Mann 1959; Roth 1949). It usually is not noted that these authors would have tolerated expansive regulation of property and commercial interests (Rose 1998: 604–5; Sax 1964: 54). Cumulatively, this gave force to the proposition that the standards of "civilized justice" required that profound respect be paid to the sanctity of private property (Borchard 1939: 61; Fachiri 1925, 1929: 50). If property rights were inviolable, international law required (a) that there be no discrimination as between nationals and foreigners (national treatment) and that, (b) even in the case of equality of treatment, there be no departure from the "minimum standard of treatment" required by the rules of civilized justice. Publicists maintained that this minimum standard was "compounded of general principles recognized by the domestic law of practically every civilized country" rather than a reflection of "the crudest municipal practice" (Borchard 1939: 61). Elihu Root's 1910 address to the American Society of International Law authoritatively promulgated these linkages between privileged versions of the local and new international standards:

> There is a standard of justice, very simple, very fundamental and of such general acceptance by all civilized countries as to form a part of the international law of the world ... If any country's system of law and administration does not conform to that standard, although the people of the country may be content or compelled to live under it, no other country can be compelled to accept it as furnishing a satisfactory measure of treatment to its citizens.    (Root 1910: 22)

Departures from the minimum standard of justice – equality of treatment being insufficient protection in this regard – authorized home states to invoke the authority of international law in order to vindicate rights denied to their nationals. In contrast to the modern investment rules regime, foreign nationals had no right of redress. These rights were invoked on their behalf by home states (Borchard 1939: 56), consistent with the proposition advanced by Grotius (1625) that the maltreatment of foreign nationals amounted to a diminution in the national wealth of home states. It was also consistent with the observation that, as foreign nationals cannot exercise political rights within host states, they reasonably should look to their home state for vindication of their rights (Borchard 1939: 57).

The decision of the Permanent Court of Arbitration in the *Norwegian Shipowners'* case (1917) bolstered the claim that international law virtually was equivalent to the constitutional standard for the protection of property established by states in the developed North. The US Congress authorized the president to requisition shipyards in the United States, taking over ship-building contracts placed by noncitizens. This gave priority to US government and private ship orders in furtherance of the war effort. A group of Norwegian ship owners claimed that property for which they had paid in part – namely, fifteen ship hulls ordered under contract – had been taken. Referring to the Fifth Amendment of the US Constitution, the arbitral tribunal pronounced it was "common ground" that the "public law of the Parties is in complete Accord with the international public law of all civilised countries." Just compensation, the tribunal concluded, was due to Norway under principles of international law just as it would be due under the principles established by the constitutional law of the United States (*Norwegian Shipowners* 1922: 324, 332, 334). In the exercise of the power of eminent domain (as it "is called, in the United States Law and Jurisprudence" [*Norwegian Shipowners* 1922: 323]), "the right of friendly alien property must always be respected" (*Norwegian Shipowners* 1922: 332). As Dolzer admits, "the tribunal appears to have examined the basic question of whether or not an expropriation had occurred, primarily in terms of United States constitutional law" rather in terms of some independent international law standard (Dolzer 1992: 693; Mendelson 1985: 416).

During this period, deviation from the principle that "no government is entitled to expropriate private property, for whatever purpose, without provision for prompt, adequate, and effective payment" (Hull 1938: 193) – the US secretary of state's famous formulation – would not be tolerated. Publicists would admit, however, that there was an international analogue to the US doctrine of police powers (Christie 1962: 338; Herz 1941: 252) that states had "full scope" to internally organize economic relations for securing their "progress and well being" (Fachiri 1925: 170). Mann's history of the international law of expropriation, for instance, acknowledges there is no unanimity regarding what amounts to a compensable taking but maintains that the common law and continental legal systems both permit interferences with property that do not rise to the level of a taking. In the United States the exception rests on the police power; in Germany on "the inherent power of the State" (Mann 1959: 215).[6] As the German exception developed in the Middle Ages, the rule permitted non-compensable interference "sometimes for the case of general statutes which affect all individuals alike and sometimes for cases of necessity" (Gierke 1987: 80). There could be no justification, however, for the appropriation of land permanently without the provision of just compensation (Fachiri 1929: 53). 稀少的，深奥的

That in the contemporary world abstruse local rules have gone global is admitted frankly in the American Law Institute's *Third Restatement of Foreign Relations Law of the United States* (1987). The *Restatement* defines the international rule by invoking US constitutional law and admits that "[a]s under United States constitutional law, the line between 'taking' and regulation is sometimes uncertain" (American Law Institute 1987: para. 99). Dezalay and Garth (1996: 175–9) have disclosed the process by which the compensation standard in the *Restatement*, distinguished from the question of what constitutes a taking, came to be drafted. Under pressure from a group of "academically-oriented lawyers active in the American Society of International Law," a compensation standard less strict than the Hull formula, whose universality was in question, was redrafted so as to remove any doubts that the Hull rule represented international legal practice. These events are relayed by Dezalay and Garth as representing the influence of the US bar in the production of international law. They lend support to the conclusion that local rules are being smuggled into play at the international level.

Others resisted an interpretation of international law that required anything more than equality as between nationals and foreigners. Much of this resistance is traceable back to the work of Argentinean jurist Carlos Calvo. His treatise (1870) articulates a vision of international law reasonably well suited to defend the interests of Latin American states against the forceful power of international capital (Lipson 1985). Calvo's doctrine mandates that aliens are not entitled to a higher degree of protection in their claims against host states than are locals, and that foreign investors are required to submit their claims to local courts rather than seek diplomatic protection from their home state (Garcia-Mora 1950: 206).[7] The doctrine is predicated on the principle of nonintervention: that "as a matter of international law, no state may intervene, diplomatically or otherwise, to enforce its citizens' private claims in a foreign state" (Sandrino 1994: 268). Reflecting on Calvo's doctrine, the Chilean jurist Alejandro Alvarez insisted that if foreigners residing in the United States and Europe could never, "for any reason whatsoever," hold more rights than nationals, why should US and European investors residing elsewhere be entitled to preferential treatment? This, after all, is what Root had insisted upon in his 1910 address. International law required only national treatment: a state could not be held responsible "in regard to a foreigner unless the law enacted by it tends directly to cause him damage as a foreigner and without justification on the grounds of general interest" (Alvarez 1927: 49).

This was a view not confined to Latin American jurists alone. States were entirely free to modify their systems of land tenure as may be required by social conditions, insisted French constitutional law professor Leon Duguit. Enactments that redistribute property and "apply indiscriminately to all land within its territory, irrespective of the nationality of the owners" could not legitimately attract the censure of foreign states (Cohen 1927: 57; Duguit 1927: 106, 109). Property rights, Duguit and others argued at this time, served social functions and landowners properly fulfilled their "social duty" when they cultivated vacant land;, otherwise, states could step in to ensure that this social function was safeguarded (1927: 131).

Despite appeals to the "universal standards of civilization," there was no evidence that uniform constitutional standards existed with regard to property. One need only have examined the property provisions of the Weimar Constitution, maintained Frankfurt am Main law professor Karl Strupp (1927: 300). The 1917 Constitution explicitly authorized expropriation in circumstances without the payment of compensation. Nor was an insistence on inviolable property rights consistent with the domestic law of many states. Calvo's doctrine, Duguit's "social function" of property, and the Weimar Constitution's property clause all influenced developments in constitutional law in Latin America in the early twentieth century (see Chapter six). Moreover, among the states claiming that there existed a minimum standard beyond national treatment required by international law, this was no more than dogma. The police powers exception to the takings rule, Sir Williams wrote for a British audience, "delivered the United States from the practical impasse to which we come if we seek to insist on an absolute rule" for the protection of private property (Wild 1939: 15; Williams 1928: 24). These very same states aggressively regulated private property. In all "civilized legal systems," wrote Morris Cohen, "there is a great deal of just expropriation or confiscation without any direct compensation" (1927: 60; Radin 1993: 131; Rose 2000: 5).

Proponents of the strict international minimum standard of treatment, both with regard to compensable takings and standard of compensation, ordinarily would not admit that the diversity of local rules could justify the transference of particularistic domestic legal doctrine to the plane of the universal. Political scientist Frederick Sherwood Dunn was more candid: for him, the debate was about preserving capitalism as a way of life. The minimum standard of justice, wrote Dunn, "is nothing more nor less than the ideas which are conceived to be essential to a continuation of the existing social and economic order of European capitalistic civilization" (Dunn 1928: 175). So long as the European and European-settler states "remain dominant in international society, it is the fundamentals of their civilization which will determine the content of the standard of justice embodied in the international legal system" (Dunn 1928: 176). Elihu Root also understood that it was the "great rules of justice" embodied in the US Constitution – premised on the idea of limited governmental power – that were being conscripted into the international minimum standard regarding the treatment of foreigners (Anghie 2004: 284–5; Williams 1928: 17). The US constitution was "a standard for the morality and the conscience of the world," Root proclaimed, which gave expression to the "eternal laws of justice and liberty" (Root 1916: 500–1). In language reminiscent of both James Madison and Adam Smith, Root declared that "the chief motive power that has moved mankind along the course of development that we call the progress of civilization has been the sum total of intelligent selfishness in a vast number of individuals, each working for his own support, his own gain, his own betterment" (Root 1913: 14). It was, for this reason, "injurious for government to attempt too much" lest it quell individual liberty and initiative (Root 1913: 15). Root's elevation of these assumptions into "eternal principles" (Cohen 1917: 14) would have the effect of transferring US constitutional values abroad and freezing, even rolling back, political solutions to distributive problems elsewhere (Anghie 2005). States, moreover, were expected to conform to the strictest possible version of the rule internal to the more powerful states without further possibility of amendment (Williams 1928: 17).

To be sure, the imposition of constitution-like limitations via an international rule of law was expected to quell the development of socialistic alternatives. But why would the international community be asked "to accept so unreservedly the theories of one side in the great economic dispute," asked Williams (1928: 21). From "the angle of human development and experimentation it may be just as well that one particular attitude to private property should not be fastened to international law," suggested Wild (1939: 20). The preferred general rule, for those resisting the new international minimum standard, was that foreign investors were entitled to no greater treatment than locals, that equality between foreigners and locals was desirable, and that, in any event, there was never any requirement to pay "just" or "full" compensation. Should states of the world be desirous of protecting alien property beyond this, they could do so by express agreement.

## RETURN OF THE STANDARDS OF CIVILIZED JUSTICE

The emergence of a world wide web of investment treaties setting high standards for the protection of foreign investment abroad might reasonably be viewed as the logical end point for this discussion. The lack of "broad international approval" has long been one of the "greatest weaknesses" of investor protections, Lipson noted, resulting in its "shaky legal basis" (1985: 176, 97). The post-1989 investment rules regime signals, it is argued, the final universal acceptance of the minimum standard of treatment long espoused by capital-exporting European and European-derived legal systems (Gunawardana 1992; Hindelang 2004). The proliferation of investment agreements, even among developing countries that have long articulated alternative readings of international law, suggests that any resistance to that interpretation now has been abandoned. For many of these developing countries, it is viewed as economically advantageous to signal their readiness to participate in the post-1989 international economic environment. The threat of noninvestment is now greater than the threats posed by foreign investment backed up by gun-boat diplomacy in times past (Beck 2005: 52; Taylor 2000: 67). As Stopford and Strange argue, the Canadian decision to join the United States in a free trade and investment agreement was not lost on developing countries: if "the weaker partner thinks the risks of *not* joining are greater and the benefits, however marginal, worthwhile," then there "must be something in it" for developing countries too (Stopford and Strange 1991: 120). Not only are economic advantages, if any, spread unevenly across these countries, but the agreements also reflect an unevenness in bargaining power between negotiating states (Sornarajah 2004: 207). These relationships, in other words, reflect "hardly a voluntary, uncoerced transaction" (Alvarez 1992: 552).

In light of the pressures to participate, we might reasonably question the extent to which the proliferation of investment rules signals a new turn to consensus in international investment law. Sornorajah argues that the absence of a multilateral agreement on investment protection standards evinces a lack of consensus on such matters (2004: 213) (hence the importance that OECD countries placed in achieving a consensus over the draft MAI). International Law Commission Special Rapporteur Dugard advises that Calvo continues to influence developments in Latin America and that "Latin American States still cling to the [Calvo] Clause [in state contracts] as an important feature of their regional approach to international law" (Dugard 2002: 15). Guzman also resists concluding that BITs establish a new rule in customary international law regarding the standard of compensation owed to foreign investors in the event of a taking. The proliferation of BITs in the 1990s can be explained as the self-interested behavior of individual states seeking "an advantage in the competition for foreign investment" rather than an expression of consensus among developing and less developed countries that the Hull formula of compensation is now the global standard (Guzman 1998: 686). Standards of compensation aside, even if BITs served as evidence of customary practice, there is still too much vagueness in their terms of protection to serve as a reliable guide to international law (Guzman 2005: 13). The standard BIT clauses that guard against "indirect" takings or that prohibit "measures tantamount to" takings are much too vague to provide any guidance. In light of their laconic wording, Dolzer surmises that states presumably will seek direction by referring back to the "general principles of law recognized by civilized nations" (2002: 76; 1986: 56). General principles are identified as a source of law in the authoritative Statute of the International Court of Justice (Art. 38[1][c]) and for which Root usually is credited with authorship, along with Phillimore (Brownlie 2003: 16).

But international law applies no clear standard in this area. Dolzer and Stevens remind us that there is "no clear definition" of indirect takings and that a "wide variety of measures are susceptible to lead to indirect expropriation" (1995: 100). Nor is there a clear distinction in international law between compensable takings and noncompensable regulations that fall within the scope of a state's police power jurisdiction. Developments in international economic law may be stepping up to fill in the void. At a time when developing countries seemingly have resigned themselves to the ascendancy of stringent rules for the protection of foreign investment, international law is generally moving in directions that may help to lock-in the post-1989 international economic environment and the general tendency toward open markets and limited government.

Higgins, for instance, has called for stricter scrutiny of measures that impact on property. She has questioned whether the distinction between regulatory noncompensable takings (in the furtherance of the police power) and compensable takings can be so easily sustained. There is a conceptual confusion in international law, she maintains, in the distinction between noncompensable regulations that pursue a "public purpose" and compensable takings. She asks whether the distinction is "intellectually viable": "Is not the State in both cases ... purporting to act in the public good? And in each case has the owner of property not suffered a loss?" Higgins insists that, under international law standards, a regulation that amounts "by virtue of its scope and effect" to a taking, could not be for a "public purpose" and so "just compensation would be due" (Higgins 1982: 331). Lipson similarly notes that there are a "whole range of state actions that affect foreign equity and profits, a range where expropriation and regulation overlap" and so the meaning of expropriation is "blurred" (1985: 25, 182). Rather than deferring to state regulation of economic subjects – the dominant mode of interpretation in US constitutional law throughout the mid-twentieth century – Higgins calls for strict scrutiny, paralleling recent trends in US constitutional law.[8]

The emergence of a literature on the subject of "constructive," "creeping," and "indirect" takings (Dolzer 1986; Mulchinski 1995: 501–2; Wallace 1983: 261; Weston 1975: 112–13) – referring to measures that cumulatively or indirectly amount to a taking – exemplifies this move to heightened scrutiny. Without abandoning entirely the presumption that states have some scope to regulate their economies, it has been urged that the public international law of expropriation capture those government actions that amount to the deprivation of foreign-based wealth, even if "indirect" or "regulatory" and even if no identifiable gains are made by other parties. According to Burns Weston, "host country deprivative 'regulations' that appear actually to retard global well-being by hindering economic development ... should be deemed 'constructive takings' (i.e, compensable events)" (Weston 1975: 177). The breadth of the proposed rule is intended to catch a variety of measures that, though falling short of outright appropriations of title, directly or indirectly exceed a not easily identifiable threshold of excessiveness.

The doctrine of conceptual severance has been embraced in international law (*Amoco* 1990: 545; *Revere Copper* 1980). Substantially impairing only a part of an enterprise can give rise to a claim for compensatory damages – the abolition of contractual rights, for instance. It has "long been recognized," announced one tribunal, "that contractual rights may be indirectly expropriated" (*Southern Pacific* 1993: paras 164–5; *Amoco* 1990: para. 108). This fits well the logic of the investment rules regime that secures protection for most of the elements that make up foreign investment – contractual expectations, real property, goodwill, and most everything else – so that the taking of part of an investment interest is equivalent to the taking of the whole (e.g., *Azurix* 2006: para. 314; *Mondev* 2003: para. 98; *Waste Management* 2004: para. 175). It usually matters not that bona fide regulatory measures, such as those protecting the environment, may have been pursued. The "obligation to pay compensation remains" (*Compañia del Desarrollo de Santa Elena* 2000: paras 72).[9]

This strict interpretive approach complements well other developments in international economic law, namely, rulings by WTO dispute settlement bodies. These panels have the responsibility of policing state compliance with a range of obligations under the WTO including national treatment and MFN rules in the Uruguay-round GATT. Dispute settlement bodies mostly have read exceptions narrowly within the GATT that permit deviations from the principle of free trade. Departures from GATT disciplines are permitted if "necessary for the protection of human, animal, or plant life or health" (Art. XX[b]).[10] Only recently has the WTO encountered a measure that qualified as a justifiable health or environmental exception.

For the most part, unilateral trade-restrictive measures, even if advancing environmental causes, simply have not been tolerated. In the *Reformulated Gasoline* case (1996), the WTO Appellate Body (AB) concluded that a failure to seek the cooperation of foreign states amounted to a disguised restriction on trade and so failed to satisfy Art. XX's "chapeau" criteria – prohibiting "arbitrary or unjustified discrimination" or a "disguised restriction on international trade" – prerequisites to the ability of states to adopt the environmental exception in Art. XX(b).[11] When it came to measures protecting dolphins from the tuna fishing industry, WTO panels would not salvage trade measures intended to promote foreign environmental conservation (*Tuna/Dolphin I* 1991) or that were intended to change the environmental policies of another country (*Tuna/Dolphin II* 1994). All less restrictive options had to be pursued before imposing such a limitation on trade. The *Shrimp/Turtle* case concerned Congressional measures to prohibit the importation of shrimp caught by trawlers that endangered sea turtle ecology. An embargo was imposed on shrimp caught without a "turtle excluding device" (TED) – this applied initially to catch from the western hemisphere and, subsequently, worldwide. The countries of India, Malaysia, Pakistan, and Thailand contested the measure before the WTO. In the final analysis, the AB acknowledged that the measure concerned an exhaustible natural resource but could not be considered justified or nonarbitrary. By insisting that identical conservation schemes be adopted abroad, the unilateral action of the United States was characterized as "coercive," "rigid," and "unbending" (*Shrimp/Turtle* 1998: paras 161, 163). The unilateral deployment of uniform trade measures in order to achieve policy change in another country (the use of TEDs by shrimp trawlers), though not prohibited per se, simply could not be justified under Art. XX.[12] Gaines argues that this interpretation showed "no understanding of how environmental protection measures operate" (Gaines 2001: 772, 798) making difficult the prospect of regulatory change for the purpose of protecting health or the environment (Parker 1999: 107). In a second report on *Shrimp/Turtle*, following the complaint of Malaysia concerning implementation of the first decision, the AB admitted that unilateralism alone would not disqualify a measure under Art. XX (*Shrimp/Turtle* 2001: para. 138). This decision together with the ruling in the *Asbestos* case (2001), upholding a French ban on Canadian asbestos, indicates that WTO jurisprudence may be taking a turn toward more leniency in the application of Art. XX exceptions (Charnovitz 2007: 695; Wai 2003: 62). Though France was found not to be in breach of the GATT, and so did not have to rely on a justifiable exception, the AB laid down an interpretation of Art. XX(b) more "deferential" and "sensitive" to regulatory choices that advance public health interests (Trebilcock and Howse 2005: 541). Among the significant findings, the AB accepted that France was protecting health under Art. XX(b) and would not scrutinize closely less restrictive measures under a proportionality analysis of "weighing and balancing" (Trebilcock and Howse 2005: 542). This recent turn suggests that the AB is a reflexive institution, responding to critiques about its strict approach to authorized exceptions to WTO disciplines (Banaker 1998; Zumbansen 2002).

Having outlined trends in international economic law that have leaned mostly in the direction of the constraining version of constitutionalism, we can now return to the argument that the "general principles of international law" help to fill out the content of the takings rule standard. It is only a short step, however, to a revival of the "great constitutions of civilization" standard. Though the law of indirect expropriation is only "very sketchy and rough," Dolzer proffers that a survey of "typical liberal" constitutions will yield fruitful results (he takes up the US, UK, French, and German national legal systems) (1986, 2002). They reveal "identical positions" with regard to permissible restrictions on the use of property. All jurisdictions permit restrictions on the economically optimal use of property; all prohibit (or limit) state regulation that denies all reasonable economically viable use; and all will permit regulation of future use only where it is necessary to protect the public from some "danger" (or nuisance) as in the exercise of the police power (Dolzer 1986: 62). This reasonably approximates a mid-twentieth-century version of the US takings rule but fails to account for movement toward a stricter version of the rule. This restatement also inadequately accounts for the UK constitutional position, where constitutional limitations with regard to property have amounted mostly to statutory presumptions (though this has changed to the extent that the Human Rights Act gives effect to European Convention on Human Rights) (Allen 1999). Last, this exercise in transnational justice conveniently reflects only the position of the most dominant economic powers. Knop has described the colonialist legacy associated with "general principles" and finds that contemporary practice tends to have the "same discriminatory effect" (2003: 456). Dolzer works within this same tradition. He acknowledges that "international rules protecting aliens have grown out of the relevant laws which have existed in the legal systems of major home states of aliens." On the basis of this "historical nexus," these systems should continue to "inform the current state of the law" (2002: 77). By declining to consider alternative constitutional arrangements for the protection of alien property, Dolzer outlines a constitutional order of investment law that serves to justify merely the established order of things.

If economic globalization is characterized as the contingent outcome of competing national experiences (Albrow 1997), the objective of this chapter has been to identify conditions intended to give rise to certain predetermined outcomes, namely, those of security and predictability with regard to protected investments. This is accomplished via constitution-like limitations on state action with regard to economic regulation. The US takings rule is an exemplar of this kind of limitation on state conduct. It is this standard that was incorporated into claims concerning the minimum standard of treatment early in the twentieth century, the outlines of which clearly are discernible in the early twenty-first century investment rules regime. Whatever the precise source of the early doctrine around physical takings, the rise of "indirect" or "regulatory" takings in the investment rules regime parallels doctrinal developments in regulatory takings law in the United States. As in earlier times, the current rules regime is premised on claims about the universality of local legal rules – claims that are successful only to the extent that they repress the conditions that give rise to privileged access to the universal (Bourdieu 2000: 70).

# CHAPTER THREE

# INVESTMENT RULES IN ACTION

I have argued that the investment rules regime has constitution-like features. The rules and institutions comprise a strategy of precommitment binding future generations to certain, predetermined norms and institutional forms, constraining unreasonably the possibilities for political practice. Like constitutions, they are difficult to amend, include binding enforcement mechanisms together with judicial review, and oftentimes are drawn from the language of domestic constitutions. Tantamount to a bill of rights for investors, international investment agreements entitle investors to sue state parties for damages before international tribunals for violations of investment strictures. The typical takings rule – the prohibition on direct or indirect expropriation and nationalization or measures "tantamount to" expropriation – limits governmental capacity in constitution-like ways while the demand of "fair and equitable treatment" as represented by the rules of civilized justice serves similarly broad constitutional functions. Premised on a distrust of political power – an idea familiar to the framers of the US Constitution – the regime institutionalizes a version of constitutionalism that is primarily concerned with freezing the regulatory status quo while inhibiting the possibilities for future political action.

Others also have observed the limiting effects of investment rules on the regulatory ability of state parties, particularly in the context of NAFTA. Wagner predicted that NAFTA's takings rule would have a "serious chilling effect on the ability and willingness of governments to implement" legitimate environmental regulations

(Wagner 1999: 467). He likened the right to sue for economic impacts of environmental regulation to a "legally enforced protection racket" (Wagner 1999: 526). The International Institute for Sustainable Development observed that NAFTA's investment disciplines had been "misappropriated" by foreign business owners seeking to prevent changes in regulatory environments (Mann and Moltke 1999: 15; cf. Banks 1999; Ganguly 1999). These concerns helped to give rise to vociferous opposition to the MAI negotiated in Paris that would have instituted similar disciplines on the twenty-nine state members of the OECD (Clark and Barlow 1997). Similar anxieties helped to mobilize opposition to the WTO in the streets of Seattle in December 1999, and later protests in Prague, Washington, Genoa, Quebec City, and elsewhere.

Many of these observations and anxieties were based upon an early assessment of NAFTA's investment chapter and related disciplines. They were informed by threatened and initiated investor-state disputes (such as the Ethyl claim that is discussed in Chapter four) but not by the rulings of arbitration tribunals. This chapter tests the hypothesis about the constitution-like effects of the investment rules regime in light of the arbitral jurisprudence. This chapter does not purport to offer up as a comprehensive review of the jurisprudence, rather, the chapter focuses on the work of selected NAFTA and other investment tribunals. Cases that might be considered foundational, such as those established to resolve the *Pope & Talbot*, *Metalclad*, *S. D. Myers*, and *Methanex* claims, are given in-depth consideration. Also the chapter doe not attempt to assess whether regulatory chill has, in fact, clouded policy making. This sort of assessment requires more than an examination of cases. Supporters of the rules regime usually point only to decided cases to argue an absence of regulatory chill (e.g., Brower, II 2003; Coe, Jr. 2003: 1438; Gaines 2002). The idea of chilling effects is derived from US free speech doctrine. It speaks to the possibility of "self-censorship" in circumstances where one has doubts about the success of defending oneself in court or fears associated with the expense of having to do so (*New York Times* 1964). So this is a phenomenon that cannot be assessed solely with reference to decided cases. What would be more useful in the international investment context, then, is a detailed investigation into the workings and practices of one or more of the NAFTA national or subnational governments in order to determine whether there has been regulatory chill in certain branches of government. A window into the inhibiting effect of regulatory chill is offered by an account of debates in the Canadian province of New Brunswick over the establishment of a new regime of public auto insurance (Shrybman and Sinclair 2004). Egregiously high premiums paid to auto insurers were a principal issue in the 2003 provincial election campaign. Upon reelection, Premier Bernard Lord struck an all-party legislative committee to consider an appropriate response to the auto insurance crisis. In its final report, the committee recommended that the province adopt a no-fault public auto insurance scheme, versions of which are in place in several other Canadian provinces (New Brunswick 2004a). The committee bravely suggested proceeding with this plan despite evidence from the Insurance Bureau of Canada (IBC) buttressed by a high-powered legal opinion that US-based private auto insurers could seek compensation for the taking of their investment interests under NAFTA's Chapter 11 (McCarthy Tétrault 2003). Ultimately, the government decided to pursue an alternative course of action. A government run monopoly, Premier Lord declared, was "not the right decision for New Brunswick," though he made no reference to NAFTA's potential chill over this regulatory proposal (New Brunswick 2004b). It is instructive that, in the days leading up to the premier's decision to yield to private insurers, IBC General Counsel Randy Bundus issued a poignant warning: "The world is a different place than it was back in the 1970s when [the provinces of] Manitoba and British Columbia took action [over auto insurance] – now we have NAFTA and GATT" (Peterson 2004).

A review of the arbitral jurisprudence suggests that fears of constitution-like discipline via NAFTA's takings rule and its associated provisions, such as fair and equitable treatment, are not without foundation. The tribunals have acknowledged that nondiscriminatory regulatory measures fall within the scope of the prohibition, and that those measures that are "substantial enough," "significantly deprive," or that "unreasonably interfere" with investment expectations will give rise to a taking under NAFTA. The scope of compensable takings remains quite broad – the rule can catch all varieties of legitimate, regulatory initiatives – while the categorical distinction between compensable and noncompensable regulatory action remains imprecise. Though many of the tribunals adopted an expansive view of the takings rule, admittedly few under discussion found there to be a compensable taking. There has been, instead, more claimant success invoking the concomitant standard of fair and equitable treatment. I argue that these standards of fairness and equity appear to be serving similar disciplinary functions as the takings rule. This migration of function from the takings rule to the fair and equitable treatment standard suggests a measure of reflexivity in the face of civil society and social movement critique, which aims to resolve legitimacy problems associated with international investment arbitration (Banakar 1998; Calliess 2002).

It should come as little surprise that the jurisprudence under NAFTA, and investment treaties generally, indicates that the overriding priority of the regime is to protect the interests of investors over the interests of state parties who may wish to pursue countervailing social policy goals. This decided tilt in favor of foreign investors reflects a mode of interpretation described as the "sole-effects" doctrine by Dolzer (2002: 79), where determinations as to the violation of investment disciplines are made solely with reference to the effects of a measure on investors. Dolzer associates this stance with the *Norwegian Shipowners'* case (1922) (discussed in Chapter two) and the *Chorzów Factory* case (1928) where the Polish government was required to pay damages, under the 1922 Geneva convention concerning Upper Silesia, for seizure of a factory in circumstances that exceeded what could be characterized as an expropriation, amounting to an "illegal act" (1926: 46–7). Sole-effects doctrine bears a strong family resemblance with the Scalian version of the takings doctrine where the impact on reasonable investment-backed expectations practically is the sole criterion for determining whether compensation is due under the US Constitution (Underkuffler 2004: 733). This is contrasted with an approach that considers public interest objectives under the rubric of proportionality analysis – a weighing of means used in light of ends sought – an infrequent occurrence in NAFTA and other investment tribunal cases. Dolzer associates this interpretive approach with a series of cases beginning with the *Oscar Chinn Case* (1934). There the Permanent Court of International Justice shielded the Belgian government from international responsibility for having taken measures, in the midst of a "severe commercial depression" (*Oscar Chinn* 1934: 71), ensuring the survival of a river transport business in which the state had an interest in circumstances where the state was entrusted with providing transportation services to the Belgian Congo (*Oscar Chinn* 1934: 78). These measures had the effect of driving the competition, namely Mr. Chinn, out of business creating a de facto monopoly. The court could not find that Belgium's actions offended the terms of the Convention of Saint Germain, guaranteeing nondiscrimination and freedom of trade and navigation in the Belgian Congo. Nor did

Belgium disregard the general principles of international law by failing to respect vested rights. No vested rights were implicated considering Mr Chinn's original position, which

> was characterized by the possession of customers and the possibility of making a profit ... Favourable business conditions and goodwill are transient circumstances, subject to inevitable changes ... no enterprise – least of all a commercial or transport enterprise, the success of which is dependent on the fluctuating level of prices and rates – can escape from the chances and hazards resulting from general economic conditions ... they are all exposed to the danger of ruin or extinction if circumstances change. (*Oscar Chinn* 1934: 88)

It is fair to say that the Scalian/sole-effects doctrine better captures the dominant tenor of the arbitral jurisprudence outlined here (Dolzer 2002: 91; Dolzer and Bloch 2003: 163). Even on the few occasions where tribunals move to a proportionality analysis, there remains a heavy burden on states to dislodge the presumption against measures that run afoul of investment disciplines. In this way, the proportionality analysis is disproportionately applied against state objectives. The tribunal decisions confirm, overall, that NAFTA and the investment rules regime generate a legal architecture institutionalizing a regime of limited government with constitution-like disciplines on state regulatory capacity.

This conclusion is fortified by the actions of two of NAFTA's state parties. Canada, some time ago, initiated a campaign to clarify aspects of NAFTA so as to better reflect "the original intentions of the drafters" (Pettigrew 2001). The other party states initially were cool to the initiative (Jack 2000a, 2001a, 2001c; McKinnon 2000; Scoffield, 2000). The overreaching of NAFTA's takings rule, however, sufficiently alarmed Congress that it moved into action when President George W. Bush sought Trade Promotion Authority (TPA) to pursue a hemispheric agreement together with a number of bilateral free trade and investment agreements. Congressional approval was tentative and this was due, in large part, to the experience under NAFTA's Chapter 11.[1] The Democratic Chair of the Finance Committee, Senator Max Baucus, together with Senator Chuck Grassley endorsed proposals that would qualify the phrase "tantamount to expropriation" in the model US takings rule to ensure that foreign investors were "accorded no greater rights than U.S. investors in the U.S." (Inside US Trade 2002a).[2] The House of Representatives endorsed similar language (Kerremans 2003: 536–7). In its final version, the Bipartisan Trade Promotion Authority Act of 2002 recognizes that US law "on the whole provides a high level of protection for investment, consistent with or greater than the level required by international law." The principal negotiating objectives of the United States regarding foreign investment, then, will be to ensure that foreign investors in the United States "are not accorded greater substantive rights with respect to investment protections than United States investors in the United States." At the same time, negotiators should "secure for investors important rights comparable to those that would be available under United States legal principles and practice" (Sec. 2102[3]; Inside US Trade 2002c). All of this, ironically, is reminiscent of the discredited Calvo doctrine.

The United States Trade Representative (USTR) followed suit, qualifying the language of the takings rule in free trade agreements with Chile, Singapore, Morocco, and others so that nondiscriminatory environmental, health, and welfare measures intended to protect the "public welfare" would not ordinarily be caught by the rule (Alden 2004; USTR 2004a). The treaties expressly incorporate the various criteria identified by the US Supreme Court in *Penn Central* in order to determine whether there has been a compensable taking (1977: 124; USTR 2003). The new standards eventually were embodied in the 2004 US model treaty and, in modified form, in a new Canadian model treaty. These developments appear to prove the very point that were made at the start by many critics of NAFTA's takings rule – that the rule is intended to mirror US takings standards. As Poirier warns, "[i]nvestment protection in the generation of FTAs [by the United States] after NAFTA will be American indeed" (2003: 898).

## TAKING STOCK

Many of the obligations undertaken in NAFTA and other BITs are organized around the idea of "nondiscrimination." States may not distinguish, for the purposes of legal regulation, between domestic and foreign investors. According to the national treatment rule, foreign investors are to be treated as if they were economic citizens within the host state. MFN status mandates that foreign investors receive the best treatment accorded by the host state to investors from any other state. Related to the principle of nondiscrimination in NAFTA are prohibitions on performance requirements, such as rules that call for the use of local labor, goods, and services. Other rules mandate not just equality of treatment, but place substantive limits on state control. Among these are the "minimum standard of treatment under international law," which includes "fair and equitable treatment," and the takings rule. The minimum standard of treatment is an omnibus standard of "civilized" justice that includes procedural and substantive components including, early in the twentieth century, standards regarding takings (Borchard 1939; Choudhury 2005; Friedmann 1956; Oppenheim 1949: para. 155d; Roth 1949; Weiler 2000). It was described, as we saw in Chapter two, as reflecting standards conceived as "essential to a continuation of the existing social and economic order of European capitalistic civilization" (Dunn 1928: 175). The contemporary version of the takings rule has been described as the "single most important goal" of the US bilateral investment treaty program (Vandevelde 1992b: 534, 1998: 621–41).

The takings rule, as noted in Chapter two, is a notoriously opaque discipline. One can search far and wide in vain for a clear and workable distinction between regulations exempt from and expropriations caught by the rule. Arbitral tribunals have expressed some frustration about this: it is "much less clear when governmental action . . . crosses the line from valid regulation to compensable taking, and it is fair to say that no one has come up with a fully satisfactory means of drawing this line" (*Feldman* 2002: para. 100; *Saluka* 2006: para. 263). This has contributed to continued questions regarding the legitimacy of NAFTA and other investment agreements. Trade scholars, too, have acknowledged puzzlement regarding the scope of the takings rule. It has been described as "unpredictable" (Dolzer 2002: 68), not "an easy task" to apply (Kunoy 2005: 467), and with "no clear answer[s]" (Newcombe 2005: 3). It has "bedevilled governments, international tribunals and international lawyers" alike (Wälde and Kolo 2001: 812). Bewilderment over the scope of the takings rule is best evinced by an opinion piece concerning the settlement of the Ethyl MMT case, discussed in Chapter four. Ostry and Soloway bemoaned the fact that the Ethyl complaint was settled so early and before an international trade tribunal could rule on whether the ban on the gasoline additive MMT amounted to an expropriation under NAFTA. Suggesting that a ruling somehow would settle the scope of the takings rule, they wrote:

> It would have clarified a great deal for legal scholars, and for others affected, if this question had been put before an arbitral tribunal: At

what point does legislation enacted under the sovereign right of a government amount to an expropriation? ... Those of us anxious to know what governments will – and won't – be allowed to do in the name of national regulation will have to monitor other cases now pending, involving U.S. companies in Mexico.  (Ostry and Soloway 1998)

Among the arbitral proceedings launched under NAFTA, the Ethyl Corporation challenge of a Canadian ban on the import and export of the toxic gasoline additive MMT is perhaps the most notorious, though a tribunal never ruled upon the substance of the claim.[3] This chapter takes up a number of cases that have been the subject of arbitration under NAFTA's Chapter 11 dispute resolution process and, parenthetically, a number of other investment treaties. These tribunals, established under the auspices of the World Bank's ICSID, the UNCITRAL, or other arbitral facilities, follow in many respects the private commercial arbitration model. Three arbitrators are appointed, one by each side of the dispute together with a neutral chair or president drawn from a roster of trade law experts chosen, according to the NAFTA Secretariat, "strictly on the basis of objectivity, reliability, sound judgment and with a general familiarity with international trade law" (2004). A number of recurring problems have been identified with the model chosen to resolve investment disputes. Members of the arbitration bar may be called upon to act as counsel, and counsel as arbitrators, giving rise to apparent, if not real, conflicts of interest (Levine 2006; Peterson 2007). Arbitrators have been described as belonging to a "club" (Sornarajah 2000: 160) with a distinct bias in favor of commercial solutions to public problems (Wälde 2005: 9). The deployment of "off-the-rack" commercial arbitration has also given rise to complaints about the general secrecy and lack of transparency in arbitral proceedings (Atik 2004: 142). There is some movement in the other direction. Greater transparency in NAFTA proceedings followed from an interpretation and joint statement of the NAFTA Free Trade Commission (FTC) (2001, 2003). New BITs signed by the United States also tend toward greater openness. Amendments to ICSID rules promulgated in April 2006 (Rules 6 and 32) call for disclosure of actual conflicts of interest and enable written submissions by third parties but permit attendance at hearings only with the consent of both parties (Rules 37 and 32). Investor-state dispute proceedings, nevertheless, involve too many "revolving doors" (Buergenthal 2006: 8) and too much secrecy (Marshall and Mann 2006).

The costs to the parties in order to run these proceedings are enormous. It is reported, for instance, that the Metalclad Corporation paid US $4 million in lawyers' and arbitrators' fees in their dispute against Mexico. Governments also incur significant costs, on average, about US $1–2 million for their lawyers, alone (OECD 2005b: 10). The tribunal in *Thunderbird* disclosed that the Mexican government had incurred US $1.5 million in legal fees, while the cost of arbitration (including arbitrators' fees and disbursements) totaled US $505,252 (2006: paras 220–1). In *Methanex*, legal costs to the government were almost US $3 million, while the Methanex Corporation claimed that its own costs were in the range of US $11–12 million (*Methanex* 2005: Pt. V. para. 12). This, perhaps, is one reason why international trade lawyers complain about third-party submissions by NGOs in the context of an investment dispute as being "effectively 'for free'" (Hunter and Barbuk 2004: 169).

Enforcement is accomplished through the aegis of arbitral tribunals established under treaty or convention in which there is no binding precedent (Schreuer 2001: 1082). Nevertheless, tribunals often "carefully examine earlier decisions and accept these as authority most of the time," but not always (*El Paso Energy* 2006: para. 39; Schreuer 2006: 17). Indeed, there is the possibility for entirely contradictory tribunal rulings to issue out of similar, if not precise, factual circumstances as in the case of *CMS* (2005) and *LG&E* (2006), discussed below. Emblematic of this possibility are the *CME* (2001) and *Lauder* (2001) cases. The Czech Republic was the subject of two separate investor disputes for having participated in freezing out a Dutch company from a broadcast licensing scheme. In *CME*, initiated by the foreign company under a Netherlands-Czech BIT, the state was held liable for the devaluation of the investment interest. In *Lauder*, brought by the principal investor under a US-Czech BIT, no liability flowed from the state action. It was not an "unnatural" result, observes Wälde, that two sets of arbitrators reached differing results (2003: 918).

Despite the potential for inconsistent awards, there are, it can fairly be said, some obvious trends issuing out of the case law. This is what arbitrator Wälde describes as an "emerging international investment law jurisprudence" (*Thunderbird* 2005 Separate Opinion [SO]: para. 15; *Waste Management* 2004: para. 98). The ensuing discussion extends across a range of claims determined by investment tribunals but, most particularly, the takings rule and the fair and equitable treatment standard. I argue that this jurisprudence, though somewhat attentive to anxieties expressed over the breadth of investor rights under NAFTA, does not assuage concerns that the investment rules regime imposes constitution-like limits on state regulatory capacity.

## "Substantial," "significant," and "unreasonable" interference

The interim award in the *Pope & Talbot* case is one of the earliest cases addressing the distinction between compensable takings and exercises of police powers jurisdiction and so helped to fill out the scope of NAFTA's takings rule. The *Azinian* tribunal (1999), which predates *Pope & Talbot*, provided some initial guidance about the scope of the rule. The Azinian claim concerned a concession contract to provide local waste disposal services to a suburb of Mexico City. The company, however, was ill equipped to live up to its contractual commitments. Assuming there was merit to the claimant's case – the tribunal found that the case was based upon misrepresentation and unconscionable conduct and so "failed in its entirety" (1999: 125) – mere contractual breaches were not sufficient to raise the dispute to the level of an international one (1999: para. 87). Investors may be disappointed in their dealings with states and national courts, the tribunal pointedly remarked, but NAFTA "was not intended to provide foreign investors with blanket protection from this kind of disappointment, and nothing in its terms so provides" (1999: 83). More was yet required to be shown before the tribunal would consider a breach of contract as a breach of NAFTA (see *Waste Management* 2004: para. 175).

The US forestry company, Pope & Talbot Inc. of Portland, Oregon, launched arbitral proceedings under NAFTA's investment chapter seeking compensation not for breach of contract but for losses suffered in the allocation of logging quotas in the province of British Columbia. These quotas were assigned to logging operators in the province pursuant to the Canada-US Softwood Lumber Agreement. In a preliminary award, the arbitral tribunal rejected Canada's motion (supported by Mexico) to dismiss Pope & Talbot's claim. Canada argued that the claim fell outside the scope of Chapter 11 as it did not concern a measure "relating to investment" in a "direct and substantial way" but merely "affected" an investor or investment interest. Alternatively, the allocation of quotas concerned a measure relating to "trade in goods." The tribunal refused this preliminary motion, finding that the measures, as applied, directly affected Pope & Talbot's ability to trade in goods and, if so, a measure primarily concerned with trade in goods can also "relate to" an investor and an investment interest under Chapter 11 (*Pope & Talbot* 2000b: para. 33).

In another preliminary decision, the tribunal ruled against Canada in its attempt to suppress the discovery of documents that Canada claimed were cabinet confidences protected by the *Canada Evidence Act*. The tribunal ruled that the act – overly protective of claims to Cabinet confidences, requiring only "certification" that they were so by government – did not control NAFTA arbitral proceedings (Appleton 2000; *Pope & Talbot* 2000c). The tribunal declared itself to be beyond the grasp of domestic law and empowered foreign investors to greater rights of disclosure than those available to Canadians in their own courts.[4]

The tribunal had issued its more substantive interim award some months earlier (2000a). Pope & Talbot claimed that the allocation of logging quotas offended national treatment, imposed performance requirements, and was a measure tantamount to expropriation. The tribunal dismissed two of the three claims. Though having the effect of deterring exports to the United States, the measures did not impose or enforce performance requirements (*Pope & Talbot* 2000a: para. 75). Nor were the measures tantamount to an expropriation under NAFTA. The substance of the national treatment claim, however, could not be conclusively determined at this stage of the proceedings and so a decision on this ground was deferred until some 8 months later.

While the arbitrators in the interim award rejected Pope & Talbot's broad interpretation of the takings rule, they accepted a number of the investor's key postulates.[5] First, the tribunal accepted that the definition of a protected "investment" under NAFTA included market access to Canada. Second, the tribunal found that the takings rule covers "non-discriminatory regulation that might be said to fall within an exercise of a state's so-called police powers." The impugned measures, however, were not "substantial enough" or "sufficiently restrictive" to give rise to a claim of expropriation (*Pope & Talbot* 2000: paras 96, 102). The focus here was predominantly on the effect of the state decision on the investor.

The tribunal found support for its interpretation of NAFTA's takings rule in the American Law Institute's *Third Restatement of the Foreign Relations Law of the United States* (1987). The *Restatement* calls for state responsibility in the event that "alien property" is subject to "taxation, regulation, or other action that is confiscatory, or that prevents, unreasonably interferes with, or unduly delays, effective enjoyment" of property (American Law Institute 1987: para. 712, comment [g]). The comment goes on to say that "As under United States constitutional law, the line between 'taking' and regulation is sometimes uncertain"[6] and the tribunal also acknowledged this difficulty in a footnote (*Pope & Talbot* 2000; 1987: para. 99, fn. 73).[7] It is precisely this distinction, familiar to US takings law jurisprudence under the Fifth and Fourteenth amendments, that NAFTA's takings rule incorporates into Canadian and Mexican law. Yet, the *Pope & Talbot* ruling appears to have gone even further. Police power regulations, according to the tribunal, may command compensation under NAFTA. These, by definition, do not attract compensation under US law (Dana and Merrill 2002: 6). This finding may not be as confused as it seems, for it is consistent with the movement toward stricter scrutiny noted in Chapter two. This is exemplified by Judge Higgins, who argues that the distinction between exercises of police powers and compensable expropriations are not "intellectually viable" (Higgins 1982: 331).[8]

The tribunal issued its award on the merits the following year, dismissing the national treatment claim (*Pope & Talbot* 2001). In doing so, the tribunal rejected the odious argument made by Pope & Talbot that the company was entitled to the best treatment accorded to lumber producer exporters throughout Canada, not simply as compared to other producer exporters in the province of British Columbia (*Pope & Talbot* 2001: para. 88). If successful, NAFTA's national treatment rule would have required uniformity with regard to measures affecting foreign investments, whereas the constitutional division of legislative power in Canada is intended to enable regulatory diversity with regard to "property and civil rights."[9] The tribunal found that the policy implementing the Softwood Lumber Accord was reasonably related to rational goals and not motivated by a desire to discriminate (*Pope & Talbot* 2001: paras 87, 102). The tribunal found fault with Canada, however, after Pope & Talbot filed its "Notice of Intent to Submit a Claim to Arbitration" in December 1998. The filing of this notice triggered a review of the company's logging quota by the government of Canada's Softwood Lumber Division. The governmental agency forthwith began treating the company as an adversary, engaging in what the tribunal described as "combat," issuing "threats," and requiring the company to suffer "unnecessary" expenditures, and "a loss of reputation in government circles" (Pope & Talbot 2001: para. 181). This behavior, the tribunal concluded, amounted to a denial of the "fair and equitable treatment" standard that is identified in NAFTA's text as an element of the minimum standard of treatment required under international law.[10] The tribunal rejected Canada's submission that only the most "egregious" behavior would be caught by the rule, following the Mexico Claims Commission in *Neer*: conduct amounting to an "outrage," "bad faith," "wilful neglect of duty," or conduct "so far short of international standards that every reasonable and impartial man would readily recognize its insufficiency" (*Neer* 1927: 556). Instead, the provision was read as imposing the requirements of international law plus the additive character of "fairness," thereby going beyond the minimum content required under customary international law (*Pope & Talbot* 2001: para. 111). The tribunal was convinced of the provision's additive nature due to the fact that the language of Art. 1105 "grew out of the provisions of bilateral commercial treaties negotiated by the United States and other industrialized countries" that address fair and equitable treatment, provisions that are independent of any treatment required under international law (*Pope & Talbot* 2001: para. 110). Moreover, the tribunal concluded, it would be absurd to treat foreign investors from non-NAFTA party states better than NAFTA investors (investors from NAFTA states could turn to the MFN rule, in any event) (*Pope & Talbot* 2001: para. 117). It was this denial of fair treatment at the hands of the government, disassociated from the company's complaint regarding lumber quotas, for which the tribunal rebuked Canada.

Within 3 months the NAFTA state parties, via the auspices of the NAFTA FTC (an interstate cabinet level oversight body), issued an interpretative note on the scope of the standard of fair and equitable treatment under Art. 1105 (though the note likely was prompted by the decision in *Metalclad*, discussed next).[11] This standard, the FTC pronounced, does not "require treatment in addition to or beyond that which is required by the customary international law minimum standard of treatment of aliens" (NAFTA FTC 2001). The Pope & Talbot tribunal returned to the question, a year later, in their award in respect of damages. If asked to choose whether the FTC note was an interpretation or amendment of NAFTA, they would choose amendment (*Pope & Talbot* 2002: para. 47). This determination was unnecessary, however, as the tribunal's interpretation of fairness as an additive element to customary international law practically was not different from the FTC's. This was because customary international law was not "frozen in amber" but evolved through state practice (*Pope & Talbot* 2002: paras 57, 59). In which case, the interpretive note could be understood as incorporating the standard of fairness that had been applied earlier by the tribunal. In any event, the behavior of Canada's Softwood Lumber Division was sufficiently "shocking and outrageous" to offend even the more onerous "egregious" standard of behavior from the *Neer* case that had been advanced by Canada (*Pope & Talbot* 2002: para. 68). The tribunal subsequently awarded the company a sum of damages for behavior associated with the verification episode far less than it had sought: US $461,566 as opposed to some US $80 million in damages that it had claimed (Chase 2002b).

### "Deprivations of reasonably-to-be-expected economic benefits"
Through its US and Mexican subsidiaries, the Metalclad Corporation of Newport Beach, California, purchased in 1993 the Mexican company COTERIN. Metalclad was intent on developing COTERIN's waste management and landfill site at Guadalcazar in the Mexican state of San Luis Potosi. COTERIN's operation of the site had raised grave concerns. The company had improperly stored industrial waste and failed to contain leakage into local water supplies. Citizens blockaded the road leading to the plant in September 1991, demanding immediate inspection of the facility (Wheat 1995). Federal investigation led to the immediate closing of the plant by order of the Mexican government. When Metalclad announced it was taking over COTERIN's operations, the local populace was mobilized to oppose reopening of the site.

Metalclad rehabilitated the Guadalcazar site, it claimed, with the express authorization and permission of the Mexican federal government (United Mexican States 2001). Metalclad was assured by federal authorities that all necessary permits were in place and that local permission was not required. The company was advised, nevertheless, that it should apply to the municipality for a construction permit merely so as "to facilitate an amicable relationship" (*Metalclad* 2000: para. 41). Without having applied for the requisite permit, the municipality of Guadalcazar ordered a halt to construction in October 1994.

Metalclad succumbed, applied for the permit, and, in November, resumed construction. The hazardous waste site opened 10 months later, in March 1995. That same month the municipality denied Metalclad's construction permit, citing denial of a similar permit to COTERIN in 1991 and 1992 and the "unanimous support for the Council's decision to deny the Construction permit as was evidenced in the public session held by this Council" (Azuela 2004: 29–30).

Metalclad claimed that this effectively closed down its hazardous waste operation (*Metalclad* 2000: para. 50). Nine months later and three days before the expiry of his term, the state governor issued an Ecological Decree declaring the site a natural area for the protection of rare cactus, at which point Metalclad abandoned the facility. Metalclad then sued under NAFTA's Chapter 11 alleging violations of the fair and equitable standard of treatment and the takings rule. The arbitration tribunal agreed and awarded the investor US $16.6 million in damages.

The tribunal, headed by Cambridge University scholar Eli Lauterpacht, found first that Mexico should be held accountable for the acts of its subnational governments – here the municipal and state governments (*Metalclad* 2000: para. 73). Next, the tribunal found that there was an absence of a clear rule with regard to the requirement that the municipality issue a construction permit. There "should be no room for doubt and uncertainty" with regard to legal requirements, the tribunal ruled. Once "authorities of the central government of any Party . . . become aware of any scope for misunderstanding or confusion in this connection, it is their duty to ensure that the correct position is promptly determined and clearly stated so that investors can proceed with all appropriate expedition in the confident belief that they are acting in accordance with all relevant laws" (*Metalclad* 2000: para. 76). This lack of transparency, predictability, and procedural fairness (Metalclad was given no notice of the town council meeting where the construction permit was denied) amounted to a denial of "treatment in accordance with international law, including fair and equitable treatment" (*Metalclad* 2000: para. 100). The tribunal, effectively, read in to Chapter 11 transparency obligations that arise only in Chapter 18, this by reason of the mention of "transparency" in Art. 102(1) as being one of NAFTA's objectives. The tribunal turned then to the expropriation claim. By "permitting or tolerating" the unfair and inequitable treatment under Art. 1105, Mexico was held to have "participated and acquiesced" in the denial of Metalclad's rights. In this way, Mexico had "taken a measure tantamount to expropriation" under Art. 1110(1) (*Metalclad* 2000: para. 104). The issuance of the Ecological Decree, the tribunal added, alone would have amounted to an expropriation requiring compensation (*Metalclad* 2001: para. 111).

The tribunal further filled out the criteria for what constitutes a taking under NAFTA (without reference to *Pope & Talbot* or to any other precedent). NAFTA's takings rule would catch not only the outright seizure of property by the host state – the most obvious case – but also "covert or incidental interference with the use of property which has the effect of depriving the owner, in whole or in significant part, of the use or reasonably-to-be-expected economic benefit of property even if not necessarily to the obvious benefit of the host State" (*Metalclad* 2001: para. 103). Nondiscriminatory exercises of regulatory power could give rise to compensation under NAFTA where the regulation wholly or significantly deprives an investor of the reasonably expected beneficial use of that investment.

The tribunal made little mention of the troubles that gave rise to the local populace's opposition to Metalclad's operation. Yet this local opposition entirely was foreseeable given the hazardous way in which Metalclad's predecessor, COTERIN, had managed hazardous waste. Metalclad had been pressed to move its waste facility to an alternative site when a new state governor took office in 1993 (and before NAFTA entered into force), but the company resisted.[12] The tribunal made no mention that Metalclad was or reasonably should have been aware that municipal permits had to be secured for this type of facility (Tamayo 2001: 77). COTERIN previously had been denied a municipal construction permit and this very decision was in the hands of Metalclad (Posadas 2001; Sands 2005: 134), though this was denied by the company (*Metalclad* 2000: para. 52).[13] The tribunal would not admit that local resistance to the operation of the facility on public health grounds and the requirement of a municipal construction permit were, even according to the tribunal's own standards, a reasonable investment-backed expectation that could not have caught Metalclad by surprise. This was "sole-effects" doctrine run amok.

More startling is the manner in which the tribunal dismissed Mexico's reply that there was no denial of the minimum standard of treatment required by international law. Mexico argued that the municipality was acting within its constitutional authority when it refused to issue a construction permit (even though representatives of the Mexican federal government appeared to have led Metalclad to believe otherwise). This constitutional authority was disputed by Metalclad's expert on Mexican law, a 1994 law graduate of the University of Arizona who was pursuing a master of laws degree in Monterrey (*Metalclad* 2001: para. 81; United Mexican States 2001: 138). The tribunal mysteriously preferred Metalclad's interpretation. Referring to a federal law that grants power to authorize hazardous waste sites to the federal government, the tribunal was of the view that federal authority "was controlling and [that] the authority of the municipality only extended to appropriate construction considerations" (*Metalclad* 2001: para. 86). In other words, Guadalcazar had no constitutional authority to refuse a permit other than for reasons having to do with the "physical construction or defects in that site" (*Metalclad* 2001: para. 86). According to the tribunal, the city did not have authority to take into account environmental concerns in the issuance of a municipal construction permit. Whatever the procedural irregularities that gave rise to Metalclad's claim, it is remarkable the confidence with which the tribunal – sitting as if it were a constitutional court – arrived at definitive conclusions regarding the constitutional authority of Mexican municipal governments. This precisely is where the state party itself offered a very different, and more authoritative, interpretation.

This aspect of the tribunal's ruling, concerning the ability of local government to make decisions about economic development, is disturbing. The tribunal purports to deny local authorities within Mexico the ability even to take into account the environmental impact of proposed economic development where approval has been obtained from the higher order of government, effectively disenfranchising local government from environmental jurisdiction. Yet, the constitution authorizes municipalities to issue construction permits and to "control and supervise the use of land within their own territories" (Art. 115, V). State governments have constitutional authority to establish municipalities and to fill out the exercise of municipal power (United Mexican States 2001: paras 415–17) and state law authorized the municipality to take into account environmental impacts in the issuance of municipal construction permits (United Mexican States 2001: 135–6). This is a constitutional fact that continues to be denied or ignored by investment law scholars and lawyers (Gaines 2002: 123; Weiler 2005b: 709, fn. 13). Textual authority aside, it surely is reasonable to expect all levels of government to be concerned about environmental impacts. The Supreme Court of Canada came to this very conclusion with regard to the Canadian constitution, where the assignment of jurisdiction over environmental matters is even less clear. The court admitted that all levels of government legitimately would want to weigh environmental repercussions in the course of governmental decision making (*Friends of the Oldman River* 1992). What the tribunal accomplished, observe Frug and Barron, was to incorporate the functional equivalent of a US interpretive canon into international investment law (2006: 44). A late nineteenth-century canon of judicial interpretation intended to preserve private property from local government action, Dillon's Rule "empowers the central government to determine the legitimacy of a city's attempt to subject private actors to novel regulations of their conduct" (Frug and Barron 2006: 4343). The tribunal's ruling in *Metalclad* mimics this antipathy to local authority in circumstances where the central government has not condoned intrusions into the private sphere.

The implications of the tribunal's ruling were mitigated somewhat by an appeal of the tribunal ruling launched by Mexico and heard by a Canadian court (as the City of Vancouver was the designated place of arbitration). Justice Tysoe vacated part of the tribunal's ruling – that part that imposed transparency obligations under the fair and equitable treatment standard and the expropriations rule (*United Mexican States* 2001: paras 72, 79).[14] Consequently, the tribunal's findings regarding the capacity of Mexican local government to consider environmental impacts became immaterial. Justice Tysoe confirmed the ruling in so far as the tribunal found a compensable taking by reason of the Governor's Ecological Decree (*United Mexican States* 2001: para. 100). The tribunal's very broad interpretation of the takings rule – including "incidental interference" that has the effect of depriving owners of a "significant part" of the "use or reasonably-to-be-expected economic benefit of property" – was shielded from judicial review as this was a question of law beyond the purview of a reviewing court. Justice Tysoe cautioned, though, that the tribunal's interpretation "is sufficiently broad ... to include legitimate rezoning of property by a municipality or other rezoning authority" (*United Mexican States* 2001: para. 99).[15]

### "Lasting deprivation ... to make use of its economic rights"

Within days of Canada's settlement with the Ethyl Corporation, S. D. Myers Inc. of Tallmadge, Ohio, initiated a claim under NAFTA for losses following a temporary ban on the export of PCB-contaminated waste to the United States for the years 1995–7 (Scoffield 1998a, 1998b). Myers was in the business of PCB remediation – the transportation, extraction, and destruction of hazardous PCB and PCB waste material. The company established a subsidiary, Myers Canada, to lobby on behalf of and promote the US-based enterprise and to arrange transportation of waste to its US waste facility.[16]

At the time that S. D. Myers began looking to Canada as a new source of business, the importation of PCB waste into the United States was prohibited by the US Environmental Protection Agency (EPA). S. D. Myers lobbied the EPA hard. In November 1995, and absent consultations with the government of Canada, the company was permitted by the EPA to import waste into the United States. The Canadian government responded by closing the border to the export of PCB waste from November 1995 until February 1997, when the EPA decision was reversed. The EPA permit order secured by S. D. Myers ultimately was overturned by a decision of the Ninth Circuit of the US Court of Appeals in July 1997 and the US border closed once again (S. D. Myers 2001: para. 128). The EPA did not have authority to issue regulations permitting the importation of PCB waste, according to the court (Gracer and Mansell 2000; Sierra Club 1997). It should be noted, then, that the complained of Canadian action was precipitated entirely by an illegal US EPA order.

S. D. Myers claimed that the government of Canada's ban on PCB exports to the United States for an almost 16-month period offended Chapter 11's fair and equitable standard of treatment, national treatment, performance requirements, and expropriation prohibitions. The government of Canada defended its temporary ban on the basis that it was merely promoting sound environmental management of hazardous waste by seeking made-in-Canada solutions to its disposal. As a signatory to the Basel Convention, Canada was required to keep the transboundary movement of hazardous waste to a minimum (S. D. Myers 2001: para. 107). S. D. Myers argued that this was a sham explanation: Canada merely was acting to protect the financial interests of Myers' principal Canadian competitor, Chem-Security, the waste management firm located in Swan Hills, Alberta. S. D. Myers sought damages in lost profits of about US $10 million.

The tribunal agreed with the claimant that Canada was motivated to impose the ban because of threats to the continuing economic viability of the Canadian Swan Hills facility rather than to comply with international environmental obligations (S. D. Myers 2001: paras 168, 178, 194). Documented commitments were made to Chem-Security to this effect (S. D. Myers 2001: para. 174). Also the tribunal was not convinced that this policy was motivated by sound environmental risk management (S. D. Myers 2001: para. 195; S. D. Myers 2001 Separate Opinion [SO]: para. 148). Disposing of hazardous waste at the S. D. Myers site in the United States was, as three Canadian Department of Environment officials noted, a "technically and environmentally sound solution for the destruction of some of Canada's PCBs" (S. D. Myers 2001: para. 173). The minister of the Environment rejected this advice, made undertakings to S. D. Myers competitors in Canada that she would close the border, and declared in the House of Commons that PCB waste would be disposed of "in Canada by Canadians" (June 9, 1995). Only afterward did she prefer to emphasize that Canada's policy was in accordance with the Basel Convention (S. D. Myers 2001: para. 185). There was, nevertheless, a reason for the distinction independent of discrimination (GAMI 2004: para. 114). Canada, the tribunal could conclude, did the right thing but for the wrong reason.

Maintaining the ability to process PCBs within Canada may have been a "legitimate goal" and consistent with the Basel Convention, the tribunal admitted, but the means employed had to be consistent with NAFTA's strictures. NAFTA permitted state parties to pursue legitimate policy objectives via alternative exempted measures, like government procurement and subsidies or grants (NAFTA: Art. 1108. 7). That these less restrictive measure were available but not adopted by Canada resulted in discriminatory treatment against Myers "in like circumstances" with Canadian competitors, and so amounted to a denial of national treatment (S. D. Myers 2001: para. 255).

Turning to the standard of fair and equitable treatment in Art. 1105(1), a breach of the standard will have occurred:

> [O]nly when it is shown that an investor has been treated in such an arbitrary and unjust manner that the treatment rises to the level that is unacceptable from an international perspective. That determination must be made in the light of the high level of deference that international law generally extends to the right of domestic authorities to regulate matters within their own borders.
>
> (S. D. Myers 2001: para. 263)

Two of the three tribunal members found that, despite this high level of deference, breach of the national treatment requirement gave rise to a breach of fair and equitable treatment (S. D. Myers 2001: para. 266, following Mann 1981: 243–4). It may have been this aspect of the decision (in addition to the ruling in Metalclad) that prompted the NAFTA parties, through an interpretive note issued by the FTC, to clarify that "a determination that there has been a breach of another provision of the NAFTA, or of a separate international agreement, does not establish that there has been a breach of Article 1105(1)" (NAFTA FTC 2001).

In a separate opinion one tribunal member, Bryan Schwartz, found that performance requirements had been imposed by Canada (S. D. Myers 2001 [SO]: para. 277) while the tribunal unanimously concluded that there was no deprivation of investor rights giving rise to an expropriation (S. D. Myers 2001: para. 288). In the course of so doing, the tribunal attempted to fill out the categorical distinction between noncompensable regulations and compensable takings. Schwartz's separate opinion admitted that the imprecise nature of Art. 1110 had precipitated vocal opposition to NAFTA and associated fears and anxieties about the decline of state sovereignty and democratic accountability. Attempting to assuage these fears, the tribunal wrote that, even if regulatory action can be caught by the takings rule, it was unlikely that "regulatory conduct by public authorities" would be "the subject of a legitimate complaint under Article 1110" though the tribunal could not "rule out that possibility" (S. D. Myers 2001: para. 281). The distinction between expropriations and regulations was an analytically helpful one, the tribunal maintained. The distinction "screens out most cases of complaints concerning economic intervention by a state and reduces the risk that governments will be subject to claims as they go about their business of managing public affairs" (S. D. Myers 2001: para. 282).

In contrast to mere regulations, expropriations usually amounted to a "lasting deprivation of the ability of an owner to make use of its economic rights," though – preferring to keep all options open – the deprivation may be "partial or temporary" (S. D. Myers 2001: para. 283; S. D. Myers 2001 [SO]: para. 217). In this case, there merely was a temporary denial of business opportunity that did not rise to the level of a compensable taking. Nor could the phrase "tantamount to expropriation" expand coverage "beyond the customary scope of the term" under international law (S. D. Myers 2001: para. 285). Citing the *Pope & Talbot* ruling, the *Myers* tribunal concluded that the word "tantamount" was intended to catch "so-called 'creeping expropriations'" rather than expand upon customary international law (S. D. Myers 2001: para. 286).

Of some interest is Schwartz's separate opinion. Recognizing that the S. D. Myers case is a "landmark one," Schwartz offered a separate opinion so as to provide "some distinctive insights or suggestions that may be of some use in the longer run" (S. D. Myers 2001 [SO]: paras 2, 90). This was an opinion directed not just to the parties, but also "to the wider public" because trade agreements like NAFTA "have an enormous impact on public affairs in many countries" (S. D. Myers 2001 [SO]: paras 33, 34). As if to prove the point being made here, Schwartz went so far as to liken these agreements to "a country's constitution": "They restrict the ways in which governments can act and they are very hard to change." While governments usually have the right to withdraw with notice, Schwartz admits that this "is often practically impossible to do": "Pulling out of a trade agreement may create too much risk of reverting to trade wars, and may upset the settled expectations of many participants in the economy." Amendment is made no easier, he writes, "just as it is usually very hard to change a provision of a domestic constitution" (S. D. Myers 2001 [SO]: para. 34).

In a far-reaching discussion, Schwartz argues that under NAFTA, free trade and environmental protection are not treated as contradictory policy goals. NAFTA is "actually environmentally friendly" and embodies a "balanced approach," Schwartz maintained (S. D. Myers 2001 [SO]: paras 25, 92). Because "[m]any of the ideas and legal phrases in NAFTA are drawn from the global trade law system that used to be called the GATT system" (S. D. Myers 2001 [SO]: paras 66, 70), Schwartz resorts to WTO jurisprudence to supplement the NAFTA text. As noted in Chapter two, the Uruguay-round GATT, Art. XX permits certain exceptions to free trade such as those "necessary to protect human, animal or plant life or health." The exceptions clause permits trade-restricting measures of this sort so long as they are "necessary" – that is, so long as they restrict trade no more than is reasonably necessary to achieve these permitted objectives (S. D. Myers 2001 [SO]: para. 93).

Schwartz claims that this principle is reflected variously in NAFTA. Art. 104, for example, permits deviations from NAFTA when complying with the Basel Convention and other "specific trade obligations." Schwartz goes so far as to say that these GATT exceptions are incorporated into Art. 1114, which permits state parties to take measures "otherwise consistent with this chapter" to "ensure that investment activity ... is undertaken in a manner sensitive to environmental concerns." The language here is not merely hortatory; rather, it is intended to remind interpreters of Chapter 11 that "means should be found to reconcile these two objectives and, if possible, to make them mutually supportive" (S. D. Myers 2001 [SO]: para. 118).

This renders NAFTA consistent with the basic approach common to the global legal trading system: "parties are free to choose high environmental standards, but should adopt and apply them in a way that avoids barriers to trade that are not necessary in order to achieve the environmental purpose" (S. D. Myers 2001 [SO]: para. 118). Schwartz acknowledges that this "reading in" of GATT Art. XX(b) into NAFTA

Chapter 11 is contentious.[17] Art. XX-type exceptions are mentioned in NAFTA only with regard to trade in goods in Chapters 3 and 4 (Art. 2101[1]). These type of exceptions have been absent from the typical US BIT (though the US model treaty that postdates this ruling suggests an interpretation of the takings rule that is less likely to catch bona fide health, environmental, and public safety measures). Nor does he mention that state parties mostly have failed to satisfy the test of necessity under GATT Art. XX (b) (the opinion also pre-dates the WTO AB ruling in *Asbestos* [2001]). As Howse admits, legal economists can almost always imagine less restrictive, welfare-maximizing alternatives (2000: 140). So while Schwartz's supplementary opinion seeks to balance investment protection with environmental concerns, the result is highly unsatisfactory in so far as he relies on a strict test of necessity that is often hard to satisfy.

Schwartz also aims to fill in the textual ambiguities of the takings rule, recognizing that the scope of the rule has "resulted in real anxiety on the part of academic critics" (*S. D. Myers* 2001 [SO]: para. 202, citing Wagner 1999). Schwartz cannot deny that some regulations will give rise to a right to compensation under Chapter 11, only that "in the vast run of cases, regulatory conduct by public authorities is not remotely the subject of legitimate complaints under Article 1110" (*S. D. Myers* 2001 [SO]: para. 207). By contrast, expropriations tend to be "severe deprivations" that upset an owner's "reasonable expectations" (*S. D. Myers* 2001 [SO]: paras 212, 213). Looking at Art. 1110 "in context" – in light, that is, of NAFTA's labor and environmental side agreements – he could not see the takings rule as a "generous invitation to impose liability on governments that are engaged in the ordinary course of protecting health, safety, the environment and other public welfare concerns" (*S. D. Myers* 2001 [SO]: para. 214). The run-of-the-mill regulation, then, will not give rise to compensation unless reasonable expectations are upset – a formulation that reflects nicely *Penn Central*'s (1978) suggested balancing act and which gets taken up in discussions of fair and equitable treatment.

In this case, Schwartz writes, "a reasonable argument" can be made that Canada's actions were expropriatory with regard to S. D. Myer's "goodwill" (*S. D. Myers* 2001 [SO]: para. 218). But Schwartz is reluctant to so find. The removal of economic rights was not "lasting" but temporary, nor was there a clear transfer of wealth from S. D. Myers to the government or to Canadian competitors (*S. D. Myers* 2001 [SO]: paras 220, 221). Moreover, it would make no practical difference if this action was labeled an expropriation – damages likely would be the same. A finding of expropriation, on the other hand, "might contribute to public misunderstanding and anxiety" about the decision and the wider implications of NAFTA (*S. D. Myers* 2001 [SO]: para. 222). Rather than risk this confusion and attracting public vitriol – while reflexively advancing the aims of arbitral legitimacy (Banakar 1998; Zumbansen 2002) – Schwartz was content to let the expropriation puzzle rest with some future tribunal.

In this supplementary opinion, Schwartz seemingly circumscribes the scope of NAFTA's takings rule, finds that the measure at issue arguably rose to the level of a taking, but declines to find for the investor on the grounds that this might cause more public anxiety about NAFTA. Schwartz also likens NAFTA's investment chapter to the BIT program and then stretches the language of NAFTA considerably beyond the usual BIT to incorporate environmental and health provisions found expressly in the GATT. He portends, to some degree, developments in the United States and Canada that would come to be reflected in their respective model investment treaties. Schwartz, however, suggests a stricter test of necessity with regard to health, environmental, and public safety measures then would appear in these model BITs.[18]

### "Unless specific commitments had been given … that the government would refrain from such regulation"

As originally conceived, the *Methanex* case looked very much like a reverse *Ethyl* one. The Methanex Corporation of Vancouver, British Columbia, sued the United States for the state of California's ban on the use of the gasoline additive methyl tertiary-butyl ether (MTBE). Methanol is the principal ingredient in MTBE, an oxygenate used to reduce gasoline emissions. The state was prompted to enquire into the safety of MTBE as a result of leeching of the substance into public drinking water supplies in various locations around California. The state legislature directed the then governor in 1997 to assess the human health and environmental risks associated with MTBE. Results from a study undertaken by the University of California would assist in this determination. The study, accompanied by public hearings and peer review, and released only days after the election of Governor Gray Davis, recommended that the use of MTBE be phased out and that there be further study of the use of other oxygenating agents such as ethanol (*Methanex* 2005: III.A.15–16). The report resulted in an executive order signed by Governor Davis that there is a "significant risk to the environment" associated with the use of MTBE. Ensuing regulations banned the sale and supply of the fuel additive.

Methanex produces methanol for the MTBE market, including fuel sold in the state of California. The statewide ban, the company claimed, amounted to an expropriation of their investment and a denial of fair and equitable treatment. The company's claim evolved over the course of the litigation, however, from one directed largely at the effects of the measures on the sale of methanol in California to a conspiracy fueled by campaign contributions from Archer Daniels Midland (ADM) of Decatur, Illinois, to Governor Davis. ADM is the principal producer of ethanol in the state, a competitor fuel additive. The "connect-the-dots" conspiracy suggested that the governor intended to single out Methanex, as the foreign producer of methanol, for discriminatory treatment so as to favor ADM. Yet the California measures banned only MTBE – they were not directed at methanol or Methanex. The company would have to establish that the measures, by virtue of their discriminatory intent, "related to" Methanex's investment. For the tribunal, this required establishing more than "mere effect," but a "legally significant connection" between the measures and the investor or an investment (Methanex 2002: para. 147). Methanex accordingly was entitled to amend its statement of claim to make these national treatment allegations which, if proved, could meet the threshold requirement of establishing that the impugned measures were made in relation to methanol and Methanex (Methanex 2002: para. 169).

Proof of subjective intent is often hard to find in discrimination cases (Ely 1980: 138; Siegel 1997: 1136). Nor is it a burden expected of investors in the rules regime (Loewen 2003: para. 132; Pope & Talbot 2001: para. 79; Tecmed 2003: para. 116), so it would seem extraordinary to require proof of this sort from the claimant. The tribunal would dispense with proof of intent, however, if the claimant otherwise could show denial of treatment required by international law (Douglas 2006: 49–50; Methanex 2005: IV.C.1). Methanex, nevertheless, was committed to proving discriminatory intent and this it failed to do, according to the tribunal in its final award. Before attending to this threshold jurisdictional question, the tribunal issued findings regarding most of Methanex's allegations. The tribunal found that there was a "serious" and "objective" scientific basis for the state measures, based upon the findings of the University of California report – they were no mere "political sham" (Methanex 2005: III.A.101). The circumstantial "six dots" implicating Governor Davis were insufficient to establish intent to harm methanol or Methanex or to favor ethanol and ADM (*Methanex* 2005: III.B.60). The inquiry into the safety of MTBE, after all, began under the stewardship of Davis's predecessor, Governor Pete Wilson. Turning to the breaches of NAFTA, there was no denial of national treatment as US-based producers of methanol also were harmed by the state ban. It was this group, and not producers of ethanol, who were "in like circumstances" with Methanex. For the purposes of the national treatment argument, the tribunal ruled, the preferred comparator group was not producers of ethanol who merely were competitors, but a group that was identical to the claimant in all respects but nationality (*Methanex* 2005: IV.B.17). There was, second, no denial of fair and equitable treatment by reason of the governor's alleged discriminatory conduct. Methanex made arguments, supported by an affidavit sworn by the late Sir Robert Jennings, that the FTC interpretation of fair and equitable treatment was intended to undermine specifically the company's NAFTA suit and that this amounted to an amendment rather than a mere interpretation of the agreement. Most every NAFTA claimant since 2001, the United States replied, "has argued that the FTC interpretation was specifically targeted against it" (*Methanex* 2005: IV.C.18). The tribunal rejected Methanex's argument as to amendment and held, moreover, that there was no rule in customary international law prohibiting differential treatment as between nationals and foreigners (*Methanex* 2005: IV.C.26). The standard of fair and equitable treatment, therefore, was construed quite strictly. The tribunal turned, finally, to the alleged expropriation of Methanex's customer base, goodwill, and market for methanol. If the allegation was to stand, Methanex would have to show that these measures were tantamount to expropriation. An "intentionally discriminatory regulation against a foreign investor fulfils a key requirement," wrote the tribunal:

> But as a matter of general international law, a non-discriminatory regulation for a public purpose, which is enacted in accordance with due process and, which affects, *inter alios*, a foreign investor or investment is not deemed expropriatory and compensable unless specific commitments had been given by the regulating government to the then putative foreign investor contemplating investment that the government refrain from such regulation. (*Methanex* 2005: IV.D.7)

There was no such specific inducement here; instead, the tribunal underscored the changing regulatory landscape at the level of states and the national government. This was a political economy "in which it was widely known, if not notorious, that governmental environmental and health protection institutions" at both levels, operating "under vigilant eyes of the media, interested corporations, non-governmental organizations and a politically active electorate, continuously monitored the use and impact of chemical compounds" that entered the environment (*Methanex* 2005: IV.D.9). It was not reasonable to assume that laws and regulations would remain static in such a political environment – the result of processes that American political scientists would describe as pluralist (Dahl 1961) and international trade lawyers would describe as mercantilist (McGinnis and Movsevian 2000). It was not a reasonable investment-backed expectation, the tribunal appeared to be saying, that MTBE would be forever safe from a ban on methanol.

The ruling, Weiler writes, though delighting NGOs would have confounded "most experts on the customary international law of expropriation" (2005: 918). Could it be, Weiler asks, that the tribunal meant to say that "compensable takings could only be found in cases of detrimental reliance on a government promise"? (Weiler 2005a: 919). This is unlikely. Indeed, the tribunal expressly stated they were contemplating only nondiscriminatory regulations with a public purpose, enacted with due process – valid exercises of a state's police power, in other words. In such instances, liability will flow only in cases where there have been express undertakings meant to induce foreign investors. The ruling leaves intact the wide variety of compensable takings Weiler and others desire to be caught by the takings rule.[19] The scope of regulatory takings, however, will have been diminished somewhat and this will have caused consternation amongst the trade and investment law community (Anzorena et al. 2006: 256–7). No worries, though, as much of the action appears to be moving from the takings rule to the requirement of fair and equitable treatment. Emblematic is the fact that the *Methanex* tribunal cited in support of its summary of the customary international law of expropriation the discussion in *Waste Management* (2004) of the minimum standard of treatment under international law, including the requirement of fair and equitable treatment.

### "That do not affect the basic expectations taken into account by the foreign investor"

It will be recalled that the *Pope & Talbot*, *Metalclad*, and *S. D. Myers* tribunals relied upon Art. 1105(1), guaranteeing the international minimum standard required by international law, including fair and equitable treatment, to find for each of the claimants. The *Pope & Talbot* tribunal even reflected upon the effect of the FTC interpretation intended to confine the content of the clause to no more than was required by customary international law. The interpretive noted added nothing new, the tribunal concluded, as customary international law was organic and evolving, incorporating concepts reflected in 2,500 treaties that made up the investment rules regime. This reading of the FTC note was endorsed by the tribunal in *Mondev* and most every tribunal since (Laird 2004; *Mondev* 2002: para. 125). In which case, whatever the content of the fair and equitable treatment standard in the 1920s, it now incorporates all varieties of international law norms, not merely the content of customary international law (*Mondev* 2002: para. 120; Weiler 2005a: 918),[20] including norms that have a family resemblance to the takings rule. The 2004 US model BIT aims to be more explicit about the limits to be placed on the clause by defining the obligation as limited to the customary international law standard, including "the obligation not to deny justice in criminal, civil, or administrative adjudicatory proceedings in accordance with the principle of due process embodied in the principal legal systems of the world" (USTR 2004b). If not additive to customary international law, the reference to "the principle of due process embodied in the principal legal systems of the world" would presume to enlarge its scope (Gantz 2004: 728).

Given this capaciousness, it is no surprise that, as Dolzer observes, "hardly any lawsuit based on an international investment treaty is filed these days without invocation of the relevant treaty clause requiring fair and equitable treatment" (2005: 87). The clause has been described by arbitral tribunals as "not clear" (*Genin* 2001: para. 367), "not adequately litigated" (ADF 2003: 183), and "abstract" (GAMI 2004: para. 92); it has been characterized by scholars as "relatively imprecise" (Schreuer 2005: 364), "nebulous" (Sornarajah 2004: 332), and "exceptionally wide" (Lowe 2002: 9), while UNCTAD describes the clause as "not automatically connot[ing] a clear set of legal prescriptions in some situations" (2004: 210). The standard has been invoked repeatedly "alongside" claims that there has been an expropriation, as an "alternative and overlapping" basis for compensation (*Waste Management* 2004: para. 86). This makes sense if we accept Dolzer's suggestion that the notion of fair and equitable treatment "is in its substance closely related to the more specific standards of an indirect expropriation" (2005: 87). Given its overlapping content, tribunals have had myriad opportunities to consider the content of this omnibus standard of treatment alongside the takings rule.

Some tribunals approached the question of its scope with some caution, admitting that the clause grants no "unfettered discretion" (*Mondev* 2002: para. 117) to "second-guess government decision making" (*S. D. Myers* 2000: para. 261) and that the threshold for finding a violation "remains high" (*Thunderbird* 2006: para. 194). On the other hand, some tribunals have been less immodest, prompting the NAFTA parties to issue their FTC interpretive note. Even this seemingly has had little effect on arbitrators in narrowing its potentially very wide grasp. Summarizing the state of play, the NAFTA *Waste Management* panel held that the standard captured behavior which is "[a]rbitrary, grossly unfair, unjust or idiosyncratic, is discriminatory and exposes the claimant to sectional or racial prejudice, or involves a lack of due process leading to an outcome which offends judicial propriety – as might be the case with a manifest failure of natural justice in judicial proceedings or a complete lack of transparency and candour in an administrative process." In "applying this standard," the tribunal added, "it is relevant that the treatment is in breach of representations made by the host State which were reasonably relied on by the claimant" (2004: para. 98). What is becoming increasingly clear is that the demand of fair and equitable treatment is serving some of the functions of a regulatory takings rule, if not swallowing up the rule entirely.

Recall the list of factors identified by the US Supreme Court in *Penn Central* in order to determine whether there has been a taking: US courts are directed to consider whether the diminution in value is attributable to the government conduct, the character of the government action, and the extent to which the regulation interferes with distinct (later modified to reasonable) investment-back expectations (1978: 124–5). The last of these factors appears to have been drawn from Michelman's path-breaking analysis in the *Harvard Law Review* (1967). In describing how courts do the work of determining when government action merits just compensation under the takings rule (1967: 1250), Michelman concluded that the question to be asked is "whether or not the measure in question can easily be seen to have practically deprived the claimant of some distinctly perceived, sharply crystallized, investment-backed expectation" (1967: 1233). It is for this reason that new zoning schemes typically grandfather established nonconforming uses, otherwise, by-laws would "totally defeat a distinctly crystallized expectation" (1967: 1233). The requirement of compensation, Michelman claimed, was premised on the assumption that property consisted of "several discrete 'things'" (the proverbial understanding of property-as-a-bundle-of-rights) and that deprivation of one of these things was "attended by a pain of a specially acute or demoralizing kind" (1967: 1234). Retroactive changes, then, were more likely to give rise to demoralization costs worthy of some compensation. This helps to explain the plurality decision in *Eastern Enterprises* (1998) where four justices held that a mandatory contribution to a health-care fund for retired coal miners and their dependents was an unconstitutional taking. Justice Kennedy preferred to rely on the law of substantive due process to find for Eastern, a doctrine which, in the late nineteenth and early twentieth centuries, looked unfavorably upon retroactive changes (Dana and Merrill 2002: 157). Under the doctrine of substantive due process, changes to laws that upset unreasonably the status quo also were constitutionally suspect.

The standard of fair and equitable treatment appears to be standing in for these sorts of constitutional disciplines. The language of the *Tecmed* tribunal, interpreting a Spain-Mexico BIT, has often been cited as the "most extensive explanation of the foundations and the substance of the standard" (Dolzer 2005: 95). Fair and equitable treatment requires that the host state "does not affect the basic expectations that were taken into account by the foreign investor to make the investment" (*Tecmed* 2003: para. 154). There may be no regulatory change that unreasonably upsets investor expectations:

> The foreign investor expects the host state to act in a consistent manner, free from ambiguity and totally transparently in its relations with the foreign investor, so that it may know beforehand any and all rules and regulations that will govern its investments, as well as the goals of the relevant policies and administrative practices or directives, to be able to plan its investment and comply with such regulations ... The foreign investor expects the host State to act consistently, i.e. without arbitrarily revoking any preexisting decisions or permits issued by the State that were relied upon by the investor to assume its commitments as well as to plan and launch its commercial and business activities. (*Tecmed* 2003: para. 154).[21]

The tribunal added, in this context, not "without the required compensation" (*Tecmed* 2003: para. 154).

That the clause will work to limit regulatory responses is made apparent in *CMS v. Argentina* (2005). Michigan-based CMS Gas participated in the wave of privatization of Argentinean public enterprise in 1995 by purchasing almost 30 percent of the public company Transportada de Gas del Norte (TGN). According to the license secured by TGN, tariffs collected by the company were to be recouped in US dollars, adjusted periodically, and converted into pesos at the time of billing (CMS 2005: paras 57, 85). The meltdown of the Argentinean economy in 2001 precipitated a variety of measures for societal self-protection – in the case of natural gas, this involved a temporary suspension of prices and then freezing of profits converted into dollars. Following devaluation of the peso (previously pegged to the US dollar), Argentina would no longer convert tariffs into US dollars (CMS 2005: para. 66). All participants in the economy were expected, according to the government, to share in the burden of restructuring. CMS instead filed a claim for damages under a US-Argentina BIT, insisting that the government had guaranteed a rate of return on its investment via the TGN license regardless of financial hardship. These actions, the company claimed, amounted to the indirect expropriation of the company's assets and, in addition, a failure to comply with the standard of "fair and equitable treatment" mandated under the treaty, all of which entitled CMS to some US $260 million in damages (CMS 2005: para. 464). Though the tribunal likened the guarantees accorded to CMS as if they were a property right (Schill 2006: 7), they found no indirect or regulatory expropriation here. Applying similar considerations as in *Pope & Talbot* (2000), the tribunal concluded that the investor was still in control of its investment, government did not manage the day-to-day operations of the company, while the investor retained full ownership and control of the company (CMS 2005: para. 263). There was, however, a denial of fair and equitable treatment. Interpreting the clause in light of the treaty preamble – to maintain a "stable framework for investment" – there could be little doubt "that a stable legal and business environment is an essential element of fair and equitable treatment" and no different from the minimum standard required by international law (CMS 2005: paras 274, 284; *Occidental* 2004: para. 183).[22] The operative legal framework, together with the operating license, was in the nature of a "guarantee" that these undertakings would bind the state far into the future (CMS 2005: para. 161).

Argentina also sought to shelter its actions by reason of a state of necessity or emergency, exceptions to investment disciplines available under both customary international law and the US-Argentina BIT. Necessity is an "exceptional" excuse available to a state if it is "the only means for the State to safeguard an essential interest against a grave and imminent peril," according to Art. 25 of the Articles on State Responsibility, which the tribunal took as an accurate summary of customary international law (CMS 2005: paras 316–17). A plea of necessity, however, will not be available where other means, even those more costly or less convenient, are available – a formulation the tribunal borrowed from the International Law Commission's comment on Art. 25 (Crawford 2002: 184).[23] Though none is elaborated, alternative means were available to Argentina (CMS 2005: para. 324). In addition, the tribunal concluded that Argentina had "significantly contributed" to the economic crisis and this, too, disentitled the state from relying on customary international law of state of necessity (CMS 2005: para. 329). The roots of the crisis, it suggested, "extend both ways and include a number of domestic as well as international dimensions" (CMS 2005: para. 329). The policy positions taken by successive administrations stretching back to the 1980s, reaching its "zenith in 2002," amounted to a significant contribution to the economic meltdown (2005: para. 329).

Neither were events in Argentina dramatic enough to warrant triggering the BIT emergency clause – events that *The Economist* likened to the Great Depression of the 1930s (*Economist* 2003). The clause was intended to protect state action in the event of "total economic and social collapse" rather than merely a "severe crisis" (CMS 2005: para. 355). In any event, the obligation to pay would have resumed as soon as conditions that gave rise to the emergency had subsided. The tribunal, Schill notes, denied "any margin of appreciation to the host state when it comes to choosing reactions to a state of emergency" (Schill 2006: 14). Where breaches resulted in "important long-term losses," the government's conduct justified a damage award equivalent to the fair market value of the investment – the usual standard of compensation in the case of a taking (CMS 2005: para. 410). The tribunal awarded CMS US $132.2 million together with interest. The company was also entitled to US $2.1 million upon transfer of its shares in TGN to Argentina (CMS 2005: paras 468–9).

All of this seems a harsh and unnecessary outcome. Schreuer notes that the fair and equitable principle need not require the host state "to freeze its legal system for the investor's benefit" (2005: 374). He suggests, for instance, that "a breach of contract resulting from serious difficulties on the part of the government to comply with its financial obligations cannot be equated with unfair and inequitable treatment" (Schreuer 2005: 380). This is not how the CMS tribunal interpreted this "relatively imprecise" standard (Schreuer 2005: 364). The CMS ruling also rendered the necessity defense "practically unavailable." According to Reinisch, states usually will have various means available to them in the face of grave and imminent peril, any number of which could be viewed as not amounting to wrongful conduct under international law (2006: 11).

It might be that the harshness of the outcome in CMS was due, in part, to the BIT "umbrella clause" that ensured that the license's specific terms could be enforced via the investment rules regime. A breach of the BIT fair and equitable treatment standard was identified by the *LG&E* tribunal, however, on almost identical facts (Reinisch 2006: 4), referring not to a license or contract but the 1992 Argentine legal framework and regulations on which the investor relied (*LG&E* 2006: para. 119).[24] In a claim for damages suffered as a result of the same emergency measures that were taken up by the Argentinean government and challenged by CMS, the tribunal found that "the stability of the legal and business framework in the State party is an essential element in the standard of what is fair and equitable treatment" (*LG&E* 2006: para. 125). The *LG&E* tribunal, however, accepted that Argentina could rely on the necessity defense in the BIT. Responding to the interests of foreign investors with measures for societal self-protection "was a legitimate way of protecting its social and economic system" (*LG&E* 2006: para. 239). Applying Art. 25 of the International Law Commission's Draft Articles on State Responsibility to facts identical to those discussed in CMS, the tribunal found no evidence to suggest Argentina had contributed to the crisis and that "an economic recovery package was the only means to respond to the crisis. Although there may have been a number of ways to draft the economic recovery plan, the evidence before the tribunal demonstrates that an across-the-board response was necessary, and the tariffs on public utilities had to be addressed" (*LG&E* 2006: para. 257). Argentina was relieved of any obligation to pay damages from the period the crisis began, in December 2001, until the election of President Kirchener on April 26, 2003, when, in the tribunal's view, the extreme crisis came to an end (*LG&E* 2006: paras 229–30). This resulted in a US$57 million award in damages.

By contrast, while paying only lip service to the economic hardship experienced by ordinary Argentineans when their economic well-being suffered, the deleterious effects on investors drove much of the analysis in *CMS*. Investors could not be expected to share in the burden of a failed economic experiment – one that companies like CMS would have endorsed actively. Recall that arbitrator Schwartz in *S. D. Myers* would have read in exceptions with regard to health and the environment, resembling exceptions in GATT Art. XX(b). This would allow for the entry of some public interest considerations that would otherwise be shut out of many analyses (*S. D. Myers* 2001 [SO]: paras 66, 70). The *Tecmed* decision, an investor–state dispute arising under a Spain–Mexico BIT, does not go so far as to incorporate GATT qualifications into investment treaty interpretation. It does, however, bring in the countervailing public interest by reading in a proportionality principle into the text of a BIT, and this has the effect of mitigating an emphasis solely on the impact of measures on an investor. The case concerned a failure to renew a permit to operate a hazardous waste facility site in the state of Sonora. The company had purchased the site at auction on the legitimate expectation that it would continue to operate, under its newly formed corporation Cytrar, as a hazardous waste site (*Tecmed* 2003: para. 88). As in *Metalclad*, however, opposition to the landfill was "widespread and aggressive," resulting in demonstrations, marches, blockades, and the filing of criminal and human rights complaints (*Tecmed* 2003: para. 108).[25] Cytrar had been guilty of a number of environmental transgressions, but the tribunal concluded that these transgressions and other public health concerns were not the real reason for the failure to renew. Rather, there were "socio-political" reasons having to do with the proximity of the site (8 km) to the local municipality of Hermosillo. The company was even prepared to relocate to another part of the state in order to placate community objections – an offer that was never taken up. So it was the location of the site, rather than its operation, which gave rise to the failure to renew (*Tecmed* 2003: para. 148).

The investor claimed primarily that there was an expropriation and denial of fair and equitable treatment. Regulatory takings fell within the terms of the treaty, according to the tribunal, as a subset of indirect de facto expropriations. These will be measures which are "irreversible and permanent, and if the asset or rights subject to such measures have been affected in such a way that '... any form of exploitation thereof...' has disappeared; i.e. the economic value of the use, enjoyment or disposition of the assets or rights affected by the administrative action or decision have been neutralized or destroyed," then there will have been a taking (*Tecmed* 2003: para. 116). Even where measures are "beneficial to society as a whole – such as environmental protection," the obligation to pay compensation remains (citing *Compañia del Desarrollo de Santa Elena* 2000: paras 72, 76). The "government's intention," the tribunal wrote, "is less important than the effects of the measure" on the investor (*Tecmed* 2003: para. 116). In this instance, the government's actions "fully and irrevocable destroyed" the investment, in which case, it amounted to an expropriation (*Tecmed* 2003: para. 117). The tribunal also found a denial of fair and equitable treatment due to the "lack of transparency" and "ambiguity and uncertainty" on the part of the host state – conduct that upset the investor's legitimate expectations (*Tecmed* 2003: paras 164, 172).

The tribunal was not content, however, examining only the effects of a measure on an investor or investment. Nor was it satisfactory to rely solely on a government's plea that it was resting its authority on police power jurisdiction. In *obiter*, the tribunal sought to determine whether such a measure was proportional to the public interest purported to be served by the measure. Having already found there to be an expropriatory measure, the analysis, curiously, began with the "due deference" that is owed to the state when it takes measures in the public interest. The tribunal quickly moved on to a consideration of "whether such measures are reasonable with respect to their goals, the deprivation of economic rights and the legitimate expectations of who suffered such deprivation [*sic*]" (*Tecmed* 2003: para. 122). These are criteria that look very much like the balancing factors articulated by the US Supreme Court in *Penn Central* (1978) and since incorporated into the 2004 US model BIT.[26] The tribunal purports to draw, however, not on US takings jurisprudence but on a ruling of the European Court of Human Rights (*James* 1986). The tribunal noted that the Strasbourg Court also considers the extent to which foreign investors are disenfranchised from participating in decisions that give rise to such measures by public authority, "partly because the investors are not entitled to exercise political rights reserved to the nationals of the State" (*Tecmed* 2003: para. 122). This is a constitutional principle identified not only in *James* (1986: para. 63) but traceable to US constitutional law doctrine (*Carolene* 1938; *McCulloch* 1819) and to the idea of "virtual representation" (Ely 1980: 83). As an organizing principle for judicial review, virtual representation asks us to focus on "whether the opportunity to participate either in the political process by which values are appropriately identified and accommodated, or in the accommodation those processes have reached, has been unduly constricted" (Ely 1980: 77). The question of whether the interests of the majority should be tied constitutionally to those on the outside – those for which "no felt community of interests" will have developed – is a question of constitutional practice which, though settled in the United States by the Fourteenth Amendment (Ely 1980: 84), purports to be settled by the investment rules regime. Whatever appeal the argument may have in the investment context, this does not justify its conversion into a basic postulate of the constitution-like regime without more, namely, without taking into account some of the following considerations. Competition for scarce capital, according to most accounts (Elkins et al. 2004; Stopford and Strange 1991), has resulted in states adopting various strategies – for instance, abandoning screening devices and regulatory measures or executing concession contracts with guaranteed rates of return – to signal that investors will be accorded the highest priority within the policy-making apparatus of the state. There are also actors within national state systems who likely will have interests tied up with those of particular investors – employees, consumers, or allied businesses. Though providing no warrant against adverse policy outcomes, they can be expected to speak for investors within national political processes. There is also the counterfactual suggesting that political voice is not of real concern to investors. Would foreign investors, it might be asked, be content solely with a voice within host national political systems rather than practically a veto? One can be reasonably confident in concluding that foreign investors would not be happy with anything less than a guarantee of the sort provided by a constitutional rule.

The standard applied by the tribunal grants states little room to maneuver, but it is one which might partially have exonerated Argentina in the CMS case. The enterprise was terminated for no reason other than political ones, the Tecmed tribunal concluded. Absent some "serious urgent situation, crisis, need or social emergency" (*Tecmed* 2003: para. 139) failure to renew the permit was not proportional to the violation of investor rights. It is noteworthy that the tribunal could find no redeeming public policy purpose being served by the government action. In its defense to civilian complaints lodged with the NAFTA Commission on Environmental Cooperation (CEC), the government of Mexico claimed that it had terminated Cytrar's operating permit because of "detected irregularities" and so had requested closure of the landfill site (CEC 2003). Though Mexico's environmental impact authorization law was not in force at the time the permit initially was granted to Cytrar, clearly there was some environmental purpose motivating the government's actions.

This is, by any account, a strict standard of review, akin to what Newcombe describes as a test of "reasonable necessity" (2005: 38). It does not look very similar to the wide margin of appreciation accorded states under European Court of Human Rights jurisprudence and upon which the *Tecmed* tribunal purported to rely (Allen 1999; Mountfield 2002). In *James* (1986) the court's analysis was guided throughout by this wide margin of appreciation. Leasehold reform legislation required the owner of some 2,000 homes in central London to sell leased property at significantly reduced rates to tenants, in some instances rendering immense profits to lessees and correspondingly less com-pensation to the owner. The state needed only to show, the court held, that there was a "reasonable relationship of proportionality" between means and ends (1986: paras 46, 50). In this instance, the property owner did not bear an "excessive burden" in light of the public interest being served by the reform measure (*Sporrong and Lönnarth* 1982: para. 73). Doing something less, such as directing the state to maintain the status quo, would have amounted to "reading [in] a test of strict necessity" into the European Convention:

> The availability of alternative solutions does not in itself render the leasehold reform legislation unjustified: it constitutes one factor, along with others, relevant for determining whether the means chosen could be regarded as reasonable and suited to achieving the legitimate aim being pursued, having regard to the need to strike a "fair balance." Provided the legislature remained within these bounds, it is not for the Court to say whether the legislation represented the best solution for dealing with the problem or whether the legislative discretion should have been exercised in another way. (*James* 1986: para. 51)

This idea of "fair balance" runs throughout the court's interpretation of the First Protocol to the European Convention on Human Rights and Fundamental Freedoms (1950). That is, in so far as state action impacts on property rights, whether via expropriation, regulatory taking, or an exercise of police power jurisdiction, the court will defer so long as the state satisfies this low-threshold proportionality requirement (van der Walt 1997: 104).

The proposal to take up proportionality analysis fits well with trends elsewhere, including those in the European Court of Justice. In his comparative review of the work of high courts making constitutional law, Beatty observes that "judges all over the world have converged on a framework of analysis," namely, that of proportionality (2004: 159). The principle of proportionality, he argues, enables judges "to resolve conflicts between majorities and minorities in a way that is equally respectful of both" (2004: 160). Though without textual support in most BITs, proportionality analysis would constitute an improvement over the sole-effects doctrine. The *Tecmed* formulation, however, suggests a strict standard of necessity of the sort that might only absolve state action in extreme circumstances. All of this underscores, as Beatty's work suggests, the constitutional quality of much that goes on under the auspices of the investment rules regime.

It should not be surprising to conclude with the observation that proportionality analysis has figured into assessments not only of whether there has been a taking but also of whether there has been a denial of fair and equitable treatment. Thomas Wälde's separate opinion in the NAFTA *Thunderbird* case (2006) suggests, first, that the doctrine of legitimate expectations, such as that applied in *Tecmed*, is subsumed under the standard of fair and equitable treatment. The doctrine, however, "is never seen as an iron-clad guarantee – comparable to a long-term concession contract with a stabilization guarantee – that policies will not change." Governments are entitled to change course, Wälde writes, but then a "balancing process takes place between the strength of legitimate expectations (stronger if an investment for the future has been committed) and the very legitimate goal of retaining 'policy space' and governmental flexibility" (*Thunderbird* 2006 [SO]: para. 102). Wälde regrettably does not provide us with clear guidance about the standard of review to be applied in such a "balancing process," other than to refer to the jurisprudence of the European Court of Justice, international economic law, and comparative administrative law (*Thunderbird* 2006 [SO]: para. 30).[27] Indeed, his two colleagues on the tribunal could not find that there was any legitimate expectation created by the Mexican government (a point on which Wälde dissented) as the government itself had relied on "incomplete" and "inaccurate" information provided by the investor (*Thunderbird* 2006: para. 151).

The work of these arbitration tribunals admittedly has been made difficult by the opacity of investment rules. Tribunals have sought to provide clarity with regard to many matters that are not at all clear and for which there is no identifiable consensus within the international community (Schwebel 2006: 4). It should have been expected that tribunals would seek guidance from national legal systems, like that of the United States – it is, after all, the "main source of case experience" on many contentious matters, such as that regarding expropriation (Wälde and Kolo 2001: 821). But they have eclipsed even these national experiences by weighing investor effects disproportionately over public interests. As Been and Beauvais demonstrate, tribunals have demanded compensation in circumstances where US courts would have been far more circumspect – for instance, by compensating investors for loss of access to markets or for property developed without requisite approvals (2003: 32, 43). Nowhere is this temerity more evident than in the Metalclad case. There the tribunal issued a ruling seemingly divorced from events on the ground that laid down expansive interpretations of the minimum standard of treatment rule and expropriations provision. The confident ability with which the tribunal dispensed with questions of Mexican constitutional law is striking.

Other elements of the arbitral jurisprudence look increasingly constitution-like. The idea of legitimate expectations, for instance, drawn from the European union and national state experience looks very much like an element of US regulatory takings doctrine and the related doctrine of substantive due process (Dana and Merrill 2002: 157). The incorporation of an omnibus standard of heightened scrutiny, together with borrowings from European high courts and constitutional jurisprudence, indicates that the significant differences between the investment rules regime and constitutional regimes are being blurred.

A handful of tribunals have ventured beyond an examination of the impact of the measure on an investor. To the extent that other factors are to be weighed in the balance (as in Tecmed), the balancing is decidedly tilted in favor of investor protection. This might make sense in light of the purpose and objects of the investment rules regime which is, after all, intended to robustly promote foreign investment. In which case, tribunal rulings in cases like Methanex (and a few others such as Loewen, Gami, and Mondev) are aberrant in the modest scope they attribute to the disciplinary effects of investment rules. It is not unreasonable to conclude that the regime of investment protection institutionalizes a constitution-like regime of limited government. As many critics justifiably feared, this is a regime in which policy alternatives are to be constrained and the imagination of alternative futures, not organized around the logic of the market, are to be actively discouraged.

**PART TWO**

PROJECTS

# CHAPTER FOUR

# HEALTH AND THE ENVIRONMENT

Economic globalization is typically portrayed as being beyond everyone's reach, including national states. Yet states are a "crucial nodal point" (Jessop 2002: 194) and a "strategic site" (Sassen 2006: 229) for the structuration of globalization. Paradoxically, states will have authored the legal regimes of precommitment that limit room for policy maneuverability (Panitch 1996b). States are critical actors within these policy regimes, governing the operation of the WTO, for instance, or as parties to investment treaties and ensuing investment disputes. The more powerful bargaining actors – typically the states of the OECD – structure these rules and institutions in ways that "best suit their development trajectory" (Weiss 2005: 724). This makes room for the regulatory capacity that developed states prefer while disabling measures that less developed and developing states may require.

The transnational regime for the protection and promotion of foreign investment can be understood, then, as an emergent form of supranational constitutional order, operating outside the internal legal orders of states, though authored by them – a phenomenon associated with the idea of "deterritorialization" (Brenner 1999: 43). I have traced the outlines of this external constitution in Part one and have suggested that the US constitutional experience retains a dominant, though not exclusive, interpretive force, at least with regard to the takings rule and its related disciplines, such as fair and equitable treatment. In this part, I fill out further the institutional ensemble that gives rise to some of the outcomes we associate with economic globalization. This requires moving, on occasion, beyond the investment rules regime to related institutional and rules-based disciplines in which law and legal institutions are deeply implicated. It also requires moving from the outside to the inside.

A move to the inside alerts us to the transformative effects of transnational law on domestic constitutional rules and structures, particularly with regard to the constitutional capacity to regulate economic subjects. The key actors promoting economic globalization expect national legal orders to undertake measures that will enhance the liberalization of markets. Where appropriate, states are expected to remove themselves from the performance of certain functions, as in the denationalization of public enterprise or the privatization of public services, conduct that Sassen labels "state work" (2006: 171, 232). The state, Cox maintains, becomes a "transmission belt from the global to the national economy" (1992: 302) so that domestic legal affairs are restructured to augment norms articulated in the transnational sphere (Robinson 2001: 173) – a phenomenon associated with the idea of "reterritorialization" (Brenner 1999: 43). This move inside represents no simple binary between external and internal, global and national (Sassen 2006: 229). Rather, the picture being drawn here is of states closely imbricated with the legal patterns of globalization. It is a matter of bringing the outside in (Walker 1993: 174). The chapters that form Part two explore these linkages by undertaking case studies of three national legal orders on differing continents. Each of these systems, in its own way, is authoring and adapting to the strictures of economic globalization.

The chapters in this part move from an emergent transnational constitutional order "outside" of states to constitutional and statutory arrangements "inside" of states that are undergoing change as a result of the pressures generated by the strong discourse of economic globalization (Bourdieu 1998: 34). There are a number of limitations inherent to this kind of undertaking. If it is accepted that states in an era of economic globalization generally are disinclined to consider genuine alternatives that stray from acceptable regulatory paths, then some of the discussion taken up here is, to some degree, hypothetical. If, in some cases, the resulting outcomes in the case of conflict between domestic constitutional law and transnational strictures may not entirely be certain, some outcomes reasonably can be anticipated.

This chapter addresses a shift in Canadian constitutional culture that may have been heralded by NAFTA's investment rules. The particular legal reform under discussion, its conflict with the investment rules regime, and the likely legal outcome, furnish concrete effects with which to test hypotheses concerning the linkages between transnational and local constitutionalism. The state strategy taken up here concerns a 1994 proposal by the Parliament of Canada that called for the "plain packaging" of cigarettes. Plain packaging demands that cigarettes be marketed and sold in plain, brown paper wrapping without the usual colors, stylized writing, and customary descriptors (such as "light" or "smooth"). Representatives of major US tobacco companies threatened to sue Canada for hundreds of millions of dollars under NAFTA's investment chapter were the government to proceed with its plain packaging initiative. A legal opinion was commissioned from former USTR Carla Hills on behalf of the tobacco companies, while Canadian international law scholar Jean-Gabriel Castel was commissioned to furnish an opinion favorable to the government's proposal. These conflicting legal opinions provide a focal point for this discussion. The opinions illustrate that the dispute ultimately would be determined by criteria familiar to US constitutional law, that is, by the categorical distinction between compensable takings and noncompensable exercises of the police power. To the extent that these distinctions do not form part of national constitutional law, states are being drawn further into the orbit of economic globalization and its regime of constitutional limitations. These effects are also being internalized within state legal and constitutional orders and so, in the last part of the chapter, I examine an instance where the disciplinary effects of the transnational legal order were coupled with domestic disciplines so as to thwart a Canadian government prohibition on the import and export of the gasoline additive MMT. The NAFTA expropriation claim by Virginia-based Ethyl Corporation against the Canadian government for banning MMT was never heard. Instead, the Canadian government settled the dispute by paying Ethyl US $13 million. The Canadian settlement was precipitated by a nonbinding ruling issued by an internal Canadian trade dispute body. This is an instance where legal standards, applicable to international trade disputes, have been internalized within Canada's legal order and perform functions complementary to those of the rules and institutions of economic globalization.

In order to better comprehend the role of states in these processes, I take up the idea of "state project." Jessop develops the notion as a way of destabilizing the state as a substantively unified system. He urges us to understand the state as a social relation which is less coherent and more the "contingent and provisional outcome of struggles to realize more or less specific 'state projects'" (1990: 9). Projects might be contradictory – there might be rival state projects issuing out of a single state system – and strategically selective – reflecting the interests of certain social interests over others (2002: 42, 1990: 268–9). This partiality structures state forms in such a way that it represents the "crystallization of past strategies as well as [the] privileging some over other current strategies" (1990: 269). Whether particular strategies will be promoted by states is determined, in part, by this strategic tilt of the state over time. State projects can fruitfully be contrasted with hegemonic projects that aim to unite state purposes under a generalized public interest or common good (2002: 42). In the chapters that follow, I outline policy innovations, such as mandatory plain packaging of cigarettes, which may be characterized as state projects as well as policy goals associated with constitutional objectives, such as land reform initiatives, that extend beyond the merely functional to embrace a hegemonic vision. For the purposes of this discussion, I assimilate both under the rubric of "state project." It is important to note that the relationship between the investment rules regime and state projects is an ambivalent one. The regime can have the effect of undermining state projects or, alternatively, might assist in the realization of projects that are harmonious with investment rules strictures – projects that have efficiency, for instance, as one of the main criteria for success (Jessop 2002: 226). Before turning to the discreet studies, I consider the idea of external effects on internal constitutional ordering via judicial interpretation and constitutional reform.

INTERNALIZING CONSTRAINTS

Transnational legal disciplines are capable of having numerous domestic legal effects on state projects (Petersmann 1991a: 422–3) and national political systems can embrace or resist these effects (Jacobs and Roberts 1987). International trade agreements, for example, may directly have the force of law according to domestic constitutional standards (as in Switzerland) or domestic constitutions themselves may be expected to conform to the demands of regional or international integration (Petersmann 1992: 3). High national courts are at the frontlines of this movement. The German Constitutional Court, for instance, grappled with the question of domestic effects of economic globalization in its famous decision concerning the EU's Maastricht Treaty (*Brunner* 1994). Both German enabling legislation and constitutional amendments giving effect to the monetary and social union were challenged as being inconsistent with the principles of democracy and sovereignty entrenched as overriding principles in the German Basic Law. The court rejected these challenges to Maastricht. National constitutional law was stretched by downplaying the scope of powers delegated upward while underscoring the preservation of state sovereignty contemplated by the union's constitutional architecture (Herdegen 1994; Stone Sweet 2004: 92–4; Weiler 1999: 288–9). Canadian courts adopted a similar posture in a case launched by the Council of Canadians and others challenging the consistency of NAFTA's investment chapter with Canada's constitution. Justice Pepall, at the trial level, characterized NAFTA as giving expression to norms of international law rather than affecting constitutional interests (*Council of Canadians* 2005: para. 41). Constitutional law was not at all implicated by NAFTA's legal order. No laws of Canada are required to be amended as a result of arbitral rulings nor are the rights of Canadians implicated (*Council of Canadians* 2005: para. 65) – a ruling that was affirmed on appeal (*Council of Canadians* 2006). In both the German and Canadian instances, transnational legal forms were contained by locating them "methodologically within historically entrenched legal disciplines" (Everson 2000: 95).

In other instances, high courts have been more complicit in the movement toward the integration of markets. Kelsey describes the Philippine Supreme Court as having succumbed to these pressures in its decision regarding accession to the WTO (1999). Despite the explicit embrace of economic nationalism in the text of the Philippines Constitution, the Supreme Court, Kelsey observes, "opted to repeal the nationalist economic principles of the Philippines Constitution" (1999: 515). The constitutional text was read so as to ensure constitutional conformity with the exigencies of economic globalization; otherwise, wrote Justice Panganiban for the court, there would be "isolation, stagnation, if not economic self-destruction" (*Tanada* 1994: 26). Despite the expectation that high courts typically will yield to powerful economic forces, there is no certainty in these matters. Scheppele describes how the Hungarian Constitutional Court came to the rescue of a vulnerable populace in the face of an IMF-induced, and hastily enacted, austerity program (*Hungarian Benefits Cases* 1995; Scheppele 2004, 2005). Those in receipt of pensions, health insurance, and other contributory social welfare measures, the court ruled, were entitled constitutionally to have those benefits continue in some form, while those receiving maternity benefits, child support, and other forms of social solidarity assistance could have those benefits eliminated but only with the appropriate notice (Scheppele 2004: 26–8). Though the court could not entirely forestall social welfare reforms, the government (and the IMF) achieved much of what it wanted while maintaining a minimal social safety net. The Hungarian government ultimately chose not to amend the constitution by way of response (Scheppele 2005: 50).

Nevertheless, political leadership in many parts of the world have been content to seek constitutional change to accommodate the strictures of investment rules and similar disciplines associated with economic globalization. Explaining the turn toward constitutional reform in the post-1989 world, Hirschl maintains that political elites, operating in conjunction with economic and judicial elites, have sought constitutional reform in order to "preserve or enhance their hegemony by insulating policy-making from popular political processes" (2004: 99). This move toward self-interested hegemonic preservation, Hirschl argues, helps to explain the current penchant for constitutional reform and the displacement of power from legislatures to the courts. Constitutional as well as quasiconstitutional reform also has been necessitated by investment rules strictures. Of particular interest is the constitutional restructuring undertaken by the Mexico in the lead up to NAFTA.

The NAFTA necessitated, at the very least, amendments to the ordinary legislation of all state parties. In this way, the free trade agreement precipitated a variety of domestic economic reforms, bringing about "restructuring and adjustment in the economy" (Doern and Tomlin 1991: 33). NAFTA, nevertheless, had a disparate impact on these legal regimes. In contrast to the modest reforms necessitated by NAFTA in the United States and Canada, Mexico's federal government undertook sweeping reform of domestic law so as to harmonize local rules with NAFTA's disciplines (Clarkson 2003). Many of those reforms, achieved via ordinary legislation or formal and informal constitutional change, were linked to Art. 27 of the Mexican constitution, described as the "most significant legal outcome of the Mexican revolution" (Murphy 1995: 59).

Art. 27 has its origins in the 1910 Revolution and Constitution of 1917. It established the "framework for a strong interventionist state" and reserved to the state exclusive control over the economic system (Sandrino 1994: 284). In addition to placing limits on foreign ownership of land and natural resources within the country, Art. 27 (Mexico's iteration of the "Calvo Clause") expressly makes foreign investment subject to the domestic law of the Mexican state. Foreign nationals who seek the protection of their home countries in order to challenge activities of the Mexican state can even forfeit their proprietary rights within Mexico (Sandrino 1994: 286).[1]

NAFTA's investment chapter imposes a variety of disciplinary measures over party states, including stringent compensation standards in the event of an expropriation enforceable before international trade tribunals, which appear incongruous with a Calvo Clause commitment. In order to avert legal uncertainty, the government of President Salinas issued a number of informal constitutional edicts in order to neutralize the full effect of Art. 27 and to assuage US and Canadian concerns. Salinas guaranteed that NAFTA would not be subject to constitutional attack (Daly 1994: 1189) and reassured investors by enacting a "Law Regarding the Making of Treaties," empowering the state to negotiate international treaties having enforceable dispute settlement mechanisms (Cánovas 1992: 391). The Mexican Chamber of Deputies, in addition, declared that submission of disputes to international tribunals "is not, in any manner, an invocation of diplomatic protection by a foreign government" and, thereby, in contravention of the Calvo Clause (Cánovas 1992: 391). In combination, the investment provisions of NAFTA, the 1992 Law Regarding Treaties, and the 1993 Foreign Investment Law, imply that the Calvo Clause has been interred until further notice, at least with regard to NAFTA investors (Daly 1994: 1187).

Up to thirty constitutional amendments were also made in the run-up to NAFTA, many of them to the "economic chapter" of the constitution (Huerta and Lujambio 1994: 64). Though the Calvo Clause as it concerns the status of foreign investors was not directly altered, other key parts of Art. 27 were amended. These were amendments that, in part, provoked the Zapatista National Liberation Army (EZLN) to armed rebellion in the state of Chiapas on New Year's Day 1994, the same day NAFTA entered into force. Article 27 is the constitutional foundation for property rights, both public and private. It made provision for the redistribution of rural lands, called *ejidos*, for collective use by indigenous campesinos. President Salinas radically altered Art. 27 in 1992, claiming chronic "underusage" of these collective lands and anticipating high volume agricultural exports to the United States and Canada.[2] These communal property provisions of Art. 27 were amended to permit individual property holding, relaxing limits on the numbers of acres held, and granting legal capacity to *ejidatarios* to enter into commercial or industrial ventures with third parties (Vargas 1994: 21). It is no coincidence, then, that the Zapatistas insisted that the Art. 27 amendments be repealed and that the "right to land ... once again be part of our constitution" (Vargas 1994: 75).

One could multiply examples of these disciplinary effects and interlinkages between transnational legal rules and domestic constitutionalism. As Fatouros writes, the "interaction of national laws and international rules is at the center of the legal regulation of FDI." Investment rules defer to national laws, supplement them and replace them "in a continuous dialectical relationship" (Fatouros 1996: 192).

One should not overstate, however, the differences between extant legal and regulatory regimes and the standards of the investment rules regime. Canada, for instance, had much less work to do in order to bring its legal regime in conformity with NAFTA's disciplines. The 1987 US-Canada Free Trade Agreement had been in place 7 years previous to NAFTA's coming into force. Various legal reforms were undertaken in order to comply with its strictures (Drache 1988: 81), among them, rolling back foreign investment screening and strengthening intellectual property protections. So Canada mostly was NAFTA compliant by the time January 1, 1994 rolled around. In addition, there already were significant affinities between US and Canadian law in so far as Canadians are respectful of property rights and are desirous of promoting foreign investment in most sectors. Though this might be so in practice, this has not been entirely the case *de jure*, for Canada has not protected property rights constitutionally. When Canadian political leaders adopted a constitutional bill of rights in 1982, they chose not to protect what might be called "pure" economic rights – those concerning contract, property, and other commercial interests. Instead, economic interests would receive protection indirectly, via provisions guaranteeing "freedom of expression" or "liberty and security" of the person (Bauman 1997) – an omission that rubs against Hirschl's elite hegemonic preservation thesis (2004: 77). Only in respect of the taking of Aboriginal property rights, courts have declared, will compensation ordinarily be required (Ziff 2005).

This is not to say that the Canadian legal system does not require compensation when private property is taken. Canada, like the United States, derives its principles of property law from the British common law. According to Blackstone, the eighteenth-century chronicler of the common law, the owner of property must be left in no worse a position than before should government exercise its power of eminent domain (Blackstone 1750: 135) – the common law, in other words, mandated a Pareto-type outcome whenever property was taken (Epstein 1985: 201). This, it is argued, can only be achieved by honoring the principle of just compensation for the taking of property. The principle was reflected in the common law rule mandating that statutes interfering with private property rights be strictly construed, and that any doubts or ambiguities found in statutory language be construed against the legislature and in favor of property owners (Maxwell 1896: 388–400). The common law presumption was that legislatures were not inclined to confiscate property without making their intentions plainly manifest (*R. v. Tener* 1985: para. 24). The important distinction between this common law rule of statutory interpretation and the US takings rule is that the former is only a presumption – it can be overridden by legislatures when their intention is made clear and plain (Cross 1987: 180; *Guardian Newspapers* 1985: 363). In Canada, then, there is no constitutional requirement that property taken by the state be for a public purpose and accompanied by the provision of just compensation (Lajoie 1971: 104).

Canadian courts, nevertheless, have taken heed of the common law presumption. In the *Manitoba Fisheries Case* (1978), considered the high-water mark in Canadian takings law, the federal government was required to provide compensation to Manitoba Fisheries, which carried on business as a fish exporter, after the government granted the exclusive right to export fish to a newly established Crown corporation. This was considered by the court to be a taking of the "goodwill" of the business rendering its physical assets "virtually useless" (*Manitoba Fisheries* 1978: 473). In the absence of a statutory pronouncement that compensation was not to be provided, the government was required to pay. This should be contrasted with the *Appleby* case (1976), where Mr. Appleby was not entitled to compensation for having fulfilled the *National Library Act* requirement that he deposit two copies of each volume he published with the National Library of Canada. The act expressly provided that the cost of the deposit would be at the publisher's own expense.

It is not the case, however, that Canadians are under constant compulsion to deliver up their property without compensation. Every jurisdiction in the country (national and subnational) provides a settled procedure by which property owners will be compensated for real property taken (Todd 1992; Ziff 2005: 347). There will be no statutory compensation forthcoming, however, in the case of regulatory takings. Limitations of use or reduction in the value of property through regulation will not give rise to a statutory requirement of compensation. Only confiscation (Bauman 1994) that amounts practically to an acquisition (*Mariner Real Estate* 1999: 730) will give rise to statutory compensation. On facts almost identical to *Lucas* – a prohibition on buildings and structures on environmentally sensitive beachfront property – the Nova Scotia Court of Appeal noted that Canadian law had taken a "fundamentally different path" than US law on the subject (*Mariner Real Estate* 1999: 732).

Ontario Justice Riddell in a 1912 address to the Iowa State Bar Association was right to state with conviction that "[i]n Canada, nobody at all is afraid that his property will be taken from him, it never is, in the ordinary case." This was because, argued Riddell, Canadians share with Americans a common commitment to "justice to all under the law" (Riddell 1912: 870). While this ordinarily is the rule, the Canadian government has seen fit to intervene in the market in ways that would have been difficult, if not impossible, in certain periods in US history (Schneiderman 2006). Government in Canada was not so much limited by the constitution as empowered to secure existing entitlements, liberate economic enterprise, and generate new wealth. Canadian constitutional design not only facilitated economic productivity through state enterprise but also sanctioned legislative intrusions into the realm of property rights as a motor of economic development. Rather than being distrustful of governmental authority (the dominant presupposition of the investment rules regime), government was viewed as a strategic player in the development of a new national economy.

PLAIN PACKAGING

Canada's *Tobacco Products Control Act* (1988) was proclaimed in force on January 1989, banning all forms of cigarette advertising and promotion in Canada. Promotion by cigarette manufacturers in the arts would have to be conducted under corporate banners, rather than under recognizable brand names. Regulations required that more effective warnings be placed in bold, black and white lettering at the top of each package. Unequivocal warnings, such as "SMOKING CAN KILL YOU," were to be placed prominently on all cigarette packages sold in Canada. In addition, the *Tobacco Sales to Young Persons Act* (1993) was enacted, prohibiting the sale of "kiddie" packs containing twenty smokes. With these kinds of regulations in place, it could feasibly be claimed that Canada had secured the means for achieving global precedent-setting reductions in tobacco consumption (Canada 1994a: 2:4). In addition to these new measures, the minister of Health proposed that the government of Canada legislate the plain packaging of cigarettes. The announcement of this initiative had been preceded by a federal tax roll-back on the sale of cigarettes in order to frustrate smuggling of contraband tobacco products from the United States (Pross and Stewart 1994: 129). Cigarette consumption being price sensitive, a decline in price likely would lead to an uptake of new smokers (Canada 1995: 157). This could be combated by the plain packaging initiative.

Cigarette packaging, it is claimed, is an effective medium of advertising. Manufacturers continue to invest in developing effective and provocative packaging for their products as well as in drawing up brand names and symbols. Manufacturers claim that they only are competing with other brands for the allegiances of existing smokers rather than attempting to lure new smokers into the marketplace (Webb 1994: 2). Critics reply that manufacturers are disingenuous – why spend so much money on developing advertising strategies, particularly ones directed at younger consumers? The plain packaging initiative could, then, have the effect of frustrating one of the more effective methods of advertising available to tobacco companies, that is, advertising by virtue of personal possession. Twenty-five to thirty times every day, smokers pull packs of cigarettes out of their pockets, bags, and purses. With 20 billion packages sold in Canada every year, this amounts to 50–60 billion "exposures" per year. According to the Non-Smokers' Rights Association, "[t]his dwarfs all other forms of tobacco advertisements" (Canada 1994a: 2:6). When packages are exposed in the presence of children, it magnifies the impact of the endorsement; it means that mom, dad, sister, or brother would rather fight than switch.

The proposed solution to this form of advertising is to mandate the plain packaging of cigarettes. The ambit of a plain packaging law remains unclear. Indications suggest that cigarettes would be sold and marketed in plain, dull packaging with only the brand name, risk warnings, and product content information permitted, all in a standard font. The use of logos, trademarks, or eye-catching fonts would be prohibited as would the words "Extra Smooth," "Finest Blend," or

"Ultra Light" (Canada 1994b). There would be no more puffery in the cigarette trade.

Research studies on plain packaging had not determined conclusively that generic packaging would reduce cigarette consumption. According to the Report of the House of Commons Standing Committee on Health, studies suggest that plain packaging makes tobacco products less attractive and appealing (Canada 1994b: 9). Consequently, the committee recommended that the federal government begin drafting a legislative framework to institute plain packaging. But the legislation would be introduced only after Health Canada concluded its own unfinished study on the effects of plain packaging at the end of that year, if its results proved favorable to the initiative (Canada 1995b: 29).

To no one's surprise, tobacco companies were unhappy with these plans. Representatives of the American tobacco giants Philip Morris International and RJR Reynolds Tobacco Company appeared before the Standing Committee on Health to indicate their displeasure. In their view, any proposed packaging legislation would run afoul of a number of international agreements to which Canada is a party, including the GATT and NAFTA. It was the expropriation provisions of NAFTA that the president of Philip Morris invoked, however, when he characterized the resulting legislation as being an unjustified taking of valuable trademarks and related investments in Canada. For this, Philip Morris and RJR Reynolds would pursue legal remedies, "including claims for compensation of hundreds of millions of dollars" (Webb 1994: 1). In their support, the tobacco manufacturers filed a legal opinion obtained from Carla Hills, former USTR who negotiated NAFTA's terms. Hills had been retained to provide her legal opinion regarding the consistency of the plain packaging proposal with a number of international agreements, among them NAFTA's investment chapter.

According to Hills, cigarette manufacturers have branded their products with distinctive trademarks and trade dress, and much of these are protected by trademarks owned or controlled by foreign investors such as Philip Morris and RJR Reynolds. Thus, her clients' interests fell within NAFTA's definition of "investment": "real estate or other property, tangible or intangible, acquired in the expectation or used for the purpose of economic benefit or other business purposes." The imposition of plain packaging would amount to a taking of their lawfully registered trademark, entitling these foreign investors to "staggering" compensation claims (Hills 1994: 19–20).

Hills acknowledged that NAFTA's expropriation provisions are qualified in one respect: the article does not apply to limitations on intellectual property rights that are authorized in Chapter 17.[3] These authorized measures could not amount to a taking under NAFTA's Chapter 11. Chapter 17 outlines the parties' obligations to protect intellectual property such as trademarks, patents, and copyrights. Hills argued, however, that the plain packaging requirement was not authorized by Chapter 17 and so could not escape the charge that it was a taking. Art. 1708(10) provides, in part, that "a party may not encumber the use of a trademark in commerce by special requirements such as use that reduces a trademark's function as an indication of source" (Hills 1994: 12–13) . Plain packaging would have the effect of encumbering trademarks by prohibiting their use altogether.

Hills's opinion also considered whether there are any exceptions to NAFTA's obligations when it comes to laws that are designed to promote health measures. Art. 2101 provides for a health exception, but only to specified parts of NAFTA. Neither the investment chapter (Chapter 11) nor the intellectual property chapter (Chapter 17) are included in this exception clause. Therefore, Hills concluded, there is no exception for measures designed to promote health that offend the investment protection or intellectual property provisions (Hills 1994: 12, 20).

In response to Hills's damaging legal opinion, the Non-Smokers' Rights Association of Canada retained a distinguished Toronto law firm to counter with an opinion on whether the proposal violated NAFTA. The law firm, in turn, retained the services of a senior professor of international law, Professor Jean-Gabriel Castel of Osgoode Hall Law School, who disagreed entirely with Hills's opinion. Castel began with the proposition that international law condones confiscation without compensation of products harmful to health (American Law Institute 1987: para 712; Christie 1962: 331–2). What was at issue here was not the alleged expropriation of intellectual property but the regulation of a harmful product (Castel 1994: 4). Castel also considered the technical question of whether an interest in a trademark is an "investment" for the purposes of NAFTA's investment chapter. Recall that a vast number of economic interests fall within the scope of NAFTA's definition of investment. Castel cast doubt on this, concluding that a trademark may not be tangible property "acquired" for a business purpose within the meaning of the definition of investment (Castel 1994: 10). Even if it was a protected investment, he argued, the regulation would be saved by the exception to the expropriation provisions, which makes those provisions inapplicable to limitations on intellectual property rights permitted under Chapter 17. Here Castel took issue with Hills's opinion that plain packaging violated the intellectual property chapter. The trademark would not be "encumbered" within the meaning of the chapter, he claimed, since plain packaging rules would entitle companies to print their brand names.[4]

As a last interpretive maneuver, Castel argued that NAFTA did not entitle any of the parties to absolute rights at the expense of a population's health and safety. Even though Chapters 17 and 11 are not mentioned explicitly in the general health exception found in Art. 2101, it was intended, Castel argued, that this article would control interpretation of the whole document. This construction of NAFTA is supported by a provision in Chapter 11 (Art. 1112[1]) which provides that, in the event of an inconsistency between Chapter 11 and any other NAFTA chapter, the other chapter shall prevail to the extent of the inconsistency. This, argued Castel, gives precedence to Chapters 9 and 21, which both recognize that a state's interest in promoting the health of its citizenry takes precedence over NAFTA rules governing the importation of goods (Castel 1994: 10).

There are considerable flaws in Castel's rejoinder to Carla Hills. One significant weakness is that there appears to be no explicit public health exception to NAFTA's takings rule (which will not have been remedied by modification of US and Canadian bilateral treaty practice, discussed in Chapter three). When the health exception is made explicitly available to the parties in NAFTA, the chapters on investment and intellectual property are excluded. As a result, Castel had to search for a way around this problem by narrowly reading some sections and expansively reading others. For example, Castel wondered whether the interests of American cigarette manufacturers would fall within the definition of investment in Chapter 11 because these interests may not be "tangible property acquired for a business purpose." But the section applies to both tangible and intangible property and applies to property acquired or "used" for the purpose of economic benefit. The verb to "use" is the same verb employed in the Canadian Trade-Mark Act (1985) to define a trademark interest ("a mark that is used by a person ..."). Assuming this were an investment caught by Chapter 11, Castel argued that the intellectual property exception to the takings rule would be available. This required, again, an exceptionally narrow reading of the paragraph that permits limitations on the use of intellectual property in Chapter 17. The two relevant paragraphs in Chapter 17: (a) prohibit encumbrances on the use of the trademark in commerce by special requirements, such as a use that reduces the trademark's function as an indication of source; and (b) permit limitations to the rights conferred on trademark holders, such as a fair use of descriptive terms, provided that such exceptions take into account the legitimate interests of the trademark owner and other persons. Plain packaging clearly would amount to an encumbrance within the meaning of the first paragraph. It likely is not an acceptable limitation under the second paragraph because it does not mandate "fair use of descriptive terms" – the initiative would prohibit the use of most terms altogether. Nor would it appear to take into account much of "the interests" of the trademark owner or other persons, such as consumers.

Castel lastly resorts to the interpretive rule that provides that in the event of an "inconsistency" between Chapter 11 and other NAFTA chapters, the other chapters shall prevail – a means of smuggling in a health exception in the investment chapter where none exists. Castel must now search for an inconsistency. Applying ordinary rules of statutory interpretation (Dreidger 1957: 124–6), it is reasonably clear that in NAFTA there is meant to be a clear distinction between expropriations, on the one hand, and regulations concerning the importation of goods that are designed to promote health, on the other hand. In the former case, no other objectives can override the stringent requirements of the takings rule. Nor does Castel's argument forestall claims by foreign investors already established in Canada that do not concern the importation of goods.

At bottom, the tension Castel wrestled with is akin to that found in US constitutional law – the constitutional tension between compensable takings and noncompensable exercises of the police power which are designed to promote health, safety, or public morals. US takings law recognizes that states are entitled to make owners of private property bear the cost of regulation under the police power, particularly when their uses impinge on the rights of others (e.g., by creating a public nuisance) (*Lingle* 2005). Private property owners should not be required to bear those costs alone in circumstances where states merely wish to take property for other public purposes, for example, establishing a new highway or an airport terminal. In those circumstances, US constitutional law requires that just compensation be provided.

This is not to say that the plain packaging initiative would attract compensation under US takings law, only that the plain packaging controversy exhibits the same tension at the heart of US doctrine. Castel argued, in effect, that a police powers type exception operates both explicitly and implicitly in NAFTA, and he offered a variety of textual interpretations which would permit a health exception for expropriations. His approach is one deferential to government initiatives that purport to regulate health. Hills, by contrast, is a strict constructionist. She strictly construed NAFTA's takings rule, narrowing the scope of the police powers exception. Castel's approach harkens back to the New Deal settlement; Hills's interpretive style is more in harmony with late twentieth-century US Supreme Court precedent (*Dolan* 1994; *Lucas* 1992; *Nollan* 1986).

For societies aspiring to regimes of democratizing constitutionalism and to pluralism in state-market relations, Castel's approach is preferable to the strict constructionist one. The problem, as we have seen, is that this approach is not justified easily by the text of NAFTA. An alternative approach to which Castel alludes is a categorical one (Michelman 1988: 1622). Regulations that fall traditionally within the scope of the state's police power are, by definition, not takings within the meaning of NAFTA. As the plain packaging initiative concerns regulations which are designed to promote health and safety, they do not, under international law nor under the domestic constitutional law of the United States and Canada, constitute unlawful takings requiring compensation. This argument compels the Canadian state to fall further into the web of US constitutional law by invoking a police power exception to the takings rule. It is also a perilous move as, even here, both scholars (Epstein 1985: 128) and courts (*Dolan* 1994) have urged that there be a precise and close relationship or nexus between the legislative objective and regulatory means used to achieve that objective. Some even claim that this revives the *Lochner* standard of review (*Dolan* 1994).

Proponents of an international standard would claim that international law traditionally has not required such a strict standard of proof. According to Christie, if a prohibition concerning the use of property "can be justified as being reasonably necessary to the performance by a State of its recognized obligations to protect the public health, safety, morals or welfare, then it would normally seem that there has been no 'taking' of property" (1962: 338). The European Court of Justice has exhibited a similar deference. The court has been inclined to treat measures which prohibit advertising of beverages with a high alcohol content as ones designed to benefit the public health. In contrast to NAFTA, however, this is an exception to the rule prohibiting restrictions on EC imports that is expressly recognized in the law of the European Economic Community.[5] It is sufficient, for the court, that the domestic law "does not appear to be manifestly unreasonable as part of a campaign against alcoholism" (*Aragonesa* 1994: 904; *E.C. Commission* 1981: para. 17).

A stricter approach to NAFTA takings would not be discordant, however, with other currents in public international law that have been discussed in Chapter two. Higgins (1982), for instance, calls upon international law to expand the doctrine of regulatory takings. Academics and jurists alike are signaling that these constitution-like limitations should be construed so as to minimize the capacity of states to intervene in the economy. Were a stricter standard of review applied, the government of Canada would be expected to show not only that plain packaging legislation was a noncompensable regulatory event but, following the lead of the US Supreme Court and recent arbitral jurisprudence (*Tecmed* 2003: para. 122), that there is some legitimate public purpose being advanced which is roughly proportionate to the impact on the tobacco companies' investment interests. In other words, some degree of relationship between plain packaging and reduction in the number of smokers would have to be shown. Here the studies extant might prove to be determinative. The Canadian House of Commons' Standing Committee on Health concluded that the "available evidence suggests that plain or generic packaging is a reasonable component of the evolving national strategy to reduce tobacco consumption." They found it significant that no study suggested otherwise (Canada 1994b: 9, 13). The Commons Committee would only recommend the institution of plain packaging on the condition that a separate federal study support the proposition that plain packaging reduces tobacco consumption (Canada 1994b: 29). The Canadian federal department, Health Canada, undertook to do this research. Authored by an expert panel and released in the following year, the study provided some support for the federal initiative. The expert panel concluded, after conducting a variety of studies and experiments, that, all other things being equal, plain packaging "would likely depress the incidence of smoking uptake by non-smoking teens, and increase the incidence of smoking cessation by teen and adult smokers." This was despite the fact that packaging was "not the most important attribute related to uptake or cessation decisions" – the price of cigarettes being a more determinative factor (Canada 1995: 158, 157).

Despite this controversy over NAFTA's strictures, the House of Commons Committee did not hesitate in recommending plain packaging. The committee merely issued a cautionary note: that "prudence should be exercised in the development of plain or generic packaging regulations for tobacco products" and that "special attention must be paid to Canada's international obligations" (Canada 1994b: 21). When Julius Katz, chief US negotiator for NAFTA, appeared on behalf of Phillip Morris and RJR Reynolds before the House of Commons Committee and the discussion turned to the terms of NAFTA, several committee members exhibited mistaken understandings about its requirements. For these members, NAFTA merely required respect for the principle of "national treatment" – as long as US and Mexican investors in tobacco companies were treated equally with Canadian ones, the proposal could not run afoul of NAFTA. This reflected the dominant understanding of NAFTA's requirements as they had been touted by its supporters (Lipsey et al. 1993). These Parliamentarians did not comprehend that NAFTA binds the parties to more than respect for the principle of national treatment and that, even if equal treatment was achieved, NAFTA could prohibit outright some regulatory initiatives. In their dissent to the Report of the Committee, the opposition Bloc Québécois members were less cautious about NAFTA's domestic effects – "plain cigarette packaging may well violate Canada's international trade obligations," they concluded (1994b: 54).

The plain packaging proposal eventually was dropped, however, and not by reason of NAFTA alone. One year after the House of Commons Committee issued its report, the Supreme Court of Canada rendered its decision in *RJR-MacDonald* (1995). The case concerned an earlier tobacco legislation (the *Tobacco Products Control Act* [1988]) which banned promotional advertising by tobacco manufacturers and mandated that health warnings be included on all cigarette packages. The court held that the ban on promotional activities, advertising, and the requirement of unattributed health warnings were unjustifiable restrictions on the constitutional guarantee of freedom of expression. The ruling goes some distance in guaranteeing the rights of manufacturers to bring their products to market, even products detrimental to public health (but see *JTI Macdonald* 1998). The ruling also suggests that the guarantee of rights in Canada's *Charter of Rights and Freedoms* complements well the ends served by NAFTA's takings rule.

Despite these setbacks, several years later the government of Canada introduced a proposal that would ban the use of misleading descriptive terms in cigarette packaging, such as the descriptors "light" and "smooth" (*Canada Gazette* 2001). The proposal prompted an immediate and predictable reply from US tobacco giant Phillip Morris. It would destroy valuable trademarks and goodwill, the company claimed, stripping tobacco manufacturers of their "property rights," tantamount to an expropriation under NAFTA (Chase 2002a; Phillip Morris 2002: 7). Having abandoned these proposed regulations, class action lawsuits have since been filed seeking damages in the hundreds of millions of dollars from tobacco companies for their deceptive product markers (NSRA 2006; Woellert 2006).

## MMT FUELS THE CONTROVERSY

There are other instances where the domestic effects of NAFTA's investment chapter have been felt in the production of Canadian public policy. Interested third party investors within the United States invoked an earlier version of the rule, in the 1987 Canada-US Free Trade Agreement, to help subvert the government of Ontario's public auto insurance plan (Campbell 1993: 92–3). The US aerospace giant, Lockheed Corporation, threatened to sue the government of Canada for the repudiation of contracts to privatize Terminal 2 at Toronto's Pearson Airport that were entered into by a previous administration (Globe and Mail 1994). This undoubtedly helped to shape the government's response in providing compensation to the consortium, of which Lockheed was a part, for cancellation of the contract. *Time* magazine threatened to invoke NAFTA's takings rule to challenge a proposed federal law that would have banned "split-run" magazines – the publication of Canadian editions of American magazines that offer cheap Canadian advertising with little Canadian content (Scoffield 1998c). Canadian public enterprise is under attack – United Parcel Service unsuccessfully claimed $230 million in lost profits as a result of Canada Post cross-subsidizing courier services with profits generated from its publicly funded regular delivery service (Jack 1999; *United Parcel Service* 2007) – as have remnants of the system for the management of agricultural products – GL Farms of Delaware claims $78 million in damages as a result of Canada's managed system of dairy supply (Chase 2006). The US investor in an abandoned iron mine site is suing for damages suffered as a result of the Ontario provincial government abandoning plans to use the open-pit mine as a landfill site for the city of Toronto's garbage (Chase 2007). One of the most notorious instances was the takings claim made by Ethyl Corporation of Richmond, Virginia (now NewMarket Corporation).

Ethyl sued the government of Canada for imposing a ban on the import and export of the toxic gasoline additive MMT. The classification of MMT as a "dangerous toxin," Ethyl claimed, amounted to an expropriation under NAFTA. Not only was there a taking, the company claimed, but there was in addition discriminatory treatment and the imposition of performance requirements, all of which amounted to US $250 million in damages (Ethyl 1997a). The manganese-based fuel additive MMT had been blended in gasoline fuel sold in Canada for almost 20 years. Invoking environmental, health, and consumer protection grounds, the federal government moved to prohibit the importation and interprovincial trade in MMT in the summer of 1997 (Curtis 1999). Seven months before the federal bill banning MMT was enacted into law, Ethyl filed its notice of intent to submit a NAFTA claim. Eight of ten Canadian provinces also voiced their objection to the federal bill before the parliamentary committee that was considering the new law. The province of Alberta (supported by three provinces) subsequently filed a complaint against the federal government under a nonbinding intergovernmental accord called the Agreement on Internal Trade (AIT). The AIT is modeled on other trade agreements, like NAFTA and the Uruguay-round GATT. Its central organizing principle is the familiar one of "nondiscrimination." Governments are prohibited from enacting laws that discriminate against goods, persons, services, and investments emanating from other provinces, which restrict or prohibit their movement or create obstacles to internal trade. Unlike in the United States, there is no dormant federal commerce power in Canada that restricts the ability of subnational units to erect nontariff barriers to the movement of goods and services. Provinces are entitled to seek resolution of complaints before dispute resolution panels as are, to a more qualified extent, business firms. Here is an instance, then, of the model rules of international economic law, though otherwise foreign to the national constitutional system, being folded into the internal legal order of the state.

A dispute panel constituted under the AIT concluded, by a vote of 4:1, that the federal ban on MMT was inconsistent with the AIT (AIT

1998c). By blocking the movement of MMT across provincial borders, the federal bill ran afoul of the agreement. The federal government conceded this point, but argued that it nevertheless had satisfied AIT standards. According to the text of the AIT, when an act in breach of the agreement pursues a "legitimate objective" and does not unduly impair or restrict interprovincial trade, the action can survive AIT scrutiny. In order to satisfy this test of proportionality, the arguments made to justify the ban were central to the government's defense. The scientific evidence in support of the ban (as in the case of plain packaging), however, was equivocal.

Airborne manganese is reported to harm the human brain and nervous system, and in high doses can lead to Parkinson's-like symptoms (Frumkin and Solomon 1997; Mergler et al. 1999). Studies show high concentrations of manganese in outdoor urban environments, but well below acceptable levels (Bhuie et al. 2005; Loranger and Zayed 1997; Zayed et al. 1996, 1999). A 1994 study commission by Health Canada did not provide the necessary scientific support for the ban. The authors concluded that manganese emissions from MMT use were not entering "the Canadian environment in quantities or under conditions that may constitute a health risk" (Wood and Egyed 1994: 64). More recent information about fine particle pollution and its adverse effects on urban populations suggests that Health Canada should have been more cautious (Boudia et al. 2006; McCarthy 1998a, 1998b). According to J. Michael Davis of the US EPA, "a reasonable basis exists for qualitative concerns regarding potential public health risks, especially for susceptible subpopulations, if MMT is used extensively in unleaded gasoline" (1999: 513). Similarly, the American Medical Association Council on Scientific Affairs deemed it "prudent and sensible to call for more research and testing before MMT is introduced widely in US gasoline supply" (Lyznicki et al. 1999: 142). Not surprisingly, the Ethyl Corporation denied any relationship between MMT exposure and danger to health (Ethyl 1997b; Lynam et al. 1999).

Besides the connection between MMT and human health, car manufacturers argued that MMT increases hydrocarbon emissions and impairs vehicle emission systems. The new generation of On-Board Devices (OBD) that control vehicle emissions are gummed up by manganese deposits caused by MMT, according to the presidents of seven of Canada's leading auto manufacturers (Curtis 1999). This, too, Ethyl disputed, claiming that the auto industry was scapegoating MMT for faulty OBD technology. Ethyl claimed that MMT boosts octane, makes cars run efficiently, and benefits the environment by reducing harmful nitrogen oxide emissions (Ethyl 1997b; Lynam et al. 1999). Soloway, for similar reasons, prefers to analyze the MMT initiative as the product of a "baptist-bootlegger" coalition made up of naïve moralists from the environmental movement and the automobile and ethanol industries seeking to transfer costs to a single vulnerable competitor (1999: 59)

For some time, the Canadian government had been facilitating discussions between the oil and auto industries regarding MMT use. They could come to no consensus on the harmful effects on vehicles or the environment. Confronted with industrial stalemate, the government moved to ban the crossborder trade in MMT (Curtis 1999). Invoking the "precautionary principle," Environment Canada argued that legislators were required to err on the side of human health and the environment. The federal act did not ban MMT outright, however, only its transborder movement. The bill was not tabled as an environmental measure and, hypothetically, MMT could still be produced and sold in any province.

The AIT panel concluded that the scientific evidence concerning the effects of MMT on vehicle emission systems and on the environment was "inconclusive." The panel conceded that there was a "reasonable basis" for believing that the federal government's objective of limiting the use of MMT was a legitimate one. But the panel was not willing to give the benefit of the doubt to the federal government in any other respect. The panel, instead, adopted a strict approach to the interpretation of the AIT – an approach consistent with tendencies in international economic law discussed in Chapter two and the one most favorable to the complaining provinces, oil refiners, and to the principle of free trade.

The text of the AIT indicates that governments should be given more leeway in environmental measures than in the case of ordinary trade restrictions. The AIT therefore directs that panels be more deferential to legislative choices in the case of environmental control. Even with these directives, the AIT panel read the agreement's requirements to promote interprovincial trade as strictly as possible. The federal government was required to show that it had satisfied each element of the relevant article: that it had "taken into account" the "need to minimize negative trade effects," that it chose among "equally effective means," and that it chose among "reasonably available means" (Art. 404.c) According to the panel, there were other equally available and reasonable alternatives that were not as trade restrictive as the federal government's ban. Moreover, cooperation, and not conflict, is an underlying principle of the AIT. Instead of engaging in federal unilateralism, the federal government should have sought the cooperation of the oil-refining provinces – mirroring precisely WTO jurisprudence regarding the environmental exception in Art. XX, discussed in Chapter two. Though the provinces succeeded in having the law declared inconsistent with the AIT, the finding had no legally binding effect. Moreover, there was still the outstanding NAFTA claim to contend with. Anticipating a similar loss before a NAFTA dispute panel, the government of Canada capitulated and issued a check for the sum of US $13 million together with an apology and an admission that MMT did not pose environmental problems (Environment Canada 1998; Ethyl 1998; McCarthy 1998b).[6]

The AIT dispute panel decision was hailed as a triumph of principle over bad science. According to jubilant editorial writers, it was case of "mad ministers thwarted" (Globe and Mail 1998b; Corcoran 1998). For Ethyl, the outcome was an unmitigated success. Not only were legal fees recouped, but the Canadian government's apology could be conscripted into its global marketing campaign. The complaints about discriminatory treatment, imposition of performance requirements, and expropriation were all rendered credible. Yet, within days of the settlement, new studies were released suggesting that exposure to low levels of manganese in MMT could cause memory impairment and nervous system disorder (McCarthy 1998b).

Despite the equivocal evidence, Canada remains one of the few countries in the world where MMT is blended into automotive fuel (though oil companies increasingly are abandoning its use: CCPA 2004). MMT was banned for 17 years in the United States by the EPA. It was not until a court ruled in 1995 that the EPA had no legal authority to consider health issues under the Clean Air Act that MMT became legally available in low concentrations (though it is still banned in California, the state with the toughest emission standards). One survey indicates that over 75 percent of US oil-refining capacity remained MMT free (Frumkin and Solomon 1997).

The 1998 decision by the AIT dispute panel, then, ultimately preempted Ethyl's NAFTA claim. The AIT was armed with enough ammunition to force the federal government to back down on their bill banning MMT. What is important to underscore is the way in which an internal Canadian trade agreement, interpreted by a panel of

Canadian trade law experts, linked up neatly with international trade and investment law disciplines. There would be no deference to government with regard to purported environmental measures, rather, every element of the agreement was to be construed in ways that were least restrictive of the overall objective of limiting governmental intervention in the economic realm. Canadian provinces are committing themselves to even greater constraints and thereby internalizing further constraints sought after by advocates of the investment rules regime. The Trade, Investment and Labour Mobility Agreement between British Columbia and Alberta[7] purports to "support ongoing trade and investment liberalization both nationally and internationally" by ensuring that neither party will enact measures that "operate to restrict or impair trade ... or investment or labour mobility" (Art. 3). Only measures that have as their purpose the achievement of a "legitimate objective," are not more restrictive than are necessary to achieve that objective, and are not disguised restrictions on trade, investment, or labor mobility may be adopted or maintained in contravention of Art. 3 (Art. 6). These and other disciplines, such as national treatment, MFN, and transparency obligations, are enforceable by both the parties and private persons before panels established under UNCITRAL rules (Art. 27). The agreement goes much further than the AIT to ensure that nationals receive rights equivalent to the constitution-like entitlements available to foreigners under investment rules.

The aim of this chapter has been to demonstrate some of the external and internal effects of the investment rules regime. The case studies taken up in this chapter suggest, first, that NAFTA has the effect of incorporating into Canadian law standards, principles, and analyses that parallel the constitutional law experience in the United States and elsewhere. To the extent that NAFTA accomplishes this task – the Parliamentary hearings on plain packaging are witness to this transformation – Canadian constitutionalism will have been significantly altered. Canadian constitutional design precipitated a wide range of energetic government action with regard to economic subjects. With the advent of the Canadian Charter of Rights and Freedoms things surely have changed, but with NAFTA matters will have been transformed. The internalization of these values, through such instruments as the nonbinding AIT, pushes the Canadian legal order further into the continental orbit of disabling constitutionalism.

# CHAPTER FIVE

# LAND AND EMPOWERMENT

If the investment rules regime is the product of interstate consensus, it is one that is "heirarchically structured" (Cox 1987: 254). In an era of economic globalization, not all states have equal access to the means of producing what are considered to be universal standards (Bourdieu 2000). Only a handful of actors operating within certain core national states over a long period of time – the "principal legal systems of the world" (USTR 2004b: Art. 5; Sohn and Baxter 1961: 547) – credibly can claim credit for their design. Drawing on particularistic national experiences, the regime's effects will also be experienced differently by states, generating opportunities for some and constraints for others. All of this suggests that the benefits and burdens of economic globalization will not be evenly distributed across the interstate system.

A vast number of states wish to participate in this regime, despite its discernible tilt, primarily as a means of signaling a ready openness to foreign investment (Elkins et al. 2004). Those branches within national states closely tied to the international economy (Cox 1992: 302; Sassen 2006: 171), in a complex mixture of consent and coercion, have generated a web of investment rules to cover almost every corner of the globe.[1] This chapter further examines the role of middle powers, such as Canada and South Africa, in the structuration of the investment rules regime. Middle powers, write Alden and Vieira, "are situated ideologically and materially within the dominant hegemonic paradigm but are limited (by both power and disposition) in their capacity to act" (2005: 1079). Canada, exemplar of a middle power

(Cox 1989: 241), energetically promoted investment treaties modeled on NAFTA standards. Though the Canadian model varied in 2004, it continues to incorporate standards long promoted by the United States as representing the principles of the law of nations. South Africa, too, actively engaged in a bilateral investment treaty program just as South Africa's multiracial democracy was constituted. That model, borrowed from a 1994 UK-South Africa BIT has also undergone some revision (TRALAC 2004). To what degree has this engagement with investment rules hampered South Africa's ability to address, as the text of its new constitution insists upon, entrenched levels of socioeconomic disadvantage?

The text of the 1995 Canada-Republic of South Africa BIT – a treaty signed but never declared in force – provides the focal point for the first part of this chapter. The treaty text, as do numbers of other South African BITs, replicates the investment rule disciplines canvassed in Chapter one and so provides a counterpoint to property provisions in the postapartheid South African Constitution. The constitution's property rights clause represents a unique compromise designed both to assuage the anxiety of the Afrikaner minority and the need to redress the legacy of dispossession represented by apartheid. Yet there are ways in which the investment rules regime might supersede, even frustrate, the objectives of the new constitution.

Trade and investment law disciplines have also required the government of South Africa to hedge the pursuit of constitutional commitments to promote equality and the lessening of apartheid's legacy of economic inequality. This is made most apparent in the plan for broad-based Black Economic Empowerment (BEE). An ANC-government initiative intended to generate a new indigenous black entrepreneurial class, the program insists that economic actors operating within South Africa promote black managers, hire black suppliers, and, excepting closely held foreign corporations operating outside of the mining sector, divest minority control to black-controlled enterprises. The BEE initiative is characterized by South Africans as merely a new form of public-private partnership, a voluntary program associated with the promotion of good governance. In the second part of the chapter, I consider the extent to which this state project has been schematized so as mostly, though not entirely, to be harmonious with investment disciplines. The discussion provides an opportunity to explore the extent of the absorption of sub-Saharan Africa into the web of investment rules.

## BITS AND LAND

Canada, together with other leading OECD economies, has actively embraced trade and investment rules. This is a noteworthy development, as Canada was long preoccupied with levels of foreign investment within its territory. The 1968 Canadian Task Force on Foreign Ownership (the "Watkins Report") reflected this deep anxiety when it reported that the "overall level of foreign ownership in Canada is significantly higher than that for any other economically developed country and higher than for most of the underdeveloped countries" (Canada 1968). Almost 60 percent of the Canadian resource and manufacturing industries has been under foreign control and most of it, since the 1950s, by companies that have their home in the United States (Rotstein 1972: 30). Though US direct investment was in decline for several decades (Niosi 1994), it has risen to high levels again – amounting to a high of 81 percent of all FDI in Canada in 1997 (Canada, DFAIT 1998b: 14) and settling to 64.1 percent of all FDI in 2005 (Canada, DFAIT 2006b: 33). Canadian direct investment, in turn, largely has been drawn to the United States, but Canadian trade policy increasingly is casting its gaze beyond the continent (Chow 1994: 37; Niosi 1994: 378). By 2005, Canadian direct investment abroad was almost ten times greater than it was in 1980 – from Cdn $28 billion to Cdn $266 billion (Canada, DFAIT 2006b: 34; Statistics Canada 1997: 34) Ostensibly to protect this growing interest in investment abroad, Canada announced in 1994 that it would begin negotiating Foreign Investment Protection Agreements (FIPAs or Canadian BITs) "based on an improved text which incorporated new obligations undertaken in NAFTA and other agreements" (Canada 1995) – these texts incorporate the key investment rule disciplines discussed in Chapter one. Canada had already begun to sign FIPAs along these lines beginning with Ukraine in 1994. Seventeen such agreements have been signed since then and are presently in force – a number of other negotiations presently are underway.

The unsettling experience with investor disputes under NAFTA (Pettigrew 2001) caused the Canadian government to vary investor protections in 2004. Up until then, there were few modifications – countries rarely seek amendments to the takings rule, for instance, nor do they seek reservations for those laws (both in force and in contemplation) that might run afoul of the prohibition. Where provision for reservation is made, they are ordinarily available for laws which do not conform with the provisions for national treatment and MFN status; they are not available for those measures that amount to expropriations. On the rare occasion when a reservation does concern expropriations, it might only address the standard of compensation, such as the date at which compensation will be paid.[2] )

As expected, no reservations to the rule against takings were listed in the 1995 Canada-South Africa BIT. The agreement does allow for mutually agreed upon nonconforming measures with regard to the requirement of national treatment. (Bargaining over this list was delayed until after the proclamation of the new South African Constitution in 1996.)These never were agreed upon and so this agreement was never declared in force. Clearly, there was concern on the part of the South African negotiators that provisions in the final constitution could be affected negatively by the BIT with Canada. Indeed, South Africa has modified investment treaty practice to address the consistency of BITs with constitutional commitments around equality, which is discussed later. It appears, however, that the expropriations prohibition has not warranted similar concern.

The negotiated transition to democracy in South Africa necessitated a number of compromises between the parties to the first phase of constitution making. Formal multiparty negotiations began in 1991 with the participation of twenty-six different political organizations (Corder 1994: 501). (But it was the positions of South Africa's primary political groups, the ruling National Party (NP) and the African National Congress (ANC) – recently legalized – that would determine its outcome (Klug 1996). In this first phase of constitution making, the groups would negotiate an interim constitution) together with the terms for a transitional government of national unity that would give rise to South Africa's first nonracial democratic elections. The 1993 interim constitution would outline a preliminary bill of rights, a division of legislative authority between the federal government and provinces, the establishment of the Constitutional Court to function as the supreme judicial authority, and the thirty-four constitutional principles (outlined in Schedule 4) that would underlie the new constitutional order.) In the second phase, a democratically elected constitutional assembly would be empowered to negotiate the terms of a final constitution. They would be guided in their work by the thirty-four constitutional principles outlined in the interim constitution (Spitz 2000: 77–86).

Central to the success of the multiparty process in the first phase of constitution making was agreement over the protection of "rights in property" in the 1993 Interim Constitution (s. 28). The ANC position on property had shifted from one of complete suspicion – this was reflected in the 1955 ANC Freedom Charter commitment to land reform and wealth redistribution via nationalization (Ebrahim 1998: 416) – to one of qualified support – reflected in the constitutional recognition of the right to "acquire, hold or dispose of property" in the 1992 proposed Bill of Rights (Chaskalson 1995: 225). Still, the ANC policy stalwartly insisted that property rights not freeze the legacy of dispossession represented by apartheid (Klug 2000: 125). The NP, for its part, insisted that property rights receive the strictest constitutional protection for fear that a democratically elected ANC government would disenfranchise white South Africans of their property (Chaskalson 1995: 224).

As the multiparty process got underway, it became clear to the ANC leadership that "the rejection of property rights would directly endanger the democratic transition" (Klug 2000: 126). Two issues around the property rights clause became central to gaining the ANC's consent. The first was to distinguish clearly between the regulation of property, in which case compensation would not be payable – typically, as in the United States, this concerns the exercise of a state's police power authority – and the expropriation or taking of property, where compensation would be due. The second, and more critical, issue was that property rights not impede the program of land restitution for the victims of forced removal from traditional lands and of land redistribution for those disenfranchised from owning property by the discriminatory laws of apartheid (ANC 1995; Chaskalson 1995: 229).

Both the interim and final constitutions attempted to reconcile the demand for protection of property and the need to provide scope for state regulation and redistribution of property. In its final version, the constitution provides no positive declaration of property rights; rather, the right is implicit in the limitations the constitution places on state activity.[3] The section distinguishes between "deprivations" of property which can be accomplished only through nonarbitrary laws of general application and expropriations of property that can be accomplished if only for "public purposes or in the public interest." Expropriations also require the provision of compensation, but this is based on a number of factors, including the history of the property, the amount of direct state investment and subsidy in the acquisition and improvement of the property, and the property's market value. Compensation is required to be ("just and equitable, reflecting an equitable balance between the public interest and the interests of those affected")(s. 25[3]). For the purposes of the section, the "public interest" is defined to include ("the nation's commitment to land reform, and to reforms to bring about equitable access to all South Africa's natural resources")(s. 25[4][a]). Last, the constitution expressly curtails the (scope of review) available under the property clause for those legislative and other measures "to achieve land, water and related reform to redress the results of past racial discrimination." The clause requires only that these measures satisfy the strictures of the general limitations clause (s. 25[8]).[4]

Three important features about the South African property rights regime deserve emphasis. (First, the drafters have attempted to distinguish between deprivations of property, which are noncompensable events, and expropriations, which are compensable)(Van der Walt 1997). There is no similar distinction in the text of the analogous guarantee in the US Fifth Amendment, rather, the distinction is implicit in the text and structure of the constitution. This has resulted in a series of ad hoc judicial pronouncements from the US Supreme Court on the question of what constitutes an exercise of the police power or a compensable taking. The South African version is marginally better than the American one to the extent that it aims to provide for this distinction in the same section. The text, however, does not identify what constitutes a deprivation as opposed to a taking, either by way of example or a list of enumerated criteria.[5] There are no clear textual signals, then, to distinguish between noncompensable and compensable events. As discussed in Chapter two, tendencies within both US jurisprudence and the law of international arbitration suggest somewhat of a narrowing of the definition of what constitutes an exercise of the police power. Judicial interpretation, therefore, is key to the mechanics of South African property rights. Chaskalson reports that the drafters were confident that the Constitutional Court would adopt a generous approach to police power jurisdiction, following trends in some other commonwealth jurisdictions (Chaskalson 1994: 134–5). Murphy (1995), Chaskalson and Lewis (1996), and Budlender (1998) were also confident that the deprivation of property rights provision would be interpreted to require only a low-level threshold of rational basis review. On the whole, Murphy argued, the provision for the protection of property rights could achieve a balance between the need for human dignity with regard to ownership and the demands of social justice (1995).

The Constitutional Court has signaled that it is attuned to this balance between the protection of property and the public interest. The Court's *Second Certification Decision* (1996) – certifying that the text of the final constitution was in substantial conformity with the thirty-four underlying principles detailed in the interim constitution – found that the property clause satisfied the standard of a "universally accepted fundamental right" (Principle II). Though the clause did not expressly protect the right of property (rather, it did so by implication) and did not provide the most stringent compensation criteria, it did not "flout any universally accepted approach." When one examines international conventions and domestic constitutions, the court declared, "one is immediately struck by the wide variety of formulations adopted to protect the right to property, as well as by the fact significant conventions and constitutions contain no protection of property at all" (*Second Certification Decision* 1996: paras 71, 73). In *Harksen*, a case arising under the interim constitution, the court denied a claim to compensation in a case where the property of an insolvent spouse vested temporarily in the state. This was an instance of a non-compensable deprivation rather than a compensable expropriation where title was permanently acquired by a public authority (*Harksen* 1998: para. 32). The court affirmed that the distinction between expropriations and deprivations "have long been recognized" in South African law but provided no further guidance in this regard (*Harksen* 1998: para. 33). In what is described as a major departure from *Harksen* (Van der Walt 2004: 868), the court in *First National Bank* (FNB) organized property clause analysis in the final constitution around the idea of "arbitrariness" (*FNB* 2002; Roux 2003: 46–3). Arbitrary deprivations will have occurred when the law "does not provide sufficient reason for the particular deprivation or is procedurally unfair." Sufficient reason will be determined by considering a "complexity of relations," including the relationship between the means and ends employed, between the purpose of the deprivation and the person affected, between the purpose of the law and the nature of the property affected, and the extent of the deprivation (*FNB* 2002: para. 100). This resembles, in some measure, the multifactor balancing approach developed by the US Supreme Court in its regulatory takings jurisprudence (Alexander 2006: 168). The standard of review ranges from simple rationality to proportionality review, which, in some cases, will render justification analysis under the general limitations clause (s. 36) redundant (*FNB* 2002: para. 100; Roux 2003: 46–24). Expropriations, according to the court's algorithm are a subset of deprivations (Currie and De Waal 2005: 536; *FNB* 2002: paras 46, 58). Consequently, any alleged taking first must be tested for arbitrariness. All of this potentially heightens the standard of review for deprivations and practically collapses the distinction between deprivations and expropriations.

At the next opportunity, in *Mkontwana* (2005), the court appeared to beat a retreat from this more robust standard of review in favor of a "thin" variety of rationality review in the case of most government action (Van der Walt 2005a: 83). Only "substantial interference" or limitation that goes beyond normal restrictions on property use 'or enjoyment found in an open and democratic society would amount to deprivation," the court declared (*Mkontwana* 2004: para. 32) – not much more helpful a formulation than Justice Holmes's measures that "go too far" (*Pennsylvania Coal* 1922: 1659). The gray area between regulations and takings remains. Indeed, it appears that the court has subsumed the doctrine of regulatory takings (in South Africa, these are called "constructive takings") into its determination of whether a deprivation may be arbitrary (Mostert 2003: 589; Roux 2003: 46–32; Van der Walt 2004: 874). This is because regulatory takings lacking in a public purpose or not in the public interest or not accompanied by just and equitable compensation would very likely be characterized as arbitrary deprivations (Roux 2003: 46–29).

A second important feature concerns the standard of compensation for takings under the South African Constitution. Here, again, the drafters attempted to distance themselves from developments elsewhere. Following the position articulated by US Secretary of State Cordell Hull (Hull 1938), much of the developed world has insisted on a standard of adequate, effective, and prompt compensation in the case of compensable takings (Khalil 1993) – the standard adopted in the Canada-South Africa BIT. In contrast, the countries of the developing world insisted on a less-stringent standard, one that provides "appropriate compensation" taking into account such factors as the public interest in the expropriation and the state's ability to pay. The Charter of Economic Rights and Duties of States (UNGA Res. 3281, 1975) affirmed the rights of each state to "regulate and supervise the activities of transnational corporations within its national jurisdiction" (s. 2[b]) and to "nationalize, expropriate or transfer ownership of foreign property, in which case appropriate compensation should be paid ... taking into account its relevant laws and regulations and all circumstances that the State considers pertinent" (s. 2[c]). In the case of controversy over the question of compensation, "it shall be settled under the domestic law of the nationalizing State and by its tribunals ..." (s. 2[c]) as Calvo (1870) had recommended in the late nineteenth century. Provisions concerning compensation under the South African Bill of Rights tilt in the direction of the more lenient standard, one akin to that traditionally advocated by developing countries. The final constitution requires that compensation be "just and equitable, reflecting an equitable balance between the public interest and the interests of those affected, having regard to all relevant circumstances" (s. 25[3]). An amount less than fair market value, then, may be deemed appropriate (Chaskalson 1993: 12–14; Currie and De Waal 2005: 557). A majority of the Constitutional Court indicated that, in the context of calculating compensation under the Expropriation Act, fair market value will form the baseline for any such assessment, after which other considerations outlined in the constitution may apply to lessen that value (*Du Toit* 2005: para. 35; Van der Walt 2005b).

A third important feature is the provision for land reform. The property rights clause may not be available in aid of an attack on land reform that seeks to redress the results of past racial discrimination. In those instances where the state impairs property for the purpose of achieving "land, water and related reform" it need only defend the measure as reasonable and justifiable and of general application taking into account a list of factors enumerated in s. 36 (the clause of the Bill of Rights that sets out criteria for justifying limitations of rights) (s. 25[8]). The relationship between this subsection and the takings rule remains ambivalent. For instance, is land or water reform that deprives an owner of the use of property an act requiring compensation and, if so, would minimal or no compensation satisfy the constitutional requirement so long as it meets the general limitations clause criteria of rationality and proportionality (Van der Walt 1997: 147; Zimmerman 2005: 415)? The property rights clause also mandates government to "foster conditions which enable citizens to gain access to land," to provide legally secure tenure or compensation, and restitution or compensation for those dispossessed of property after June 19, 1913 (s.25[5]–[7]). The Bill of Rights more generally guarantees to everyone the right "to have access to adequate housing" and the state is required to take reasonable measures, "within its available resources, to achieve the progressive realization of this right" (s. 26; *Port Elizabeth Municipality* 2005; *Grootboom* 2000). These constitutionally sanctio‐ned policy options for achieving socioeconomic reform in South Africa signal a constitutional regime in tension with developments in international investment law.

How might these constitutional constraints and obligations link up with binational, regional, or transnational commitments, such as South Africa's BIT with Canada? In other words, what are the dif‐ferences between these sorts of BITs and the South African Consti‐tution such that the former might have the effect of disciplining the latter? At a high level of generality, it is clear that the constraints concerning expropriation and nationalization in the BIT are more onerous than those found in the text of the constitution. As a result, foreign investors from Canada would be treated preferentially. South African nationals and non-Canadian foreign investors who could not avail themselves of similar BIT provisions (or a MFN clause) would have less protection from state interference with their investments. In addition, Canadian foreign investors would be given standing under the BIT to have prompt review under the laws of South Africa of any state action in breach of the agreement. Foreign investors have standing to sue in South African courts in addition to any standing they may have under the constitution, a local double check on the state regulation of investment interests.

The definition of "investment" in the BIT seemingly is much broader than the definition of "property" in the constitution. Property is defined in the negative – it is "not limited to land" (s. 25[4][b]). Though it may be the case, wrote Justice Ackermann, that a "corporeal moveable must – as must the ownership of land – lie at the heart of our consti‐tutional concept of property" (*First National Bank* 2002: para. 51), it is likely that South African courts will not confine the property clause to physically tangible interests but will adopt "a fairly wide conception of property" (Roux 2003: 46–11; Van der Walt 2004: 866) drawn from the constitutional property experience of liberal democracies elsewhere (Van der Walt 1997). Constitutionally protected property interests may even extend as far as the definition of "investment" in the BIT, defined expansively to include "any kind of asset" owned or controlled by an investor of one contracting party situated in the other con‐tracting party's territory. Without limiting the scope of protected investments, the BIT definition includes movable and immovable property; shares, stock, bonds and debentures; money, claims to money, and claims to performance under contract; goodwill; intellectual property rights; and rights to undertake any commercial activity.)

The Canada-South Africa BIT does not distinguish between deprivations and expropriations. Moreover, the BIT takings rule seemingly is (broader:) it prohibits nationalization or expropriation or "measures having an effect equivalent to" nationalization or expropriation, which covers indirect or regulatory takings. It is not at all clear that the equivalent doctrine of "constructive takings" in South Africa will be as expansive (*Steinberg* 2001: para. 9; Van der Walt 2002). Van der Walt (2004) is hopeful that this possibility remains. It also may be the case, as Roux suggests, that the doctrine of "arbitrary deprivations") will swallow up the very idea of a regulatory takings doctrine (Roux 2003: 46–32). Though the distinction between deprivations and expropriations may be hard to sustain in practice, the constitutional provisions have the virtue of at least attempting to carve out noncompensable regulations from the takings rule.

The constitutional provision permits (a greater range) of expropriations than does the BIT. For example, takings are not permitted under the BIT unless they are for a "public purpose." Attentive to the possibility that a public purpose test may not be sufficient to cover state transfers of property from one private owner to other private (or nonstate) owners (Chaskalson 1995: 137–8; but see *Kelo* 2005), the constitution permits takings for public purposes or (in the "public interest") (s. 25[2][a]). As an additional precaution, the public interest is defined to include "the nation's commitment to land reform, and to reforms to bring about equitable access to all South Africa's natural resources" (s. 25[4][a]). If, as was feared by the drafters of the final constitution, the inclusion solely of a public purpose test (as in the interim constitution) might preclude land redistribution measures, then the BIT potentially could block certain attempts at land reform in which Canadian investments were implicated.

The standard of compensation available in the event of a taking also reveals important differences. Under the BIT, compensation is required to be consistent with the standard of "prompt, adequate and effective" compensation. Compensation must be based on the "genuine value of the investment ... payable from the date of expropriation at a normal commercial rate of interest ... without delay ... effectively realizable and freely transferable." This stringent standard, usually the norm in BITs (Parra 1996: 29), is in contrast to the constitutional provisions regarding compensation. As mentioned, the standard concerning the "amount, timing, and manner of payment must be just and equitable reflecting an equitable balance between the public interest and the interests of those affected" having regard to all relevant factors, including the market value of the property (s. 25[1][3]). The South African constitutional standard of compensation signals, in some cases, provision of amounts less than market value, payable less than immediately, nor fully realizable and transferable (Du Toit 2003).

In each of these areas – the scope of protected interests, the attempt to distinguish between deprivations and expropriations, the provision for land and water reform, and the standard of compensation – the constraints concerning expropriation and nationalization in the BIT are more onerous than those found in the text of the new South African Constitution. Taken together, the BIT expropriations rule suggests the application of standards discordant with the stated goals of the South African property rights regime.

What difference might this make to South Africans? In the case of direct investment, it could undermine constitutional objectives foundational to the democratic transition in South Africa. It might be observed that Canadian direct investment in South Africa is sufficiently negligible that it should warrant little cause for concern. The South African government, nevertheless, should have proceeded with caution. An increasing proportion of Canadian investment abroad has been directed to South Africa. Canadian direct investment rose tenfold, from Cdn $19 million to Cdn $196 million, between 1989 and 1998. At year end 2005, Canadian investment in South Africa was estimated at Cdn $119 million (Canada, DFAIT 2006a). Second, the potential pool of investors that have standing to sue under the investment treaty is much larger than the pool of companies actually investing in South Africa. As a significant percentage of Canadian enterprises with investments abroad are themselves under foreign control or allied to foreign corporations, Canadian subsidiaries, connected to transnational parent enterprises with resources to sue, can act as vehicles for disciplining rogue governments that hinder investment interests. Beyond Canadian firms and investors, South Africa has signed onto over thirty BITs, beginning with the United Kingdom in 1994, many of which contain similar guarantees to foreign investors making their homes in these states. In order to take advantage of these protections, companies doing business in South Africa may choose to "migrate" to jurisdictions that have entered into BITs with South Africa (Aguas del Tunari 2005: para. 174). Together with the MFN rule, which mandates that any new treaty partner be entitled to treatment no less favorable than that available to other foreign investors in South Africa, there will be multiple opportunities to hinder South African policy objectives.

At the national level, the South African Constitutional Court, which has final authority to interpret the property rights clause, may resist interpretations that distort the transformative aspirations of the domestic property rights regime. But the court may not be immune entirely from pressures to conform to transnational disciplines (Davis 1999: 17, 2006: 317) and may seek to harmonize, to the extent that it does not violate the literal text of the constitution, the property rule with investment rules. Indeed, the final constitution instructs courts to take international law and foreign law into account when interpreting legislation or the Bill of Rights (Strydom and Hopkins 2005).[7] It is instructive that the ANC government has not been entirely successful in resisting the internal effects of investment law disciplines.

## EQUALITY PROMOTION AND BLACK ECONOMIC EMPOWERMENT

On coming to power in historic elections in 1994, the ANC committed the government to policies that appear seemingly dissonant with national constitutional obligations regarding the promotion of equality. South Africa hastily entered into BITs not only with Canada but also with a variety of Western European, African, and Latin American countries, using a UK model treaty as a prototype (TRALAC 2004: 10). Signaling South Africa's commitment to concluding and participating in the Uruguay-round GATT, an ANC delegate accompanied outgoing Minister of Trade and Industry, Derek Keys, to meetings in Marrakesh in April 1994 (Hirsch 2005: 72). One of the key products of the Uruguay-round GATT, the agreement on TRIPs, sets high levels of protection for patent and trademark holders, amounting practically to a transfer wealth from the South to large pharmaceutical companies in the North (Drahos and Braithwaite 2002: 11; Stiglitz and Charlton 2005: 48), undermining South Africa's ability to respond to the HIV/AIDS pandemic. Enthusiastically embracing trade and investment disciplines in the hope of attracting foreign investment (Klug 2005: 126), TRIPs subsequently was incorporated domestically by virtue of 1997 amendments to South African patent laws (Dugard 2000: 353; Forman 2007: 206–7).[8] Though intended to be TRIPs compliant, the

*Medicines and Related Substances Amendments Act* (Act 90 of 1997) was also aimed at facilitating access to low-cost medicines. This prompted legal action under the South African Constitution by the ever-vigilant pharmaceutical industry (PMA 1999), galvanizing opposition and even subsequent amendment to TRIPS (Correa 2006: 400; Drahos and Braithwaite 2002: 8; Sell 2003: 157). In addition to national treatment obligations that are part of the Uruguay-round GATT policed by the WTO, South Africa is a signatory to the agreement on TRIMs also under WTO supervision. The agreement commits South Africa not to impose local content or purchasing requirements or other sorts of trade-distorting performance requirements in relation to trade in goods that are "mandatory" or "compliance with which is necessary to obtain an advantage" (TRIMs Annex). South Africa refrained, however, from joining in the plurilateral Uruguay-round Agreement on Government Procurement (GPA), which imposes strict requirements on government purchasing.

Widespread fears about the ANC project of nationalization (Marais 1998: 146) gave way to the embrace of a multipronged program of economic liberalism, including policies to promote the generation of a new black entrepreneurial middle class. From 1994 onward, it has been the aim of the ANC to deracialize the economy by facilitating BEE.[9] Initially, ANC leadership believed that this could be achieved through the ordinary operation of market processes – this was to be a "market-driven" rather than "confiscatory" process, writes Gelb (2004: 1). Investor confidence would be maintained with the adoption of neo-liberal economic policy in the 1997 "Growth, Employment and Redistribution" (GEAR) strategy – a strategy that was more about growth rather than about redistribution (Gumede 2005: 87) – signaling to the investment community the ANC's commitment to dominant economic orthodoxy (Marais 2002: 86). The international business community was largely assuaged (Handley 2005: 233).

GEAR's economic projections were vastly overwrought – beyond a number of core resource industries, the South African economy lagged (Gqubule 2006, c.2). Foreign direct investment plunged, job losses were staggering, and wealth disparities worsened (Marais 2002: 87–9) – it is reported that South Africa now has one of the highest unemployment rates in the world (Rodrik 2006: 2). GEAR is hardly mentioned amongst polite company. It is almost absent entirely from the Department of Trade and Industry (DTI) "BEE Strategy Document." In its place are mentioned the ANC Freedom Charter of 1955 and the Reconstruction and Development Program (RDP) of 1994 (DTI 2003). Originally formulated by the trade union movement (Marais 1998, c.6), the RDP was embraced by the ANC in elections that year, and abandoned 2 years later with the unilateral adoption of GEAR. Markets alone, President Thabo Mbeki has concluded, are no longer reliable engines for black economic improvement. Government now is expected to come to the aid of empowering of black business (Marais 2002: 97).

The BEE program represents a modest attempt at generating a new entrepreneurial class of black South Africans. The program aims to steer economic growth in such a way as to benefit a wider swath, but not too wide a slice, of indigenous South African society. It is intended to give as little offense as possible to the actors and institutions of economic globalization. The reform of South Africa mining laws (an early expression of BEE) admittedly resulted in the alienation of the mining establishment and, perhaps, abridgement of investor rights. This is discussed further below. Since then, the ANC government has developed a more cooperative scheme for developing codes of good behavior that advance BEE and which aims to steer clear of investment rules disciplines. Just to ensure that much of BEE remains immune from investor suits, South Africa has modified its BIT practice so as to shield from certain investment disciplines measures intended to "promote the achievement of equality." The BEE program, nevertheless, does not question the operating assumptions about the importance of markets and the continuing pursuit of neoliberal economic policy (Ponte et al. 2006: 49). To the extent that BEE really is about generating a new class of black entrepreneurs, the Mbeki plan is consistent with the principal outlines of current economic orthodoxy. A multiracial entrepreneurial class has the advantage of distancing powerful business interests from the legacy of apartheid (MacDonald 2004: 646) and deterring calls for more radical redistribution of wealth. Yet, paradoxically, broad-based BEE calls upon the state to flex its muscle in ways that test the outer limits of permissible policy options under the legally enforceable regime for the promotion and protection of foreign investment.

The BEE program unquestionably is in furtherance of national constitutional commitments. The 1996 Constitution, in myriad ways, promotes equality not only of opportunity but also of outcome: "legislative and other measures designed to protect or advance persons, or categories of persons, disadvantaged by unfair discrimination may be taken" (s. 9[2]). The state is expected to perform a variety of redistributive functions, including taking measures to foster access to property (s. 25[5]), land and water reform (s. 25[8]), rights to adequate housing (s. 26), rights to health care, sufficient food and water, social security (s. 27), and education (s. 28). Procurement expressly is mentioned in the constitution: while it is to be "fair, equitable, transparent, competitive and cost-effective," any organ of the state may take measures to prefer categories and the advancement of persons "disadvantaged by unfair discrimination" (s. 217). The federal government is required, by the terms of this section of the constitution, to implement national framework legislation to achieve these objectives.[10] Its constitutional lineage is admitted in the preamble to the BEE Act, which expressly declares that the bill is intended to "promote the achievement of the constitutional right to equality" (also DTI 2003: 1.3).

Despite this lineage, BEE garnered very bad press early on. In its earliest manifestations, it privileged a small group of former ANC activists and so the program was severely discredited. "BEE-llionaires" and a few other "wanna BEEs" (Cronin 2004) – often former ANC leadership – were handpicked to buy equity shares in a variety of white-owned businesses. Other share-equity ventures were less than successful. Some in the new black shareholding class defaulted on loans secured only by rising dividends that would never materialize. Voting rights were circumscribed while black directorships involved no "operational control over productive assets" (Gelb 2004: 2). Often, white-owned companies merely established BEE corporate "fronts." Transactions were tainted and the program's beneficiaries were few.

Corruption and cronyism prompted Archbishop Desmond Tutu to condemn BEE for benefiting only a small "recycled elite" (Meldrum 2004). Under prodding from the Black Business Council and its independent BEE Commission Report (2001), the Mbeki government embraced, after some initial hesitation,[11] the objective of an "integrated" national BEE program that was "broad-based." The BEE Commission Report called for a "State-driven programme" as "[m]arkets tend to reinforce an existing distribution of incomes and assets" (BEE Commission 2001: 2). The objective now is to broaden the base of economic empowerment by measuring sectoral progress along the lines not only of equity ownership but also by increasing the number of black-controlled enterprises ("direct empowerment"), encouraging the hiring and promotion of blacks into executive and managerial ranks ("human resource development"), and by measuring levels of procurement by private industry from black-owned businesses ("indirect empowerment") (DTI 2004: 12). The strategy is intended to be inclusive. The framework legislation defines "black people" as including Africans, coloreds, and Indians and declares that economic empowerment should benefit all black people including women, workers, youth, people with disabilities, and people in rural areas (South Africa 2003). Both the public and private sectors are expected to comply with "codes of good practice," which refine BEE objectives and generate indicators (s. 9). Progress will be measured using BEE "scorecards" (DTI 2003). Companies are expected to develop, in conjunction with government, sectoral "transformation Charters" in particular industries. Charters in the mining, construction, and financial services sectors have been gazetted and new charters have been formulated for the agriculture, tourism, and information and communications technology sectors. Even a draft charter for the legal profession is being circulated (Tempkin 2007).

There is a heavy emphasis on voluntarism. These transformation charters, according to the BEE Act, will have "been developed by major stakeholders in the sector" (s. 12). The process is described as an "inclusive" one and all enterprises operating in South Africa are expected to "participate" in the establishment of "innovative partnerships." BEE, in short, is associated with the ideas of "soft regulation" and of "good governance" (BEE Experts 2006: 10; Rittich 2006: 223–24) – proposals that might be characterized as "third way," purporting to drive a path between the binary of left and right (Giddens 1994; McLennan 2004). Soft law, notes Cutler, "provides normative guidance, but remains largely optional" (2003: 187). Yet, despite an emphasis on stakeholders and alliances with business, the program undeniably is state driven, even coercive in parts. This was most evident in the process leading up to the release of the 2002 mining charter. This was a document formulated largely by government and its initial draft badly received by equity markets (Gelb 2004: 2). The target of 51 percent ownership by historically disadvantaged South Africans (note the broadened class of beneficiaries) by 2012 was reduced to a more modest 26 percent (SA Mining Charter 4.7). The final charter sets targets of 40 percent in management and 10 percent participation of women in the industry by 2007 (SA Mining Charter 4.2) and commits industry to give historically disadvantaged South Africans "preferred supplier status" (SA Mining Charter 4.6). BEE took the form of hard law in the Mineral and Petroleum Resources Development Act No. 28 of 2002. Mining companies are expected to promote BEE when applying for, or converting existing rights, into new rights under the act, and this has given rise to investor controversy, discussed later. If the government took an active lead in the draft of the first mining charter and in framework legislation for subsurface rights, later charters were both industry led and often without accompanying statutory obligations. DTI Deputy Director General Lionel October explained to *Business Day* that BEE is "not a legal requirement" and that, once this is explained to foreign firms, their objections dissolve (Rose 2004).[12]

Many companies have taken up the BEE program with gusto. Deutschebank divested itself of 25 percent control over its South African operation to black-owned enterprise. Others have been slow to get with the program. The energy company Sasol included BEE among the "risk factors" of doing business in South Africa in its 2003 US Securities and Exchange Commission filing. The company has changed course and is reported to have "embraced" BEE (Reed 2005a, 2005b). Diamond producer de Beers has entered into joint ventures with black operators while the mining group Anglo-American appointed its first black chief executive of South African operations, Lazarus Zim (Wachman 2005) and agreed to sell 27 percent ownership in a new coal subsidiary to black-owned enterprise (Matthews 2007). US-based multinationals have joined the pack: Merrill Lynch in 2006 sold an 8.5 percent stake in its South African operations to its black employees and a consortium of black women professionals (Gunnion 2006). Not all South African-based US subsidiaries endorse BEE. The results of a 2004 survey by the American Chamber of Commerce in South Africa suggests that 74 percent of US companies in South Africa view divestiture expectations under BEE as having "negatively affected their investment decisions" (Rose 2004). Talks leading toward a comprehensive US-South African Customs Union (SACU)[13] trade and investment agreement broke down, in some measure, because of the perceived difficulty US investors would have with aspects of BEE (Inside US Trade 2004). Based on discussions with various foreign investors, Katz maintains nevertheless that investors "support the objectives of BEE" (Katz 2006: 41).

Despite the dominant discourse of voluntarism and good governance, government holds in reserve financial rewards for those companies that perform well on their scorecards through the power of government procurement. The BEE Act mandates that "every organ of the state and public entity" will take BEE measurements into account in granting not only procurement contracts, but licenses, concessions, the sale of state-owned enterprise, and in entering into private sector partnerships (s. 10). The DTI describes preferential procurement using performance on BEE scorecards as an "effective instrument to promote BEE in our economy" (DTI 2003: 3.5.5).[14] With 120 billion Rand in government contracts awarded every year and plans to privatize state-owned enterprise, there is much that government can do to sway market operations (Gumede 2005: 227–28). The UK management group Proudfoot, for instance, sold off a 51 percent stake in its South African operation to empowerment companies in February 2005 fearing "the increased likelihood of exclusion from future government and public sector work without appropriate empowerment accreditation and broad-based ownership" (Wadula 2005). "You will not be able to do business in South Africa," declared the director of issuer services at the Johannesburg Stock Exchange, John Burke, "if you are not compliant" (Stokes 2007). This determined use of the financial stick of government probably is not misplaced, at least with regard to local firms: data shows that promotion of black managers has best been achieved in the trade, tourism, and recreation sector (from 14 to 28 percent in 2000), and this Gelb and Black suggest, may be "perhaps due to regulatory and public sector procurement requirements" (2004: 207). It has proven a less effective lever for promoting BEE in foreign investor affiliates (Vickers 2003: 8) and in sectors such as metals and engineering (Ponte et al. 2006: 24).

Surveillance of business performance is expected to improve, particularly for those companies involved in "fronting," with the authorization of a new oversight body to verify the accreditation of ratings agencies (*Mail and Guardian* 2006). This is expected to combat "fly-by-night" verification agencies that have sprung up in order to mask fronting and other deceptions that undermine progress toward BEE. Codes of Good Practice have also been approved, and they adhere to the basic principles of broad-based BEE. Foreign multinational firms operating outside of the mining and resources sectors that do not have a global practice of selling equity, however, scored a pretty big victory by being exempt from ownership requirements. Rather than having to divest 25 percent ownership to black enterprises, closely held foreign corporations may generate alternative "equity equivalents" to make up for lack of minority ownership (Southey 2006). So despite the seeming willingness of many large multinationals to address BEE targets, some are reluctant to part with equity. This is the case, for instance, in South Africa's successful automobile industry, where Toyota and BMW are promising to promote empowerment in ways other than divestiture (Rumney 2006). The minister for Trade and Industry, Mandisi Mpahlwa, admitted that foreign investors had to be appeased in the codes: "we had to be mindful that we also have to position South Africa in a global environment where there is fierce competition for investment" (Southey 2006).

Broad-based BEE, in sum, is designed to offend, as little as possible, foreign investors and the legal regime for their protection. It is, for the most part, a measured and modest attempt at reversing the apartheid-era project of economic inequality. Aspects of BEE, consequently, can be expected to survive investment rules disciplines. The human resources component of BEE, for instance, which concerns the hiring and promotion of black managers and employees mostly seems benign. Many states actively encourage the hiring of disadvantaged persons distinguished by race and class, etc., and many firms already will be complying with these sorts of requirements within their home states. In the United States, for instance, government contracts have been used for minority set-aside schemes and these have been exempted from trade and investment treaty disciplines, in addition to the GPA, by the United States (Corr and Zissis 1999: 346; McCrudden 1999: 20). As the United States argued in defense of its "Buy America" policy in the *ADF* case (2001), "in point of fact, domestic requirements for government procurement are in place 'in most, if not all countries'" (*ADF* 2001: para. 94).

Nevertheless, rewarding foreign investors with licenses, concessions, or the selling off of state-owned enterprise could run up against the principle of national treatment and fair and equitable treatment in so far as foreign nationals – including the subset of foreign black-owned companies – either are disentitled from participating in the program or are at a disadvantage as compared with local competitors who are similarly situated. Much will turn on the comparator group chosen for the purposes of discrimination analysis. Peterson, for instance, suggests that the group most similarly situated to foreign investors are those with investments in enterprises not owned or controlled by historically disadvantaged South Africans. This then would not give rise to discriminatory treatment (2006c: 31). Others will point to the adverse impact on foreign companies which are less likely to do as well on their BEE score cards than locally owned or controlled black firms. They cannot compete effectively, for instance, in processes for the selling off of state-owned enterprise. Even if the program is construed as nondiscriminatory on its face, as its burdens fall on all large firms, foreign or national, its benefits are available only to the few – by definition, it is intended to promote black indigenous entrepreneurs who are nationals of South Africa – thereby disfavoring foreign nationals and so triggering the obligation of national treatment.

Rewarding firms that procure from local suppliers or local labor may also run afoul of investment disciplines. Firms may prefer to contract for the supply of materials on an international, rather than a national, basis and so may insist on being exempt from this requirement. To the extent that many of the South African BITs are silent about performance requirements, it may be that investors only will have recourse to TRIMs disciplines (in so far as they restrict trade in goods), enforced before the WTO through the aegis of the firm's home state. Mortensen (2006) has identified other WTO disciplines that may be offended by BEE, including the national treatment rules in GATS and the GATT, which would subject BEE to WTO dispute settlement, entitling injured states, but not investors, to take retaliatory measures if successful.

The prospects are that any number of investor disputes could render BEE fiscally unsustainable.[15] Though South Africans were confident that they could trade on the goodwill of the global community and so avoid these sorts of disputes – the possibility that South Africa could degenerate into another Zimbabwe looms large in this sort of calculation – South Africa nevertheless modified investor language so as to accommodate the policy instruments envisaged to promote BEE. In treaties with China, Iran, Russia, and the Czech Republic, among others, the requirements of national treatment, MFN, and fair and equitable treatment are subject to the exception of laws or measures, "taken pursuant to Article 9 of the Constitution ... the purpose of which is to promote the achievement of equality in its territory, or designed to protect of advance persons, or categories of persons, disadvantaged by unfair discrimination" (2000 South Africa-Iran BIT).[16] The equality exception, importantly, does not extend to measures that might be considered equivalent to expropriation or nationalization. This omission might have the effect of thwarting expectations regarding divestiture to black-owned enterprises in the pursuit of BEE. Moreover, as a consequence of those 1990s treaties in which the "promotion of equality" is not exempted from general investment rules disciplines, BEE could be imperiled.

This threat is magnified following enactment of the Mineral and Petroleum Resources Development Act of 2002. The mining law, which entered into force in May 2004, declares that the state is the custodian of mineral and petroleum resources on behalf of all South Africans (s. 3), consequently, underlying title to subsurface resources now resides with the state. Owners of existing mining rights are required under the act to convert to "new order rights" in which successful conversion is dependent upon compliance with BEE objectives (Maluleke 2004]).[17] The executive director of Anglo-American in 2002 alluded to the possibility of launching a claim under the South Africa-UK BIT for the alteration of mining rights under the act but acknowledged that political considerations militated against it (Peterson and Gray 2003: 25). Instead, four foreign mining companies, including Placer Dome of Canada and Lonmin of the United Kingdom, filed notice under South African law of their intention to sue for the expropriation of their mining rights under the constitution (Phasiwe 2004). The first transnational investment dispute challenging the mining law was filed in January 2007 by Italian investors in Finstone, a Luxembourg-based granite mining enterprise (ICSID Case No. ARB (AF)/07/1; Creamer 2007). They claim that the company has been stripped of mining rights which amounts to an expropriation and that the "forced" divestiture of 26 percent of the enterprise to historically disadvantaged South Africans amounts to a denial of fair and equitable treatment (Ryan 2007). The investors have invoked BITs signed by South Africa with Italy and Belgium which builds on the UK model and which does not have an equality promoting exception (Peterson 2007). This is a claim that would be considered less sympathetically by the South African Constitutional Court, South African mining lawyer Peter Leon surmises, given the potential amount of compensation involved. As if to prove the point made in the first part of this chapter, Leon observes that an "international arbitration tribunal will not have those implications in mind" (Ryan 2007).

The object of this chapter has been to trace the activities of middle powers, like Canada and South Africa, in knitting together a worldwide investment rules regime. The process is operating in spaces both within and without state systems, in which states are mostly complicit. The outcome of this process has the potential of posing real constraints on the progress of policy in countries facing the task of political and economic reconstruction. Outside the state, a close reading of the text of the Canada-South Africa BIT (or similar BITs previously signed with a number of European states) suggests the potential for conflict between constitutional aspirations in the postapartheid era and the exigencies of economic globalization. Within states, the problem is intensified in places like South Africa where constitutional commitments to the promotion of equality elbow up against a narrow range of available policy options to spread economic wealth to those economically and socially disadvantaged by apartheid. The ANC government mostly has embraced the soft law of voluntarism and good governance in the promotion of broad-based BEE, the principal vehicle for remedying apartheid's legacy of economic inequality. This modest plan, intended to generate an indigenous black business class, is, for the most part, designed to offend as little as possible the investment rules regime. The South African government may have misstepped, in this regard, by linking the conversion of mineral rights to the promotion of BEE – merely an instance of hard law complementing soft. By releasing firms that do not have a global practice of selling equity abroad from the obligation of divesting equity ownership to black-owned firms in the Codes of Good Practice, South Africa has signaled that it is not its intention to "overly interfere unduly with the private sector" (BEE Experts 2006: 10). South Africa continues, then, to do the work of states in an age of economic globalization, coding as "national" key aspects of the new normative order of transnational legality (Sassen 2006: 223). As a consequence, South Africa's internal policy options will have been shaped by the external environment for the promotion and protection of foreign investment. State projects, like broad-based BEE, likely will serve as weak vehicles for economic redistribution in a country rife with inequality, while narrowing the available range of preferred policy options.

# CHAPTER SIX

# PRIVATIZATION AND DEMOCRATIZATION

In the post-1989 global scene, political alternatives have narrowed in scope. The shape of the structures that influence political and economic life are now predetermined by the seeming global consensus that states must be made safe for trade and foreign investment. It is this context that narrows political alternatives to two dominant visions that address relations between state and market taking shape through state projects. The first is the state capitalist mode, designed to enhance the capacity for state control and public participation (Petras 1977). The other is the neoliberal mode, which places legal limits on the state's regulatory capacity (the direction in which many third-way proposals also lean) (Beck 2005: 162–3).[1] Contemporary debates about the direction of constitutional design in an era of economic globalization, then, are better understood in light of the interplay between these two dominant visions of political-economic thought, state capitalist, and neoliberal.

The model of constitutional design embraced traditionally by countries from the South envisages a regime of constitutional rules and structures that facilitate the exercise of government power through state building and national enterprise. This is a view approximating the "state capitalist" approach: that constitutions give expression to great national goals and state projects and that constitutions are not just about limiting government action, but about enabling self-government. This is a model of institutional design that recognizes "the indispensable guiding role of the state in the development of the nation's productive forces" (Cox 1996: 201). While state capitalism concedes the world market as the background context against which political choices are made, the project assumes that the state has a role to play in facilitating national competitiveness and in enabling the widest distribution of wealth across the social stratum of society. When it takes a "more radical form," writes Cox, state capitalism tends "toward the prospect of internal socialism sustained by capitalist success in world-market competition" (Cox 1996: 202).

This approach to constitutionalism can take shape through different forms of constitutional design, but two come primarily to mind. The first places no substantive limits on government intervention in the market. The description of the nineteenth-century British Constitution by A.V. Dicey (1885) approximates this design – Parliament, according to Dicey can make or unmake any law whatsoever. The second institutional form facilitating energetic government is one that specifically articulates, in constitutional language, the capacity of the state to intervene in the market. The Latin American model best exemplifies this use of constitutionalism for the purpose of state building.

Latin American constitutions have committed governments to certain state projects – mandating nationalization or management of key economic sectors – that bind successive governments to the maintenance of national goals and objectives. Constitutional rules may also expressly enable state intervention in the market for the purposes of wealth redistribution, through rules permitting the expropriation or nationalization of property subject to the provision of "appropriate" compensation, for instance. This form of constitutional project also has its inside and outside dimensions: constitutional rules protect national political power from the external pressures generated by foreign economic power. Much of the twentieth-century Latin American constitutional experience has been preoccupied with the appropriate measure of influence acceptable to Latin American development and constitutional design.

Beginning in the 1990s, state capitalism fell into disfavor. Many countries in Latin America abandoned aspects of constitutional design that mandated public control over the economy or enabled nationalization of key economic sectors. In Colombia, for instance, the constitution now permits the privatization of key public sectors and services, with the proviso that share offerings first be made to public sector workers and, via statute, to customers and local communities. Other residues of old-style constitutionalism remained, such as a property clause that permitted the taking of property, for reasons of equity, without the provision of just compensation. These remnants became the subject of further constitutional consideration and subsequent amendment. These two constitutional stipulations in the Colombian constitution – one having to do with privatization, the other with property more generally – are the subject of this chapter. The object is to track the erosion of these remnants of state capitalist constitutional design as they run up against the strictures of investment rules. In the face of resurgent social-democrat and left-populist governments in much of Latin America in the mid-2000s (Castañeda 2006), these strictures might also pose an impediment to reversing, or at least ameliorating, some of the detrimental effects of economic globalization.

Rapidly undertaken privatization – the transfer of key state resources or services from public to private hands – is considered a key indicator of success amongst the neoliberal set (Stiglitz 2002: 54). Programs of privatization can take a variety of forms. I discuss in the third part of the chapter programs concerning the divestiture of state assets through the sale of shares or assets to employees and employee associations. I do not presume to discuss the assumed benefits of privately over publicly owned enterprises (Stiglitz 1994: 179; Vilas 1995: 131)[2]; rather, the discussion proceeds on the assumption that enabling employee access to public property is a defensible policy objective that is achievable in the privatization context. The privatization discussion is preceded, in the first part, with a review of the Calvo doctrine and, in the second part, with reflection on pertinent twentieth-century constitutional moments in Colombian history. Finally, in Part four, I turn to the 1991 constitutional property provisions that deviated from the hegemonic formulation found in most contemporary BITs.

Can constitutional rules in the state capitalist mode that redistribute property ownership more widely, by granting ownership preference to employees of privatized enterprises, or that promote the social function of property by permitting expropriation in terms less advantageous to property owners, survive the pressures generated by the regime of transnational rules for the promotion and protection of foreign investment? Given the decided structural tilt of the contemporary rules regime, this may prove to be difficult. Yet the regime, or more precisely, the band of elites that help to constitute its rules and structures, are aware of their legitimacy problems – they are reflexive and so have some measure of adaptability. Rather than generating an entirely autonomous system of law, the actors and institutions that make up the investment rules regime have the capacity to monitor continually their behavior so as to maintain their legitimizing aspirations (Banakar 1998; Zumbansen 2006: 743). For these reasons, it turns out that both the failed MAI and the stalled 2006 US-Colombia BIT (discussed in Part three) are better able to accommodate solidaristic aspirations in the context of privatization.

In some ways, the dysfunctional present and past of Colombian politics makes this constitution a poor subject for a case study. Indeed, the Colombian case points to the insufficiency of constitutional rules as a mechanism for achieving peaceful social change. But the interesting point about the Colombian case is that Colombians in 1991 massively overhauled their constitutional structure, abandoning the constitutional framework that had been in place since 1886. The fact that this very recent exercise in constitution making was already under significant pressure to change provides us with a window through which to watch this confrontation between the old and new constitutionalism. Further comparative study likely will show that the Colombian constitutional experience is representative of the larger Latin American constitutional experience of the 1980s and 1990s, one in which the neoliberal model has been in the ascendance.

## THE CALVO DOCTRINE

A number of pressures generated this shift in emphasis from the public to the private, from state building to state divestiture, in Latin American constitutionalism.[3] For one, the 1980s debt crisis precipitated the adoption of structural adjustment programs under the active encouragement of the World Bank. A policy of selling off state enterprises has been a central plank in the bank's strategy. For another, with the fall of the Soviet empire, there seemingly were fewer political options available other than privatization for those states wishing to improve the material conditions of their citizens and desirous of securing the political success of state managers. Moreover, numerous benefits were expected to fall upon states that take up programs of privatization, including increased foreign investment, overall efficiency gains, and technology transfers. At the very least, privatizing states could anticipate a huge financial windfall, the proceeds of which could be used to pay down the public debt. The shift in emphasis from public undertaking to private enterprise reflected the dominant discourse "subscribed to by corporate capital and most governments ... that competitiveness in the world economy is the ultimate criterion of policy" (Cox 1999: 27). The formation of all public policy is subordinated to this goal of enhancing the structural competitiveness of the national economy.

Since the late 1980s, the countries of Latin America have undertaken large-scale constitutional reform in order to relieve state agencies of the obligation of protecting the national "patrimony" – industries and public services considered vital to the future of the state, such as electric power, oil and gas development, communication, and transportation services. I have already mentioned Art. 27 of the 1917 Mexican Constitution in Chapter four. This article mandates state monopoly over the hydrocarbon and petroleum industries. Though these key sectors were exempted from NAFTA's disciplines, foreign investment rules have been relaxed to permit investment in the natural gas industry (Guislain 1997: 247). Outside the parameters of NAFTA, it is reported that the Mexican government has entered into "highly complex financing transactions to bypass constitutional restrictions in the oil industry" (Chua 1995: 290); nonetheless, components of Art. 27 were amended in the lead up to NAFTA. These included provisions that had prohibited the privatization of public commercial banks (Guislain 1997: 35) and rules that protected *ejidos*, communal land holdings, which now can be broken up into individual parcels for the purpose of commercial enterprise, factors that precipitated the armed rebellion in Chiapas on New Year's Day 1994 (Vargas 1994).

All of this amounts to an abandonment of the traditional Latin American model, traceable back to the work of Argentinean jurist Carlos Calvo (1870) discussed in Chapter two. Prompted by the dismal Latin American experience with an interventionist international capital, Calvo argued that the countries of Latin America were entitled to the same degree of respect for their internal sovereignty as were the United States and the countries of Europe. Among Calvo's precepts was the proposition that states should be free, within reason, from interference in the conduct of their domestic policy. From this, he could argue that foreign nationals could not lay claim to greater protection in their disputes with sovereign states than the citizens of these same countries (a version of national treatment). Foreign nationals who chose to establish themselves within the territorial confines of the host state – through direct investment, for instance – were entitled to no greater protection from state action than were those nationals residing within the acting state (Shea 1955). These precepts came to be reflected in the Mexican Constitution's Calvo Clause, which prohibits foreign investors from seeking the protection of their home state in any dispute with the Mexican state. These and other rules mostly were abandoned by the Mexican government in the lead up to NAFTA via a series of nonconstitutional and legislative edicts (Daly 1994: 1187).

A variety of other Latin American countries took up Calvo's doctrine (Tamburini 2002; Wiesner 1993). The 1991 Colombian Constitution, for instance, declares that "it is the duty of both citizens and aliens to obey the Constitution and the laws, and to respect and obey authorities" (Art. 4). Numerous provisions concerning the expropriation of property also gave expression to the doctrine. One of its last vestiges was to be found in the 1991 Colombian Constitution. The property clause, until amended in 1999, authorized the legislative expropriation of property "for reasons of equity" and without the payment of compensation, a determination which was not judicially reviewable (Art. 58).[4]

Constitutional declarations of exclusive state ownership and control also gave expression to this principle of equality as between states (Chua 1995: 272). Constitutional constraints could serve the purpose both of giving expression to important national objectives and confining successive governments from bending too easily to the pressures of foreign investors and diplomatic overtures (Lipson 1985: 54). The Calvo doctrine, though, never was acceptable to the United States and other European powers (Shea 1955: 20). In the contemporary world, many states in Latin America appear to have abandoned their hostility to international arbitration by signing on to BITs and ratifying conventions for the resolution of investment disputes (Cremades 2005; Naón 2005). Indeed, Naón argues that Calvo's edicts never precluded agreement between equal states who wished to resort to the international arbitration of disputes (2005: 137). There remains, nevertheless, an ever-growing adverse reaction to the investment rules regime (in states like Argentina and Brazil) and this is being made manifest in the placement of roadblocks to the completion of a Free Trade Area of the Americas (FTAA). The report of the special rapporteur to the International Law Commission, John Dugard, confirms that the version of the Calvo Clause requiring the exhaustion of local remedies in the event of a contractual dispute between a foreign investor and the host state remains an "important feature ... of the [Latin American] regional approach to international law" (Dugard 2002: 15).

## CONSTITUTIONS OLD AND NEW

The Colombia Constitution is a modern constitutional text which aspires to secure important national social objectives, but which has been encountering significant pressures to conform to new trans-national norms. The Colombian model is also an interesting case study as it combines two distinctive features, described by Sanín and Jaramillo (2005: 193): "stability of macroinstitutional forms and a long tradition of diffuse, chronic and scathing armed conflicts." Indeed, Colombia ranks as one of the most violent societies in the world (Garfield and Arboldea 2003: 36), and this makes it difficult, if not impossible, to achieve many of the aims and objectives sought to be secured by constitutional reform. The "efficacy of law is very precarious" in Colombia, write Uprimny and García-Villegas (2005: 82), and this suggests real limits to achieving social change through constitutional reform in societies riven by violence. The inability to achieve these changes lies beyond the scope of this discussion. Instead, I focus in this part on the constitutional reforms of 1936 and 1991 both as they pertain to property rights, generally, and to privatization, more particularly. This history is pertinent to the sections that follow.

### 1936 reforms

The reforms of 1936 have been portrayed as Colombia's "New Deal." The radical Liberal administration of President Alfonso López Pumarejo had wrested control of government from the Conservatives who held power for decades (Stoller 1995). Lopez instituted a variety of social reforms – this is why the period is known as the *Revolución en marcha* – including tax and agrarian reform, and the constitutional changes of 1936. Art. 26 of the constitution enshrined the notion that "property is a social function which implies obligations." It also provided that, in the event of a conflict between private interests and laws passed for reasons of "public utility or social interest," the private must give way to the public.

The 1936 constitutional reforms enabled the state to expropriate property for the purposes of "public utility or social interest." This could be achieved under judicial supervision with the provision of prior compensation or, for reasons of equity, without compensation by a vote of an absolute majority (two-thirds) of the Senate and House of Representatives (Gibson 1948: 367).[5]

Recognizing that private ownership implies a degree of social obligation – that property serves a social function – is a conventional idea in postrealist legal thought (Singer 2000). But the intellectual origins of this reform in Colombia is often traced back to the work of French constitutional theorist Léon Duguit (1918), discussed in Chapter two (Karst 1964: 346; Stoller 1995: 391).[6] Duguit outlined a theory of the state familiar to British and American progressives of the late nineteenth and early twentieth centuries (Laski 1917–18). The authority of the state is justified by the function it performs, and according to Duguit, that function was to provide for certain social needs. Private property was justifiable to the extent it served and was limited by this social mission (Duguit 1923: 13, 295).

Despite its seemingly foreign origins, Kenneth Karst argues that this approach to property comports well with Latin American understandings. The principle that property fulfills a social function, for instance, has doctrinal support in the notion that the underlying title to all lands lies in the state (Karst 1964: 356). The idea is given expression in Art. 27 of the 1917 Mexican Constitution and Arts. 165–6 of the Bolivian Constitution: all private property is contingent on a transfer of title from the "Nation" – the guardian of all lands and waters. If all rights of ownership emanate from the state, then, according to Art. 27, "it properly depends for its continuance upon the satisfaction of community needs" (Karst 1964: 356). It is entirely consistent with Latin American constitutionalism, then, to ascribe social functions and obligations to property holders. A number of texts recognize this social function: the Venezuelan constitutional guarantee of the right to private property is subject to the "public benefit and the general interest" (Art. 99), while the Chilean Constitution declares that the social function of property includes the requirements of the nation's general interest, security, public use, health and environmental conservation (Art. 19, para. 24) (Daintith and Sah 1993: 474; Hendrix 1995: 7).

In the Colombian context, property as a social function gave constitutional expression to the Lockean edict that land must not remain idle but must be utilized productively (Tully 1995). Hirschman (1965) traces the lineages of this notion to Colombian cultural politics. The socially condoned practice of settling (or colonizing) the seemingly empty and unproductive lands of the interior of Colombia resulted in the highly inequitable concentration of land in the hands of large (*hacienda*) land owners. Legislation giving effect to the 1936 constitutional reform (Act 200) was consistent with an ideology of Lockean productivity. The law was intended to divest speculative property owners of their uncultivated rural lands by authorizing the expropriation of plots that remained idle for more than 10 years. Act 200, wrote Hirschman, "established the fundamental principle that a presumption of private property exists in favor of those who occupy the land and make 'economic use' of it" (Hirschman 1965: 150).

As Hirschman shows, the agrarian reform movement of the 1930s and its successor program of the 1960s[7] made little "progress." Certainly, the election of Lopez's successor, Eduardo Santos, helped to retard the advance of agrarian land reform (Kalmanovitz 2003). But the 1936 constitutional reforms, if seemingly radical, were never intended to be effective, Hirschman concludes (1965: 197). His 1963 study of Colombian agrarian reform closes with the observation that the passage of progressive land reform laws in Colombia "may have been facilitated by the long tradition of issuing well-meaning and socially advanced laws and decrees which turn out to be ineffective because of enforcement or clever obstruction" (1965: 211). Other work on the period confirms these suspicions. There appears to have been no widespread belief in the 1930s that the solution to economic inequality lay in constitutional reform, or that the 1886 Constitution somehow impeded the achievement of effective social and economic change. The impulse for constitutional reform in 1936, in other words, was "primarily political rather than socioeconomic" (Stoller 1995: 393; Palacios 2006).

Though no meaningful land reform was realized, the 1936 constitutional changes enabled the state to undertake modest agrarian reform in the 1960s. In so far as these reforms impinged on property rights, the Colombian Constitutional Court had jurisdiction to review the actions of the Instituto Colombiano de Reforma Agraria (INCORA), the body charged with expropriating land under the 1961 agrarian law. The institute was mildly activist: by 1963, it had instigated 108 lawsuits seeking revocation of title or the invalidation of claims to land (Smith 1967: 89). Property owners were being compensated by the state at market value with the provision of government bonds, redeemable at some time in the future; the property owner alleging that the state had expropriated property without "prior indemnification." If the state bonds were not immediately realizable, it was argued that this did not satisfy the constitutional requirement of prior compensation in Art. 26.

In finding for the state, the court reflected on the meaning of the social function of property: "The social function ... accentuated the subordination of ownership to community interests, to the point that the guarantee given in the Constitution in favor of property rights is conditioned [on] the extent to which the rights correspond to the needs of the community" (Karst 1966: 560). In light of this constitutional "prevalence of social interests over private ones, in all instances and circumstances," the court found that the provision of compensation in the form of bonds satisfied the constitutional require-ment of Art. 30 (Karst 1966: 559).

In the following decades, the state made only modest advances in agrarian reform at the very same time as peasants were being forced to migrate from their lands because of paramilitary conflict. Colombian efforts at land reform in these periods have been described as marginal both in magnitude and in impact (Balcazar et al. 2001: 30). At present, the land reform agenda, if timely 50 years ago, is now confined to the redistribution of expropriated lands of Colombian drug traffickers (Act 793 of 202; Kalmanovitz 2001: 252).

Karst noted in 1964 that talk about social function was largely restricted to rural land. The "similar performance of social function might, with equal reason," he wrote, "be demanded of other property" (Karst 1964: 347). The 1991 Colombian Constitution includes provi-sions for the privatization of public enterprise and underlying these provisions is the principle that property serves social functions, simi-larly subordinating private property to community interests.

## 1991 Colombian Constitution

Colombia is regarded as one of the few Latin American countries that did not experience severe financial turmoil in the 1980s – it has had lower debt ratios and only moderate fiscal deficits (Easterly 1995). The relative success of the Colombian economy did not spare successive governments from engaging in programs of austerity, initially self-induced, and aided, subsequently, by IMF adjustment programs in 1987 (Giugale 2003: 16; Kalmanovitz 2003: 549; Ocampo 1987: 257).

The 1990 program of economic liberalization (*apertura*), signaled Colombia's openness to foreign investment and commitment to a modest program of privatization (Pacuzzi 1994: 449–50). According to the government's report to the WTO in 1996: "The purpose of the privatization of public sector assets is to free the Government resources tied up in activities that could be carried out more efficien-tly by the private sector and to transfer them [i.e., government resources] to sectors where Government intervention is essential, for example, education, health, justice and security" (WTO 1996: 166). Privatization, in other words, could increase revenue flows, reduce the deficit, and help to subsidize social reform (Pacuzzi 1994: 468).

One of the catalysts for this program of economic and social change was to be the achievement of constitutional reform of 1991. This task was undertaken by a multiparty constitutional assembly, composed of seventy elected delegates, widely representative of various constituencies in Colombian political life, including the Conservative and Liberal labor parties, indigenous peoples, and four representatives of demobilized guerrilla groups, including the M-19 guerrilla movement. It has been described as the "first body in Colombia to work by seeking consensus" (Fox and Stetson 1992: 145) and its successful negotiation of a new constitution for Colombia as "stunning" (Banks and Alvarez 1991: 45).[8] It was hoped that the new constitution could provide a framework for neutralizing the major sources of corruption and instability in Colombia – continuing armed resistance by Marxist guerillas and political violence instigated by the drug traffic in cocaine.

The 1991 Constitution, then, amounts to a remarkable achievement by a fractious assembly in a country riven by violence and instability in all sectors of political life. The idea of *estado social de derecho* – an admixture of social state and rule of law – gives expression to the role of the state captured in the new constitution (Cepeda 1998: 86). The text guarantees a variety of social and economic rights, in addition to the recognition of indigenous self-government. While private property is given general protection, the democratization of property also is envisaged.[9] The constitution declares that the state "will promote access to property" (Art. 60). It is also "the duty of the state to promote the gradual access of agricultural workers to landed property in individual or associational form" (Art. 64). Aboriginal communal land rights are recognized (Art. 329) and these lands are "inalienable, imprescriptible, and not subject to seizure" (Art. 63). Contrary to the seemingly universal tendencies in international investment law, the constitution also permitted the expropriation of property without the provision of compensation (Art. 58). The constitutional property provisions, however, would not withstand homogenizing pressures of the rules regime and so were the subject of subsequent amendment, discussed in Part four of this chapter.

Nonetheless, a program of privatization of public sector assets and responsibilities is expressly contemplated. The 1991 Constitution endorses the internationalization of economic relations (Art. 227) and permits Congress to authorize the government to "sell national assets" (Art. 150.9). While "public health and environmental protection" are declared to be "public services for which the state is responsible," the constitution permits "private entities ... to exercise oversight and control over them" (Art. 49). Social security is a guaranteed "irrevocable right" which "may be provided by public or private entities" (Art. 48). Last, as the state is obliged to promote "access to property," when a state enterprise is privatized it is obliged to offer employees, trade unions, pension funds, and cooperatives (the *sector solidario*) shares at a minimum price and under special credit conditions (Art. 60).[10] Privatization in the Colombian Constitution, then, aspires to disperse property ownership to a wider stratum of the population rather than concentrating it in the hands of foreign investors or the already affluent.[11]

The Constitutional Court halted the planned privatization of financial institutions because the scheme failed to comply with the requirements of Art. 60 (Linares and Aldana 1997). As the share offering to the solidarity sector was limited to 15 percent, and as preferential conditions also were attached to offers to current shareholders, the scheme violated the constitutional commitment to the "democratization" of public property (C-037/94 and C-452/95). Nevertheless, by 1996 the Colombian government had privatized approximately 100 state-owned or -controlled entities (WTO 1996: 9), including more than six banks, savings and loan corporations, the national port authority, thermoelectric and hydroelectric plants, and railway interests (Linares and Aldana 1997). With the exception of telecommunications, writes Giugale, "the private sector has a major role in all subsectors," such as oil, gas, coal, power, water, and the like (2003: 11). Resisting policy directions in the neighboring states of Bolivia and Ecuador, President Uribe announced in July 2006 that the government would sell off a 20 percent stake in the state-owned oil company, Ecopetrol (Webb-Vidal 2006). Uribe's push for further privatization, even if only partial, runs counter to much public opinion in Latin America. Sixty-three percent of those surveyed disagreed or strongly disagreed with the proposition that "privatization of State companies has been beneficial" with "absolute gains in welfare for the poor" (Birdsall and Nellis 2005: 2, 26). Nor is this how privatization has been experienced on the ground, with riots and demonstrations associated with privatization initiatives in Bolivia, Ecuador, Peru, and Brazil, some of them giving rise to investment disputes. Uribe's partial privatization plan provoked the labor movement to call for a national strike (Webb-Vidal 2006).

The participation of the solidarity sector in privatization has been mixed. In the case of the privatization of thermal electric plants, the sector was able to purchase over 60 percent of an interest (Linares and Aldana 1997). In other instances, the program has had, and will continue to have, little effect. Considering the low rates of unionization in Colombia (about 8 percent) (PRS 1996), and continuing violence directed at the trade union movement (*Financial Times* 2006), the poorest workers will not be organized nor have the fiscal capacity to purchase shares (Pacuzzi 1994: 476).[12]

On the other hand, for the disciplinarians of economic globalization, privatization in Colombia has moved too slowly. The majority of public services continue to be delivered by the state. The Pastrana administration (1998–2002) promised to step up privatization, according to one report, and so rolled "out the red carpet for foreign investors" (Vogel 1999). President Pastrana aimed to privatize seventeen state-owned power companies, a state interest in a large coal operation and also partner with investors in new infrastructure development (roads, highways, airports). The government estimated in 1999 that it would earn at least US$ 3.1 billion from privatizations (Vogel 1999). Much of this was never realized – *apertura*, according to a World Bank analysis, "never really occurred" (Giugale 2003: 14).

Related to the Colombian program of privatization is the relaxation of the rules for the admission of foreign investment. Investment screening has ceased, there are few restrictions on the patriation of profits, national treatment has been granted to all foreign investors, and 100 percent foreign ownership is permitted in most sectors (National Trade Data Bank 1996; WTO 2006: 19). Yet at least one major irritant for foreign investment remained as of 1991, and it was a vestige of the notion that property performs social functions. It is that, until its subsequent amendment in 1999, the constitution authorized the state to expropriate property without the payment of compensation. For "reasons of equity" – a determination that could not be the subject of judicial review – the legislature, authorized by a two-thirds absolute majority in both chambers of Congress, could expropriate property without prior compensation.

How would this new constitutional regime, particularly its provisions regarding privatization and the social function of property, stack up against the investment rules regime reflecting the neoliberal consensus around the admission and treatment of foreign investment? I take up this question in the following section.

## NATIONAL TREATMENT RULES

I focus here on two related instruments of transnational rule – BITs and the draft MAI – and their effect on domestic constitutional rules such as those found in the new Colombian Constitution. Privatization rules that prefer local workers or associations, unless specifically exempted, likely run afoul of the obligation of "national treatment" found in both investment instruments. National treatment requires that there be no discrimination against foreign investors resident in the other party state: that nonnational investors be treated as if they were nationals. It is for this reason that privatization processes preferring the solidarity sector were identified as nonconforming in a November 2006 Colombia-US Trade Promotion Agreement (TPA) that stalled in Congress, lacking the requisite Congressional approval. Absent these country-specific reservations (UNCTAD 2006c), the disciplines of the typical BIT, such as those signed by Colombia prior to 2006, could forestall preferred privatization processes. The MAI, with its detailed provisions regarding privatization, may have turned out to be a more tolerable instrument in this regard, as I discuss below.

It is interesting to surmise whether national treatment obligations subvert or undermine constitutional commitments. International trade scholars have long argued that national treatment does not require any particular minimum standard of treatment, only equality of treatment as between local and foreign investors. States, they have argued, continue to have the ability to legislate in any area whatsoever – national sovereignty, then, is not impinged in any substantive way. When constitutional text authorizes or commits a state to prefer nationals, however, the national treatment rule could have the effect of undoing the constitutional commitment. No longer is the obligation of nondiscrimination simply a version of formal equality that is neutral with regard to legislative objectives. It is this constitutional context that makes the national treatment obligation cut close to the bone of national sovereignty (Hart 1987: 55).

### The bilateral regime

BITs usually do not contain express provisions regarding processes for the divestiture of state enterprises. Typically, BIT obligations are not triggered until a foreign investor enters the host state. In order to enter that jurisdictional space, investors must comply with all the usual laws or regulations. The sale of public assets to private owners, with the exception of US and Canadian BITs, ordinarily will not activate national treatment obligations (nondiscrimination against foreign investors) unless the nonnational investor already has entered the host state. In other words, privatization schemes that impinge on the ability of foreign investor participation will not offend the national treatment rule unless the investor is already established in the country. The OECD considered this question in 1991: whether the principle of national treatment, as defined in its 1976 standard investment code, should apply to the "privatisation of enterprises previously under public ownership." The OECD concluded that the undertaking should come into play whenever areas "previously under monopoly are opened up. In such cases, access to move into these areas should then be provided on a non-discriminatory basis as between private domestic and foreign-controlled enterprises already established in the country in question" (OECD 1991: 27).

States use various model rules to guarantee national treatment – some APEC countries exclude the commitment while others, like Canada and the United States, exempt certain sectors (UNCTAD 2006a: 34–5, 2006c: 25–7) – but most, when they do, speak to a similar idea of nondiscrimination by the host state on the basis of nationality (UNCTAD 2004b: 161). This is how it is expressed in the 2004 US model rule, which was taken up in the proposed 2006 US-Colombia TPA: "Each party shall accord to investors of the other Party treatment no less favorable than that it accords, in like circumstances, to its own investors with respect to the establishment, acquisition, expansion, management, conduct, operation, and sale or other disposition of investments in its territory" (US Department of State 2004: Art. 3).

Would the constitutionally-mandated privatization rule in Colombia, which requires preferential share offerings to employees, trade unions, and cooperatives, offend the principle of national treatment for those investors already established within Colombia? Leaving aside the problematic question of applying equality rights analysis to frustrate the achievement of rational economic and political objectives (Sornarajah 2004: 153), the answer again turns on the comparator group chosen for the purposes establishing that there has been treatment in "like circumstances." One option is to look to the class of potential foreign investors who would want to participate in the privatization scheme, but who would not be entitled to participate. This group would not be treated as favorably as local investors, though in like circumstances, and so would be discriminatory on the basis of nationality. If the object is to find a comparator group most like the group of local investors (*Feldman* 2002; *Methanex* 2005), perhaps the more fitting comparators are potential investors, both foreign and local, who happen to be affiliated with employers (rather than employees) or other non-solidarity pension funds. This might amount to discrimination on the grounds of employment status or some other such ground, but not on the ground of nationality. Yet another option is to consider as the "most-like" group foreign employee and other associational investors who are treated less well than similar local groups (though there is some question whether foreign employee and trade associations would want to challenge such a measure). This might be the group closest to the preferred solidarity sector group and they might be considered to be suffering discriminatory treatment as a consequence of nationality. According to tribunals deciding such cases, measures will be caught by the national treatment rule even if not intentionally discriminatory. Preferred share offerings to the solidarity sector, under this third formulation, likely would be inconsistent with the principle of national treatment. It certainly would be inconsistent under the first formulation if the group "foreign investor" were considered most like local investors. The draft MAI text, which I turn to next, helps to shed light on this question. According to the negotiating parties there, any preferential scheme would have been contrary to the broadly drafted national treatment rule.

This understanding of the BIT rules suggests that the constitutionally-mandated privatization rule in Colombia, which requires preferential share offerings to employees, trade unions, and cooperatives likely offend the principle of national treatment. Preferred share offerings to this sector run contrary to the principle of national treatment: that foreign investors be treated no less favorably than domestic enterprises and investors. US BIT standards broaden the likelihood of conflict with the domestic constitutional regime. These standards require non-discrimination in the *admission or establishment* of investments, not merely equal treatment after admission (UNCTAD 2004b: 168). Those nonresident foreign investors who wish merely to establish a presence in the host country are entitled to equal treatment with domestic nationals even before they make any investment. Colombian constitutional requirements and their legislative articulation would more likely be in conflict with this more stringent standard.

This is precisely why the proposed US-Colombian TPA listed, as a nonconforming measure to the requirement of national treatment, preferred share offerings to the solidarity sector in the wake of privatization (see Annex 1 referring to Act 226 of 1995, Arts 3 & 11). Were the TPA to provide otherwise, the Colombian Constitutional Court likely would have found that, in so far as the treaty deactivates constitutional obligations, it is not in conformity with the constitution. Indeed, as we learn later, the Colombian Constitutional Court has shown itself somewhat impervious to the pressures of economic globalization. The same cannot be said for the government of Colombia.

### The multilateral regime

How might Colombian constitutional rules regarding privatization have fared against the terms of the draft MAI? The twenty-nine member countries of the OECD undertook the task of completing an enforceable agreement for the protection and promotion of foreign direct investment in September 1995. It is not that investment flows between these countries had been frustrated; rather, the objective was to set very high standards for the protection of investment which countries in the so-called developing world would be pressured to embrace. The web of bilateral agreements then could be filled in by this new multilateral instrument.

Negotiations in Paris came to a halt, in part, because of resistance to the agreement in the US Congress, the withdrawal of France from the negotiating table, and also because of the coordinated action of citizen organizations in Canada, France, New Zealand, and elsewhere (Vallely 1999) (discussed further in Chapter seven). There is little likelihood that the exercise will continue under the auspices of the OECD, though it is probable that negotiations will shift to a venue like the WTO. A multilateral agreement on investment initially was on the agenda at the WTO, included as one of the Singapore issues, only to fall unceremoniously off the table (Stiglitz and Charlton 2005: 263). It is worthwhile, then, to review the provisions of the MAI as they concern privatization, particularly as the draft text contains provisions that expressly contemplate rules for the treatment of foreign investors in the case of a divestiture of state assets.

It is particularly interesting that, although a number of key issues were resolved in negotiations, the draft provisions concerning privatization were among the least settled. In fact, the provisions concerning privatization suggest substantive disagreement between some of the negotiating parties. If the draft text signals what remained in dispute at the OECD negotiations, it also makes difficult drawing any definitive conclusions about what consensus would have emerged on this issue among the negotiating parties.

A number of matters were not in dispute. As national treatment and MFN treatment would be accorded to investors in the establishment phase (Art. III) – the US BIT standard – processes of privatization would ordinarily be caught by the rule. But the parties felt it desirable to spell out how these obligations applied specifically in the privatization context.[13] It was agreed that the privatization disciplines in the MAI would require that national treatment and MFN status be accorded in all manner of privatization, "irrespective of the method of privatization chosen" (public offering, direct sale, etc.) and to all phases of the process. In dispute was the extent to which "special share arrangements," such as management/employee buy-outs, "golden shares" (reserved for government), and special schemes for the public, offended national treatment and MFN treatment (Ahnlid 1997: 24).

For the negotiating parties, it was not that these arrangements did not on their face offend the principle of nondiscrimination – they did – rather, disagreement appeared to turn on the manner in which this was to be acknowledged in the text. Most delegations appeared willing to exempt special share arrangements, adopting the more restrictive definition of national treatment: so long as foreign investors are treated no more worse than other excluded domestic investors, there is no discrimination. Others preferred that the obligation of non-discrimination remain in effect, but that those states concerned about privatization in certain areas designate as reservations (either bound, in which case no new sectors could be added, or unbound, anticipating future sectoral exceptions) special share arrangements in those sectors (Ahnlid 1997: 24; eSilva 1997: 35).

The proposed text accepted by a large number of delegations would have rendered special share arrangements compatible with the commitment to national treatment and MFN treatment unless they expressly offended MFN or discriminated against investments "in like circumstances" on the grounds of "nationality or permanent residency." The explanation provided by the OECD (predating the April 1998 draft text under discussion here) was that so long as foreign investors "are not put in a more disadvantageous position than domestic investors which do not qualify for such privatisation schemes" then these measures would be considered nondiscriminatory (OECD 1996:7).

With the clarification offered by this explanatory text, it may have been that a comprehensive code would have provided more certainty and more equity with regard to preferred share options for employees and their associations than the standard BIT text.

A minority of the delegations preferred the option of designating certain sectors as exceptions. Exempting privatization processes from MAI disciplines may similarly have avoided constitutional conflict. In large measure, this would have depended on the specificity of those reservations. The expectation of the MAI negotiators was that the agreement would "standstill" investment measures – the agreement would provide an "irreversible minimum standard" from which states could not deviate (Witherell 1995: 11). The agreement would also "rollback" reservations and exceptions, "with a view to their eventual elimination," according to a predetermined time table, for instance (Witherell 1995: 11). Over time, then, even a positive list of exempted enterprises or sectors would be subject to erosion due to commitments in the MAI text or state peer pressure. While the proposed US-Colombian TPA would not have been subject to similar rollback, the agreement was intended to amount to an irreversible minimum standard. No further exemptions or qualifications would be expected to arise, requiring an improbable degree of ex ante knowledge about what policy direction citizens and their governments might wish to pursue (Cho and Dubash 2005: 149).

## CONSTITUTIONALISM UNDER PRESSURE

If I have portrayed the Colombian Constitution as being mostly at odds with the investment rules regime, this would not be a representative portrait. The constitutional amendments of 1991 endeavored to free the state from a number of public welfare obligations. The amendments represented a new style of constitutionalism for Colombia more con-genial to post-1989 economic developments. Vestiges of the old-style of constitutionalism remained, however. It is in these spaces that conflict with the dominant discourse of neoliberalism would be expected to materialize. There is little evidence that the Colombian government can resist pressures to reform these remnants of old-style constitutionalism.

Differing branches of the state may respond differently to the pres-sures generated by economic globalization. As Jessop argues, there is little unity with regard to state structures, only different combinations of constraint and opportunity that impact on differing social actors (1990: 256). In a recent episode of constitutional conflict, the Colombian Constitutional Court resisted adopting interpretive approaches more compatible with the dominant discourse of economic globalization. The government of Colombia was not capable of similar resistance; instead, the government responded by amending the constitution. In this way, economic globalization's strictures are being articulated not only outside of states, but are also being internalized within, even as differing branches respond differently to these exigencies.

The episode giving rise to amendment concerned the expropriations rule of the 1991 Colombian constitution. A series of BITs, including a 1994 Colombian-UK BIT, appeared to be in direct conflict with it. The 1994 BIT contained the usual provisions concerning national treatment, MFN treatment, and prohibitions on expropriations and nationalizations. Expropriation and nationalization were prohibited unless it was for a public purpose, nondiscriminatory, and accompanied by the payment of "prompt, adequate and effective compensation," fully realizable and transferable (the "Hull formula"). The Constitution of Colombia required that the treaty be presented to the Colombian Constitutional Court for its certification. There is a strong tradition of constitutional review in Colombia, and the court has been able to captivate on this legitimacy in the aftermath of the 1991 constitutional settlement. The historic weakness of social movements coupled with weak institutions for political representation has enabled the court to assume a much more prominent role than previously had been the case. Upriminy and García-Villegas even talk about the "emancipatory potential" of some of the Constitutional Court's progressive rulings in the domains of indigenous rights, gay and lesbian rights, and poor people's rights, which have helped to generate popular support for the court as an institution (Upriminy and García-Villegas 2005: 71).

Flexing its constitutional muscle, the court held by a majority of six to three that the BIT was contrary to the constitution in two respects (C-358/96). First, the BIT had the effect of deactivating provisions of the Colombian Constitution – the constitution permits, in the interests of equity, expropriation without the payment of any compensation. The government could not waive the exercise of a power delegated to it by the constitution by conceding the payment of prompt, adequate, and effective compensation. Second, the investment treaty offended the equality provisions of the constitution by granting to citizens of British nationality preferential treatment in respect of expropriations, preferred treatment not available to Colombian nationals. The BIT, in other words, offended Calvo's edict that foreign nationals not be entitled to preferential treatment over domestic nationals (Weizman 1998: 116).[14]

The majority of the Constitutional Court resisted the government's argument that the differential treatment of foreign investors was justified by reason of the fact that they are excluded from the political process – an idea familiar to US constitutional analysis (Ely 1980; *Carolene Products* 1938) and more recently taken up by the European Court of Human Rights (*James* 1986) and the *Tecmed* tribunal (2004). As foreigners are precluded from exercising the privileges of citizenship, the government argued, they are "not tied to the political destiny of the country." The majority preferred to remain faithful to Calvo's edict, expressed in Art. 4 of the constitution, that nationals and foreigners alike are expected to adhere to the constitution.

The three minority judges adopted an entirely different interpretive approach, one more befitting of the disciplinary global environment. They were of the opinion that the BIT was in conformity with constitutional requirements. The BIT generally was in accord with the constitutional rule regarding compensation. Only the possibility of nonpayment of compensation for "reasons of equity," an eventuality denied by the UK-Colombia BIT, could give rise to irreconcilable constitutional conflict. The minority found that the state was entitled to circumscribe its own discretionary power through treaty. Here, the state could elect not to exercise a constitutional authority in order to stimulate foreign investment.

The minority's judicial orientation was, by their own admission, cognizant of the "new conception of sovereignty" that results from the globalization of economic relations. According to the minority,

> In the current moment of world development, economic prosperity can only be achieved through clear strategies of market conquest, of attraction, protection and promotion of foreign investors and of insertion in international markets. Protectionism at all costs and policies which dissuade foreign investment, implemented with the intention of defending sovereignty and national interests, become counter-productive instruments which tend to increase poverty and worsen internal levels of social well-being. In sum, sovereignty can only be fully defended through a political economy which reconciles national needs and interests with the inexorable tendency toward internationalization of economies. (C-358/96: 65)[15]

The minority understood that the 1991 Constitution "was no stranger to these ideas." Rather, "it adopts a clear basic political decision in favour of economic integration of the country in world markets and the internationalization of the economic relations of the Colombian state" (C-358/96: 65). Without a doubt, the minority wrote, the majority decision would lead to amendment of the offending clause. Despite other reasonable interpretive possibilities, the majority had issued a "death sentence" to the constitutional provision.

The minority was not wrong about the likely consequence of the Constitutional Court's ruling in this case and subsequent certification decisions respecting Colombian BITs with Cuba (C-379/96), Peru (C-008/97), and Spain (C-494/98). Anxious to reassure foreign investors that Colombia is open beyond question to foreign investment, the government pledged to remove this remnant of a bygone era. No government in modern Colombia history has expropriated foreign property – the Municipality of Cali had only threatened to expropriate property owned by the American and Foreign Power Co. in 1947 (USDC 1953: 12) – nor had investors expressed any concern that the risk of expropriation was high in Colombia (National Trade Data Bank 1996). There is also some doubt, as I argued in Chapter two, that any benefits ultimately would accrue to Colombia as a consequence. Nevertheless, the Colombian government remained intent on removing the offending language from the constitution, deploying investment policy and constitutional reform to "symbolize a commitment to economic liberalism" (Vandevelde 1998: 628). Two paragraphs of constitutional text were repealed in August 1999. The constitutional property clause no longer permits expropriation without the payment of compensation, thereby solving both the equality and property law concerns.[16] Here, then, was a clear instance of the new constitutionalism disciplining deviant constitutional norms – interference with private property and investment rights simply was beyond the pale, requiring constitutional overhaul.

Though the state capitalist model of constitutional design fell into disfavor, only to see modest revival after 2000, it faces an uneasy future with the model of governance represented by the investment rules regime. The Colombian constitutional treatment of privatization remains, to date, untested against the strictures of the investment rules regime. It is acknowledged as a nonconforming measure in the stalled US-Colombia TPA but it appears not to be similarly shielded from the disciplines of a 2000 Chile-Colombia BIT. The encounter between investment rules and constitutional property rules suggests that the outcome in the case of privatization likely will not favor diversity in national rule making. The outcome, however, would be different when tested against the preliminary draft of the MAI. That multilateral instrument suggested a more tolerant approach to alternatives to privatization. We should keep in mind, however, that preferred share option schemes remain inconsistent with the key precepts of the investment rules regime and that MAI disciplines were intended to tighten their grip over time, eliminating exceptions through standstill and rollback.

The conflict outlined above is not confined to the level of constitutional analysis. It has resonance in the context of ordinary legislative rules for the privatization of state enterprise. But the constitutional context heightens the quality of the conflict. Constitutions are intended to have a level of fixity outside of politics; that is, they are intended to standardize the enduring rules of the game. As such, they should be able to withstand the pressures generated by particular class interests within states and the pressures generated by the material interests of other states. But constitutions are also within politics, and so provide a focal point of real conflict about alternative futures. Constitutions, in other words, both shape politics and are shaped by politics (Dearlove 1989: 534).

In this environment, are not domestic constitutions a reasonable resource with which to countervail the investment rules regime? We should be mindful again of the fact that states are the principal authors of this regime which limits their capacity to regulate privatizations and intervene in the marketplace. So rather than seeking to further constrain state action through constitutional limits, perhaps the better option is to loosen binding precommitments. This means having states unlock themselves from the regime of investment rules – a difficult matter in so far as most BITs remain in force for periods of up to 10 years for those investments established during the time a treaty was in force. The draft MAI would have locked states in to at least a 20-year commitment.

The failed MAI talks, though, should hearten those who wish to free states from a predetermined constitutional course of economic conduct. By removing themselves from the room, the French delegation was able to effectively scuttle negotiations. So rather than bypassing the state, we should better understand the ways in which states are implicated in the structuration of the investment rules regime. Citizens, presumably, can aim to undo constraints, both domestic and transnational, concerning the democratization of property and the promotion of self-rule. In the next part, the discussion turns to the capacity of citizens to countervail the force of the transnational rules regime. In light of the constitution-like rules of investment discipline, this turns out to be more difficult than might be imagined.

# PART THREE

## RESISTANCE

# CHAPTER SEVEN

# CITIZENSHIP

The dominant themes that emerge from a review of the literature on globalization are those of speed, movement, and uncertainty. Zygmunt Bauman, for instance, equates globalization with a "political economy of uncertainty" that gives rise to political regimes of "permanent and ubiquitous" insecurity (Bauman 1999: 173–4). There is in much of this literature an indifference toward the structural elements that help to generate the phenomenon we associate with economic globalization. As we have seen in the foregoing chapters, the elements of predictability and surety are goals that the transnational regime for the protection and promotion of trade and investment aims to secure. These features of rootedness and fixity would appear to contradict much of the current diagnoses of globalization.

A focus on legal rules and institutions not only helps us to comprehend the mechanisms by which economic globalization is being made material, but also brings to the foreground the concept of place. The physicality of economic globalization – the head offices, plants, and sweatshops – recalls the ongoing importance of place which is often displaced by the so-called compression of time and space. Disrupting dominant understandings and relocating the centrality of place might furnish openings to contest, even to resist, economic globalization.

Not that contestation and resistance will be any easier. Institutionalizing the rigid legal regime for the protection and promotion of foreign investment makes opposition difficult to sustain. Limiting state capacity with regard to the market inhibits Polanyi's "double movement" – the ability of society to take self-protective measures with regard to land, labor, and money (Polanyi 1957: 76). It is this capacity for societal self-protection that is under threat by the constitution-like features of the investment rules regime.

This chapter inquires into those places where alternative futures might be imagined and pursued in places above and below the national state system. These possibilities are examined through the idea of "citizenship" and the citizenship regime flowing from the ensemble of legal rules and institutions I have associated with economic globalization (Jenson 1997: 631). By taking seriously the "present actualities of our institutions" (Shklar 1991: 9), a particular view of citizenship follows from the institutional logic of the investment rules regime, and this is taken up in the first part of the chapter. It is a version of citizenship propelled by the values of the market and a regime constructed around the typical market citizen: white, male, English-speaking, and residing in a North Atlantic country. There will be many who fall outside the rubric of this regime. They should be considered the "subaltern," those who fall outside of "capitalism's logic" and who have no established agency in the West's culture of consumerism (Spivak 1993: 78). Following Aristotle's formulation that the constitution defines the possibilities for good citizenship, not the good individual (Aristotle 1995: $1276^{b}16$), what emerges is not an idealized citizenship regime, but a constrained and partial version – a snapshot of a regime in the process of formation.

Economic globalization is fraught with contradiction. These antinomies offer potential openings for resistance. Within the realm of market citizenship, then, there remain spaces where alternative futures might be explored. The balance of the chapter explores three such places, from the perspective of (a) consumer citizenship, (b) local or subnational citizenship, and (c) computer-mediated (or "wired") citizenship. The possibilities for citizenship practice are examined in the concrete contexts of, in the case of the consumer, the boycott against the Nike Corporation; in the case of the subnational citizen, anti-Burma purchasing by-laws in the state of Massachusetts; and, in the case of the wired citizen, the transnational social movement opposing the MAI. What emerges is a version of citizenship that is enabled mostly with regard to those activities that correspond to the value of market civilization (Gill 1995). Citizenship practices that subvert market dominance are more likely to be constrained, even prohibited, by investment rules and their complementary national manifestations.

In undertaking this analysis, we should be reminded that this is a regime in flux, constitutive of and constituted by citizenship practices (Silbey 2005: 334). Though the analysis is, in this way, preliminary, there is some urgency to understanding the capacity of citizens to mobilize and change the world. Lewis Lapham alarmingly describes contemporary American society as being "composed of citizens in name only, 'ostensible citizens' united by little else except the possession of a credit card and a password to the Internet" (Lapham 2001: 12). Even if hyperbolic, this diagnosis is increasingly pertinent to other parts of the world as the rules and structures of economic globalization are becoming fixed and frozen, dislocating and constraining alternative relations between the market, the state, and citizenry.

The chapter turns, first, to a discussion of a conception of citizenship. This is not one defined solely by traditional state apparatus and its concern with the administration of immigration and naturalization; rather, this is a conception of citizenship understood as residing outside the boundaries of the national state (Bosniak 2000; Sassen 1997). By tracking the implications of the new legal architecture giving effect to economic globalization, we can identify the outlines of a provisional citizenship regime in formation. This regime gives rise to a version of citizenship with identifiable rights and membership in a particular and privileged community. I then turn to those spaces out of which alternative conceptions of citizenship might arise. These spaces, it has been argued, provide resources with which to countervail the new provisional regime. The alternative conceptions of citizenship turn out to be quite limited in scope, all of which help to underscore the contracted political space implied by the rules and structures of economic globalization.

## MARKET CITIZENSHIP

I begin with Jenson's dynamic understanding of citizenship as "the institutionalization of a set of practices by which states use public power to shape and regulate markets and communities" (Jenson 1997: 630). It is Jenson's premise that institutions matter, for it is institutions that give substance to the idea and practice of citizenship. The rules and institutions of economic globalization similarly matter by generating both new constraints and new opportunities for individuals and groups to pursue social and political possibilities. If we follow Shklar's advice that "it is unconvincing and ultimately an uninteresting flight from politics" to disregard institutional effects (Shklar 1991: 9), then we should follow the logic of the present ensemble of institutions that arise outside of and interact with the legal structures of the national state.

Most contemporary discussions of citizenship begin instead with T.H. Marshall's classic formulation in "Citizenship and Social Class." Marshall there traced the evolution of citizenship rights from the establishment of civil rights in the eighteenth century (implying individual economic freedom through the law), political rights in the nineteenth (through expansion of the franchise), and social rights in the twentieth (via the satisfaction of basic entitlements). Marshall understood citizenship as having "entitlement" and "integrative" aspects (Marshall 1965: 101). Citizens were defined by a set of legal rights (the entitlement aspect) that were ascribed to them not only as individuals but also as members of a political community (the integrative aspect). These two elements of citizenship – rights and identity (Lehning 1997: 108) – are helpful tools in delineating the kind of citizen contemplated by the logic of the institutions of economic globalization.

The constitutive elements of a citizenship regime are, of course, experienced differentially. The variables of gender, ethnicity, race, or wealth make the experience of citizenship felt differently, both in terms of the rights exercisable and in terms of the community of political belonging which may, or may not, be included within officially sponsored definitions (Young 1990). Aristotle, from another direction, acknowledged that there are "several kinds of citizens," both within and across cities (1995: 1278$^a$34). Leaving aside the degraded status of slaves and "workmen" in Greek city-states, Aristotle distinguished between citizens "proper" – those who were fit to rule and be ruled (1995: 1277$^b$7) – and "imperfect" citizens or citizens "of a kind," like children and women (1995: 1275$^a$5, 1277$^b$39).[1] Even in the eighteenth century – the defining period for the regime of Marshall's civil rights – members of a political community did not play identical roles; there were, Koselleck describes, the "more exalted members" and the "lesser members" (1988: 87).

For Aristotle, it was citizens proper who ruled for the common advantage of all, including on behalf of the class of imperfect citizens. According to Keyt, the distinction implies a body of second-class citizens "whose advantage is included within the common advantage" (Aristotle 1995: 134). Analogizing to the contemporary world, full citizenship status is accorded to the class of individual who acts on behalf of the public interest – the global entrepreneur. Before pursuing this analogy further, let me reiterate the institutional framework outlined in prior chapters that gives rise to the idea of the market citizen.

This is a regime that accords an extraordinary number of rights – one of the hallmarks of citizenship – to foreign investors and is a model widely adopted in all parts of the globe (Lauterpacht 1997). Investment rules are intended to foster the establishment of foreign-owned enterprises in countries host to foreign investment by securing the highest conceivable protections to foreign investors in the form of justiciable rights enforceable before international trade tribunals and domestic courts of law. The rules regime is made manifest in a worldwide web of investment protection agreements. Foreign investors are entitled to "nondiscrimination" in the application and interpretation of local rules and regulations that may negatively impact on investment. States, in other words, must treat foreign investors equivalent to nationals within the host state. This helps to generate the legal fiction that foreign investors are equal in status and rights to domestic citizens. States party to these agreements also undertake substantive commitments that limit their capacity to act in relation to the market, such as via the takings rule and the standard of fair and equitable treatment. These rights of nondiscrimination and nondimunition are binding commitments enforceable by foreign investors themselves. The extended scope of covered investment interests together with substantive limits placed on state activity and investor standing to enforce legally these commitments has entitled business firms to meddle significantly in the regulatory capacity of states. While providing high levels of security to investment interests, investment rules destabilize the capacity for self-government by constraining the possibility for regulatory innovation and, in an age of increasing disparities of wealth, the capacity for societal self-protection.

A particular kind of citizen is presupposed by this trade and investment rules regime. Events at Seattle and elsewhere would suggest that the new model citizen is made up of ministers for international trade who tote briefcases under cover of tear gas. It is true that lines of authority flow easily between these sectors of government and powerful economic interests (Cox 1992: 302). The underlying theme of the investment rules regime, however, is to separate economic from political power and it is the remaining residue of citizenship that is the focus of discussion here.

The citizens proper contemplated by this new configuration are "market" or "economic" citizens. The rights accorded to market citizens are akin to Marshall's eighteenth-century "civil rights" to contract and own property. As in the eighteenth century, there is an exalted and a lesser, a first and a second class of citizens. There is, on the one hand, the foreign investor and trader – an integral member of the "transnational capitalist class" (Sklair 2001) or "mercatocracy" (Cutler 2003: 185) – and, on the other hand, an aggregate of wage earners or consumers – the class of imperfect or qualified citizens whose advantage is calculated as part of the "common advantage."

The transnational capitalist class is composed of differing fractions each performing distinct functions: managers and professionals, investors and bankers, advertisers and lawyers (Sklair 1996: 3). Having mastered the compression of time and space, global capitalists are the main beneficiary of new technological advances, enabling the production of value added from anywhere (Reich 1991). The foreign business firm and its operatives, then, are the agents expressly contemplated by the trade and investment rules regime, for they are the bearers of certain rights. This class of person, both natural and artificial, with investment interest in tow, presumptively is entitled to establish a presence in any foreign market (an enforceable right in US and Canadian investment agreements). Once having established that presence, an investor has the right to full and equal participation in the market without fear of discrimination or favor. It is a version of citizenship familiar to the US constitutional experience under the dormant commerce clause doctrine. The US Constitution (Art. 1, s. 8, cl. 3) entitles Congress "to regulate commerce with foreign nations, and among the several States." The federal commerce clause has been interpreted not only as a positive grant of federal power but also as a negative prohibition on states interfering with interstate trade. State measures that discriminate against out-of-state interests either directly or indirectly are unconstitutional; measures that impose an unreasonable burden on interstate commerce are also constitutionally suspect (Sunstein 1993: 30). These constitutional limitations are justified on a number of grounds, but one reason is that a national economic union demands it. According to Regan (1986), a prohibition on state protectionism makes sense because it promotes the "concept of union." Protectionism is, for Regan, "inconsistent with the very idea of political union" (Regan 1986: 1113). More commonly, it is said that the dormant commerce clause reinforces political processes by ensuring that out-of-state interests are taken into account in the formulation of local rules (Farber and Hudec 1994; Tushnet 1979). This theory of political process – ensuring that those without the right to participate in ordinary political processes are virtually represented (*Carolene Products* 1938) – fits well, Farber and Hudec argue, the Uruguay-round GATT (in addition to the investment rules regime) as it rests "on a collective perception that ruthless treatment of the economic interests of out-siders is inconsistent with the conditions of peaceful international society" (Farber and Hudec 1994: 1405).[2] Likening foreign investors to the citizens of a large national unit, then, mandates that investor interests are accorded high priority in the formulation of public policy. The risk and uncertainty generated by host country politics is some-what removed – states are prohibited from taking a variety of measures that impair to any significant degree the value of that investment. This account of the citizenship regime is flawed, however, to the extent that there is no governing democratic community – a "political union" – analogous to the US federal government capable of attaining some of the objectives forbidden to states by the dormant commerce clause. Howse wisely points out that, unlike in the US case, "there is no real democratic escape" from the results of the world trading and invest-ment system (Howse 2000: 143). The order of the world thereby is reversed. If the international realm was considered lawless – the outside considered "alien and strange, mysterious and threatening" (Walker 1993: 174) – and the national as tame and orderly, the investment rules regime has managed to turn these understandings upside down.

## CONSUMER CITIZENSHIP

The foreign investor's lesser counterpart is the consumer. Consumers are not expressly included within the legal regime but they are understood to be a main beneficiary of expanded global free trade and investment. Indeed, without at least these benefits flowing to con-sumers, the legitimacy of the investment rules regime would be liable to break down.

The consumer dimension to economic citizenship is characterized by an ability to consume goods and services from any place and to travel anywhere (Lash and Urry 1994: 310). This is how globalization is experienced by many people in Western societies: as giving effect to the right, for instance, to sing karaoke, eat Thai, and dance to the latest CD of Cuban *son*. This understanding is reinforced by work in cultural studies which contends that consumption provides pleasure for those who face obstacles in most other areas of life and a space of freedom to generate new identities and communities of meaning (Hall 1996). Consumer freedom, according to this account, has the effect of integrating individuals within social worlds that are constructed around symbols, objects, and brands that express difference and belonging.

For wage-earners with disposable income, one can purchase the freedom to belong. Participation requires only proof of purchase together with a stamped, self-addressed envelope. This meshes easily with dominant political discourse. Constraints on purchasing power, like "high" taxes, are to be resisted and so the relation between consumption and public expenditure becomes a hostile one (Williams 1961: 325). There are, of course, those who are too poor to be consumers, those who are "flawed consumers" or "inadequate citizens" (Bauman 1998: 38). They fail to experience the fullness of membership in North Atlantic societies.

In this regime of market citizenship, consumers are complicit with transnational capital – the relation between production and consumption is obscured but it is not severed. This relationship is unstable, however, as consumption increasingly is being offered as a site of resistance to countervail patterns of economic globalization (Wai 2003). "Citizens are discovering," according to Beck, "that the act of purchase can always and everywhere be a direct ballot paper" (2000: 70, 2005: 74). Consumer activism offers women, for instance, "new areas of authority and expertise, new sources of income, and a new sense of consumer rights" (Nava 1987: 208). Consider, for instance, the publication of guides to informed consumerism, the rise of ethical investment funds, or the sale of shade-grown, fair-trade coffee at high-end coffee shops. Consumer spending remains, nevertheless, for many, outside the "sphere of pure leisure" and part of the domestic labor that sustains the family (McRobbie 1991: 8). Once consumption is politicized and transformed by collective action, however, it becomes a more potent brew with which to influence transnational forces of production.

The Nike Corporation of Portland, Oregon, faced just this sort of collective action when consumers learned of labor practices associated with the production of Nike footwear and sporting goods. There were reports of "union crackdowns" in factories in South Korea and Indonesia, "starvation wages" and "military intimidation" in Indonesia and China, and beatings in Vietnamese factories (Klein 1999: 328). Allegations that child labor was being used in the production of Nike products either were blamed on local subcontractors or, as Nike CEO Phil Knight suggested in Michael Moore's film, *The Big One*, were welcomed for providing a less brutal existence to those over 14 years of age in the developing world (Maslin 1998).

News reports about the "sweat behind the swoosh" (Klein 1999: 375) resulted in the mobilization of groups from all over the United States, Canada, and Europe conducting largely decentralized actions against Nike at local retailers, malls, and big-box stores (Klein 1999: 366). College and university campuses offered a locus for more concerted action, reprimanding universities that contracted with Nike for sportswear purchases and tying future contracts to improved labor conditions. Protests and collective action made some difference: Phil Knight promised not to hire anyone under 18, wages rose in Indonesia in the wake of the Asian financial crisis, and a clamp down on subcontractor's abuse of workers was undertaken (Klein 1999: 375–6).

Consumer activism takes place usually at points of purchase. The problem with contemporary economic globalization is that modes of production appear as "authentically global abstraction[s]" (Dirlik 1994: 350). This makes oppositional politics difficult to mobilize other than at places like malls, mega-stores, or at universities in the case of bulk institutional purchases. Naomi Klein, nevertheless, maintains that "there's plenty that can be done on the sidewalk or in the mall parking lot" (1999: 366). The Workers Rights Consortium, with 158 college and university members, offers a model for monitoring local production practices that may overcome the seeming abstraction of economic globalization, making transnational actors more accountable and better corporate "citizens."

The consortium issued a report in January 2001 detailing the abuse of worker's rights in the wake of a turbulent labor dispute at the Korean-owned Kukdong factory in the state of Puebla, Mexico, where both Nike and Reebok manufacture products. The consortium reported that children under 16 were employed for more than 6 hour a day in contravention of Mexican law and that, once the labor dispute began, labor leaders were fired and workers beaten by state police. Nike called for independent monitoring of the situation but, according to *The New York Times* report, "appeared to agree with the consortium" regarding the abuse of worker's rights at Kukdong (Greenhouse 2001). Kukdong subsequently transformed itself into the Mexmode company and entered into a collective agreement with an independent trade union in 2002 (Erlich 2002). Labor conditions since have improved.

According to one Mexmode worker, the "treatment by the Koreans is not very good, but it's not as bad as it was before" (NPR 2001) – "they still scream at us, but less than before" (Featherstone 2002: 88).

The Nike campaign suggests that "activism at the point of consumption" (Nava 1991: 167) is a strategically powerful tool for securing change with regard to corporate conduct – for making corporations "better citizens." Consumer activism as a site of resistance has its ethical and practical limits, however. The critical voting requirement is that one has purchasing power – individuals and groups can register their preferences through patterns of consumption only if they have economic wealth and sufficient amounts of it to make a difference. Moreover, the mobilization of resources required to achieve success at Kukdong seems daunting: a delegation of eight experts donated their time to the consortium, traveled to Puebla for 4 days, interviewed over sixty workers and managers, and produced a lengthy legal brief (WRC 2001). As Massing reminds us, "[a]ll of this work was required to improve the conditions at just one plant," yet "Nike have hundreds of factories around the world" (Massing 2001). This kind of intensive organizing from abroad seems difficult to sustain (Seidman 2007: 136–37). Moreover, the vitality of consumer activism likely dissipates once "fair trade" measures sufficiently gain ground in transnational subcontracting practices – no small achievement, to be sure, but a strategy with a due date. Consumer citizenship, after all, is subtly linked to the more exalted version of economic citizenship comprised of transnational business actors.

We might want to disrupt this relationship by imagining other spaces for agency where imperfect citizens of contemporary market societies can oppose economic globalization, not merely making it more humane. One possibility resides in local self-government, in provincial, state, and municipal forms of government. This strategy is opportunistic of neoliberal forms of governance, promoted by institutions like the World Bank, which champion the devolution of political power to subnational units (World Bank 1997). The next section explores local self-government as offering a site for alternative citizenship practice.

## SUBNATIONAL CITIZENSHIP

Local self-government reflects arrangements that divide authority between national and the subnational political units. This is a version of federalism which has some resonance in contemporary political thought

(Hirst 1994; Taylor 1993: 107) and that was best articulated by the British 'political pluralists' in the early part of the twentieth century. The pluralists formulated an alternative conception to that of the unified British Crown. The state, they argued, is one of the myriad of associations and groups – both territorial and nonterritorial – that aspire to secure the allegiance of citizens. The individual, wrote Harold Laski, "is a point towards which a thousand associations converge" (Laski 1919: 92).

Laski's understanding of citizenship drew on the Aristotelian notion of self-rule, for it was in these sites of associational activity that self-government was learned and practiced. It was not at its highest and most central peaks – in the figure of the Crown – that politics was lived, rather, it was on the shop floor, in local government, or in the halls of the university. All of this associational activity exposed the federal underpinnings of society and it was the task of modern political authority to recognize this fact of federalism.

The pluralists admitted that political life was not entirely constituted by subnational associations. There are commonalities of interest that need coordination by the national state. The satisfaction of basic needs – like food, education, clothing, and shelter, for instance – could be organized by centralized political authority. In Laski's decentralized federation, the role of the central state was to guarantee the provision of essential necessities that sustained life (Laski 1938: 69). The central state would not promote the development of national identity, rather, it would facilitate participation in the local sites that forged more meaningful associations. Identities, in contrast to work in cultural studies, were formed outside of the calculus of consumption.

Does devolution through federal forms provide any kind of antidote to the regime of economic citizenship? If Eric Hobsbawm is right, the national subunit poses no threat to transnational forces. Though smaller political units are potentially better able than large ones to narrow the distance between ruler and ruled, they are less capable of responding to decisions taken by nonstate entities, like transnational corporations (Hobsbawm 1996: 63–5). Subnational units may also offer political orientations fully consonant with the regime of economic citizenship. Whatever the political orientation of the government in power locally, they will be practically as bound by the strictures of the investment and trading rules regime as their national government. Proposals to devolve power to local institutions, then, fit well with neoliberal institutional design, the political project associated with economic globalization. Sending authority downward from central political institutions helps to keep national political power at bay.

But subnational units, like states, provinces, and cities, also provide discursive sites with which to explore political alternatives. This is particularly significant at a time when national governments are dominated by that branch of the state concerned with promoting trade and investment, a goal to which all other departments of government are rendered subordinate (Sassen 1997: 22–3). The pluralist image of government exploits the potential for disunity within the state structure, including its subnational parts. Rather than being irreducibly unified in its objectives, the state is viewed as being comprised of a plurality of institutions each of which exhibits a strategic selectivity with regard to different political actors – individuals, business firms, and groups (Jessop 1990: 260). It makes sense, then, that local government will provide important openings to pursue oppositional politics. If national governments, Castells writes, "tend to focus on managing the strategic challenges posed by the globalization of wealth, communication, and power," they will permit "lower levels of governance to take responsibility for linking up with society by managing everyday life's issues, so as to rebuild legitimacy through decentralization" (1997: 272). Individuals and groups with few resources are able to mobilize at low cost and place pressure on local political actors who may be more responsive than national actors to these political inputs. Once "this decentralization of power occurs," Castells postulates, "local and regional governments may seize the initiative on behalf of their populations, and may engage in developmental strategies vis-à-vis the global system, eventually coming into competition with their own parent states" (1997: 272).

This, arguably, was one of the phenomenon at work in the fight against the MAI. At the same time that the Canadian government aggressively pursued a multilateral agreement for the protection of investment at the OECD, the provincial government of British Columbia undertook a full-scale examination of the MAI holding lengthy hearings and issuing a report in opposition to the federal stance. Numerous major Canadian municipalities issued resolutions expressing concern about the MAI's potential impact on local government authority with regard to such matters as land use planning and government procurement. The US Western Governors Association commissioned a detailed study of the MAI which resulted in calls for the modification of the text so as to preserve state legislative authority in a wide variety of areas (Stumberg 1998). None of these actions alone threatened to destabilize economic globalization's regime of rules and institutions, though they gave effective expression to a growing unease with its manifestation in the MAI.

In another such instance, Massachusetts' selective purchasing law challenged the military regime in Burma via the purchasing power of a large US state. Massachusetts, along with twenty-one other state and local governments, mandated that subordinate agencies not purchase goods and services from enterprises that conducted business with the brutal military regime of Myanmar, formerly known as Burma (Stumberg 2000: 110). Many state and local governments in the United States have enacted "selective purchasing" laws that target regimes in Nigeria, Indonesia, China, Burma, and even Switzerland (Winston 1998). Most are modeled on antiapartheid laws of the 1980s, when nineteen states and sixty-two local governments participated in state purchasing boycotts (Stumberg 1998: 543). Like the university-based consumer boycott movement, Burma laws have been initiated in many college towns, though the cities of New York, San Francisco, and Los Angeles joined in the fight. They are a species of collective sub-national engagement with international issues labeled the "municipal foreign policy movement" (Frug and Barron 2006: 27).

The EU and Japan filed complaints with the WTO claiming that the Massachusetts law violated the 1994 GPA, forbidding states from using noneconomic criteria in bidding for government contracts. At the same time, the National Foreign Trade Council, a consortium of US businesses, thirty-four of whom were on the state's restricted purchase list of companies doing business in Burma, challenged the constitutionality of the Massachusetts law (Greenhouse 2000). At the US Supreme Court, Justice Souter, writing for the majority, found that the state law was preempted by a federal law entitling the president to control economic sanctions against Burma. By virtue of the supremacy clause, federal law preempted state law where the state measure "stands as an obstacle to the accomplishment of Congress's full objectives under the Act." The state law subverted the intention of Congress to pursue a less restrictive course of action, as the president was delegated wide discretion over the course sanctions against Burma would take. Though the national and state law sought common ends, they deployed "conflicting means." The court described the state law as undermining the president's capacity to act and to "speak for the Nation with one voice in dealing with other governments." The decision significantly is at odds with the general orientation of the court's jurisprudence with regard to states' rights. As Tushnet notes, the court usually has preferred to narrow the scope of national authority rather than to widen it at the expense of state power (2000: 14).[3]

The court did not go so far, as did lower courts, as to deny to states the capacity to pursue foreign policy objectives. Rather than granting a broad federal power of preemption, the court confined the decision to the specific facts of the case. The thrust of the decision, however, is to make it less likely that these kinds of state or municipal laws will have as beneficial an effect. Though there may be little direct investment by US-based companies in Burma, Stumberg has documented how they can indirectly benefit from the abuse of human rights (Stumberg 2000: 183). In which case, states now will be limited in the range of measures they can pursue by way of local response. In Stumberg's estimation, allowable measures might include selective purchasing directed only at a few specific companies, or nonprocurement measures like the requirement of business disclosure, shareholder resolutions to develop standards with regard to corporate conduct, and political speech, such as resolutions condemning violations of human rights in Burma (Stumberg 2000: 130). These alternatives are likely to prove less successful than the broad selective purchasing laws taken up by Massachusetts and others. Yet the gains could have been significant: state governments spent US $730 billion on procurement in 1996 while the federal government spent only US $199 billion (Stumberg 2000: 117). Consumer power through procurement – representing the purchasing power of subnational political communities – likely has been removed from the arsenal in the United States and for those states party to the GPA (Frug and Barron 2006: 28).[4] In an age of economic globalization, one could have predicted the result in the Massachusetts Burma law case. It is to be expected that globalization will require national governments to "rein in their subnational units to the extent that subnational law might interfere with transnational operation" (Tushnet 2000: 14). Other sorts of, more congenial, municipal engagement with the transnational, such as tourism or trade promotion, are less likely to clash with these expectations.

Federalism poses a threat to economic citizenship in another direction. To the extent that political power is transferred not only downward but also upward, to new global forms of government, transnational corporate power might be more effectively tamed. These new forms of political power and authority – federal or confederal in design – could structure relations between citizens, states, and transnational corporations in ways that individual citizens and states, because of collective action problems, could not. David Held, for instance, contemplates a democratic cosmopolitan order of a confederal type along the lines of Kant's *Perpetual Peace* (Held 1995: 231). The EU is oft cited as an emergent constitutional order with a federal structure that can serve as a model for world government. Indeed, the European Parliament issued a joint five-committee report calling for the cessation of MAI negotiations until a review had been conducted of its implications (Mabey 1999: 65). As the debate around the "democratic deficit" in Europe shows, however, democratic accountability proportionately becomes more problematic the more power is transferred upward, even when mediated by the subsidiarity principle. Moreover, some commentators warn that the EU primarily is about the "free" European market, and much less about European citizenship. The reigning project of integration into "a single market without a single state" is not a democratic and federalist one, Streeck maintains (1995: 413–14; Greven 2000: 45). The movement toward a European Constitution, though derailed by reason of 2005 referenda results in France and the Netherlands, may yet succeed if it moves beyond the thin citizenship strategy of merely conferring rights without democracy on European subjects (Brunkhorst 2006).

## COMPUTER-MEDIATED CITIZENSHIP

I turn now to another variant of citizenship left to imperfect citizens of the North Atlantic economies. It underlies much of what has been discussed in so far as it is facilitative of the other possibilities for citizenship discussed above – the movement toward consumer boycotts has been aided substantially by it as have support for local oppositional movements like the one in Chiapas (Castells 1997). I am thinking here of technological innovations that have given rise to the Internet and other forms of computer-mediated communication. The impact of this technological revolution has been so profound that it should qualify, on its own, as a space within which the possibilities for citizenship can be pursued.

Although culturally specific to affluent societies with access to expensive computers and modems, computer-mediated communication is being made widely, if unevenly (Tobey 2006), available in North Atlantic societies and the Far East (Castells 1996: 345–51; Dorday and

Mellor 2001: 175). In order to participate in cyberspace communications, actors must have purchasing power in order to secure access to the proper hardware and software, together with connectivity through Internet service providers. Complementary to this growing devolution is an ever-increasing concentration of media power, made manifest in the escalation of vertical and horizontal integration.[5] Measuring the growing concentration in the Internet sector's "core instrumentalities and infrastructure" in the United States, including hardware, software, Internet service provision, and content, Noam finds that there are "pronounced horizontal and vertical trends of concentration" in this sector (2003: 12). If Apple is known as a hardware and software provider, for instance, it now dominates as a music-content provider and if Google is reliably known as a search engine it also increasingly provides content and software. The spread of new technologies "world wide" by these powerful economic players fits well the narrative of inexorable movement associated with economic globalization.

The computer revolution remains a highly ambiguous phenomenon, however. Beck describes it as "creat[ing] proximity over distance, and distances within proximity" (2000: 74). It is not solely an individuating activity, however, as one connects up with networks of people through computer bulletin boards or the worldwide web, devolving authority and generating counterpublics with the participation of an ever-growing number of users. In this way, computer technology is a global phenomenon generating, some argue, "virtual communities" of users (Rheingold 1993). Summarizing the empirical data on the impact of the Internet on social relations, Benkler observes not so much the generation of new communities as a "thickening of preexisting relations with friends, family and neighbors" and "the emergence of greater scope for limited purpose, loose relationships" (2006: 357). Where transnational political mobilization is attempted, new technologies give rise, it is argued, to a new "global civil society" (Beck 2000). The Internet, some have claimed, both "decentres and continues citizenship in a different form" (Smith and Smythe 1999: 87).

These sorts of claims about the impact of technology on citizenship practices were heard in the aftermath of the successful campaign to defeat the MAI. As discussed in Chapter six, the MAI was a compendium of investment rules being negotiated at the OECD by its twenty-nine member states. The cynical intention of these states was to encompass the widest range of protections for foreign investment into one agreement – building on the NAFTA model in this regard – which countries in the so-called developing world would then be pressured to adopt as their own (Picciotto 1999). In this way, the OECD-led agreement would set global standards in investment protection without having to dilute the text to appease the sentiments of less-affluent countries. The draft agreement far exceeded NAFTA in terms of the scope of its protections and, generally, as concerns the disciplines it imposed on member states (one exception is discussed in Chapter six). It was described by some as "NAFTA on steroids" or "the EU on crack" (Vallely 1999).

Negotiations in Paris came to halt and then were suspended entirely in November 1998 as a result of a number of factors: there was a measure of resistance to the agreement in the US Congress while the French delegation withdrew from the negotiating table over cultural concerns. The MAI's spectacular failure most often was attributed to the coordinated action of citizen organizations in Canada, the United States, France, New Zealand, and elsewhere. In an unprecedented transnational campaign, citizen groups successfully cast the MAI as the egregious eclipse of democratic rights by corporate rule (Clarke and Barlow 1997). Critical to the success of the anti-MAI campaign was the Internet. This is how the lead Canadian government negotiator William Dymond understood events (Dymond 1999: 50) as have some social activists (Notes from Nowhere 2003: 65). Feature stories in the British *Independent on Sunday* described "How the Web Saved the World" (Vallely 1999) and, in the Canadian *Globe and Mail*, "How the Net Killed the MAI" (Drohan 1998). Even a careful analyst like Sassen described mobilization against the MAI as "largely a digital event" (2006: 339). In their study of the campaign to oppose the MAI, Smith and Smythe conclude that, though NGOs were not solely responsible for the defeat of the MAI, Internet technology "contributed to the capacity of groups to communicate, to quickly mobilize, and widely disseminate critical information outside the control of national elites." In these ways, they write, the Internet facilitated and enhanced the "growth of a global civil society and global citizenship" (Smith and Smythe 1999: 101).

Confining the discussion solely to claims about the capacity of the Internet to generate new forms of citizenship around resistance to the MAI, this assessment seems overblown. First, the Internet did not create the network of activists, led by the International Forum on Globalization (IFG), which helped to mobilize the fight against the MAI. Face-to-face meetings between national leaders developed the trust necessary to undertake the transnational campaign (as in the Seattle WTO protests [Bennett 2005: 145]). Maude Barlow, head of the council of Canadians and a member of the board of directors of the IFG, disagrees that the MAI killed the Internet; rather, "We killed it using the Internet as a tool" (Johnston and Laxer 2003: 62). Opposition to the MAI more effectively was organized at the national level (Diebert 2002). According to Tony Clarke of the Polaris Institute and a member of the IFG Board, even with the coordinated action of the network of international NGOs, the transnational movement "was gradually finding itself losing its ground to the country-based campaigns ... where the real strength was" (Johnston and Laxer 2003). The Internet was facilitative, then, of politics going on at local and national levels (Van Aelst and Walgrave 2005). It helped to coordinate collective action but did not dislodge the traditional politics of contention (Tilly and Tarrow 2007: 13).

The campaign, as it emerged, focused on putting pressure on the national governments negotiating the draft MAI to withdraw their delegations. This describes well what happened in Canada, which provided an effective home base for opposition to the MAI. The release of the draft text to the *Globe and Mail* by Tony Clarke of the Polaris Institute on April 3, 1997, precipitated frontpage headlines (Eggertson 1997).[6] Canada's short-lived experience with NAFTA's investment rules proved instructive to activists in Canada – particularly the Ethyl Corporation claim discussed in Chapter four – which was then communicated to the network of organizations based in other countries. Canadian opposition to the MAI was sufficiently effective that the federal government considered it necessary to hold Parliamentary hearings on the agreement in December 1997 under the auspices of the Standing Committee on Foreign Affairs and International Trade. The committee's report asked that Canada's negotiators ensure protection for Canadian culture, the environment, labor standards, health, education, and social services provided by both levels of government (Canada, House of Commons 1997b).

Nevertheless, the committee was not convinced that the MAI posed any greater threat to the regulatory capacity of the state than that which already existed under Canadian law. The committee agreed with the testimony of Canada's chief negotiator William Dymond on this point. If there was a chilling effect on regulatory innovation, Dymond maintained, it surely arose because of the right of corporations to sue under Canadian law (Canada, House of Commons 1997a). This was manifestly incorrect, at least as regards the takings rule. As we saw in Chapter four, Canadian law does not protect property owners in the event of regulatory action that significantly impairs an investment interest (*Mariner Real Estate* 1999).

Negotiations bogged down not just because of the stronger reservations and exceptions that Canada was now seeking. The failure of President Clinton to get fast track authority from Congress to finalize the agreement together with the resolute objections of the French delegation to the draft text helped to undermine the proceedings. Ultimately, it was the unilateral withdrawal of France from the table, on the grounds that its requested cultural exemption would not be accommodated, that put a halt to the negotiations.[7]

It cannot fairly be said, then, that the Net killed the MAI. Nor can it be said that, in the fight to oppose the MAI, the Internet generated a new form of "global citizenship." Rather, it was a confluence of events, including the coordinated action of national social movements communicating easily over the Internet, which resulted in the death of the agreement. It was a "campaign," rather than a new site of citizenship, that was facilitated by the Internet (Armstrong and Moulitsas 2006: 172; Tarrow 2005: 138). This is a species of coordinated activity in which "local initiatives become part of a global network of activism" but which do not lose their "focus on specific local struggles" (Sassen 2003: 12, 2006: 375). This is no version of global citizenship, Sassen reminds us, for actors "may well remain domestic and particularistic in their orientation" but it does represent, for her, a nascent form of global politics "through the knowing multiplication of local practices" (2003: 13, 2006: 366).

Each of the three possible forms of citizenship examined in this chapter do not significantly undermine, indeed may correspond well to, the rules and structures of economic globalization. Consumer citizenship remains a viable, but constrained, route to opposition that requires purchasing power. Wired citizenship similarly facilitates coordinated political action within and across specific locales, but there remains some question of whether these mobilizing effects can endure beyond short-run particular campaigns. Subnational citizenship remains not only the most promising but also the most difficult vehicle for opposition. Both national and transnational rules help to suppress this kind of opposition. Exercises of subnational citizenship political power are enabled, however, to the extent that they concern matters that do not threaten the imperatives of economic globalization. As the World Bank (1997) would prefer, local governments should be entrusted with the ability, for instance, of contracting out to private actors for the provision of basic services but they should not be entrusted with the ability of taking a position that would impede the progress toward privatization. Each site helps to facilitate political action both inside and outside of formal national political systems, but the case of the MAI is instructive: it suggests that the governing "community of fate" for many activists opposing economic globalization remains the national state.

Though we should be cautious about the prospects of national states resisting the pressures associated with economic globalization, it is the interstate system itself that is constructing the legal regime of rules and structures that bind states to these predetermined and limited forms of politics. States, consequently, have the capacity to undo that which is being done. There is no better example of this than the day the French delegation left the MAI negotiating table in Paris. While negotiations had been stalled due to coordinated social movement action, public pressure, and US waffling, the withdrawal of France effectively terminated discussions. States still have the power to say "no."

For those concerned with the problems of democracy, self-government, and the future of the redistributive state, the regime of market citizenship presents a bleak picture. It is, of course, only one conception of citizenship vying for supremacy, though the economic and social processes associated with market citizenship render it a powerful and profound one. As Stephen Gill reminds us, however, "we are still a long way from an approximation of a pervasively neoliberal world order where market discipline is virtually automatic, where state forms have become more fully marketized and commodified in outlook, and where social identities and interests have become reduced to the formula: self equals rational economic person" (Gill 1996: 210). There continue to be spaces in which political action, the pursuit of rights, and a sense of community and identity – some of the key markers of citizenship – can be realized, but not fully. Not so long as the regime of economic citizenship is "fixed, fast-frozen" in the realm of quasiconstitutional law, prohibiting and constraining the possibility of imagining alternative futures.

# CHAPTER EIGHT

# THE RULE OF LAW

How we represent the phenomenon associated with economic globalization matters, for it affects how we "interpret and then act with respect to the world" (Harvey 1990: 205). The rapid circulation of capital freed from the confines of the local and the territorial, mediated via new communication technologies, compressing both time and space – these are the sorts of things we ordinarily associate with the term "economic globalization." Analysts of globalization seem drawn to these themes of high-speed interconnectedness, to uncontainable and unrestrainable economic processes. Benjamin Barber maintains, for instance, that there is not now a new world order but a "global disorder," in which economic actors are free to wreak havoc in an anarchic world (Barber 2002). Scheuerman describes the high-speed global economy as one where powerful transnational forces rely "overwhelmingly on ad hoc, discretionary, closed, and non-transparent legal forms" to facilitate movement across time and space. These arbitrary legal forms are "fundamentally inconsistent with a minimally defensible conception of the rule of law" (Scheuerman 1999a: 3).

Under the thrall of the compression of time and space, analysts overlook the fact that economic globalization is not as much about producing uncertainty as about locking in regulatory frameworks, freezing existing distributions of wealth, and securing certainty for already affluent economic interests. The legal regimes associated with economic globalization are concerned with pinning states down, through the guise of international economic law, to a narrow field of political possibilities. This political economy of certainty is being secured, in part, via the establishment of a transnational regime for the protection and promotion of foreign investment that I have been describing in this book, a regime constituted by the web of interlocking and legally binding agreements intended to provide the most stringent legal protections for foreign investment abroad.

Legal protection for foreign investment is concerned less with movement than with rootedness (though freedom to move and establish investment interests is of some importance) (Sauvé and Schwanen 1996). The investment rules regime is intended to protect established investments abroad far into the future by locking countries into predictable regulatory frameworks. The objective is to bind states to a version of economic liberalism, to impose the discipline of the "rule of law" on state regulation of markets – domestic legal rules thereby are rendered predictable and certain. This rule-of-law regime promotes economic liberty, mandates equal treatment or "nondiscrimination," fair and equitable treatment, and prohibits expropriation or measures "tantamount to" expropriation. These are legal rules intended to slow down or paralyze certain political processes.

The rule-of-law ideal, admittedly, is exceedingly pliable. Tamanaha has identified three familiar themes that run through the rule-of-law tradition. The first and broadest understanding of the rule of law is that of government limited by law: that government must play by the rules it lays down (2004: 115). Second, are those rules associated with formal legality. Broken down into their constituent elements, they include publicity, equality, generality, nonretroactivity, and access to judicial review (2004: 119). The third Tamanaha associates with the idea of the "rule of law, not man" (2004: 133) – that impartial judges, rather than partial and self-interested political actors, will interpret and apply legal norms and procedures. This chapter focuses mostly on the cluster of rules associated with formal legality and, in particular, the requirements of equality and generality: that legislative action is limited to the enactment of general legal pronouncements directed at no specific economic actors. Hayek championed these requirements by mandating that states enact general rules directed at no one particular person – states only are entitled to lay down the "Rules of the Road," not to "order people where to go" (Hayek 1944: 74, 944). Contemporary trade law, it has been argued, similarly is in need of the corrective treatment offered by the "rule of law."[1] John Weekes, Canada's former ambassador to the WTO, invokes Hayek's formulation when he claims that the world trading system lays down the "rules of the road for international trade" and ensures that "the rule of law prevails in an important area of international relations" (Weekes 1999: 33). I argue, in the first part of this chapter, that the investment rules regime is intended precisely to institute rule-of-law disciplines by insulating key aspects of economic life from the pressures of majoritarian politics.

The "rule of law" is an antidote prescribed not only by international trade law scholars but also by critical theorists like Scheuerman (1999a). If it is correct to claim that a regime for the protection of foreign investment is being erected under the guise of the rule of law, might it not be worthwhile to transfigure the rule of law so as to thwart dominant neoliberal understandings? E. P. Thompson famously described the rule of law as being a "cultural achievement of universal significance" (Thompson 1975: 265). Operating on the "plane of the universal" (Hunt 1990: 321; Gramsci 1971: 371), the rule of law remains a resource available to social movements to countervail the power of dominant social and economic forces. The rule of law thereby becomes an arena of struggle and contestation (Bartholomew and Hunt 1990: 51; Thompson 1975: 262–5)[2] in which transnational corporate power can be reigned in (Picciotto 1998). The "Tobin Tax," intended to slow down the movement of capital by attaching a small fee on all currency transactions worldwide (Helleiner 1993), is one such instance where corporate restlessness might be tamed.[3]

There are interesting affinities between this kind of proposal for the rule of law and debates amongst Weimar legal theorists in the early part of the twentieth century. The Weimar Republic Constitution – Germany's first democratic constitution resulting, ultimately, in the rise and fall of the Third Reich – attempted to reconcile economic liberal with social democratic and corporatist constitutional formulations. Responding to reactionary and conservative interpretations of the Weimar constitutional order by Carl Schmitt and others, the critical theorist Franz Neumann formulated an understanding of the rule of law and its requirement of "generality." Neumann argued that the significance of the rule of law, in the context of widespread social and political inequality, was to freeze existing distributions of power and wealth (Neumann 1937). Neumann and labor lawyer Otto Kircheimer insisted that the Weimar Constitution, rather than constituting the bourgeois legal order, exemplified the "social rule of law" (Kircheimer 1930). The function of the social rule of law was to uncover and rectify socioeconomic relations of domination and subordination, to realize what Neumann called "social freedom" or "self-determination" (Neumann 1930: 39).[4] Under conditions of democratic pluralism, the Weimar Constitution condoned departure from the formal requirements of the rule of law by permitting, among other things, the redistribution of private property. This interpretive move – shifting the rule of law from nineteenth-century understandings rooted in economic liberalism to social democratic formulations dedicated to "economic freedom" of the laboring classes – ultimately failed. Scheuerman similarly promotes the formal requirements of the rule of law as a means of taming transnational production in the global economy.

Neumann's diagnosis of the rule of law in conditions of what he called "monopoly capitalism" resonates in today's integrated and interconnected world where the disjunctures between rich and poor, both within and across national states, is intensifying. Even accepting that the rule of law remains a powerful resource open to contestation, an embrace of the formal requirements of equality and generality in conditions of wide and concentrated disparities of wealth is not entirely mindful of the lessons of Weimar. A contemporary insistence upon satisfying formal legal requirements may have similar effects as in Weimar, I argue in the second part, by limiting the capacity of democratic publics to mitigate the negative effects of economic globalization. I turn first to a discussion of the late nineteenth-century genealogy of the contemporary rule of law.

THE NEOLIBERAL RULE OF LAW

I have argued in earlier parts of this book that the principal legal rules for the protection of foreign investment are intended to freeze politics and inhibit the imagination of alternative futures. Likened to a new form of constitutionalism, the regime inhibits the possibilities for political action by enacting binding constraints, in the form of general legal principles, on the ability of states to intervene in the market. These rules operate both outside of states – as independent legal regimes that discipline state action – and within, through the agency of constitutional and statutory reform and oftentimes judicial review.

The investment rules regime purports to institute the "rule of law" in the domain of foreign investment. National governments are cabined by a variety of legal restraints. Not only are legal rules rendered more transparent, accessible, and prospective – features usually associated with the rule of law – but legal regulation of foreign investment is made more secure by the requirements of equality, generality, and access to judicial review. It is these elements of the rule-of-law idea, and its relationship to late nineteenth-century constitutional thought, that is emphasized here. The requirements of equality and generality preclude singling out any one interest for special treatment – the burden or benefit of the law must apply generally and to no one specifically. This is precisely the prevailing understanding of the takings rule: it is a rule designed to ensure that, when government undertakes a public program of action, it does not leave "associated costs disproportionately concentrated upon one or a few persons" (Michelman 1967: 1165). Radin has noted that the takings rule poses a crisis of sorts for the ideal of the rule of law "because no one has been able to bring the issue [of what constitutes a taking] satisfactorily under a general rule or a regime of general rules" (1993: 160). That is, as there is no certainty, predictability, or generality to the rule as it has developed in the United States, the takings rule itself cannot satisfy the prerequisites of the rule of law. It is ironic, then, that investors will insist on a rule limiting government action which lacks many of the attributes of the rule of law.

Premised on a distrust of legislative majorities (McGinnis and Movsevian 2000), there are clear affinities between the contemporary rule-of-law project and its antecedents in the late nineteenth century. The "rule of law" in this earlier period maximized liberty by delineating clear boundaries between impartial, public-regarding regulation, and partial or "class" legislation (Gillman 1993: 10; Sugarman 1983: 108). Legislation on behalf of a "temporary, or factious majority" incongruent with the interests of the larger public could be checked by the rule of law enforced by judges (Dicey 1890: 506). As a genre of "classical legal thought" (Horwitz 1992; Kennedy 1980), the rule-of-law idea confidently distinguished between the private and the public, carving out a realm of personal liberty free of public interference – free from the "unrestricted power of wage earners" (Dicey 1920: 310).

Oxford legal scholar Albert Venn Dicey famously outlined the rule-of-law idea in his *Introduction to the Study of the Law of the Constitution* (1885). It was represented by a series of "kindred conceptions" foundational to English constitutionalism (1909: 183). According to the first, England was governed by nonarbitrary "regular law." This supremacy of law meant that laws properly established had the force of law. Second, legal rules governed all equally without exemption, including the law makers so that, as we usually say, no one is above the law. Third, the constitution was the sum of the "ordinary law of the land," including decisions made by courts in the ordinary course of private litigation. This last conception best captured the English sense of legality, a trait which he, and Alexis de Tocqueville before him, had observed also in the United States (1908: 183).

In his study, Dicey expressed great admiration for the US Constitution. Federalism in the United States ensured "weak government." It was "unfavourable to the interference or to the activity of government" and so was "incompatible with schemes for wide social innovation" (1908: 169). Coupled with a prohibition on certain legislative enactments – such as the inability of states to "impair the obligation of contract" – the US Constitution fostered a spirit of legality that guaranteed the widest berth for liberty. As America afforded "the best example of a conservative democracy" (Dicey 1886: 53), this model for checking legislative excesses was of great interest to Dicey and other "educated Englishmen" of his time (Maine 1909: 110). Dicey would not go so far, however, as to recommend federalism and a bill of rights for England – this was "not the work of a day or of a year," he cautioned (1890: 506). Rather, judicial review through the guise of the rule of law provided a means of policing democratic despotism (Schneiderman 1998). Parliament ordinarily was considered supreme, but as it spoke through statute, "from the moment that Parliament has uttered its will as lawgiver, that will becomes subject to the interpretation put upon it by the judges of the land" (1909: 338). So the rule of law by judges ensured that all Parliamentary enactments were subject to the careful scrutiny of a conservative judiciary. As Dicey explained elsewhere, this oversight role would be performed by persons, for the most part, "of a conservative disposition" (1920: 364). It followed that judges would be the protectors of individual rights as against encroachments by the state (Hibbits 1994: 18). This reconceptualization of the judicial role through the rule of law emerged, for Dicey, as a prophylactic for the prevention of class rule (Sugarman 1983: 109–10).

A preoccupation with the maximization of liberty through boundary policing – a feature common to classical legal thought of the late nineteenth century – was prevalent in US constitutional writing as well (Horwitz 1992). Though anxiety with coerced economic leveling has animated much US constitutional thought, it featured prominently in the work of University of Michigan scholar Thomas M. Cooley. Cooley admired greatly the English common law record of "freedom, order, enterprise and thrift" (1868: 21). American constitutionalism, Cooley maintained, should be construed in light of the "great fountain" that was the common law. According to the common law, special privileges were "obnoxious" and so "[e]quality of rights, privileges, and capacities unquestionably should be the aim of the law" (1868: 390–1). "Security can be found only in general principles," Cooley maintained – "[c]onstitutional law can know no favoritism" (1878: 239). Constitutional limitations, like the requirement of "due process of law," meant that "every citizen shall hold his life, liberty, and immunities under the protection of general rules which govern society" (1868: 354).

Cooley admitted that states could regulate private business so as to protect the public from harmful nuisance under the "police power." These regulations, too, ordinarily should be addressed to no one in particular. There would be exceptions, however, such as when the state grants special privileges for the performance of some activity in which the public has an interest – the operation of a bridge, pier, or warehouse, for instance (1878: 252). Then there will be occasions, rare for Cooley, in which interference with private right is accomplished not through general rules but through particularistic regulation. This is never more the case than when the state grants a monopoly or exclusive right of franchise, when some public interest otherwise cannot be realized than through public delegation to private authority (1878: 260). On these occasions "equality of right under the government [defensibly] is disturbed" (1878: 260).

If the state could grant exclusive authority to carry out some grand scheme on behalf of the public interest, it could never do so with regard to the "ordinary occupations of life." Nor should the state intervene in the case of what Cooley calls "virtual monopolies," where by "superior industry, enterprise, skill and thrift" a person has secured special advantages due solely to their own initiative (1878: 266, 268). On these occasions, constitutional limitations dictate that the state cannot interfere with private business under the pretense of public interest. The "fundamental rule," according to Cooley, was that the state refrain from interfering with individuals reaping the benefits of competitive capitalism (1878: 256). This was particularly so in the case of contracts of employment, which should be protected "with the same jealous care" as protection from "unlawful confinement behind bolts and bars" (1878: 270). This anxiety with partial legislation culminated famously in the *Lochner* case (1905), where a New York state law limiting the hours of work for bakery workers was declared unconstitutional. According to Justice Peckham, the law could not be justified on any basis other than as a "mere meddlesome" interference with individual rights and so amounted to an unreasonable interference with freedom of contract.

The contemporary rule-of-law project does not go so far as to claim a freedom from interference in contracts of employment (much as contemporary US takings jurisprudence does not, for the most part, resurrect *Lochner*). Rather, it seeks to restrain state regulatory capacity to unreasonably upset expected returns on investment. As Rubins and Kinsella put it, "when local mandatory laws … make doing business more costly or difficult" (2005: 50), investment rules can step in to mandate state immobilization in certain sectors. The case of *CMS Gas v. Argentina*, discussed in Chapter three, well represents this aspect of the regime at work. This is one of approximately thirty investment disputes faced by Argentina in the wake of the collapse of the peso in 2000. The tribunal in CMS, it will be recalled, held Argentina to the most exacting standards in the treatment of foreign investment in circumstances comparable to the Great Depression of the 1930s. According to the state, stability and predictability could not take priority over measures for societal self-protection in the wake of an economic meltdown. Foreign investors, therefore, were expected to share in the economic disruption experienced by all other economic sectors in Argentina. The investment tribunal disagreed, likening the gas transportation license issued to CMS in Argentina's privatization heydays as if it were a "guarantee" which the state would have to honor irrespective of the "collapsing economic situation" (*CMS Gas* 2005: paras 161, 165). The economic realities on the ground provided no valid legal excuse for Argentina's failure to comply with investment rules strictures (*CMS Gas* 2005: para. 212).[5]

This desire to tame state action is not confined to the investment rules regime. Jackson helpfully distinguishes between power-oriented and rule-oriented approaches in diplomacy and sees a gradual evolution from a power-based approach to a rules-based one. Jackson maintains that there is a strong argument to be made that, in international economic affairs, a rule-oriented approach will be preferred "for its stability and predictability of governmental activity." (1997: 109–11, 2006: 88–90). This state of affairs has been achieved, according to Jackson and others, with the establishment of a world trade "constitution" under the WTO secured, above all, by "an intricate set of constraints imposed by a variety of 'rules' or legal norms" overseen by the WTO (Jackson 1997: 339, 2006: 205–6; Petersmann 2000). Even in the realm of customary international economic law (*lex mercatoria* or the law merchant) there is a thrust toward rule formation. Traditionally conceived as "vague and open-ended" (Scheuerman 1999a: 7), Dezalay and Garth (1996) describe a transnational struggle centered in the international arbitration centers of Paris and Geneva between the flexible, case-by-case determinations of *lex mercatoria* and a rigid, more predictable, rule-bound approach favored by Anglo-American trade lawyers. Dezalay and Garth report that the rule-of-law side is winning (1996: c. 4). Finally, the World Bank has linked "good governance" to the rule of law and its institutional supports that protect property and markets from "arbitrary government action" (World Bank 1997: 41, 99; Rittich 2002: 67). By arbitrary government action, the bank means not merely outright corruption but a range of activity including "unpredictable" rule making or "ad hoc regulations and taxes." Stability and predictability in legal rules and institutions, it is claimed, are the hallmarks of a successful developing market associated with the rule of law (North 1990). Increasing the number of checking points on domestic political processes via the rule of law – slowing down politics and restraining "constant legislative changes" (World Bank 1997: 100) – is the stated objective of the bank's good governance strategy. By subordinating political to economic processes, the bank makes clear that democratic politics are less important than securing the conditions for the entry of foreign direct investment.

Having a better appreciation of the contours of the investment rules regime and its "rule-of-law" aspirations, I turn next to debates amongst Weimar legal theorists concerning the *Rechsstaat* or the rule of law, the requirement of generality, and the protection of property rights. This account, once again, offers an alternative to the predominant neoliberal formulation of property rights and the rule of law. Despite the break from the constitutional past presented by the text of the Weimar Constitution, we find this alternative rule-of-law vision frustrated by a legal profession dearly attached to the idea of the rule of law as placing limits on government, rather than enabling state action.

## THE SOCIAL RULE OF LAW

The idea that positive state action must meet certain formal requirements – that laws should be nondiscriminatory and general in their operation – has a distinguished lineage in Western political and legal thought. Originating in the ethical ideal of the equality of all citizens, the modern variant has the rule of law performing a limiting function on state action. As Neumann describes it, "individual rights may be interfered with by the state only if the state can prove its claim by reference to a general law that regulates an indeterminate number of future cases." The rule of law prohibits retroactivity and insists on the strict separation of legislative from judicial powers (Neumann 1953: 200).

The rule of law performed a number of critical functions for Neumann, including an ethical role of promoting equality, an ideological role of masking private power, and an efficiency role ensuring that economic processes were rendered "calculable and predictable" (Neumann 1986: 213, 1937: 116). But legal rules were capable of undergoing functional alteration, and so Neumann explored the application of the rule of law in changing social and legal contexts. Every legal decree, Neumann wrote, "can remain under some circumstances unchanged for centuries, while the content and social meaning of a legal institution can experience decisive transformation" (Neumann 1930: 33). This was the case in so far as the rule of law and its requirement of generality were concerned.

The rule of law was intended to guarantee certainty and security in commercial relations in the context of competitive markets. The underlying foundation for the rule of law was "free competition" and the existence of a "large number of competitors of roughly equal strength who compete in a free market" (Neumann 1937: 116). If the state were to intervene in the market, it would have to do so in calculable and predictable ways so as to impair self-maximizing economic choices as little as possible. What should happen, however, if economic conditions shift from a market with roughly equal competitors to one where economic power is concentrated in the hands of the few – what Neumann called a situation of "monopoly capitalism"?[6] The rule of law, Neumann argued, "becomes absurd in the economic sphere if the legislator is dealing not with equally strong competitors but with monopolies which reverse the principle of the free market" (Neumann 1937: 127). Even Cooley admitted that in a "monopolistically organized system the general law cannot be supreme" (1878: 260). This is because "if the state is confronted only by a monopoly, it is pointless to regulate this monopoly by a general law" (Neumann 1937: 126). The law must regulate by way of "individual facts" rather than developing "general norms" (Neumann 1934: 71). In such a context, wrote Neumann, the "individual measure" becomes "the only appropriate expression of the sovereign power" (Neumann 1937: 126). Legal expressions of liberty thus "lose their significance" (Neumann 1931: 48) and the formal requirements of equality and generality of law are "destroyed" (Neumann 1934: 71).

Though structured to accommodate competition amongst roughly equal competitors, the legal system faced a situation of monopoly capitalism, a condition which began for Neumann with the constitution of the Weimar Republic in 1919. In an era of monopoly capitalism, laboring classes increasingly make "demands which can only be met at the cost of the property of the possessing bourgeoisie" (Neumann 1934: 71). Weimar legal institutions precisely were designed, Neumann urged, to promote a social-democratic conception of the rule of law, to secure the advancement of laboring persons. The Weimar Constitution thus mandated appropriately enacted and specific legal measures to address the context of monopoly capitalism – measures that would, in certain circumstances, interfere with the "liberty, property and security of the bourgeoisie" (Neumann 1930: 33). An incessant preoccupation with general principles, on the other hand, would "support the power position of the monopolies" by shielding private interests from the social reforms achievable by positive law (Neumann 1937: 131).

The effect of applying the rule of law and the requirement of generality in an environment of wide economic disparity is to bar interference with the existing distribution of wealth and power – it is to privilege the status quo and to "disguise [the] revival of natural law" through the rule of law, argued Neumann (1937: 127). This precisely was the consequence of constitutional interpretation urged by the reactionary legal theorist, Carl Schmitt (1926). Building on arguments made 2 years earlier by Heinrich Triepel (Triepel 1924 in Caldwell 1997: 148–53), Schmitt insisted that the term "equality before the law" in the Weimar Constitution entitled the legislature to create only general laws and not measures directed at specific individuals. Schmitt developed this thesis in a pamphlet responding to proposals to expropriate, via referendum, royal property owned by the monarchs of the former Länder (Caldwell 1997: 104–5; Scheuerman 1999b: 210). The proposed measures interfered with the independence of the judiciary and the right to fair trial,[7] argued Schmitt, by interceding in present and future litigation pending before the courts and by rendering judges superfluous and subordinate to government (Schmitt 1926: 10). The measures also violated the equality and property provisions of the constitution.[8] Expropriations could only be pursued if done on a "lawful basis" and, according to Schmitt, it was not "lawful" to intervene in specific, concrete cases (Schmitt 1926: 18). The principle of equality mandated, similarly, that legislators be prohibited from enacting situation-specific laws. As the bourgeois liberal legal order was founded upon the separation of powers and the principle of equality, these constitutional foundations mandated that laws only be general in their formulation (Schmitt 1993: 288–94). Otherwise, constitutional rights were secure only for those successful factions who had convinced the prevailing parliamentary majority to enact laws on their behalf. Schmitt reserved for the state the ability to enact nongeneral laws only in the exceptional case of a state of emergency, where constitutional rights are suspended (Schmitt 1927: 23).

Schmitt's coy professional legalism purported to defend the integrity of the Weimar Constitution. This was a legal opinion offered to "bourgeois democrats" that "takes the Weimar constitution seriously," Schmitt concluded in his pamphlet (Schmitt 1927: 26). Yet Schmitt had already undertaken a full-scale assault on liberal legal values in other work (Schmitt 1922, 1923). His arguments, Scheuerman notes, were "purely strategic" (Scheuerman 1999b: 211). The legal analysis nevertheless was consistent with Schmitt's approach to Weimar constitutional interpretation, which privileged political sovereignty – in so far as it gave expression to the unified will of a homogenous people (Schmitt 1923: 9) – over any surplus constitutional text (Scheuerman 1999b: c.3; Schmitt 1993: 267). The Weimar Constitution, according to Schmitt, gave expression to a bourgeois political order – to the liberal constitutional ideals of personal liberty, private property, and liberty of contract, commerce, and employment (Schmitt 1993: 263) – that was antecedent to any particular constitutional text (Preuss 1999: 158). Individual freedoms and even the rule of law were superfluous parts unless they promoted the strong underlying unity and homogeneity of the people (Bockenforde 1998: 44). If the "sovereign" ("he who decides on the exception") (Schmitt 1922: 5) is the "decisive entity" that represents this underlying homogeneity and defends the integrity of the "fighting collectivity" (Schmitt 1932: 39, 28), then the requirement of the "generality of laws" ultimately is empty. It is in this context, where politics is defined by a "friend-enemy" distinction, that Schmitt could claim that "all law is situational law" (Schmitt 1922: 13). Schmitt's legal opinion is not a defense, then, of the rule of law *simpliciter* but a strategic offensive against pluralist constitutional interpretation undermining an antecedent homogeneity which valued economic liberty. In this way, Schmitt's argument is intended precisely to limit state action in the economic sphere (Kennedy 2004: 139; Neumann 1937: 125).

Weimar-era courts enthusiastically took up this counsel and used the constitutional property clause to strike at all variety of state and municipal regulation of vested private rights (Caldwell 1997: 158).[9] According to Kircheimer, the courts "widened the expropriation concept to such an extent that the state has been made liable to pay compensation for every interference of private property" (Kircheimer 1969: 57, 1930: 122). For Weimar-era courts, expropriations requiring the payment of compensation included a law mandating the payment of a levy upon surrendering foreign exchange, a revenue law reducing the payment of dues owed to landowners by mine owners, and a law forbidding excavation of private lands (Caldwell 1997: 156–7; Kircheimer 1930). This was despite the qualified nature of property rights in the text, the social obligations property rights were intended to serve, and the constitutional mandate of the "socialization" of property. The Weimar property clause "dissolved the categories of the bourgeois constitutional schema," wrote Kircheimer (1930: 113). Neumann insisted that the constitution "was the creation of the working class" (Neumann 1930: 37) and that it was "indefensible to divorce the postulate of the generality of the law from the postulated social order" as Schmitt proposed (Neumann 1986: 24). The social-democratic part of the constitution was not mere surplusage but had substantive legal content. If the object of the property clause was not to secure private property but to secure "the advancement" of laboring people (Neumann 1930: 37), then it "runs counter to the essence of the Weimar constitution when laws which penalize an economically stronger class are in the name of justice rejected as arbitrary" (Kircheimer 1930: 108).

The property clause undoubtedly was intended to break down the public–private distinction, enable legislative intervention in economic matters, and signal that the economic status quo would not be entitled to privileged status in judicial interpretation. The "economic life" chapter of the Weimar Constitution, and its correlative interpretive approach of the "social rule of law," offered a novel institutional form for the transformation of legal and social practice. Despite the reasonably clear drafting effort (Caldwell 1997: 105) – indeed, as we saw in Chapter two, the Weimar property clause for this reason was used as a model in many Latin American Constitutions – the enterprise was thwarted by a number of factors, including reactionary legal scholars and a judiciary schooled in the value of free enterprise. Reminiscent of Anglo-American classical legal thought of the late nineteenth century, according to these authorities legislative interventions in the economy deserved the strictest of constitutional scrutiny (Horwitz 1992: c.1; Unger 1996: 24).

## TAMING THE RULE OF LAW

The rule-of-law project taken up by the investment rules regime seems, then, to perform similar functions as the rule of law did in the hands of the judges of Weimar Germany. The revival of rule-of-law rhetoric in contemporary times signals the restoration of classical legal thought, now in the guise of contemporary economic liberalism. The requirement of generality today aims to preserve the power position of transnational economic actors, often at the expense of state measures for societal self-protection (Polanyi 1944: 76). For this reason, Neumann's diagnosis of the rule of law in a regime of "monopoly capitalism" seems apt. We might liken "monopoly capitalism" to modern "corporate society" where giant business conglomerates and cartels dominate economic life (Cotterrell 1996: 456). While many of the social and economic conditions giving rise to Neumann's analysis are different – the Weimar Republic was in a state of constant crisis – it could be said that the economic field is dominated now more than ever by a small number of economic actors, originating mostly from the triad of North America, Europe, Japan, and, increasingly, China. Growing FDI, spurred on by privatization, vertical and horizontal integration in all aspects of production and distribution ("merger mania") results in highly concentrated levels of economic power.[10] This concentration of wealth also means increasing disparity both within and across national borders. According to recent U.N. Human Development Reports, the "greatest benefits of globalization have been garnered by a fortunate few" (UNDP 1997). The gap between the average citizen in the poorest and the richest states on the planet "is wide and getting wider" (UNDP 2005: 36–7). The three richest men on the planet, the UNHDP reports, have combined private assets larger than the GNP of the 48 poorest countries (UNDP 1998). "The level of inequality worldwide is grotesque," they conclude (UNDP 2002: 19). The landscape of the world economy, according to the UNCTAD, "has already become polarized" (UNCTAD 1997b: 82). An increasing divergence in global wealth suggests that, in

Neumann's time as in our own, the benefits of the rule of law have not accrued to the vast majority of the world's population.

So long as the contemporary situation is characterized by speed and uncertainty, instead of fixity and surety as in the case of protections for FDI, the structuration of economic globalization via the rule of law will go unnoticed. It is for these reasons that Scheuerman and others misrecognize the contemporary situation. What of taming economic globalization through the rule of law by placing legal limits on corporate activities so as to enhance personal security and strengthen economic and social standards (Scheuerman 1999a: 19)? This links up to proposals to reform investment rules so that they promote economic development which specifically advantages poor people in the South rather than simply enriching those in the North (Ghosh 2005). Mann and von Moltke, for instance, have developed a Model International Agreement on Investment for Sustainable Development which aims to "reconceptualize from the ground up" the investment rules regime (2005: v). Their model takes the "priorities of developing countries as its starting point" and explicitly recognizes the important regulatory role of governments in managing sustainable economic development (2005: v, 11).[11] What are the prospects of reforming the regime of investment rules in this direction, that is, from the ground up?

We might liken rules to resources open to counter claims which, when formulated in terms cognizable to a legal and political order, legitimates demands not previously acknowledged. The rule of law, it might be argued, is open to alternative formulations and constitutes thereby an arena of "struggle and contestation" for progressive action (Bartholomew and Hunt 1990: 50–1). We must be reminded, however, that the content of this resource is not neutral vis-à-vis the balance of class forces in society. The rules and institutions that give effect to the rule of law will have a "structural selectivity" (Jessop 1990; Bartholomew and Hunt 1990: 52). This means that legal regimes will privilege certain social actors while constraining the actions of others differentially. Social agents configure transformative strategies in light of the opportunities offered by this system of opportunities and constraints.

Has such a conjunctural moment arisen,[12] where the legal regime of investment rules are reformable in a direction which will limit corporate power more and state capacity less? This largely is a strategic question answerable only with reference to specific sociopolitical contexts. In the aftermath of the protests at the WTO ministerial meeting in Seattle, the claims of the labor and environmental movements to tame economic globalization are considered among the most serious challenges today facing the world trading and investment system.[13] Even after 9/11, resistance to the constraints of economic globalization continues to pose a challenge to the transnational regime for the regulation of state conduct (Wayne 2001). Road blocks on the way to a FTAA erected by Brazil and Argentina, among other states, signal a reluctance to bind political authority any further than is necessary to attract foreign investment. New prototypes in investment protections, such as an exemption for equality-promoting measures in South African BITs, signals an openness on the part of some states to revisiting the principles that lie behind standard investor protections. The United States has reformed its model treaty to allow greater scope for nondiscriminatory regulatory measures that may impact negatively on investment interests. There also is on the table a model for doing away entirely with investor-to-state disputes, as in the 2004 US-Australia free trade and investment agreement.

There are limits to this sort of openness. At the same time as the US reforms its investment treaty program to create greater scope for state action, it reinforces the constitutional underpinnings of the program, promoting the US model of constitutional limitations world wide. The US-Australia model appears to be of a singular sort. The Australian Department of Foreign Affairs and Trade explains the omission of an investor-to-state dispute mechanism on the basis of "the Parties' open economic environments," their "shared legal traditions, and the confidence of investors in the fairness and integrity of their respective legal systems." Other legal systems with which the United States recently has entered into treaties – Chile, Morocco, Jordan, Central America, Uruguay – are considered less trustworthy. These states, moreover, were not members of the 'coalition of the willing' that participated in the invasion of Iraq. They also are less likely to be home to foreign investors filing troublesome suits for regulatory takings against the United States.

The failure to remove agricultural tariff barriers in the Doha round, which would have opened up agricultural markets to developing and less-developed states, signals less than a full commitment to meeting the needs of developing states. The chilly reception given to the position advanced by the Group of 20 developing nations during the Doha round, led by India and Brazil, that protections remain in place for vulnerable subsistence farmers, suggests closed-mindedness about matters of trade that can spill over into related matters of investment (Blustein 2006).

There is further cause for concern. The appropriation of rule-of-law discourse so as to countervail transnational economic power leads to the danger of fortifying core elements of the investment rules regime at the expense of national initiatives to secure better living conditions for the less powerful – precisely the lesson that Neumann insists that we learn from Weimar-era legal debates. We have seen how, in Chapter five, the new South African constitution authorizes the state to undertake land and water reform so as to undo some of the economic evils of apartheid. Yet this constitutional objective likely runs afoul of the investment rules regime and its version of the rule of law. In Colombia, the constitution provides for privatization of state assets but on the condition that workers associations receive preference in the sale of those enterprises. As we saw in Chapter six, absent an express exception, this too likely offends the rules regime. These and other measures (often times not expressed in domestic constitutional text) require the utilization of "situation-specific" laws that directly or indirectly discriminate against foreign investors. The rule-of-law project expressed in the investment rules regime likely would prohibit them.

This is not to deny the appeal of the rule-of-law ideal to body politics in various parts of the world (Rodríguez 2001), or to suggest that the rule of law is "imprisoned within the historical circumstances of its origin" (Sypnowich 1999: 185). We might agree with Cotterrell that the rule of law has an ethical function to perform: that the rule of law provides "a minimum yardstick of social and political equality" but that it "cannot be the sole or even dominant guide for all state action in the corporate society" (Cotterrell 1995: 173; Raz 1970).[14] It is reasonable to expect that democratic publics will choose, some time soon, to countervail private economic power through legal means. So long as there is an absence of international democratic fora where transnational collective action can freeze and rollback current concentrations of economic power and guarantee social and economic minima, it also seems reasonable that citizens will look to national states as the appropriate vehicle to mitigate some of the deleterious effects of economic globalization. This legal regulation should exhibit some of the features attributed to the rule of law, with its constituent elements such as publicity, transparency, and procedural fairness, features associated with the elements of formal legality (Tamanaha 2004: 119). One can envisage a thinner version of the rule of law enabling measures for societal self-protection (Daniels 1995) in contrast to the more disabling and robust one promoted by rules and institutions of neoliberal globalization. The strategy is to rule through law, then, rather than to embrace rule-of-law discourse. We can assume that resulting legal obligations, following Habermas, will be premised on a system of rules that is respectful of the basic individual rights that facilitate public participation and democratic deliberation (1996: 125). In this way, employing the legal medium to achieve democratic self-rule promotes fairness and openness, the hoped-for consequences of so-called rule-of-law legal systems.

The objective here has been to mark the presence of a contemporary rule-of-law regime to protect and promote foreign investment that is intended to shield the market from the intrusion of vulgar democratic politics. It also has been to problematize the capacity of transforming the strong discourse of the rule of law (Bourdieu 1998: 95) at this juncture. While a rules-based trading and investment system seems a laudable objective, care must be taken in the reconstruction of a legal order that privileges the market over much else. In the transnational arena, the rule of law continues to serve the interests of a privileged few. These significant deficiencies in the transnational regime together with the stated objective of permanently rolling back the state in so far as it is an expression of deliberative public authority suggests that demo-cratic forces can do without rule-of-law rhetoric. It seems, at least, perilous to embrace it.

# CHAPTER NINE

# CONCLUSION: A WORLD OF POSSIBILITIES

I have argued the patterns of protection codified in the investment rules regime resemble national constitution patterns. The protection of investment protection through general legal entitlements enforceable by rights holders with access to international dispute settlement resembles the structure of rights protection found in the bills of rights of many national jurisdictions. I have argued, more specifically, that the investment rules regime replicates patterns of protection observable within US constitutional law. Though important parallels can be found in other national legal systems (the idea of the police power, for instance), the rules regime is better understood as modeled on, though more expansive in its protections than, the US constitutional experience.

The problem is that the rules regime draws on the wrong US experience. An alternative chapter in US history suggests a different kind of model, one where the state plays an active role in the development of a national economy. In the antebellum United States (the period roughly from 1800 to 1860), capital was scarce and the so the state, together with private partners, energetically constructed the infrastructure for a single national market. Constitutional law in this period, rather than blocking options and preserving vested interests, kept open the channels of change (Hurst 1956: 27).

The dominant narrative in US constitutional law moves in the other direction: beginning with the framers in 1787, the US constitutional experience primarily is understood as preserving the sacred rights of property and liberty (Scheiber 1989: 217). Underkuffler (2003) helpfully contrasts two conceptions of American property rights that have been competing for supremacy. In the first, "common" conception, property is understood as static and unyielding to collective power associated with politics (2003: 40). In the second, "operative" conception, change is envisaged "as part of the idea of property" (2003: 48). It is the operative conception of property, Underkuffler argues, that resolves takings claims in the United States, though it is the common and absolutist conception of property that is associated with the US constitutional idea of property. The "reigning paradigms of American politics," Novack writes, conspire to produce "a gross overemphasis on individual rights, constitutional limitations, and the invisible hand; and a terminal neglect of the positive activities and public responsibilities of American government over time" (1996: 7).

By examining this mostly forgotten period of social and legal change, other models for the successful pursuit of economic development materialize. Rather than understanding the contemporary legal scene as inevitable – conceiving of the modern world as pursuing a single, unceasing path, transpiring in open borders and free markets – we examine here counterfactuals that open up "multiple trajectories of possibility" (Gordon 1989: 97). Part one pursues one of the roads not yet taken. This repressed history – where the state played an active role as facilitator in the development of a national economy in conditions of capital scarcity – suggests a pattern of state behavior at odds with dominant discourse. This alternative discourse should facilitate discussions of an alternative rules regime modeled on experiences other than the dominant United States one. History, in this way, becomes a resource for imagining alternative futures in an age of economic globalization.

The commonly accepted objective of the investment rules regime is to promote inward direct investment for those countries without ready access to pools of capital. FDI is understood to be a viable means of attracting "scarce development capital" for the purposes of national economic development (Sauvé 1996: 41). By erecting barriers to state action – those which forestall the relaxation of investment rules strictures – together with unremitting enforcement of the highest standards for the protection of FDI, it is expected that investors will be attracted to locales otherwise neglected.

As the reach of investment rules regime continues to expand, however, few of the benefits expected to be gained by open borders and free-flowing investment, as I argued in Chapter two, have accrued to those countries rushing to embrace the strictures of the rules regime. As the negative impact of unrestrained market mechanisms is being felt in considerable parts the globe – through diminished purchasing power, declining employment levels, and growing disparities of wealth (Stiglitz 2002: 248) – a legal incapacity to usher in what Polanyi called the "double movement, " to the extent that these measures unreasonably impair investment interests, may be catastrophic for many people in the world.

Binding precommitment strategies – constitution-like rules – seem out of proportion, then, to the actual objectives of securing increased FDI. While surely providing high levels of stability to investment interests, they destabilize the functioning of democratic processes, represented by other constitutional rules. Given the relatively small percentage of FDI traveling South, it is correct to say, following Unger, that foreign investors exert "an influence out of all proportion to [their] size" (Unger 1998: 151).

It might be preferable, instead, to move away from investment protections that equate investment interests to constitutional property rights. By way of conclusion, I consider a couple of nonconstitutional arrangements that help to safeguard some of the interests of foreign investors but that do not unreasonably handcuff the operation of processes I have associated with democratizing constitutionalism.

ALTERNATIVE HISTORY

I have claimed that the investment rules regime is an instance of what Santos calls "globalized localism" – an example of local rules having successfully gone global (Santos 2002: 179). In this instance, the local rules are traceable back at least to classical legal conceptions of property rights dominant in the *Lochner* era, where clear and bright lines were presumed to exist between public and private purposes (Horwitz 1992). In this part, I take up another version of the local rule largely forgotten; a history that has been blocked by the dominant narrative about rights in the United States (Scheiber 1989: 217). I recover here a lost chapter: the so-called commonwealth period, running roughly from 1800 to 1860 (Hurst 1956: 53). The commonwealth idea refers to the promotion of the general interest through legislative reform, an idea prevalent in many states including in the leading jurisdiction of the Commonwealth of Massachusetts (Handlin and Handlin 1969: 30–1; Levy 1957: 305).

In the period before the American civil war, it was considered a reasonable-investment backed expectation that property rights would be limited by the state or its delegates in the interests of national development. Regulatory change in this kind of environment not only was expected, it was welcomed. Representative of this view was the dictum of an 1857 New Hampshire court: "Every man, when he embarks in any business or makes an investment of property, must do it at the risk of such changes as time and the progress of the age may introduce" (*Petition of Mt. Washington Road Co.* 1857: 146).

According to Hurst, property in this period was valued for its "dynamic" rather than its "static" features: property "in motion or at risk" was valued over property merely secure or at rest (1956: 182, 1964: 32). Legal rules consequently were designed and interpreted to enable the release of public and private energies putting property to optimally productive use. If property remained idle, it was susceptible to public control. A similar phenomenon could be observed in Latin America, as we saw in Chapter seven, where property was declared constitutionally to serve a public or "social function" (Hirschman 1965). Massachusetts Chief Justice Lemuel Shaw gave expression to this view: that (all property . . . is derived directly or indirectly from the government, and held subject to the common good and the general welfare" (*Commonwealth* 1851: 83–4; Levy 1957: 309).

It is not that all property merely was held at the sufferance of the state. Rather, law in the commonwealth era had less to do with protecting interests than with promoting ventures (Hurst 1956: 24). For much of the nineteenth century, scarcity of capital was acutely felt. There was no lack of raw materials, Hurst notes, as there was "an abundance of land, timber, minerals and waterpower" (Hurst 1956: 7, 1964: 10). Public opinion was obsessed with debt and taxes and so expenditure through taxation, though necessary, was both impractical (Hurst 1964: 10) and looked on with some disfavor (Handlin and Handlin 1969: 86, 242). Instead, the state would actively promote national development through its steering function, granting privileges and concessions to private enterprise, acting in concert with states, to pursue great public works. According to Hurst: "Until the '90s the country was . . . hard-pressed to find mobile capital sufficient to realize on its opportunities. This situation spelled the great importance of the power of the purse – the power to tax and spend – and the power to dispose of public lands" (Hurst 1960: 46, 1964: 12).[1]

States in this period devolved authority to companies engaged in the construction of infrastructure projects "vitally necessary to the common weal" (Scheiber 1973: 243). State legislatures accomplished these objectives by granting special charters of incorporation for various business purposes. Hartz reveals that in the period 1790–1860, Pennsylvania granted 2,333 charters through special acts of the legislature – well over half of them concerned transportation (1948: 38). In the building of roads, railways, bridges, and canals, states granted extraordinary privileges to business enterprises whose private economic interests merged with those of the public. These privileges included the authority to charge tolls or to take private property for the purpose of advancing a right of way or for supplying materials necessary for construction (Freyer 1981: 1267). Ordinarily, private enterprises reciprocally would undertake a number of obligations. In the case of a turnpike charter in Massachusetts, the company was obliged to build a road according to certain specifications; the road would be held in private hands for only a limited period of time; and the terms of the charter were alterable with the consent of the legislature. The company had to guarantee free passage to churchgoers, militiamen, and farmers, while the state could lower toll charges unilaterally after a period of 20 years (the period in which the company could realize a reasonable rate of return). The state could dissolve the company "as soon as the body had earned its costs plus an average annual return of 12 to 15 per cent" (Handlin and Handlin 1969: 112).

Charters did not grant entrenched entitlements to business enterprises. States reserved the right to repeal or amend the rights and privileges granted to corporations (Hurst 1956: 29). In the *Charles River Bridge* case (1837), the US Supreme Court affirmed the capacity of the Commonwealth of Massachusetts to impair an existing franchise. The proprietors of the Charles River Bridge sought to put a halt to the issuance of a franchise by the state for the building of a new bridge – the West Boston Bridge – that would be in direct competition with their own existing undertaking. The Charles River Bridge company relied on the decision in the *Dartmouth College* case (1819) where Chief Justice Marshall held corporate charters protected from alteration by the constitution's contract clause. In this way, the bridge proprietors claimed, the rights granted under charter were irrevocable and unalterable. Chief Justice Taney for the court declared that no monopoly or other power could be implied by the existing corporate charter.

Instead, the bridge company should expect that the state will intervene on behalf of the "rights" of the larger community (1837).

States even would delegate their power of eminent domain to rail-roads and builders of roads and waterways to allow for maximum returns from the investment of scarce resources of manpower and money (Hurst 1964: 183). In the calculation of just compensation, courts would take into account presumed gains to the public attributable to the construction of the local undertaking. This amounted, according to Scheiber, to the extraction of "involuntary subsidies" for public enterprise (1971: 363). The Supreme Court of Massachusetts in 1831, for instance, articulated the legal presumption that one "is compen-sated by sharing in the advantages arising from such beneficial legis-lation" (*Baker* [1831]). The practice of "offsetting" the value of benefits gained from losses suffered ensured that the just compensation rule was not strictly applied (Scheiber 1971: 364). Courts, then, largely abstained from interfering in affairs of states. Freyer's study of local assessment procedures reveals that companies often would settle pri-vately with landowners or accept the judgment of an assessment process (1981: 1271). It was rare that there was "an outright refusal to allow compensation" on the part of the company (1981: 1279). Chief Justice Shaw of Massachusetts, for his part, resisted the offsetting rule and demanded a closer connection between the benefit accrued and the harm suffered. Claims about "general prosperity" were too remote; what was required was that the company show some "direct" or "peculiar" benefit (Levy 1957: 132). Generally, though, all that was required was that there be some procedure for determining the provision of com-pensation ("due process") and some faithful adherence to this process (Scheiber 1973: 238).

The law performed an enabling function, generating a framework for action and the release of private energies. Rather than limiting state capacity, the object of constitutional and statutory law was to "keep open the channels of change" and to enlarge the "practical range of options in the face of limiting circumstance," wrote Hurst (1956: 27, 53). In the early part of the nineteenth century, the majority of state constitutions did not protect private property from state interference. State courts instead would derive the requirement of public purpose and just compensation from natural law theories and the text of the Fifth Amendment (which was binding only on the federal government) (Scheiber 1971: 362). Still, these requirements were read loosely: only physical takings with an accompanying transfer of title were deemed compensable (Scheiber 1971: 383). Partial or indirect takings – the mere regulation of private rights – were not compensable events (Levy 1957: 133). Nor did the US Supreme Court actively intervene in this area of state law: it did not even register on the question of eminent domain before 1870.[2] Even then, "it tended to leave very wide discretionary powers to the states" (Scheiber 1971: 381).

It was only in the 1850s that state constitutional conventions began reforming their constitutions in the direction of the "classical" rule, stipulating, for instance, that compensation be provided irrespective of the benefit received (Horwitz 1977: 65–6). Increasingly, fears of "leveling" (lawyer Daniel Webster's words) through the redistribution of wealth provoked concerns about the commonwealth mode of economic development (Horwitz 1977: 260). With the introduction of the Fourteenth Amendment in the period after the civil war, states now were constitutionally bound to respect liberty of contract and private property. Corwin describes the end of the era in this way: "That distrust of legislative majorities in which constitutional limitations were conceived, from being the obsession of a superior class, became, with advancing prosperity, the prepossession of a nation, and the doctrine of vested rights was secure" (1914: 51).

To sum up, in the commonwealth period capital was scarce and law was conscripted to help mobilize the national economy in directions that promoted popular understandings of the public good. Constitutional law was no impediment – indeed, it was formulated to advance – the release of public and private energies. This enabling function of the law permitted states to impinge on vested rights, such as the right to property. Though compensation was required to be provided in the case of a physical taking, so long as states adhered to some procedure in responding to claims for compensation, courts would not interfere. Moreover, states were entitled to lay down the conditions under which private profits were to be accumulated. All that rightly could be expected was that there would be a reasonable return on investment; there was no entitlement to interminable profits. There simply was no doctrine of regulatory takings. In the commonwealth period, regulatory changes were to be anticipated, if not welcomed. So rather than arresting national economic development, US constitutional law got out of the way.

The pattern of legal behavior in the antebellum United States nicely fits earlier conceptions of the rights to property. These conceptions are often cited in support of the rigid contemporary legal regime. Both

Grotius and Vattel, for instance, were firm advocates of government price regulation (Sax 1964: 54). Blackstone would permit the diminution of the "absolute" right of property, so long as this was "necessary and expedient for the general advantage of the public" (1979: 121). By way of example, Blackstone in his *Commentaries* discusses a statute of King Charles II which prescribed that the dead be buried in woolens. This was a law, Blackstone write, "consistent with public liberty, for it encourages the staple trade, on which in great measure depends the universal good of the nation" (1979: 122). Blackstone built on Locke's earlier formulation that, once beyond the state of nature and organized into political communities, governments were entitled to regulate property even in the minutest detail (Laslett 1988: 105). It also is a view of constitutionalism in accord with other regimes, like the Canadian one, where an energetic state helps to steer national economic development along certain lines and where property and "pure" economic rights receive no special constitutional recognition (Schneiderman 2006). It perhaps best approximates the model of democratizing constitutionalism discussed in Chapter one.

ALTERNATIVE FUTURES

The spread of investment rules world wide in the post-1989 universe was motivated less by concern that countries would expropriate investments of vulnerable foreign business firms. Rather, it was the diminution in the value of investment interests through regulatory innovation which appears to have animated investment rules disciplines (Wälde and Dow 2000: 4). This remains a controversial use of investment rules. The controversy turns, in part, on the difficulty of identifying the sorts of measures that impair investor rights significantly enough to warrant compensation, in contrast to those that would not.

The benefit of heightened scrutiny of measures impacting on investor rights, it is said, is that they serve as a check on political forces that may aim their sights on foreign investors. Historically, as Chua shows, this kind of targeting has been done primarily for the purposes of securing the fortunes of political actors representing majority ethnic groupings in developing and less developed countries (1995). At their best, then, investor rights act as a prophylactic to ethnic and race conflict. Treanor connects the US takings rule to the objective of shielding "vulnerable groups" from discriminatory takings (1995: 856; Levmore 1990: 310). In this way, the rule identifies failures in the political process that single out minorities whose interests are blocked or not represented in the formulation of state policy (Ely 1980). McGinnis and Movsevian go even further and draw direct analogies between international trade rules and US constitutional law. These rules enhance democratic processes by undermining factionalism generally in national politics, they argue. By restraining the role of protectionist interest groups from extracting rents and concessions from national governments, transnational rules "accomplish similar goals of Madisonian constitutionalism on a global scale" (2000: 515). In which case, the WTO, they maintain, serves similar constitutional functions as US constitutional structures by prohibiting discrimination against out-of-state traders. As Howse points out (2000), however, it is incongruent to think that foreign economic interests are entitled to protection as great as out-of-state interests are under the US dormant commerce clause. In the United States, the federal government has the capacity to achieve overriding national objectives that are prohibited to state governments. There is no transnational counterpart to the US Congress. Moreover, trade and investment rules often are less deferential to local rule making than even the US Supreme Court is in the case of state rules that impede interstate commerce.[3] The whole edifice of investment rules seems, then, out of balance.

Instead of seeking transnational rules that check factionalism of all sorts, we might imagine nonconstitutional alternatives that address more compelling "fairness" concerns (Franck 1995) – those regulations that single out disadvantaged individuals or groups for particular treatment or target the property rights of vulnerable minorities (Dagan 1999). States, even ones most faithful to republican and democratic precepts, retain the capacity of engaging in political acts that are commonly associated with Schmitt's friend-enemy distinction: of declaring foreigners as adversaries and, in so doing, threatening their very livelihood (Mouffe 1993: 114, 127). If the constitution-like dictates of the investment rules regime is one of the most drastic means by which states can signal openness to foreign investment in an age where competition for inward foreign investment is both necessary and intense, a rebalancing of that relationship may be in order. This can be achieved by identifying a number of alternative measures that offer some (though certainly not complete) protection to foreign investors but that do not mandate constitutional strictures for their enforcement. Two are suggested here – antidiscrimination laws and insurance – though there others available at the national level

231

(processes of judicial review of administrative action such as *amparo* in Mexico or *tutela* in Colombia) or even at the regional level (as in the law of the European Union).

A first strategy is to look to antidiscrimination laws as a viable nonconstitutional alternative that advances the interests of vulnerable economic actors who might be singled out solely because of their foreignness (Kaplow 1986: 574). Laws prohibiting discrimination, both direct and indirect, in the formulation and application of state policy can discipline state action in ways that can prevent the targeting of minority groupings distinguished on the basis of race, ethnicity, or national origin. In those countries with functioning human rights oversight bodies, these sorts of discriminatory activities usually are forbidden outright; they are not merely prohibited as a corollary to the requirement of compensation as under the takings rule. For those countries without national human rights institutions, there is no shortage of models available – including those in Asia (Cardenas 2002) – that are focused on protecting vulnerable groups coupled with a mandate to handle the resolution of individual complaints.[4] Laws or state practices that deny property rights on the basis of discriminatory treatment can fairly be assessed under such an instrument as does the UN Human Rights Committee, operating under the auspices of the International Covenant on Civil and Political Rights. While the right to property is not protected under the Covenant, "a confiscation of private property or the failure by a State party to pay compensation for such confiscation" if done in discriminatory fashion can give rise to a finding of discrimination (*Simenuk* 1992: para. 11.3). The investment rules regime also purports to be organized around the principle of "nondiscrimination." The regime, however, equates discrimination on the basis of one's investment portfolio with noxious discrimination on the grounds of race, ethnicity, or national origin. This faulty equation is avoided in antidiscrimination prohibitions found commonly in statutory human rights codes. Chua, as mentioned, has identified that cycles of nationalization in the global South often target the wealth of minority ethnic communities (1995). Though they may be nationals, they are viewed, often in times of economic crisis, as strangers within. Statutory human rights codes would prohibit the targeting of minority wealth if the primary object of a state measure is to harm economically a vulnerable group distinguished on the basis of race, nationality, etc., rather than to regulate wealth-creating activities that happen to impact negatively on foreign investors – admittedly, sometimes a difficult distinction to apply in practice (Levmore 1990).

As a back stop, particularly for those host states without functioning human rights bureaucracies, foreign investment insurance programs, both public and private, remain a viable alternative to the constitution-like commitments represented by investment rules. Insurance programs provide security to foreign investors by indemnifying companies for most of the losses sustained by host state action that amount to expropriation under international law. Though takings rules have been characterized as a form of government-sponsored insurance (Blume and Rubinfield 1984), insurance supported by investor contributions is a more efficient means of guaranteeing investments. Having investors contribute to a compensation scheme (by paying insurance premiums) mitigates the problem of moral hazard – though not entirely (Wells and Ahmed 2007: 246) – and helps to ensure that investors will assume only reasonable investment risks (Been and Beauvais 2003: 115; Kaplow 1986: 529; Levinson 2000: 392).

The burgeoning private insurance market will guarantee investments from political risks like expropriation and nationalization, though premiums are higher and contracts are for shorter terms than those of national and multilateral investment guarantee agencies (Comeaux and Kinsella 1994: 45). The Multilateral Investment Guarantee Agency (MIGA), established in 1988 and administered by the World Bank, makes political risk insurance available to foreign investors resident in 157 member countries. Investors contribute to the fund by paying premiums in annual installments (Shihata 1988: 168–9), while member countries bear the brunt of the risk by contributing to MIGA's authorized capital fund. Noncommercial insurable events include expropriations, defined as those acts or omissions depriving investors of ownership and control of their investments, including so-called creeping expropriations (Shihata 1988: 124–9). Significantly, MIGA will not cover losses sustained by non-discriminatory regulatory measures of general application – measures that may fall into the class of so-called regulatory takings (Been and Beauvais 2003: 112; Comeaux and Kinsella 1994: 41; Shihata 1988: 127). In the event of an expropriation, MIGA reimburses investors for a portion of the loss (up to US $200 million for a term of 15 years) and then assumes any claim against the host state, but most often will seek to negotiate terms of settlement between states and investors. Until recently, MIGA proudly boasted that it had issued over 475 guarantees since 1988 yet paid out only one claim (to the now-discredited Enron Corporation for a suspended power project in Java, Indonesia) (MIGA 2001; Wells and Ahmed 2007: c.15; West and Tarazona 2001: 214). It has since become embroiled, however, in more than a dozen investment disputes, a number of them resulting from the economic meltdown in Argentina (MIGA 2006: 34).

Many jurisdictions will have national counterparts to MIGA – investment guarantee agencies that back risky investments overseas made by nationals within the home state. In the United States, the Overseas Private Investment Corporation (OPIC) provides insurance and export financing to US citizens and corporations. OPIC will insure investments against expropriation up to US $200 million per project for a term of up to 20 years. The standard subrogation rights apply, in which case OPIC will assume any rights the compensated investor may have against the host state (O'Sullivan 2005). OPIC only guarantees investments in countries that have entered into BITs with the United States. This not only significantly narrows the range of eligible investments but also reinforces the constitution-like entitlements to which the investment rules regime gives rise. We could look, then, to other country models, such as Japan, Germany, and Australia (Rubins and Kinsella 2005: 89–97) operating under the Berne Union, an umbrella group of credit and investment insurers, which do not require that a bilateral treaty be in place before insurance is issued (International Union of Credit and Investment Insurers 2003). It is noteworthy that in Yackee's empirical study of the relation between BITs and FDI, he found that the existence of MIGA and OPIC insured projects suggested greater likelihood of FDI as a percentage of GDP. This is the first evidence, Yackee notes, to suggest that "investment insurance serves to promote investment that would not otherwise have taken place," rather than merely subsidizing investment decisions already made (2006: 61).

There is a further potential advantage to embracing nonconstitutional alternatives as a means of shielding investors from some, but not all, host state measures that have substantial negative impacts on their investments. It could generate greater interest in ordinary legal reforms that benefit citizens and investors alike, such as the model of human rights enforcement described above. Daniels hypothesizes that generating legal enclaves for foreign investors "siphons off the investor voice from the enterprise of creating good and generalized rule of law institutions" in the host country (2004: 4). Investors become not only less interested in host state legal developments, they demand contractual concessions from host states that are likely "to limit the state's capacity to respond to legitimate public policy concerns through the creation of credible, transparent and participatory regulatory institutions" (2004: 31). So as to illustrate the point, Daniels points to public infrastructure concession contracts which have given rise to vociferous opposition by local national publics and subsequent investor-state disputes. Contracts typically are nontransparent commitments for a lengthy term of years, lacking in public legitimacy, and freezing regulatory regimes possibly at the expense of socially desirable regulatory changes (2004: 34; Ayine et al. 2005).[5] Tobin and Rose-Ackerman similarly suggest that a world replete with BITs "reduces the interest of MNCs in property rights reform and enforcement in developing countries" (2004: 10). When foreign investors "bypass local law and lower their risk through BITs, developing country governments may have lost a major incentive to strengthen their domestic property rights regimes" (2004: 34).

While Tobin and Rose-Ackerman anticipate strengthened property rights commitments, the rule of law idea Daniels promotes is a "thinly conceived" one – a "minimalist" and "procedurally oriented" conception (Daniels and Trebilcock 2005: 107). This is in contrast to the more robust version of the rule of law associated with the neoliberal program of economic globalization, described in Chapter nine, and to which Tobin and Rose-Ackerman appear to subscribe. Instead of freezing regulatory frameworks, the thinner version aims to promote access to justice, such as to courts, administrative tribunals (including human rights bodies), and the legal profession. In this way, Daniels purports to avoid charges of "legal imperialism" and counterproductive interventions in national policy decision making (2004: 15).

Despite the availability of nonconstitutional alternatives, investments would remain vulnerable to the risks associated with regulatory change. Nonconstitutional protections will not lessen anxieties that the value of investment interests will be diminished through legal reform. Nevertheless, these alternatives restore the equilibrium between the economy and democracy. They encourage and even protect foreign investment – in the case of antidiscrimination laws, they prohibit outright actions that target foreign investors by reason of ethnicity, race or national origin – while leaving open the channels of change to self-governing political communities who may elect to innovate in relations between state and market.

An openness to change, one of the great virtues of democratic society, as de Tocqueville observed, more than ever is a feature worthy of preservation in this age of economic globalization. What is required is a shift of emphasis away from investor protections to one of institutionalizing democratizing constitutionalism. Constitutional ordering organized around principles of openness to change and to difference is given expression at the state level via rules and structures that empower the public sphere and remain agnostic about many societal conflicts, particularly those concerning markets and citizens. Constitutions can be expected to exhibit the *minima legalia* for societal dispute resolution, including guarantees of freedom of speech, public fora for communicative activity, and the institutionalization of rules and institutions for mediating intersocietal conflict (Frankenburg 2000: 22). Veto points should be avoided or kept to an absolute minimum. The state thereby remains available to perform all variety of functions, and these may be delegated upward or downward.

The state might perform functions similar to those postulated by Santos, who envisages the state as the "newest social movement," "transformed into a field of institutional experimentation" (Santos 2002: 489, 492). Santos claims that regulatory functions, previously performed by states, now are the responsibility of nonstate actors working either to privatize or to broaden participatory decision making. In this environment, states should be expected to engage in meta-regulation, performing the key function of articulating and coordinating new "public, non-state spheres" (Santos 2002: 490). It is critical, however, that the state's range-of-movement remain open –irreversible institutional prescriptions, Santo warns, are to be avoided (Santos 2002: 492).

Nor need these expressions of sovereignty take exclusively an internal form. One could foresee, building on the European experience, the generation of regional or confederal arrangements where democratic self-legislation takes place at multiple levels (Hirst 1994). Inspired by Kant's "Perpetual Peace" (1991), Habermas (2006) and Beck (2005) both imagine a nascent cosmopolitan consciousness emerging out of national outlooks, previously concealed by the "hidden transnationality of national myths" (Beck 2005: 41). One could envisage, as this book's premises suggest, a constitutional order of a sort operating outside the confines of national states (Habermas 2006: 138). Irrespective of whether we accept that states have been forever changed by the experience of economic globalization, we should understand existing state forms as contingent devices for self-legislation and constitutional authorship. In which case, new hybrid forms of representation may yet emerge out of the maelstrom.

In this light, investment treaties can even be conceived anew. They could, for instance, take on the role of ensuring that investors have a voice in the construction of state policy. *Audi alteram partem* – hearing the other side (Wade and Forsyth 2004: 476) – might be the organizing principle of a new regime of investor protection (Tully 2002: 218). This would have the beneficial effect of restoring the capacity of self-governing democracies to regulate markets and allowing states the ability to stimulate national economic development along similar paths as those used in the past. This is not, at bottom, an argument, though, that states must replicate any particular path to generate economic growth, much less the US pattern – this is one of the disquieting themes of the current investment rules regime. This is an argument, rather, that we keep open the variety of paths available to developing and less developed economies, admitting that there is no one model to national economic success. The parameters of these commitments can be negotiated between investors, governments, and publics attuned to the possibility of both mutual economic gain and a commitment to the value of more democratic possibilities.

# NOTES

## INTRODUCTION: THE NEW CONSTITUTIONAL ORDER

1 The idea of a national community engaging in self-binding precommitment is problematic, however (Elster 1992: 37). In the case of constitutionalism, it is future generations that are intended to be bound by present-day framing exercises. Nor are constitutional rules self-executing. Waldron notes that precommitment means being subservient not to the will of the framers but to a later generation of judges who put into operation the original binding act (Waldron 1998: 278). The constraints on judicial review posed by text, precedent, and modes of legal argumentation vitiate somewhat this concern with judicial authorship.

2 Ingeborg Maus, for instance, cannot imagine how citizen involvement in legislative decision making at the cosmopolitan level could be achieved. What could "the right to petition or to demonstrate mean vis-à-vis a world parliament"? (2006: 473, 477).

3 The phrase "alternative futures" is borrowed from Charles Taylor (1993). By "markets," I refer to spaces where "the forces of supply and demand in an economy determine prices, output and methods of production via the automatic adjustment of price movements" (Boyer and Drache 1996: 3).

4 I am mindful of Holmes's and Sunstein's account of property rights as publicly funded rights: property owners are "comparatively strong only as a result of government support, that is, because of deftly crafted laws, enforced at public expense, that enable them to acquire and to hold onto what is 'theirs'" (1999: 230). Their account of the state's ability to regulate property for redistributive purposes (rather than merely for the purposes of taxation), however, appears to go no further than to say that "reasonable people can disagree about the advantages and disadvantages" of differing systems of private property (1999: 231).

5 Absent an unlikely coherence and unity to state action, there may likely be rival state projects that complement well investment rules strictures.

## THE INVESTMENT RULES REGIME

1 In the 2005 China-Germany BIT, existing nonconforming measures within China are exempt from the requirement of national treatment. China undertakes, however, to take steps to "progressively remove" them (protocol #3).

2 The 2005 China-Germany BIT deems measures "taken for reasons of public security and order, public health or morality" as not amounting to "treatment less favorable" for the purposes of the national treatment and MFN requirements. Also, in the model German BIT, MFN treatment does not extend to the favored treatment required by membership in the EU. In the MAI negotiations, the EC sought a similar exemption from this basic tenet and was a cause for concern among the other negotiating states (Picciotto 1998: 759). For a fuller discussion of regional economic arrangements and their impact on MFN treatment, see UNCTAD (2004c).

3 Parallel importing permits the importation of the least costly version of a drug from licensed manufacturers or distributors in third countries; compulsory licensing entitles non-patent owners to produce patented pharmaceutical drugs. See discussion in Correa 2007: 78ff and 313ff.

4 As Tarullo notes, trade law disciplines politics by ensuring that only "normal" government functions are tolerated. That which are considered normal are those functions for which there is a US government analogy (Tarullo 1987: 577–8).

5 UNCTAD reports that over the last few decades the Triad share of inward FDI has fluctuated from 60 to 70 percent. Europe increasingly is dominating that share (almost half of all global inward and outward FDI), while the US FDI has declined and Japan remains a marginal host country for FDI (UNCTAD 2006b: 6).

6 Cass might liken this to "constitutionalism," a term she associates with the "set of values" typically found in liberal constitutional design, such as rights and the rule of law (2005: 28).

## THE TAKINGS RULE

1 Though the Fifth Amendment applies only to Congressional action, the same rule binds states pursuant to the Fourteenth Amendment.

2 It has been suggested that Holmes J. did not mean to be referring to the takings clause (which was not yet considered as applying to the states via the Fourteenth Amendment); rather, Holmes J. meant to be describing a deprivation under the due process clause of the Fourteenth Amendment. See White (1993: 402–3) and Note (1994: 775–6).

3 Dana and Merrill identify six factors, taken together from *Penn Central* and *Pennsylvania Coal* (2002: 132). In addition to the three already mentioned, they add: "(4) whether the regulation is a noxious use of property; (5) whether the regulation provides an average reciprocity of advantage among property owners; and (6) whether the regulation destroys a recognized property right."

4 Gregory Alexander shows, however, that the bundle-of-rights metaphor appeared first in John Lewis's classic treatise on eminent domain. Lewis invoked the metaphor to support the notion that deprivation of any element of ownership required compensation (1997: 322–3).

5 In both *Nollan* (1986) and *Dolan* (1994), the court explained in *Lingle* (2005), the dedications of property were so onerous that they "would be deemed *per se* physical takings" (though they constituted a "special application" of the doctrine of unconstitutional conditions) (2005: 17–18). The doctrine of unconstitutional conditions provides that "the government may not require a person to give up a constitutional right – here the right to receive just compensation when property is taken for a public use – in exchange for a discretionary benefit conferred by the government where the benefit has little or no relationship to the property" (*Dolan* 1994: 385, quoted in *Lingle* 2005: 18).

6 There surely are important affinities between police powers as it is understood in US constitutional law and eighteenth-century continental notions of "police." There was the common concern with securing the conditions for prosperity, good government, and the promotion of the common good. The idea of police, as it developed in Europe, was both an end and an "administrative means of achieving that end" (Tomlins 1993: 40).

7 Grigera Naón (2005: 137) notes that, though foreign aliens may have been precluded, under Calvo's doctrine, from pursuing their claims under international law, Calvo was not opposed to the peaceful resolution of disputes through international arbitration whenever states consented to this jurisdiction.

8 This passage from Higgins (1982) is quoted with approval in *Azurix* (2006: para. 310).

9 The *Santa Elena* case (2000) concerns the valuation of property that the Republic of Costa Rica admittedly had taken. The ICSID panel announced, however, that compensation was required to be paid even in the case of bona fide environmental measures and that there are a "wide spectrum of measures" that could amount to a taking (*Compañía del Desarrollo de Santa Elena* 2000: paras 72, 76).

10 Departures from GATT disciplines are also permitted if they "relat[e] to the conservation of exhaustible natural resources" so long as they do not "constitute a means of arbitrary or unjustifiable discrimination between countries where the same conditions prevail" or amount to a "disguised restriction on international trade" (Art. XX[g]). This "in relation to" test is easier to satisfy than the test of "necessity" under Art. XX(b): the measure need only be "reasonable" rather than the least restrictive alternative (*Shrimp/Turtle* 1998: para. 141).

11 The AB ruling in *Reformulated Gasoline* concerned the Art. XX(g) exception – measures "relating to the conservation of exhaustible natural resources" – that would have been available to the United States, so long as they also met the chapeau criteria, which they failed to do.

12 In a second report on *Shrimp/Turtle*, following the complaint of Malaysia concerning implementation of the first decision, the AB confirmed that unilateralism alone will not disqualify a measure under Art. XX (*Shrimp-Turtle* 2001: para. 138).

## INVESTMENT RULES IN ACTION

1 This coolness was precipitated, in part, by a "hard-hitting" documentary that Bill Moyers had aired on PBS (Inside US Trade 2002a). Moyers's documentary shed light on "secret" tribunals established under NAFTA that could hamper the ability of states to regulate in the interests of protecting workers or the environment. Particular attention was paid in the documentary to the pending suit against the State of California by the Canadian company Methanex.

2 Senator John Kerry's amendment would have gone further, limiting the "provision on expropriation, including by ensuring that payment of compensation is not required for regulatory measures that cause mere diminution in the value of private property." It would have also ensured that the standard for minimum treatment required by international law "shall grant no greater legal rights than United States citizens possess under the due process clause of the United States constitution." No foreign investor could succeed in challenging any federal, state, or local measure "that protects public health, safety and welfare, the environment or public morals" unless it is demonstrated that "the measure was enacted or applied primarily for the purpose of discriminating against foreign investors or investments" or violates due process (148 Cong. Rec. S4504, May 16, 2002). Kerry's amendment was defeated (Inside US Trade 2002b) whereas Baucus-Grassley was easily approved (148 Cong. Rec. S4298).

3 An arbitral tribunal did issue a ruling refusing Canada's challenge to the tribunal's jurisdiction to hear Ethyl's complaint. See *Ethyl Corporation v. Government of Canada (MMT)* and the discussion in Gaillard (2000) and Wilson (2000).

4 The tribunal, in its award on the merits, "deplores the decision of Canada in this matter" and declared that "Canada's refusal to disclose or identify documents in these circumstances is at variance with the practice of other NAFTA parties, at least of the United States, [and] that refusal could well result in a denial of equality of treatment of investors and investments of the Parties bringing claims under Chapter 11" (*Pope & Talbot* 2001: para. 193).

5 The tribunal did not accept the investor's submission that "measures of general application which have the effect of substantially interfering" with protected investments give rise to a compensable taking (*Pope & Talbot* 2000: paras 103–4).

6 American Law Institute (1987: para. 99). For a glimpse at the political nature of the restatement drafting process, particularly in the context of expropriations, see Dezalay and Garth (1996: 175–9).

7 The tribunal in LG&E also took note of the American Law Institute's restatement of U.S. law on this subject (2006: para. 196).

8 This purported conceptual confusion identified by Higgins was quoted approvingly in *Azurix* (2006: para. 310).

9 This would seem to be the point of NAFTA Art. 1102(3), that the requirement of national treatment "means, with respect to a state or province, treatment no less favorable than the most favorable treatment accorded, in like circumstances, by that state or province to investors, and to investments of investors, of the Party of which it forms a part."

10 Art. 1105(1) provides: Each Party shall accord to investments of investors of another Party treatment in accordance with international law, including fair and equitable treatment and full protection and security. This interpretation was rejected both by Justice Tysoe in *United Mexican States* (2001: para. 65) and the NAFTA FTC Interpretive Note (2001).

11 Pursuant to NAFTA Art. 1131(2).

12 According to Tamayo (2001: 75), having already invested several millions of dollars acquiring a large percentage of COTERIN's stock, Metalclad was banking on the ratification of NAFTA's and Mexico's "tradition of political centralism" to overcome opposition to reopening of the facility.

13 It was not the case, as Gaines (2002: 111) suggests (echoing Metalclad's claim), that the municipalities' decision was motivated by opposition to foreign-owned corporation taking over the site.

14 The same point was made by the state parties in an "interpretive note" issued 2 months after the court's ruling (NAFTA FTC 2001). Weiler argues that the *Metalclad* tribunal relied on grounds other than just transparency in finding a denial of fair and equitable treatment, in which case, it was inappropriate for Justice Tysoe to annul all of the tribunal's findings regarding Art. 1105 (2005b: 718).

15 Mexico subsequently delivered a cheque in the amount of US $15.6 million to Metalclad (*New York Times* 2001b).

16 On the issue of whether Myers was an investor with an investment under Chapter 11, the tribunal ruled that it fell within the terms of NAFTA. It would "not accept that an otherwise meritorious claim should fail solely by reason of the corporate structure adopted by a claimant in order to organise the way in which it conducts its business affairs" (*S. D. Myers* 2001: para. 229). According to tribunal member Schwartz, Myers and its affiliate were ready "to carry out many business steps within Canadian boundaries, including assessment of a customer's problems, recommending solutions, assisting with drainage of contaminated equipment and arranging for transportation" (*S. D. Myers* 2001 [SO]: para. 194).

17 The incorporation of WTO standards into the interpretation of NAFTA's national treatment standard was rejected, for instance, in *Methanex* (2005: IV.B.37).

18 *S. D. Myers* was the subject of an application for judicial review to the Federal Court of Canada. That application was dismissed. See *A. G. Can. v. S. D. Myers* (2004).

19 It is noteworthy that Paulsson and Douglas, in their review of tribunal decisions pre-*Methanex*, summarize the indirect expropriation rule in much the same way as does the *Methanex* tribunal but with specific reference to "legitimate expectations." They add that this "is by no means an exclusive test to be applied to all types of alleged indirect expropriations in isolation of other relevant factors. It is, nonetheless, a useful guiding principle that appears to cover many of the situations that have come before modern investment treaty tribunals" (2004: 157).

20 The content of international law, as defined by Art. 39 of the authoritative Statute of the International Court of Justice, includes international conventions, international custom (as evinced by *opinion juris*), and the general principles of law recognized by civilized nations (discussed in Chapter two). Judicial decisions and the writings of "highly qualified publicists" are available as a "subsidiary means for the determination of rules of law" (Brownlie 2003: 5). Once the international minimum standard is untethered from the norms of customary international law, all will inform the content of the standard of fair and equitable treatment.

21 Douglas notes that the *Tecmed* tribunal issued no "standard" but the "description of a perfect public regulation in a perfect world, to which all states should aspire but very few (if any) will attain" (2006: 28).

22 The fair and equitable treatment standard clause at issue in CMS, unlike the NAFTA standard, was not tied in the BIT to the minimum standard required by customary international law.

23 The tribunal in *LG&E* (2006) took a far less restrictive view of the necessity exception in the context of Argentina's "severe economic crisis." Though the response was not the only one available, suspending the calculation of tariffs in US dollars and periodically adjusting them "was a legitimate way of protecting its social and economic system" (2006: paras 238–40).

24 The violation of these specific statutory commitments also gave rise to an abrogation of the BIT's umbrella clause in *LG&E* (2006: para. 175).

25 Curiously, the tribunal elsewhere concludes that the community opposition to the landfill, "however intense, aggressive and sustained – was [not] in any way massive or went any further than the positions assumed by some individuals or the members of some groups that were opposed to the landfill" (*Tecmed* 2003: para. 144). The tribunal notes that only 200–400 people, out of a population of almost 1 million, participated in demonstrations (*Tecmed* 2003: para. 144)

26 Coe, Jr. and Rubins (2005: 651) agree that the *Tecmed* standard is close to the regulatory takings jurisprudence of the US Supreme Court, but they misidentify the standard by invoking only the per se categorical rule in *Lucas* (1992) of total economic wipeout. See discussion in Chapter three.

27 In an earlier essay, Wälde and Kolo undertake a comparative review of proportionality tests in the realm of regulatory takings in a similar cursory fashion (2001: 831–4). For a discussion of the evolving doctrine of legitimate expectations in UK administrative law, moving from a

procedural to a substantive conception, see Wade and Forsyth (2004: 500–5) and Le Seuer et al. (1999: 287–96), and, from a comparative perspective, Schønberg (2000: 149–50).

## HEALTH AND THE ENVIRONMENT

1 In addition to its appearance in the 1917 Mexican Constitution, Calvo's doctrine emerged as a central plank of the new International Economic Order (UNGA 3171 of 1973) and the UN Charter of Economic Rights and Duties of States (1974). Art. 2 of the Charter provides that the laws governing nationalization and expropriation and compensation are those of the nationalizing state and not those of international law. Further, see Dugard (2002).

2 As the president declared in his 1991 State of the Nation address: "In the past, land distribution was the path to justice; today it is unproductive and impoverishing" (Smith 1992: 20).

3 The article does not apply to the "revocation, limitation, or creation of intellectual property rights, to the extent that such ... revocation, limitation, or creation is consistent with Chapter Seventeen" (Art. 1110.7).

4 This purportedly fell within the wording of Art. 1708(12): "A Party may provide limited exceptions to the rights conferred by trademark, such as fair use of descriptive terms, provided that such exceptions take into account the legitimate interests of the trademark owner and of other persons."

5 Art. 30 of the EEC prohibits measures which restrict imports whereas Art. 36 expressly exempts from Art. 30 such measures which have as their purpose the protection of public health. The burden placed on parties under s. 36 is to show that the measure falls within the scope of the section and that it is not arbitrary or a disguised (colorable) restriction, and is proportional in its effects (the least restrictive means). See *Commission* (1983) and discussion in Wyatt and Dashwood (1993: 225–33).

6 The federal Environment minister wrote to Ethyl that "current scientific information fails to demonstrate that MMT impairs the proper functioning of automobile on-board diagnostic systems. Furthermore, there is no new scientific evidence to modify the conclusions drawn by Health Canada in 1994 that MMT poses no health risk" (McCarthy 1998b).

7 Dated April 2006 and entering into force April 1, 2007.

## LAND AND EMPOWERMENT

1 Though the US constitutional experience is most instructive in comprehending the meaning of its strictures, the US was not aggressively signing agreements until after the collapse of WTO talks at Cancun in 2003 (Mayne 2005: 4; Stiglitz 2006: 96). Vandevelde explains that this was a result of US hesitation in signing agreements that set less than the highest standards of protection (Vandevelde 1992b).

2 See, e.g., the 1997 Thailand-Canada BIT. While the usual standard of prompt, adequate, and effective compensation based on fair market value remains, provisions concerning the date at which compensation is payable are subject to the ordinary laws of Thailand. In the case of expropriation of immovables within Thailand, compensation is to be determined by a committee established in accordance with the Immovable Property Expropriation Act, and, in the case of movables, determined by the Civil and Commercial Code (Art. VIII. 2.b).

3 The section provides:

(1) No one may be deprived of property except in terms of law of general application, and no law may permit arbitrary deprivation of property.

(2) Property may be expropriated only in terms of law of general application –
(a) for public purposes or in the public interest; and
(b) subject to compensation, the amount, timing, and manner of payment, of which must be agreed, or decided or approved by a court.

(3) The amount, timing, and manner of payment, of compensation must be just and equitable, reflecting an equitable balance between the public interest and the interests of those affected, having regard to all relevant factors, including –
(a) the current use of the property;
(b) the history of the acquisition and use of the property;
(c) the market value of the property;
(d) the extent of direct state investment and subsidy in the acquisition and beneficial capital improvement of the property; and
(e) the purpose of the expropriation.

(4) For the purposes of this section –
(a) the public interest includes the nation's commitment to land reform, and to reforms to bring about equitable access to all South Africa's natural resources; and
(b) property is not limited to land.

(5) The state must take reasonable legislative and other measures, within its available resources, to foster conditions which enable citizens to gain access to land on an equitable basis.

(6) A person or community whose tenure of land is legally insecure as a result of past racially discriminatory laws or practices is entitled, to the extent provided by an Act of Parliament, either to tenure which is legally secure, or to comparable redress.

(7) A person or community dispossessed of property after 19 June 1913 as a result of past racially discriminatory laws or practices is entitled, to the extent provided by an Act of Parliament, either to restitution of that property, or to equitable redress.

(8) No provision of this section may impede the state from taking legislative and other measures to achieve land, water and related reform, in order to redress the results of past racial discrimination,

provided that any departure from the provisions of this section is in accordance with the provisions of section 36(1).

(9) Parliament must enact the legislation referred to in subsections (6).

4 The limitations clause provides:

(1) The rights in the Bill of Rights may be limited only in terms of law of general application to the extent that the limitation is reasonable and justifiable in an open and democratic society based on human dignity, equality and freedom, taking into account all relevant factors, including –
   (a) the nature of the right;
   (b) the importance of the purpose of the limitation;
   (c) the nature and extent of the limitation;
   (d) the relation between the limitation and its purpose; and
   (e) less restrictive means to achieve the purpose.

(2) Except as provided in subsection (1) or in any other provision of the Constitution, no law may limit any right entrenched in the Bill of Rights.

Van der Walt (1997) insisted that both deprivations and expropriations provisions would be subject to the general limitations clause in s. 36. Moreover, he wrote, as expropriations are a form of deprivation (1997: 19), lawful expropriations also must satisfy the deprivation clause requirement of generality and nonarbitrariness (1997: 95). The Constitutional Court appears to have agreed with these propositions in the case of arbitrary deprivations in *First National Bank* (2002: paras 46, 57, 70).

5 The ANC *Draft Bill of Rights: Preliminary Revised Version* of February 1993 provided for a more exacting provision in this regard. See s. 13(8) summarized in Van der Walt (1994: 482).

6 Up to 37 percent in 1969 to a low of 18 percent in 1991, but on the rise again (Chow 1994: 38–40; Statistics Canada 1997: 14). There is, at present, a concern over the "hollowing art" of corporate Canada as more firms are acquired by foreign companies. See Martin and Nixon 2007.

7 Courts are mandated to interpret the Bill of Rights "having regard to public international law applicable to the protection of the rights entrenched in this Chapter, and may have regard to comparative foreign case law" (s. 39[1]). Elsewhere courts are instructed to prefer interpretations of legislation that are consistent with international law (s. 233). Other provisions concerning the status of international agreements (s. 231) and the status of customary international law (s. 232) may also have application here. See discussion of Mahomed J. concerning provisions of the interim constitution (*AZAPO* 1996: 687–91).

8 TRIPs was ratified by Parliament in 1995 (Berger 2002: 197). It would not have the force of law, however, until incorporated via legislative enactment into domestic law (*Azapo* 1996: para. 26)

9 Though the ANC were slow to embrace this favored corporate buzzword (Hirsch 2005: 117).

10 Section 217 provides as follows:

(1) When an organ of state in the national, provincial or local sphere of government, or any other institution identified in national legislation, contracts for goods or services, it must do so in accordance with a system which is fair, equitable, transparent, competitive and cost-effective.

(2) Subsection (1) does not prevent the organs of state or institutions referred to in that subsection from implementing a procurement policy providing for –

(a) categories of preference in the allocation of contracts; and

(b) the protection or advancement of persons, or categories of persons, disadvantaged by unfair discrimination.

(3) National legislation must prescribe a framework within which the policy referred to in subsection (2) may be implemented.

11 Finance Minister Trevor Manuel is reported to have described the BEE Commission report as a "text out of the Communist Manifesto" and, for Trade and Industry Minister Alec Irwin, demanding too large a role for the state. See Gumede (2002: 212).

12 BEE commitments have been codified in a number of statutory instruments, such as the Lotteries Act of 1997, the Competition Act of 1998, and the Gas Act of 2001, amongst others, in addition to the Mineral and Petroleum Resources Development Act of 2002, discussed below. See Lester (2007, 118) and Gqubule (2006, 116).

13 The SACU includes the countries of South Africa, Botswana, Lesotho, Namibia, and Swaziland.

14 In the mining sector, the charter suggests that the awarding of mining licenses and concessions will be based on the "scorecard approach" (4.11).

15 Estimates of mining expropriation claims run more than R 100 billion (Ryan 2007).

16 There might be concern that MFN status will render redundant the promotion of equality exception in recent BITs. The MFN clause, if available to foreign investors with investments covered by new model BITs which are intended to shield BEE from many investment disciplines, would entitle them to treatment no less favorable than that available to investors within EU member states or other states in which there is no "promotion of equality" exception. This problem may be solved in so far as the exception applies to MFN in addition to national treatment.

17 Namely, "to substantially and meaningfully expand opportunities for historically disadvantaged South Africans" (s. 2[d]).

## PRIVATIZATION AND DEMOCRATIZATION

1 The "third way," as developed by Giddens (1994) purports to drive a path through the binary of left and right, which is imperfectly represented by these two models. As appropriated by New Labour, third-way thinking seems entirely pragmatic – "what works is what's best" (Nexus 1998) – and

an excuse for the prevalence of markets over the state (Giddens 2001: 13). McLennan observes that "the sheer weight of diversity involved [in Third Way thinking], and the different levels of abstraction enclosed, threaten to bring the entire edifice crashing to the ground" (2004: 488).

2 Stiglitz argues that the case for privatization "is a political one," not an economic one (1994: 173). Government can "*potentially* almost always improve upon the market's resource allocation" (1994: 179). Nor do I discuss here the benefits or pitfalls of this particular form of privatization over other methods, like unrestricted sales to outsiders or equal-access vouchers. Among the perils, it has been claimed that selling shares to employee "insiders" fails to bring new capital or new skills to divested companies (Gray 1996: 188), a case of "private benefits being had at private cost" (Cass 1988: 514; Edwards 1995: 179).

3 Edwards identifies "[t[he failure of so-called heterodox programs in Argentina, Brazil and Peru; the experience of the East Asian economies; the advice of multilateral institutions; and the example of Chile" as factors contributing toward the "emerging consensus" (1995: 48).

4 Similarly, Colombia entered a reservation concerning the takings rule in the 1995 Colombia, Mexico, and Venezuela (G-3) free trade agreement (Annex to Art. 17–08). Venezuela withdrew in May 2006 from the agreement. This reservation was not withdrawn following the 1999 constitutional amendment to Colombia property clause (WTO 2006: 21).

5 Article 26: Private property and other rights legally acquired in accordance with civil law by natural or juridic persons shall be guaranteed, nor may they be disavowed by later laws. When the enforcement of a law passed for reasons of public utility or social interest conflicts with the rights of individuals, private interests must give way to the public or social interests.

Property is a social function which implies obligations.

For reasons of public utility or social interest, as defined by the legislature, property may be expropriated by judicial decree with prior indemnification.

6 Inspiration was also drawn from the Mexican Constitution of 1917, the Weimar Constitution of 1919, and the Spanish Constitution of 1931. See Sáchica (1989: 263). Excerpts from Duguit's influential 1911 lecture in Buenos Aires are reproduced in Constaín (1959: 253–8).

7 New land reform initiatives were undertaken in the 1960s, following a plebiscite in 1957 affirming the constitutional reforms of 1936. Little progress was achieved. Property was more unequally distributed by 1970 than before; larger agricultural holdings occupied even more of the national territory (Jaramillo 1998, 51–2; Kline 1996, 39). The Constitutional Assembly recalled the "repugnant corruption" of forced expropriations: it was "a great business" to expropriate and to be expropriated (quoted in C-358/96 at 42).

8 The two remaining major armed resistance movements, the Colombian Revolutionary Armed Forces (FARC) and the National Liberation Army (ELN), both refused to participate (Leger 1994: 72–3) – it is said that the guerrilla war reduces GDP by at least 2 percent a year (Swafford 1999).

9 Article 58: Private property and other rights acquired in accordance with civil laws may not be ignored or infringed upon by subsequent laws. When in the application of a law passed on account of public utility or social interest and recognized as essential a conflict should occur about the rights of individuals, the private interest will have to give precedence to the public or social interest.

Property is a social function which implies obligations. As such an ecological function is inherent to it.

The state will protect and promote associational and collective forms of property.

Because of public necessity or social interest defined by the legislative, expropriation will be possible by means of a judicial determination and prior indemnification. The latter will be determined in consultation with the interests of the community and of the affected party. In cases determined by the legislative, said expropriations may be pursued by administrative means, subject to subsequent contentious administrative action at law, including with respect to price.

Still, the legislative, for reasons of equity, may determine those cases in which there is no ground for indemnification through an affirmative vote of the absolute majority vote of the members of both chambers.

10 Article 60: When the state sells its interest in an enterprise, it will take measures promoting democratization of the ownership of its shares and will offer its workers or the collective and worker's organizations special terms to make it possible for them to accede to the said proprietary shares.

11 According to the Colombian Constitutional Court, Art. 60 is designed to prevent the privatization procedure followed "in many countries" in which privatization is "converted into the transfer of public property, for a fraction of its worth, to the richest sectors of society" (C-452/95). It is intended, in other words, as a special rule to promote access to property (C-075/06, s. 11). Similar provisions can be found in Art. 111 of the 1992 Paraguayan Constitution which provides: "When the State decides to transfer public enterprises or its shareholdings therein to the private sector, it shall confer a preferential right on the employees and other operators directly connected with those enterprises. The manner in which this preemptive right is granted shall be regulated by law" (Guislain 1997: 37).

12 This helps to explain Act 812 of 2003. In order to further the democratization of property through privatization, the law facilitates the acquisition of public service companies by customers or by local communities, in addition to the solidarity sector.

13 Four country delegations, however, "reserved their position on all privatisation obligations" (fn. 41).

14 One solution is to confer the same advantages on domestic nationals, though this may not satisfy the constitutional requirement; alternatively, on all investors regardless of nationality. According to Vandevelde, this would "ensure genuine investment neutrality and create a host state constituency in support of an enduring liberal investment regime" (Vandevelde 1998: 639).

15 Translation by Moira Gracey.

16 The amendment, by Acto Legislativo 1/99 of August 4, 1999, excised the provisions concerning equitable expropriation: "Con todo, el legislador, por razones de equidad, podrá determinar los casos en que no haya lugar al pago de indemnización, mediante el voto favorable de la mayoría absoluta de los miembros de una y otra Cámara. Las razones de equidad, así como los motivos de utilidad pública o de interés social, invocados por el legislador, no serán controvertibles judicialmente [Still, the legislative, for reasons of equity, may determine those cases in which there is no ground for indemnification through an affirmative vote of the absolute majority vote of the members of both chambers. Reasons of equity, as well as motives of public necessity or social interest invoked by the legislative, will not be judicially reviewable.]"

## CITIZENSHIP

1 Commercial trade relationships did not ordinarily give rise to even imperfect citizenship status unless a resident foreign trader had a "patron" within the city walls (Aristotle 1995: 1275$^a$5).

2 Regan does not endorse this understanding of the clause as it would call for review not only in interstate commerce cases but in every case where out-of-state interests require virtual representation (1986: 1164).

3 Tushnet suggests that the tension between the court's federalism decisions and preemption law "may flow from globalization itself, and [that] it might be impossible to eliminate that tension by limiting the national government's power to preempt" (2000: 14).

4 The complaint by Japan and the E.U. that the Burma law violated the terms of the WTO agreement concerning procurement (GPA) added a further transnational legal dimension to the controversy. This "diplomatic tension" helped underscore, for the Court, the alleged usurpation of federal authority. It might also serve as an effective precedent in the case of any other less restrictive measures being adopted at the local level. We should expect private parties to attempt to mobilize foreign states to take action under the GPA or under bilateral investment treaties against measures that threaten the free movement of their goods, capital, and investment (Stumberg 2000: 125).

5 Held et al. write that "above the plethora of local and national culture industries, a group of around 20–30 very large MNCs dominate global markets for entertainment, news, television, etc., and they have acquired a very significant cultural economic and cultural presence on nearly every continent" (1999: 347).

6 On the circumstances in which the draft text arrived in Clarke's hands, see Johnston and Laxer (2003: 53).

7 According to Dymond, the real reason for France's withdrawal was French Prime Minister Lionel Jospin's desire to appease the Communists and Greens in his coalition at little political cost, given the negligible

public support for the initiative among French business and NGO groups (Dymond 1999: 32).

## THE RULE OF LAW

1 Domestic trade law is replete with "non-transparent, discriminatory, disproportionately harmful and . . . illegal trade policy instruments which often elude effective parliamentary and judicial control" (Petersmann 1992: 19).

2 For a trenchant critique of a discursive politics of rights, see Fudge and Glasbeek (1992). They note that formulating political demands in the form of rights claims is hardly novel. Placing emphasis on courts and constitutional litigation, argue Fudge and Glasbeek, is misguided for "[c]hanges external to law drive the politics of litigation, not the other way around" (1992: 58).

3 Named after noted economist James Tobin, the Tobin Tax came within six votes of being adopted in the European Parliament in 2000. See *New York Times* (2000: A19).

4 The objective of the social Rechsstaat, for Neumann, was the realization of social freedom. "Social freedom means that workers will determine their own working life; the alien power of the owners to command labour through their control of the means of production must give way to self-determination" (1930: 39).

5 In the subsequent decision of *LG&E* (2006), which is discussed in Chapter three, a tribunal excused Argentina based on the defense of necessity on virtually identical facts.

6 Neumann meant by a monopolistic market position "economic domination which allows the proprietor's market performance (price, contractual terms, quality of the goods and turnover) to differ from the situation of free competition, in order that they might gain higher profits" (1931: 62).

7 Articles 102 and 105 of the Weimar Constitution.

8 Articles 109 and 153 of the Weimar Constitution.

9 On the function of judges in "mass democracy and monopoly economy," see Neumann (1934: 72).

10 This is reflected in the rising percentage in the 1990s of mergers and acquisitions within OECD countries. In 1996, 47 percent of global foreign direct investment (where the majority interest is foreign owned) concerned mergers and acquisitions. These are "increasingly the major means of entering foreign markets in the 1990s" (UNCTAD 1997: 9). In the period 1986–90, this accounted for 70 percent of all FDI (Held et al. 1999: 243–5).

11 The model agreement can be found at Mann et al. (2005).

12 I am following Jessop who defines conjunctural moment as "elements in a social formation that can be altered by a given agent (or set of agents) during a given time period" (Jessop 1982: 253). Althusser theorized the conjuncture to refer to the "character of more or less dominant or subordinate and therefore more or less 'paradoxical' determination of a

given structure in the current mechanism of the whole" (Althusser and Balibar 1970: 106–7).

13 For a review of the debates, see Trebilcock and Howse (2005), chapters 15 and 16.

14 Scheuerman acknowledges the need to tame the formal requirements of the rule of law in his *Between the Norm and the Exception* (1994: 118).

## CONCLUSION: A WORLD OF POSSIBILITIES

1 A word needs to be said here – though Hurst makes little mention of it (1964: 9, 28) – about the failure to compensate for the taking of Aboriginal lands in North America. It was these "great tracts of land" (Locke 1988) which made up the "abundance" of resources available for exploitation by the state and its private partners. First Nations were not members in the original compact that made up the citizens of the United States. They would not have been presumed to have tacitly consented to the taking of their lands without compensation for the purposes of national development – the Lockean premise underlying much of the legal thought of the period (Tully 1995: 73). The animating idea for these takings was the unrealized potential of these "waste" lands. Seemingly unaware of their potential wealth, these tracts of land still lay in "common" and were available to settlers to appropriate through the productive practices of European agriculture. It was the perceived failure to properly exploit these rich resources, coupled with ethnocentric formulations about "civilization," which fueled politicolegal understandings of the period. According to Locke's version, they [First Nations] "who are rich in land ... for want of improving it by labour have not one hundredth part of the Conveniences we enjoy." Thus, a "King of a large and fruitful territory there feeds, lodges, and is clad worse than a day labourer in *England*" (Locke 1988: para. 2:41). English colonial presuppositions operating in Hurst's work are discussed in Tomlins (2003).

2 Mark Graber (2000) has identified a series of early- to mid-nineteenth century cases where the US Supreme Court exercised its power of judicial review to undo "naked land transfers" – addressing a taking of private property from one owner and transferring it to another. In these cases, the Court effectively would declare federal and state measures unconstitutional without uttering the word (2000: 103). The string of cases Graber discusses do not appear to concern public infrastructure projects of the sort I have been describing in this part.

3 McGinnis and Movesian acknowledge the constitutional analogy is "not exact," and so maintain that no "regulatory superstructure" is required at the transnational level to enforce labour or environmental standards (2000: 543). They urge, nevertheless, a process-based standard of review as regards discriminatory conduct – including a least restrictive means requirement – that runs afoul of WTO disciplines. This standard of review, they insist, would facilitate democracy rather than constrain it. As noted

in Chapter three, it is not difficult to imagine welfare-maximizing less restrictive alternatives (Howse 2000: 140). The Canadian constitutional context is instructive in this regard. Governments are entitled to limit constitutional rights and freedoms in those instances where they have, among other things, chosen the least restrictive means of limiting rights. After 20 years of experience under the charter, applying this limb of the justification process has emerged as the most controversial as it is the standard against which governments too often have faltered.

4 These bodies build on the "Paris Principles," developed under the auspices of the United Nations Commission on Human Rights, that provide a benchmark for human rights institutions. See Lindsnæs and Lindholt (1999), International Council on Human Rights Policy (2000).

5 For these reasons, concession contracts raise some of the same problems associated with investment treaties, though limited to the life of the concession. If democracies like the United States reserve the right unilaterally to change the contractual conditions under which businesses operate (Franck 1995: 444), we should expect, then, that similar considerations will apply to new and emergent democracis.

# BIBLIOGRAPHY

Ackerman, Bruce. 1991. *Foundations: We the People.* Cambridge: Harvard University Press.

African National Congress. 1995. *Preliminary Submission on Land Rights* (September 10) [Unpublished].

*Agrarian Reform in Roumania and the Case of the Hungarian Optants in Transylvania before the League of Nations.* 1927.

Ahnlid, Anders. 1997. "New Disciplines," in OECD Working Papers, vol. V (No. 96). *Proceedings of the Special Session on the Multilateral Agreement on Investment Held in Paris on 17 September 1997.* Paris: OECD, pp. 23–5.

Albrow, Martin. 1997. *The Global Age.* Stanford, CA: Stanford University Press.

Alden, Chris and Marco Antonio Vieira. 2005. "The New Diplomacy of the South: South Africa, Brazil, India and Trilateralism," *Third World Quarterly* 26: 1077–95.

Alden, Edward. 2002. "U.S. Does About-Face on Expropriation," *The National Post* (October 2), FP 16.

2005. "US Faces Tough Talks with Egypt in Its Push for Regional Trade Accords," *The Financial Post* (September 29), p. 6.

Alexander, Gregory S. 1997. *Commodity and Propriety: Competing Visions of Property in American Legal Thought, 1776–1970.* Chicago: Chicago University Press.

2006. *The Global Debate over Constitutional Property: Lessons for American Takings Jurisprudence.* Chicago: University of Chicago Press.

All URLs are current as of September 21, 2007, unless otherwise indicated.

Alexandroff, Alan S. 2006. "Introduction," in Alexandroff (ed.), *Investor Protection in the NAFTA and Beyond: Private Interest and Public Purpose*. Toronto: C. D. Howe Institute, pp. 1–25.

Alexandrov, Stanimir A. 2005. "The Baby Boom of Treaty-Based Arbitrations and the Jurisdiction of ICSID Tribunals," *Journal of World Investment and Trade* 6: 387–412.

Allen, Tom. 1999. "The Human Rights Act (UK) and Property Law," in Janet McLean (ed.), *Property and the Constitution*. Oxford: Hart, pp. 147–69.

Althusser, Louis and Etienne Balibar. 1970. *Reading Capital*, trans. Ben Brewster. New York: Pantheon Books.

Alvarez, Alejandro. 1927. "The Agrarian Reform: The Hungarian–Roumanian Controversy before the Council of the League of Nations," in *Agrarian Reform in Roumania* (1927), pp. 41–57.

Alvarez, José E. 1992. "Remarks," *American Society of International Law Proceedings* 86: 550–6.

Alvaro, Alexander. 1991. "Why Property Rights Were Excluded from the Canadian Charter of Rights and Freedoms," *Canadian Journal of Political Science* 24: 309–429.

American Law Institute. 1987. *Restatement of the Law Third, the Foreign Relations of the United States*, vol. 2. St. Paul: The American Law Institute.

Anderson, Chandler P. 1927. "Basis of the Law Against Confiscating Foreign-Owned Property," *American Journal of International Law* 21: 525–33.

Anderson, Gavin W. 2005. *Constitutional Rights After Globalization*. Oxford: Hart Publishing.

Andrews, Edmund L. 2001. "Backing U.P.S. Complaint, Europeans Fine German Postal Service," *The New York Times* (March 21), p. C6.

Angell, Marcia. 2004. "The Truth about Drug Companies," *The New York Review of Books* (July 15).

Anghie, Anthony. 2004. *Imperialism, Sovereignty and the Making of International Law*. Cambridge: Cambridge University Press.

Anzorena, C. Ignacio Súarez, Robert Wisner, Jack J. Coe, Jr., Claudia T. Salomon, and Keria S. Gans. 2006. "International Commercial Dispute Resolution," *International Lawyer* 40: 251–62.

Appleton, Barry. 2000. "NAFTA Ruling Will Force Governments to Disclose," *The Lawyers Weekly* (September 29), p. 16.

2001. "Canada Is Encouraging Old-Fashioned Trade Barriers," *Financial Post* (March 23), p. C19.

2006. "Deliberation on the NAFTA Decade: Confronting Facts and Fiction in Light of Recent NAFTA Decisions," in Alexandroff (ed.), pp. 27–60.

Arendt, Hannah. 1959. *The Human Condition.* Garden City: Doubleday Anchor Books.

Aristotle. 1995. *Politics Books II and IV*, trans. Richard Robinson. Oxford: Clarendon Press.

Armstrong, Jerome and Markos Moulitsas Zúniga. 2006. *Crashing the Gate: Netroots, Grassroots, and the Rise of People-Powered Politics.* White River Junction, VT: Chelsea Green.

Arrighi, Giovanni and Beverley J. Silver. 1999. *Chaos and Governance in the Modern World System.* Minneapolis: University of Minnesota Press.

Atik, Jeffrey. 2004. "Legitimacy, Transparency and NGO Participation in the NAFTA Chapter 11 Process," in Weiler (ed.), pp. 135–50.

Ayine, Dominic, Hernán Blanco, Lorenzo Cotula, et al. 2005. "Lifting the Lid on Foreign Investment Contracts: The Real Deal for Sustainable Development," *Sustainable Markets Briefing Paper* (No. 1, September), International Institute for Sustainable Development online at www.iied.org/pubs/pdf/full/16007IIED.pdf

Azuela, Antonio. 2004. "Con olor a NAFTA. El caso Metalclad y la nueva geografía del Derecho Mexicano" (Paper prepared for the International Congress "Culturas y Sistemas Juridicos Comparados," Legal Research Institute, UNAM, Mexico City, January).

Bakan, Joel, Bruce Ryder, Margot Young, and David Schneiderman. 1995. "Developments in Constitutional Law: The 1993–94 Term," *Supreme Court Law Review* (2d) 6: 67–126.

Balcazar, Alvaro, Nelson López, Martha Lucía Orozco, and Margarita Vega. 2001. *Colombia: alvanes y lecciones de su experienca en reforma agraria.* Santiago de Chile: CEPAL.

Banakar, Reza. 1998. "Reflexive Legitimacy in International Arbitration," in Volkmar gessner and Ali Cem Budak (eds), *Emerging Legal Certainty: Empirical Studies on the Globalization of Law.* Aldershot: Ashgate, pp. 347–98.

Banks, Kevin. 1999. "NAFTA's Article 1110: Can Regulation Be Expropriation?" *NAFTA: Law and Business Review of the Americas* 5: 499–521.

Banks, William C. and Edgar Alvarez. 1991. "The New Colombian Constitution: Democratic Victory or Popular Surrender?," *University of Miami Inter-American Law Review* 23: 38–92.

Barber, Benjamin R. 2002. "A Failure of Democracy, Not Capitalism," *The New York Times* (July 29), p. A19.

Bartholomew, Amy and Alan Hunt. 1990. "What's Wrong With Rights?" *Law and Inequality* 9: 1–58.

Bauman R. J. 1994. "Exotic Expropriations: Government Action and Compensation," *The Advocate* 52: 561.

Bauman, Richard. 1997. "Business, Economic Rights and the Charter," in David Schneiderman and Kate Sutherland (eds), *Charting the Consequences: The Impact of Charter Rights on Canadian Law and Politics*. Toronto: University of Toronto Press, pp. 58–108.

Bauman, Zygmunt. 1998. *Work, Consumerism and the New Poor*. Buckingham: Open University Press.

1999. *In Search of Politics*. Stanford, CA: Stanford University Press.

Baxi, Upendra. 1998. "Voices of Suffering and the Future of Human Rights," *Transnational Law and Contemporary Problems* 8: 113–169.

2006. *The Future of Human Rights*, 2nd edn. New Delhi: Oxford University Press.

Beatty, David M. 2004. *The Ultimate Rule of Law*. Oxford: Oxford University Press.

Beaufort Wijnholds, J. Onno de, and Lex Hoodguin. 1994. "Central Bank Autonomy: Policy Issue," in J. Onno de Beaufort Wijnholds, Sylvester C. W. Eijffinger, and Lex H. Hoodguin (eds), *A Framework for Monetary Stability*. Dordrecht: Kluwer, pp. 74–95.

Beck, Ulrich. 2000. *What Is Globalization?* Cambridge: Polity Press.

2005. *Power in the Global Age*. Cambridge: Polity Press.

Been, Vicki and Joel C. Beauvais. 2003. "The Global Fifth Amendment: NAFTA's Investment Protections and the Misguided Quest for an International 'Regulatory Takings' Doctrine," *New York University Law Review* 78: 30–143.

Benhabib, Seyla, ed. 1996. *Democracy and Difference: Contesting the Boundaries of the Political*. Princeton, NJ: Princeton University Press.

Benkler, Yochai. 2006. *The Wealth of Networks: How Social Production Transforms Markets and Freedom*. New Haven, CT: Yale University Press.

Bennett, W. Lance. 2005. "Communicating Global Activism: Strengths and Vulnerabilities of Networked Politics," in Van de Donk et al. (eds), 2005, pp. 123–46.

Berger, Jonathan. 2002. "Tripping Over Patents: AIDS, Access to Treatment and the Manufacturing of Scarcity," *Connecticut Journal of International Law* 17: 157–248.

Bhagwati, Jagdish. 2004. "Don't Cry for Cancun," *Foreign Affairs* (January 1) 83(1): 52–63.

Bhuie, A. K., O. A. Ogunseitan, R. R. White, M. Sain, and D. N. Roy. 2005. "Modeling the Environmental Fate of Manganese from Methycyclopentadienyl manganese tricarbonyl in Urban Landscapes," *The Science of the Total Environment* 339(1–3): 167–78.

Birdsall, Nancy and John Nellis. 2005. "Privatization Reality Check: Distributional Effects on Developing Countries," in John Nellis and Nancy Birdsall (eds), *Reality Check: The Distributional Impact of*

*Privatization in Developing Countries.* Washington: Center for Global Development, pp. 1–30.

Bishop R. Doak, James Crawford, and W. Michael Reisman. 2005. *Foreign Investment Disputes: Cases, Materials and Commentary.* The Hague: Kluwer International.

Blackett, Adelle. 1999. "Whither Social Clause? Human Rights, Trade Theory and Treaty Interpretation," *Columbia Human Rights Law Review* 31: 1–80.

Blackstone, William. 1750 [1979]. *Commentaries on the Laws of England.* Chicago: University of Chicago Press.

Block, Fred. 1987. *Revising State Theory: Essays in Politics and Postindustrialism.* Philadelphia: Temple University Press.

Blume, Lawrence and Rubinfield Daniel L. 1984. "Compensation for Takings: An Economic Analysis," *California Law Review* 72: 569–627.

Blustein, Paul. 2006. "Trade Deal Looks More Like a Distant Dream," *The Washington Post* (July 4), p. D1.

Bockenforde, Ernst-Wolfgang. 1998. "The Concept of the Political: A Key to Understanding Carl Schmitt's Constitutional Theory," in Dyzenhaus (ed.), pp. 37–55.

Bohman, James. 1996. *Public Deliberation: Pluralism, Complexity, and Democracy.* Cambridge: MIT Press.

Bollyky, Thomas J. 2002. "Balancing Private Rights and Public Obligations: Constitutionally Mandated Compulsory Licensing of HIV/AIDS Related Treatments in South Africa," *South African Journal on Human Rights* 18: 530–69.

Borchard, Edwin. 1939. "The 'Minimum Standard' of the Treatment of Aliens," *American Society of International Law Proceedings* 33: 51–63.

Bordo, Michael D. and Finn E. Kydland. 1996. "The Gold Standard as Commitment Mechanism," in Tamim Bayoumi, Barry Eichengreen, and Mark P. Talyor (eds), *Modern Perspectives on the Gold Standard.* Cambridge, NY: Cambridge University Press, pp. 55–100.

Bosniak, Linda. 2000. "Citizenship Denationalized," *Indiana Journal of Global Legal Studies* 7: 447–509.

Boudia, N., R. Halley, G. Kennedy, J. Lambert, L. Gareau, and J. Zayed. 2006. "Manganese Concentrations in the Air of the Montreal (Canada) Subway in Relation to Surface Automobile Traffic Density," *Science of the Total Environment* 366(1): 143–7.

Bourdieu, Pierre. 1998. *Acts of Resistance: Against the Tyranny of the Market.* New York: New Press.

2000. *Pascalian Meditations.* Stanford, CA: Stanford University Press.

Boyer, Robert and Daniel Drache. 1996. "Introduction," in Boyer and Drache (eds), pp. 1–27.

Boyer, Robert and Daniel Drache (eds) 1996. *States against Markets: The Limits of Globalization.* London: Routledge.

Braithwaite, John and Peter Drahos. 2000. *Global Business Regulation*. Cambridge: Cambridge University Press.

Brenner, Neil. 1999. "Beyond State-Centrism? Space, Territoriality, and Geographical Scale in Globalization Studies," *Theory and Society* 28: 39–78.

Broude, Henry W. 1964. "The Role of the State in American Economic Development, 1820–1890," in Scheiber (ed.), pp. 114–35.

Brower, Charles H. II. 2003. "Structure, Legitimacy, and NAFTA's Investment Chapter," *Vanderbilt Journal of Transnational Law* 36: 37–94.

Brownlie, Ian. 1995. "International Law at the Fiftieth Anniversary of the United Nations: General Course on Public International Law," *Recueil des cours*, vol. 255. The Hague: Martinus Nijhoff, pp. 9–228.

2003. *Principles of Public International Law*, 6th edn. Oxford: Oxford University Press.

Brunkhorst, Hauke. 2006. "The Legitimation Crisis of the European Union," *Constellations* 13: 165–80.

Buchanan, James M. 1991. "The Domain of Constitutional Political Economy," in Buchanan (ed.), *The Economics and the Ethics of Constitutional Order*. Ann Arbor: University of Michigan Press, pp. 3–18.

Buchanan, James M., and Gordon Tullock. 1962. *The Calculus of Consent: Logical Foundations of Constitutional Democracy*. Ann Arbor: University of Michigan Press.

Budlender, Geoff. 1998. "The Constitutional Protection of Property Rights: Overview and Commentary," in Geoff Budlender, Johan Latsky, and Theunis Roux (eds), *Juta's New Land Law*. Kenwyn: Juta.

Buergenthal, Thomas. 2006. "The Proliferation of Disputes, Dispute Settlement Procedures and Respect for the Rule of Law" online at transnational-dispute-management.com (December) 3(5).

Burin, Frederic S. and Kurt L. Shell, eds. 1969. *Politics, Law, and Social Change*. New York: Columbia University Press.

*Business Day*. 2006. "Cabinet Approves BEE Codes" (December 7), online at www.businessday.co.za

Caldwell, Peter C. 1997. *Popular Sovereignty and the Crisis of German Constitutional Law: The Theory and Practice of Weimar Constitutionalism*. Durham, NC: Duke University Press.

Calliess, Gralf-Peter. 2002. "Reflexive Transnational Law: The Privatisation of Civil Law and the Civilisation of Private Law," *Zeitschrift fr Rechtssoziologie* 23: 185–216.

Calvo, Carlos [Charles] M. 1870. *Le Droit International Théorique et Practique*, 2nd edn. Paris: Amyot.

Campbell, Bruce. 1993. "Restructuring the Economy: Canada into the Free Trade Era," in Ricardo Grinspun and Maxwell A. Cameron (eds),

*The Political Economy of North American Free Trade*. Montreal: McGill-Queen's University Press, pp. 89–104.

Canada, Department of Foreign Affairs and International Trade. 1994. *Press Release*.

1998a. *Visit to Canada by Nelson Mandela, President of South Africa, September 24–25, 1998: Background Information*.

1998b. Trade and Economic Analysis Division. *Developments in Canada's Trade and Foreign Investment in 1997*.

2006a. "Canadian Direct Investment Abroad," online at www.dfait-maeci.gc.ca/eet/foreign-statements-en.asp

2006b. *Seventh Annual Report on Canada's State of Trade: Trade Update*. Ottawa: Minister of Public Works and Government Services Canada, online at www.international.gc.ca/eet/trade/state-of-trade-en.asp

Canada, Department of Health, Expert Panel Report. 1995. *When Packages Can't Speak: Possible Impacts of Plain and Generic Packaging of Tobacco Products* (March).

Canada Gazette. 2001. "Notice" (December 1), p. 4299.

Canada, House of Commons. 1994a. "Minutes and Proceedings of Evidence of the Standing Committee on Health" (April 14).

Standing Committee on Health. 1994b. *Towards Zero: Generic Packaging of Tobacco Products*. Ottawa (June).

Sub-Committee on International Trade, Trade Disputes and Investment. 1997a. "Proceedings and Evidence."

Sub-Committee on International Trade, Trade Disputes and Investment. 1997b. Report (December 17).

Canada, Internal Trade Secretariat. 1998c. *Report of the Article 1704 Panel Concerning a Dispute between Alberta and Canada Regarding the Manganese-Based Fuel Additives Act* (June 12), Winnipeg, Manitoba.

Canada, Report of the Task Force on the Structure of Canadian Industry. 1968. *Foreign Ownership and the Structure of Canadian Industry*. Ottawa: The Privy Council Office.

Canadian Centre for Policy Alternatives. 2004. "Filling Our Tanks (and Our Brains) with the Wrong Fuel," *The CCPA Monitor* (September), online at http://policyalternatives.ca/index.cfm?act=news&call=880&do=article&pA=BB736455

Cánovas, Antonio Garza. 1992. "Introductory Note," *International Legal Materials* 31: 390–6.

Carbonneau. Thomas. 2002. "The Ballad of Transborder Arbitration," *University of Miami Law Review* 56: 773–829.

Cardenas, Sonia. 2002. "National Human Rights Commissions in Asia," *Human Rights Review* 4: 30–51.

Cass, Deborah Z. 2005. *The Constitutionalization of the World Trade Organization*. Oxford: Oxford University Press.

Cass, Ronald A. 1988. "Privatization: Politics, Law, and Theory," *Marquette Law Review* 71: 449–523.

Castañeda, Jorge G. 2006. "Latin America's Left Turn" *Foreign Affairs* (May-June): 29–43.

Castel, J.-G. 1994. "Legal Opinion for Fasken Campbell Godfrey" (May 30).

Castells, Manuel. 1996. *The Rise of the Network Society*. Oxford: Blackwells. 1997. *The Power of Identity*. Oxford: Blackwells.

Cepeda, Manuel José. 1998. "Democracy, State and Society in the 1991 Constitution: The Role of the Constitutional Court," in Eduardo Posada-Carbó (ed.), *Colombia: The Politics of Reforming the State*. London: Macmillan Press, pp. 71–95.

Cerny, Philip. 1997. "Paradoxes of the Competition State: The Dynamics of Political Globalization," *Government and Opposition* 32: 251–74.

Chang, Ha-Joon. 2002. *Kicking Away the Ladder: Development Strategy in Historical Perspective*. London: Anthem Press.

Charnovitz, Steve. 2007. "Trade and the Environment in the WTO," *Journal of International Economic Law* 10: 685–706.

Chase, Stephen. 2001. "Ottawa Faces Suit Over Banned Pesticide," *The Globe and Mail* (December 10), p. B1.

2002a. "Tobacco Firm Warns 'Mild' Cigarette Ban May Violate NAFTA," *The Globe and Mail* (March 16), p. A6.

2002b. "Ottawa Loses Pope Lumber Spat," *The Globe and Mail* (June 1), p. E1.

2004. "Canada Could Lose Face Over Bill, Lewis Says" *The Globe and Mail* (November 25), p. A9.

2006. "U.S. Dairy Suing Ottawa Over Milk Exports" *The Globe and Mail* (February 28), p. B3.

2007. "Investor Uses NAFTA to Sue Ottawa Over Landfill Site," *The Globe and Mail* (January 29), p. B3.

Chaskalson, Matthew. 1994. "The Property Clause: Section 28 of the Constitution," *South African Journal on Human Rights* 10: 131–9.

1995. "Stumbling towards Section 28: Negotiations Over Property Rights at the Multiparty Talks," *South African Journal of Human Rights* 11: 222–40.

Chaskalson, Matthew and Carol Lewis. 1996. "Property," in Chaskalson et al. (1996).

Chaskalson, Matthew, Janet Kentridge, Jonathan Klaaren, Gilbert Marcus, Derek Spitz, and Stuart Woolman. 1996. *Constitutional Law of South Africa*. Kenwyn: Juta.

Cho, Albert H. and Navroz K. Dubash. 2005. "Will Investment Rules Shrink Policy Space for Sustainable Development? Evidence from the Electricity Sector," in Kevin P. Gallagher (ed.), *Putting Development First: The Importance of Policy Space in the WTO and International Financial Institutions*. London: Zed Books.

Choudhury, Barnali. 2005. "Evolution or Devolution? – Defining Fair and Equitable Treatment in International Investment Law," *Journal of World Investment and Trade* 6: 263–96.

Chow, Franklin. 1994. "Recent Trends in Canadian Direct Investment Abroad: The Rise of Canadian Multinationals," in Steven Globerman (ed.), *Canadian-Based Multinationals.* Calgary: University of Calgary Press, pp. 35–62.

Christie, G. C. 1962. "What Constitutes a Taking of Property Under International Law?" *British Yearbook of International Law* 28: 307–38.

Chua, Amy. 1995. "The Privatization-Nationalization Cycle: The Link between Markets and Ethnicity in Developing Countries," *Columbia Law Review* 95: 223–303.

Clarke, Tony and Maude Barlow. 1997. *MAI: The Multilateral Agreement and the Threat to Canadian Sovereignty.* Toronto: Stoddart.

Clarkson, Stephen 1993. "Constitutionalizing the Canadian-American Relationship," in Duncan Cameron and Mel Watkins (eds), *Canada Under Free Trade.* Toronto: James Lorimer, pp. 3–20.

1998. "Somewhat Less than Meets the Eye: NAFTA as Constitution," Presented at the International Sociological Association Annual Meeting, July 27, 1998.

2002. *Uncle Sam and US: Globalization, Neoconservatism and the Canadian State.* Toronto: Toronto University Press.

2003. "NAFTA and the WTO's Role in Transforming Mexico's Economic System," in Joseph S. Tulchin and Andrew D. Selee (eds), *Mexico's Politics and Society in Transition.* Boulder, CO: Lynne Rienner.

Closa, Carlos. 1998. "European Union Citizenship and Supranational Democracy," in Albert Weale and Michael Nentwich (eds), *Political Theory and the European Union: Legitimacy, Constitutional Choice and Citizenship.* London: Routledge, pp. 172–86.

Coe, Jr. Jack. 2003. "Taking Stock of NAFTA Chapter 11 in its Tenth Year: An Interim Sketch of Selected Themes, Issues, and Methods," *Vanderbilt Journal of Transnational Law* 36: 1381–460.

Coe, Jr. Jack and Noah Rubins. 2005. "Regulatory Expropriations and the *Tecmed* Case: Context and Contributions," in Weiler (ed.) (2005), pp. 597–667.

Cohen, Morris R. 1917. "The Legal Calvinism of Elihu Root," in Cohen (1982), pp. 12–18.

1927. "Property and Sovereignty," *Cornell Law Review* 13: 8, in Cohen (1982), pp. 41–68.

1982. *Law and Social Order: Essays in Legal Philosophy.* New Brunswick: Transaction Books.

Comeaux, Paul and Stephan Kinsella. 1994. "Reducing Political Risk in Developing Countries: Bilateral Investment Treaties, Stabilization

Clauses, and MIGA and OPIC Investment Insurance," *New York Law School Journal of International and Comparative Law* 15: 1–48.

Commission on Environmental Cooperation (CEC). 2003. "CEC Receives Mexico's Response to Cytrar III Submission" (November 28), online at http://www.cec.org/news/details/index.cfm?varlan'english

Constaín, Alfredo. 1959. *Elementos Derecho Constitucional.* Bogota: Temis.

Cooley, Thomas M. 1868. *A Treatise on the Constitutional Limitations which Rest upon the Legislative Power of the States of the American Union.* Boston: Little Brown.

1878. "Limits to State Control of Private Business," *Princeton Review* (New Series 1) March: 233–71.

Cooper, Christopher. 2006. "Court's Eminent Domain Edict Is a Flash-Point on State Ballots," *The Wall Street Journal* (August 7), p. A4.

Corcoran, Terence. 1998. "Free Trade and Good Science Rule" *The Globe and Mail* (January 21, 1998), p. B2.

2001. "Ottawa's Campaign to Sabotage NAFTA," *The Financial Post* (February 23).

Corder, Hugh. 1994. "Towards a South African Constitution," *Modern Law Review* 57: 491–533.

Corr, Christopher F. and Kristina Zissis. 1999. "Convergence and Opportunity: The WTO Government Procurement Agreement and U.S. Procurement Reform," *New York Law School Journal of International and Comparative Law* 18: 303–56.

Correa, Carlos M. 2006. "Implications of Bilateral Free Trade Agreements on Access to Medicines," *Bulletin of the World Health Organization* 84(5): 399–404.

2007. *Trade Related Aspects of Intellectual Property Rights: A Commentrary on the TRIPS Agreement.* Oxford: Oxford University Press.

Corwin, Edward S. 1914. "The Basic Doctrine of American Constitutional Law," in Richard Loss (ed.), *Corwin on the Constitution, Volume Three: On Liberty Against Government.* Ithaca: Cornell University Press, pp. 27–51.

COSATU. 1996–7. "The Social Clause." *The Shopsteward* 5(6) (December-January), online at www.cosatu.org.za/shop/shop0506.html# THE%20SOCIAL%20CLAUSE

Cotterrell, Roger. 1995. "Social Foundations of the Rule of Law: Franz Neumann and Otto Kirchheimer," in R. Cotterrell (ed.), *Law's Community: Legal Theory in Sociological Perspective.* Oxford: Clarendon Press.

1996. "The Rule of Law in Transition: Revisiting Franz Neumann's Sociology of Legality," *Social and Legal Studies* 5(4): 451–70.

Cox, Robert W. 1987. *Production, Power and World Order: Social Forces in the Making of History.* New York: Columbia University Press.

1989. "Middlepowermanship, Japan, and Future World Order," in Cox and Sinclair, pp. 241–75.

1992. "Global Perestroika," in Cox and Sinclair, pp. 296–313.

1996. "The Global Political Economy and Social Choice" in Cox and Sinclair, pp. 191–208.

1999. "Civil Society at the Turn of the Millennium: Prospects for an Alternative World Order," *Review of International Studies* 25: 3–28.

Cox, Robert W. and Timothy J. Sinclair. 1996. *Approaches to World Order*. Cambridge, NY: Cambridge University Press.

Crawford, James, ed. 2002. *The International Law Commission's Articles on State Responsibility: Introduction, Text, and Commentaries*. Cambridge: Cambridge University Press.

Creamer, Terence. 2007. "Italy Raises Concern about SA's Mine Law, But Takes Hands-Off Position in Granite Dispute," *Mining Weekly* (March 15), online at http://www.miningweekly.co.za/article.php?a_id=105736

Cremades, Bernardo M. 2005. "The Resurgence of the Calvo Doctrine in Latin America," transnational-dispute-management.com (November) 2(5).

Cronin, Jeremy. 2004. "BEE-llionaires and Wanna-BEEs" *Mail & Guardian* (October 20).

Cross, Sir Rupert. 1987. *Statutory Interpretation*, 2nd edn. by Bell and Engle (eds). London: Butterworths.

Currie, Iain and Johan de Waal. 2005. *The Bill of Rights Handbook*, 5th edn. Lansdowne: Juta.

Curtis, Jennifer. 1999. "Big Oil vs. Big Auto," Report on *Business Magazine* (March), pp. 62–71.

Cutler, A. Claire. 2003. *Private Power and Global Authority: Transnational Merchant Law in the Global Political Economy*. Cambridge: Cambridge University Press.

Dagan, Hanoch. 1999. "Takings and Distributive Justice," *Virginia Law Review* 85: 741–804.

Dahl, Robert A. 1961. *Who Governs? Democracy and Power in an American City*. New Haven, CT: Yale University Press.

Daintith, Terence and Monica Sah. 1993. "Privatisation and the Economic Neutrality of the Constitution," *Public Law* 1993: 465–87.

Daly, Justine. 1994. "Has Mexico Crossed the Border on State Responsibility for Economic Injury to Aliens? Foreign Investment and the Calvo Clause in Mexico after NAFTA," *St. Mary's Law Journal* 25: 1147–93.

Dana, David A. and Thomas W. Merrill. 2002. *Property: Takings*. New York: Foundation Press.

Daniels, Ronald J. 2004. "Defecting on Development: Bilateral Investment Treaties and the Subversion of the Rule of Law in the Developing World," Faculty Workshop, Faculty of Law, University of Toronto (November 29), online at http://www.unisi.it/lawandeconomics/stile2004/daniels.pdf

Daniels, Ronald J. and Michael Trebilcock. 2005. "The Political Economy of Rule of Law Reform in Developing Countries," *Michigan Journal of International Law* 26: 99–140.

Davey, Monica. 2006. "Liberals Find Ray of Hope in Ballot Measures," *The New York Times* (November 9), p. P16.

Davis, Dennis. 1999. *Democracy and Deliberation*. Kenwyn: Juta.

  2006. "Adjudicating the Socio-Economic Rights in the South African Constitution: Towards 'Deference Lite'?" *South African Journal on Human Rights* 22: 301–27.

Davis, Lance and Robert J. Cull. 2000. "International Capital Movements, Domestic Capital Markets, and American Economic Growth," in Engerman and Gallman (eds), pp. 733–812.

Dearlove, John. 1989. "Bringing the Constitution Back In: Political Science and the State," *Political Studies* 37: 521–39.

Del Castillo, Carlos Pérez. 2003. "The General Council Chairperson's Statement," online at www.wto.org/english/news_e/news03_e/trips_stat_28aug03_e.htm

Denis, Claude. 1997. *We Are Not You: First Nations and Canadian Modernity*. Peterborough: Broadview Press.

Dewey, John. 1954. *The Public and Its Problems*. Athens, Ohio: The Swallow Press.

Dezalay, Yves and Bryant G. Garth. 1996. *Dealing in Virtue: International Commercial Arbitration and the Construction of a Transnational Legal Order*. Chicago: University of Chicago Press.

  2002. "Legitimating the New Orthodoxy," in Dezalay and Garth (eds), pp. 306–34.

  eds. 2002. *Global Prescriptions: The production, Exportation, and Importation of a New Legal Orthodoxy*. Ann Arbor: University of Michigan Press.

Dicey, Albert Venn. 1885. *Introduction to the Law of the Constitution*. London: Macmillan.

  1886. "Americomania in English Politics," *The Nation* 42: 52–3.

  1890. "Ought the Referendum Be Introduced in England?" *Contemporary Review* 57: 489–507.

Diebert, Ronald J. 2002. "Civil Society Activism on the World Wide Web: The Case of the Anti-MAI Lobby," in David R. Cameron and Janice Gross Stein (eds), *Street Protests and Fantasy Parks: Globalization, Culture, and the State*. Vancouver: UBC Press, pp. 88–108.

Dirlik, Arif. 1994. "The Postcolonial Aura: Third World Criticism in an Age of Global Capitalism," *Critical Inquiry* 20: 328–56.

Dodge, William S. 2006. "Investor-State Dispute Settlement between Developed Countries: Reflections on the Australia-United States Free Trade Agreement" *Vanderbilt Journal of Transnational Law* 39: 1–37.

Doern, G. Bruce and Brian W. Tomlin. 1991. *Faith & Fear: The Free Trade Story.* Toronto: Stoddart.

Dolzer, Rudolf. 1981. "New Foundations of the Law of Expropriations of Alien Property," *American Journal of International Law* 75: 553–89.

1986. "Indirect Expropriation of Alien Property," *ICSID Review – Foreign Investment Law Journal* 1: 41–65.

1992. "Norwegian Shipowners' Claims Arbitration," *Encyclopaedia of Public International Law,* vol. III. Amsterdam: Elsevier.

2002. "Indirect Expropriations: New Developments?" *New York University Environmental Law Journal* 11: 64–93.

2005. "Fair and Equitable Treatment: A Key Standard in Investment Treaties" *International Law* 39: 87–106.

Dolzer, Rudolf and Felix Bloch. 2003. "Indirect Expropriation: Conceptual Realignments?" *International Law Forum* 5: 155–65.

Dolzer, Rudolf and Margarete Stevens. 1995. *Bilateral Investment Treaties.* The Hague: Martinus Nijhoff.

Dorday, Alan and Mary Mellor. 2001. "Grassroots Environmental Movements: Mobilisation in an Information Age," in Frank Webster (ed.), *Culture and Politics in the Information Age.* London: Routledge.

Dorf, Michael C. and Charles F. Sabel. 1998. "A Constitution of Democratic Experimentalism," *Columbia Law Review* 98: 267–473.

Douglas, Zachary. 2006. "Nothing if Not Critical for Investment Treaty Arbitration: *Occidental*, Eureko and *Methanex*," *Arbitration International* 22: 27–51.

Downs, Anthony. 1957. *An Economic Theory of Democracy.* New York: Harper & Row.

Drache, Daniel P. 1998. "The Mulroney-Reagan Accord: The Economics of Continental Power," in March Gold and David Leyton-Brown (eds), *Trade-Offs on Free Trade: The Canada-U.S. Free Trade Agreement.* Toronto: Carswell, pp. 79–88.

Drahos, Peter. 2002. "Negotiating Intellectual Property Rights: Between Coercion and Dialogue," in Drahos and Mayne (eds), pp. 161–82.

Drahos, Peter and John Braithwaite. 2002. *Information Feudalism: Who Owns the Knowledge Economy?* London: Earthscan Publications.

Drahos, Peter and Ruth Mayne, eds. 2002. *Global Intellectual Property Rights: Knowledge, Access and Development.* Hampshire: Palgrave Macmillan.

Dreidger, Elmer A. 1957. *The Composition of Legislation.* Ottawa: Queen's Printer.

Drohan, Madelaine. 1998. "How the Net Killed the MAI," *The Globe and Mail* (July 3), pp. A1, A13.

Dugard, John. 2002. "Third Report on Diplomatic Protection," International Law Commission 54th Session, U.N. Doc. A/CN.4/523/Add.1 online at http://daccessdds.un.org/doc/UNDOC/GEN/N02/336/86/PDF/N0233686. pdf?OpenElement

Duguit, Léon. 1918. *Manuel de droit constitutionnel*, 3e. ed. Paris: Anciennes Librarie Fontemoing & Cie, Éditeurs.

Dumberry, Patrick. 2001. "The NAFTA Investment Dispute Settlement Mechanism: A Review of the Latest Case Law," *Journal of World Investment* 2: 151–195.

Dunleavy, Patrick. 1991. *Democracy, Bureaucracy and Public Choice: Economic Explanations in Political Science*. New York: Prentice Hall.

Dunn, Frederick Sherwood. 1928. "International Law and Private Property Rights," *Columbia Law Review* 28: 166–80.

Dymond, William. 1999. "The MAI: A Sad and Melancholy Tale," in Fen Osler Hampson, Martin Rudner, and Michael Hart (eds), *Canada among Nations 1999: A Big League Player?* Don Mills: Oxford University Press, pp. 25–53.

Dyzenhaus, David (ed.) 1998. *Law as Politics: Carl Schmitt's Critique of Liberalism*. Durham, NC: Duke University Press.

ed. 1999. *Recrafting the Rule of Law: The Limits of Legal Order*. Oxford: Hart.

Easterly, William. 1995. "Colombia: Avoiding Crises through Fiscal Policy," in William Easterly, Carlos Alfredo Rodríguez, and Klaus Schmidt-Hebbel (eds), *Public Sector Deficits and Macroeconomic Performance*. Oxford: Oxford University Press, pp. 225–72.

Ebrahim, Hassen. 1998. *The Soul of a Nation: Constitution-Making in South Africa*. Cape Town: Oxford University Press.

*Economist*. 1999a. "The Face of Mammon" (December 4), p. 67.

1999b. "Clueless in Seattle" (December 4), p. 17.

2003. "Liberty's Great Advance," (June 26).

2006. "Land Battles" (September 23), p. 41.

Edwards, Sebastien. 1995. *Crisis and Reform in Latin America*. Oxford: Oxford University Press.

Eggertson, Laura. 1997. "Treaty to Trim Ottawa's Power," *The Globe and Mail* (April 3), p. A1.

Eichengreen, Barry. 1996. *Globalizing Capital: A History of the International Monetary System*. Princeton, NJ: Princeton University Press.

Eisenstadt, S. N. 1999. *The Paradoxes of Democracy: Fragility, Continuity and Change*. Washington and Baltimore: Woodrow Wilson Centre and Johns Hopkins University Press.

Elkins, Zachary, Andrew Guzman, and Beth Simmons. 2004. "Competing for Capital: The Diffusion of Bilateral Investment Treaties, 1996–2000," Boalt Working Papers in Public Law, Paper 124, online at http://repositories.cdlib.org/boaltwp/124

Elster, Jon. 1984. *Ulysses and the Sirens: Studies in Rationality and Irrationality.* Cambridge: Cambridge University Press.

1988. "Consequences of Constitutional Choice: Reflections on Tocqueville," in Elster and Slagstad (eds), pp. 81–102.

1992. "Intemporal Choice and Political Thought," in George Lowenstein and Jon Elster (eds), *Choice Over Time.* New York: Russell Sage Foundation.

2000. *Ulysses Unbound.* Cambridge: Cambridge University Press.

Elster, Jon and Rune Slagstad, eds. 1988. *Constitutionalism and Democracy.* NY: Cambridge University Press.

Ely, John Hart. 1980. *Democracy and Distrust: A Theory of Judicial Review.* Cambridge, MA: Harvard University Press.

Engerman, Stanley L. and Robert E. Gallman, eds. 2000. *The Cambridge Economic History of the United States, vol. II: The Long Nineteenth Century.* NY: Cambridge University Press.

Environment Canada. 1998. "News Release: Government to Act on Agreement on Internal Trade (AIT) Panel Report on MMT," online at www.ec.gc.ca/press/mmt98_n_e.htm

*Environmental Health Perspectives.* 1998. "Is Airborne Manganese a Hazard" (February) 106(2): A57–A58.

Epstein, Richard A. 1985. *Takings: Private Property and the Power of Eminent Domain.* Cambridge, MA: Harvard University Press.

1992. "Property, Speech and the Politics of Distrust," in Geoffrey R. Stone, Richard A. Epstein, and Cass R. Sunstein (eds), *The Bill of Rights in the Modern State.* Chicago: University of Chicago Press, pp. 41–89.

2006. *How Progressives Rewrote the Constitution.* Washington: Cato Institute.

Erlich, Reese. 2002. "A Case of Mexican Labor Reform," *St. Petersburg Times* (July 5), p. 11A.

eSilva, Madalena Oliveira. 1997. "OECD Working Papers, Vol. V: Multilateral Agreement on Investment State of Play in April 1997" (No. 51). Paris: OECD, pp. 33–7.

Ethyl Corporation. 1997a. "Ethyl Files Claim to Seek not Less than U.S.$250 Million," at http://www.ethyl.com/news/4-17-97.html (last accessed November 30, 1999).

1997b. "Ethyl, Canada and MMT: Let's Set the Record Straight," at http://www.ethyl.com/news/4-18-97.html (last accessed November 30, 1999).

1998. "Ethyl Welcomes Government of Canada Decision," at http://www/ethyl.com/news/7-20-98.html (last accessed November 30, 1999).

Everson, Michelle. 2000. "Beyond the *Bunesverfassungsgericht*: On the Necessary Cunning of Constitutional Reasoning," in Zenon Bańkowski and Andrew Scott (eds), *The European Union and Its Order: The Legal Theory of European Integration.* Oxford: Blackwell, pp. 91–112.

Fachiri, Alexander P. 1925. "Expropriation and International Law," *British Yearbook of International Law* 6: 159–71.

1929. "International Law and the Property of Aliens," *British Yearbook of International Law* 10: 32–55.

Farber, Daniel A. and Robert E. Hudec. 1994. "Free Trade and the Regulatory State: A GATT's-Eye View of the Dormant Commerce Clause," *Vanderbilt Law Review* 47: 1401–40.

Fatouros, A. A. 1996. "Towards an International Agreement on Foreign Direct Investment?" in OECD (1996), pp. 47–67.

Featherstone, Liz and United Students against Sweatshops. 2002. *Students Against Sweatshops*. London: Verso.

*Financial Post.* 1997. "Multilateral Investment Pact Serves Canada's Interests" (November 7), p. 16.

*Financial Times.* 2006. "Colombia Unionists Face Deadly Threat" (June 7), p. 6.

Fishlow, Albert. 2000. "Internal Transportation in the Nineteenth and Early Twentieth Centuries," in Engerman and Gallman (eds), pp. 543–642.

Fletcher, Frederick J. and Donald C. Wallace. 1985. "Federal-Provincial Relations and the Making of Public Policy in Canada: A Review of the Case Studies," in Richard Simeon (ed.), *Division of Powers and Public Policy*. Toronto: University of Toronto Press.

Forbath, William E. 1991. *Law and the Shaping of the American Labour Movement.* Cambridge, MA: Harvard University Press.

Forman, Lisa. 2006. "The Power of Human Rights to Increase Access to AIDS Medicines: International Human Rights Law, TRIPS, and a South African Case Study" A thesis submitted in conformity with the requirements for the Degree of Juridical Science, Graduate Department of the Faculty of Law, University of Toronto.

Fox, Donald T. and Anne Stetson. 1992. "The 1991 Constitutional Reform: Prospects for Democracy and the Rule of Law in Colombia," *Case Western Journal of International Law* 24: 139.

Franck, Thomas M. 1995. *Fairness in International Law and Institutions.* Oxford: Clarendon Press.

Frankenburg, Gunther. 2000. "Tocqueville's Question: The Role of a Constitution in the Process of Integration," *Ratio Juris* 13(1): 1–30.

Freeman, Alan. 1994. "U.S. Firms Considers Pearson Challenge" (July 20), p. A1.

Freyer, Tony. 1981. "Reassessing the Impact of Eminent Domain in Early American Economic Development," *Wisconsin Law Review* 36: 1263–86.

Friedmann, W. 1956. "Some Aspects of Social Organization in International Law," *American Journal of International Law* 50: 475–513.

Frug, Gerald E. and David J. Barron. 2006. "International Local Government Law," *The Urban Lawyer* 38: 1–62.

Frumkin, H. and G. Solomon. 1997. "Manganese in the U.S. Gasoline Supply," *American Journal of Industrial Medicine* 31(1): 107–15.

Fudge, Judy and Harry Glasbeek. 1992. "The Politics of Rights: A Politics with Little Class," *Social and Legal Studies* 1: 45–70.

Gaillard, Emmanuel. 2000. "A Strong Start for NAFTA," *New York Law Journal* (February 3), p. 3.

Gaines, Sanford. 2001. "The WTO's Reading of the GATT Article XX Chapeau: A Disguised Restriction on Environmental Measures," *University of Pennsylvania Journal of International Economic Law* 22: 739–858.

2006. "*Methanex Corp.* v. *United States*," *American Journal of International Law* 100: 683–9.

Ganguly, Samrat. 1999. "The Investor-State Dispute Mechanism (ISDM) and a Sovereign's Power to Protect Public Health," *Columbia Journal of Transnational Law* 38: 113–68.

Gantz, David. 2004. "The Evolution of FTA Investment Provisions: From NAFTA to the United States-Chile Free Trade Agreement," *American University International Law Review* 19: 679–767.

Garcia-Mora, Manuel R. 1950. "The Calvo Clause in Latin American Constitutions and International Law," *Marquette Law Review* 33: 205–19.

Garfield, Elise and Jairo Arboleda. 2003. "Violence, Sustainable Peace, and Development," in Giugale et al. (eds), pp. 35–58.

Gauchet, Marcel. 2000. "A New Age of Personality: An Essay on the Psychology of Our Times," *Thesis Eleven* 60: 23–41.

Gelb, Stephen. 2004. "Creating a Black Business Class in South Africa," *CNEM Newsletter* (#7 Summer).

Gelb, Stephen and Anthony Black. 2004. "Foreign Direct Investment in South Africa," in Saul Estrin and Klau E. Meyer (eds), *Investment Strategies in Emerging Markets*. Cheltenham: Edward Elgar, pp. 174–208.

General Agreement on Tariffs and Trade (GATT) – Multilateral Trade Negotiations, The Uruguay Round. 1994. "Agreement on Trade-Related Aspects of Intellectual Property Rights, Including Trade in Counterfeit Goods," *International Legal Materials* 33: 81–111.

Ghosh, Jayati. 2005. "The Right to Development and International Economic Regimes," in Arjun Sengupta, Archna Negi, and Moushumi Basu (eds), *Reflections on the Right to Development*. New Delhi: Sage, pp. 276–304.

Gibson, William Marion. 1948. *The Constitutions of Colombia*. Durham, NC: Duke University Press.

Giddens, Anthony. 1993. *New Rules for Sociological Method*, 2nd edn. Stanford, CA: Stanford University Press.

1994. *Beyond Left and Right: The Future of Radical Politics*. Stanford, CA: Stanford University Press.

2001. *The Global Third Way Debate*. Cambridge: Polity.

Gierke, Otto. 1987. *Political Theories of the Middle Age*, trans. F.W. Maitland. Cambridge: Cambridge University Press.

Gill, Stephen. 1995. "Globalisation, Market Civilisation, and Disciplinary Neoliberalism," *Millennium: Journal of International Studies* 24: 399–423.

——— 1996. "Globalization, Democratization, and the Politics of Indifference," in James H. Mittleman (ed.), *Globalization: Critical Reflections*. Boulder, CO: Lynne Reiner.

——— 2003. *Power and Resistance in the New World Order*. Hampshire: Palgrave Macmillan.

Gillman, Howard. 1993. *The Constitution Besieged: The Rise and Decline of Lochner Era Police Powers Jurisprudence*. Durham, NC: Duke University Press.

Gills, Barry. 1997. "Whither Democracy? Globalization and the 'New Hellenism,'" in Carolien Thomas and Peter Wilkin (eds), *Globalization and the South*. Houndsmills: Macmillan, pp. 60–75.

Giugale, Marcelo M. 2003. "Colombia: The Economic Foundation of Peace," in Giugale et al. (eds), pp. 1–32.

Giugale, Marcelo M, Olivier Lafourcade, and Connie Luff, eds. 2003. *Colombia: The Economic Foundation of Peace*. Washington: World Bank.

*Globe & Mail*. 1998. "Mad Minsters Thwarted" (July 21), p. A14.

Goldstein, Judith L., Miles Kahler, Robert O. Keohane, and Anne-Marie Slaughter. 2001. "Introduction: Legalization and World Politics," in Goldstein et al. (eds), *Legalization and World Politics*. Cambridge: MIT Press, pp. 1–16.

Gqubule, Duma, ed. 2006. *Making Mistakes Righting Wrongs: Insights into Black Economic Empowerment*. Johannesburg and Cape Town: Jonathan Ball.

Graber, Mark. 2000. "Naked Land Transfers and American Constitutional Development," *Vanderbilt Law Review* 53: 73–121.

Gracer, Jeffrey and Robert Mansell. 2000. "NAFTA Liability Imposed on Canada," *New York Law Journal* (December 18), p. 9.

Gramsci, Antonio. 1971. *Selections from the Prison Notebooks*, ed. and trans. Q. Hoare and G. Nowell Smith. New York: International.

Gray, Cheryl W. 1996. "In Search of Owners: Privatization and Corporate Governance in Transition Economies," *The World Bank Research Observer* 11: 179–87.

Green, Thomas Hill. 1881 [1986]. "Liberal Legislation and Freedom of Contract," in Paul Harris, and John Murrow (eds), *Lecture on the Principles of Political Obligation*. Cambridge: Cambridge University Press, pp. 194–212.

Greenhouse, Linda. 2000. "Justices Overturn a State Law on Myanmar," *The New York Times* (June 20), p. A23.

Greenhouse, Steven. 2001. "Rights Group Scores Success with Nike," *The New York Times* (January 27), p. B2.

Greven, Michael Th. 2000. "Can the European Union Finally become a Democracy?" in Michael Th. Greven and Louis W. Pauly (eds), *Democracy Beyond the State? The European Dilemma and the Emerging Global Order*. Toronto: University of Toronto Press, pp. 35–61.

Grigera Naón, Horacio A. 2005. "Arbitration in Latin America: Progress and Setbacks," *Arbitration International* 21: 127–215.

Grinspun, Ricardo and Robert Kreklewich. 1994. "Consolidating Neoliberal Reforms: 'Free Trade' as a Conditioning Framework," *Studies in Political Economy* 43: 33.

Grotius, Hugo. 1625. *The Rights of War and Peace*, 3 vols. Ed. R. Tuck. Indianapolis: Liberty Fund, 2005.

Guislain, Pierre. 1997. *The Privatization Challenge: A Strategic, Legal, and Institutional Analysis of the International Experience*. Washington: World Bank.

Gugler, Philippe and Vladimir Tomsik. 2006. "International Agreement on Foreign Investments: North American vs. European Approach," Faculty of Economics, University of Fribourg, Working Paper No. 392, online at www.ssrn.com

Gumede, William Mervin. 2005. *Thabo Mbeki and the Battle for the Soul of the ANC*. Cape Town: Zebra Press.

Gunawardana, Asoka de Z. 1992. "The Inception and Growth of Bilateral Investment Promotion and Protection Treaties," *American Society of International Law Proceedings* 86: 544–55.

Gunnion, Stephen. 2006. "Merril Lynch seals empowerment deal," *Business Day* (February 9) at http://www.businessday.co.za/articles/frontpage. aspx?ID=BD4A152279

Gunson, Phil. 2006. "Venezuela Poised to Take Control of Idle Mines," *Financial Times* (June 17–18), p. 2.

Guzman, Andrew T. 1998. "Why LDCs Sign Treaties that Hurt Them: Explaining the Popularity of Bilateral Investment Treaties," *Virginia Journal of International Law* 38: 639–88.

2005. "Saving Customary International Law" (June 15), online at www. ssrn.com

Habermas, Jürgen. 1996. *Between Facts and Norms: Contributions to a Discourse Theory of Law and Democracy*, trans. William Rehg. Cambridge: MIT Press.

1998a. *The Inclusion of the Other: Studies in Political Theory*, ed. Ciaran Cronin and Pablo de Greiff. Cambridge: MIT Press.

1998b. "Three Normative Models of Democracy" in Habermas (1998a).

2001. "The Postnational Constellation and the Future of Democracy," in *The Postnational Constellation: Political Essays*, trans. and ed. Max Pensky. Cambridge: MIT Press.

2002. "The European Nation-State and the Pressures of Globalization," trans. G.M. Goshgarian, in Pablo De Grieff and Ciaran Cronin (eds), *Global Justice and Transnational Politics*. Cambridge: MIT Press, pp. 217–34.

2006. "Does the Constitutionalization of International Law Still Have a Chance?" in Jürgen Habermas (ed.), *The Divided West*, trans. Ciaran Cronin. Cambridge: Polity Press.

Haggard, Steven. 2000. *The Political Economy of the Asian Financial Crisis*. Washington, DC: The Institute for International Economics.

Hale, Robert L. 1943. "Bargaining, Duress, and Economic Liberty," *Columbia Law Review* 43: 603–28.

Hall, Stuart. 1996. "The Meaning of New Times," in David Morley and Kuan-Hsing Chen (eds), *Stuart Hall: Critical Dialogues in Cultural Studies*. London: Routledge, pp. 223–37.

Hallward-Driemeier, Mary. 2003. "Do Bilateral Investment Treaties Attract Foreign Direct Investment? Only a Bit ... and They Could Bite" Policy Research Working Paper No. 3121. Washington, DC: World Bank online at http://www-wds.worldbank.org/external/default/WDSContentServer/IW3P/IB/2003/09/23/000094946_03091104060047/Rendered/PDF/multi0page.pdf

Hamilton, Alexander, John Jay, and James Madison. 1961. *The Federalist Papers*, ed. Clinton Rossiter. New York: New American Library.

Handley, Antoinette. 2005. "Business, Government and Economic Policymaking in the New South Africa, 1999–2000," *Journal of Modern African Studies* 43(2): 211–39.

Handlin, Oscar and Mary Flug Handlin. 1969. *Commonwealth: A Study of the Role of Government in the American Economy: Massachusetts, 1774–1861*, rev. edn. Cambridge, MA: Harvard University Press.

Hart, Michael M. 1987. "The Mercantilist's Lament: National Treatment and Modern Trade Negotiations," *Journal of World Trade Law* 21: 37–61.

1996. *A Multilateral Agreement on Foreign Direct Investment: Why Now?* in Sauvé and Schwanen (eds), pp. 36–99.

Hartz, Louis. 1948. *Economic Policy and Democratic Thought: Pennsylvania, 1776–1860*. Cambridge, MA: Harvard University Press.

Harvey, David. *The Condition of Postmodernity*. Cambridge, MA: Blackwell.

2000. *Resources of Hope*. Berkeley: University of California Press.

2005. *A Brief History of Neoliberalism*. Oxford: Oxford University Press.

Hawthorn, Geoffrey. 1995. "The Crises of Southern States," in John Dunn (ed.), *Contemporary Crisis of the Nation State?* Oxford: Blackwell, pp. 130–45.

Hay, Colin and David Marsh. 2000. "Introduction: Demystifying Globalization," in Colin Hay and David Marsh (eds), *Demystifying Globalization*. Houndsmills: Macmillan.

Hay, Colin and Matthew Watson. 1999. "Globalisation: 'Sceptical' Notes on the 1999 Reith Lectures," *Political Quarterly* 418–25.

Hayek, Friederich. 1944. *The Road to Serfdom*. Chicago: University of Chicago Press.

Held, David. 1995. *Democracy and the Global Order: From the Modern State to Cosmopolitan Governance*. Cambridge: Polity Press.

Held, David and Ayse Kaya, eds. 2007. *Global Inequality: Patterns and Explanations*. Cambridge: Polity Press.

Held, David, Anthony McGrew, David Goldblatt, and Jonathan Perraton. 1999. *Global Transformations: Politics, Economics and Culture*. Stanford, CA: Stanford University Press.

Helleiner, Eric. 1996. "Post-Globalization: Is the Financial Liberalization Trend Likely to Be Reversed?" in Boyer and Drache (eds), pp. 193–210.

Hendrix, Steven E. 1995. "Property Law Innovation in Latin America with Some Recommendations," *Boston College International and Comparative Law Review* 18: 1–58.

Herdegen, Matthias. 1994. "Maastricht and the German Constitutional Court: Constitutional Restraints for an 'Ever Closer Union,'" *Common Market Law Review* 31: 235–49.

Herz, John H. 1941. "Expropriation of Foreign Property," *American Journal of International Law* 35: 243–62.

Heywood, Mark. 2001. "Debunking 'Conglomo-Talk': A Case Study of the *Amicus Curiae* as an Instrument for Advocacy, Investigation and Mobilisation," *Law, Democracy and Development* 5: 133–62, online at www.tac.org.za/Documents/MedicineActCourtCase/Debunking_Conglomo.rtf

Hibbits, Bernard J. 1994. "The Politics of Principle: Albert Venn Dicey and the Rule of Law," *Anglo-American Law Review* 23: 1–31.

Higgins, Rosalyn. 1982. "The Taking of Property by the State: Recent Developments in International Law," *Recueil des Cours* 176: 259–391.

Hills, Carla A. 1994. "Legal Opinion for R. J. Reynolds Tobacco Company and Phillip Morris International Inc." (May 3) [Unpublished].

Hindelang, Steffen. 2004. "Bilateral Investment Treaties, Custom and a Healthy Investment Climate: The Question of whether BITs Influence Customary International Law Revisited," *Journal of World Investment and Trade* 5: 789–809.

Hirsch, Alan. 2005. *Season of Hope: Economic Reform Under Mandela and Mbeki*. Scotsville and Ottawa: University of KwaZulu-Natal Press and International Development Research Centre online at www.idrc.ca/openebooks/215-5

Hirschl, Ran. 2004. *Towards Juristocracy: The Origins and Consequences of the New Constitutionalism*. Cambridge, MA: Harvard University Press.

Hirschman, Albert O. 1945. *National Power and the Structure of Foreign Trade*. Berkeley: University of California Press.

1965. *Journeys toward Progress: Studies of Economic Policy-Making in Latin America*. Garden City, NY: Anchor Books.

Hirst, Paul. 1994. *Associative Democracy: New Forms of Economic and Social Governance*. Cambridge: Polity Press.

Hirst, Paul and Grahame Thompson. 1999. *Globalization in Question: The International Economy and the Possibilities of Governance*, 2nd edn. Cambridge: Polity Press.

Hobhouse, L. T. 1911. *Liberalism*. London: Williams and Norgate.

Hobsbawm, Eric. 1996. "The Future of the State" in Cynthia Hewitt (ed.), *Social Futures, Global Visions*. Oxford: Blackwell.

Holmes, Stephen. 1988. "Precommitment and the Paradox of Democracy," in Elster and Slagstad (eds), pp. 195–240.

Holmes, Stephen and Cass R. Sunstein. 1999. *The Cost of Rights: Why Liberty Depends on Taxes*. New York: W.W. Norton.

Horn, Norbert and Stefan Kröll, eds. *Arbitrating Foreign Investment Disputes*. The Hague: Kluwer Law International.

Horwitz, Morton J. 1977. *The Transformation of American Law, 1780–1860*. Cambridge, MA: Harvard University Press.

1992. *The Transformation of American Law 1870–1960: The Crisis of Legal Orthodoxy*. New York: Oxford University Press.

Howse, Robert. 2000. "Managing the Interface between International Trade Law and the Regulatory State: What Lessons Should (and Should Not) Be Drawn from the Jurisprudence of the United States Dormant Commerce Clause," in Thomas Cottier and Petros C. Mavroidis (eds), *Regulatory Barriers and the Principle of Non-Discrimination in World Trade Law*. Ann Arbor: University of Michigan Press, pp. 140–66.

2002. "The Appellate Body Rulings in the Shrimp/Turtle Case: A New Legal Baseline for the Trade and Environment Debate," *Columbia Journal of Environmental Law* 27: 491–521.

Huerta, Carla and Alonso Lujambio. 1994. "NAFTA: Recent Constitutional Amendments, Sovereignty Today, and the Future of Federalism in Mexico," *Constitutional Forum* 5: 63–7.

Hull, Cordell. 1938. "Mexico-United States: Expropriation by Mexico of Agrarian Properties Owned by American Citizens," *American Journal of International Law*, Supp. 32(4): 181–207.

Hunt, Alan. 1990. "Rights and Social Movements: Counter-Hegemonic Strategies," *Journal of Law and Society* 17(3): 309–28.

Hunter, Martin and Alexei Barbuk. 2004. "Procedural Aspects of Non-Disputing Party Interventions in Chapter 11 Arbitrations" in Weiler (ed.), pp. 151–78.

Hurst, James Willard. 1956. *Law and the Conditions of Freedom in Nineteenth-Century United States*. Madison: The University of Wisconsin Press.

1960. *Law and Social Process in United States History*. Ann Arbor: University of Michigan Law School.

1964. *Law and Economic Growth: The Legal History of the Lumber Industry in Wisconsin, 1836–1915*. Cambridge, MA: Harvard University Press.

Ihedru, Okechukwu C. 2004. "Black Economic Empowerment and Nation-Building in Post-Apartheid South Africa," *Journal of Modern African Studies* 42: 1–30.

Inside U.S. Trade. 2002a. "Baucus, Grassley Split on Government Veto for Investor-State Disputes" (March 29), at www.insidetrade.com

2002b. "Kerry Defeat Boosts Industry Case in Interagency Debate" (May 24), online at www.insidetrade.com

2002c. "Final Trade Package Further Weakens Limits on Investor Protections" (August 2), online at www.insidetrade.com

2004. "August Round of SACU Talks Delayed, USTR Says No New Date Set" (July 9), online at www.insidetrade.com

International Council on Human Rights Policy. 2000. *Performance and Legitimacy: National Human Rights Institutions*. Versoix, Switzerland: International Council on Human Rights Policy.

International Law Association. 1926. "Report of the Protection of Private Property Committee," in *Some Opinions* (1920), pp. 13–26.

International Monetary Fund (IMF). 2007. *World Economic Outlook*. Washington, DC: The Fund.

International Union of Credit and Investment Insurers. 2003. *Berne Union Yearbook*. London: Berne Union.

Jack, Ian. 1999. "UPS Suing Ottawa for $230M," *The National Post* (April 22), p. D1.

2000a. "Ottawa Wants to Trim NAFTA Powers," *National Post* (May 30), p. A9.

2000b. "Tribunal Tells Ottawa to Release Secret Papers," *National Post* (September 8), p. A3.

2001a. "Canada Loses Bid to Change NAFTA Chapter11," *Financial Post* (April 5), p. C4.

2001b. "Prime Minister Contradicts Trade on Chapter 11," *Financial Post* (24 April), p. C8.

2001c. "New Debate on Controversial NAFTA Clause," *Financial Post* (March 6), p. C4.

Jackson, John H. 1997. *The World Trading System: Law and Policy of International Economic Relations*, 2nd edn. Cambridge, MA: MIT Press.

2006. *Sovereignty, the WTO and Changing Fundamentals of International Law*. Cambridge: Cambridge University Press.

Jacobs, Francis G. and Shelley Roberts, eds. 1987. *The Effect of Treaties in Domestic Law: The United Kingdom National Committee of Comparative Law*, vol. 7. London: Sweet & Maxwell.

Jaramillo, Carlos Felipe. 1998. *Liberalization, Crisis, and Change in Colombian Agriculture*. Boulder, CO: Westview Press.

Jenson, Jane. 1997. "Fated to Live in Interesting Times: Canada's Changing Citizenship Regimes," *Canadian Journal of Political Science* 30: 627–45.

Jessop, Bob. 1982. *The Capitalist State*. New York: New York University Press.

1990. *State Theory: Putting Capitalist States in their Place*. University Park: Pennsylvania State University Press.

2002. *The Future of the Capitalist State*. Cambridge: Polity Press.

Johnston, Josée and Gordon Laxer. 2003. "Solidarity in the Age of Globalization: Lessons from the Anti-MAI and Zapaztista Struggles," *Theory and Society* 32: 39–91.

Jones, Alan. 1967. "Thomas M. Cooley and 'Laissez-Faire Constitutionalism': A Reconsideration," *Journal of American History* 53: 751–71.

Kahn, Paul. 1992. *Legitimacy and History: Self-Government in American Constitutional Theory*. New Haven, CT: Yale University Press.

Kalmanovitz, Salomón. 2001. "Colombian Institutions in the Twentieth Century," *International Journal of Politics, Culture and Society* 14: 235–55.

2003. *Economía y Nación: Una Breva Historia de Colombia*, Nueva ed. Bogota: Grupo Editoria Norma.

Kant, Immanuel. 1991. "Perpetual Peace: A Philosophical Sketch," in *Political Writings*, trans. H. B. Nesbit, 2nd edn. Cambridge: Cambridge University Press, pp. 93–130.

Kantor, Mark. 2004. "The New Draft Model U.S. BIT: Noteworthy Developments," *Journal of International Arbitration* 21: 383–96.

Kaplow, Louis. 1986. "An Economic Analysis of Legal Transitions," *Harvard Law Review* 99: 509–617.

Karl, Joachim. 1996. "The Promotion and Protection of German Foreign Investment Abroad," *ICSID Review* 11: 1–36.

Karst, Kenneth L. 1964. "Latin-American Land Reform: The Uses of Confiscation," *Michigan Law Review* 63: 327–72.

1966. *Latin American Legal Institutions: Problems for Comparative Study*. Los Angeles: Latin American Center, University of Los Angeles.

Katz, Michael. 2006. "BEE and the Foreign Investor," *New Agenda: South African Journal of Social and Economic Policy* 22: 41–3.

Kelman, Mark. 1999. *Strategy or Principle? The Choice between Taxation and Regulation*. Ann Arbor: University of Michigan Press.

Kelsey, Jane. 1999. "Global Economic Policy-Making: A New Constitutionalism?" *Otago Law Review* 9: 535–55.

Kennedy, Duncan. 1980. "Toward an Historical Understanding of Legal Consciousness: The Case of Classical Legal Thought in America, 1850–1940," *Research in Law and Sociology* 3: 3–24.

Kennedy, Ellen. 2005. *Constitutional Failure: Carl Schmitt in Weimar*. Durham, NC: Duke University Press.

Keohane, Robert O. 1982 [1999]. "The Demand for International Regimes," in Charles Lipson and Benjamin J. Cohen (eds), *Theory and Structure in International Political Economy*. Cambridge, MA: MIT Press, pp. 147–77.

Kerremans, Bart. 2003. "Coping with the Nettlesome Dilemma: The Long Road to the U.S. Trade Act of 2002," *Journal of World Investment* 4: 517–51.

Khalil, Mohammed I. 1993. "Treatment of Foreign Investment in Bilateral Investment Treaties," in Shihata (ed.), pp. 221–335.

Kircheimer, Otto. 1930. "The Limits of Expropriation," in Tribe (ed.), pp. 33–74.

1969. "Weimar – And What Then?" in Burin and Shell (ed.), pp. 57–.

Klein, Naomi. 1999. *No Logo: Taking Aim at the Brand Bullies*. New York: Picador.

Kline, Harvey F. 1996. "Colombia: Building Democracy in the Midst of Violence and Drugs," in Jorge I. Dominguez and Abraham F. Lowenthal (eds), *Constructing Democratic Governance: South America in the 1990s*. Baltimore: Johns Hopkins University Press, pp. 20–41.

Klug, Heinz. 1996. "Participating in the Design: Constitution-Making in South Africa," *Review of Constitutional Studies* 3: 18–59.

2000. *Constituting Democracy: Law, Globalism and South Africa's Political Reconstruction*. Cambridge: Cambridge University Press.

2002. "Hybrid(ity) Rules: Creating Local Law in a Globalized World," in Dezalay and Garth (eds), pp. 276–305.

2005. "Campaigning for Life: Building a New Transnational Solidarity in the Face of HIV/AIDS and TRIPS," in Santos and Rodríguez-Garavito (eds), pp. 118–39.

Knop, Karen. 2003. "Reflections of Thomas Franck, Race and Nationalism (1960): 'General Principles of Law' and Situated Generality," *New York University Journal of International Law and Politics* 35: 437.

Koselleck, Reinhart. 1988. *Critique and Crisis: Enlightenment and the Pathogenesis of Modern Society*. Oxford: Berg.

Koskenniemi, Martti. 2007. "The Fate of Public International Law: Between Technique and Politics," *The Modern Law Review* 70: 1–30.

Krasner, Stephen D. 1983. "Structural Causes and Regime Consequences: Regimes as Intervening Variables," in Stephen D. Krasner (ed.), *International Regimes*. Ithaca, NY: Cornell University Press, pp. 1–21.

Kunoy, Bjørn. 2005. "Developments in Indirect Expropriation Case Law in ICSID Transnational Arbitration," *Journal of World International Trade* 6: 467–91.

Kymlicka, Will. 1995. *Multicultural Citizenship*. Oxford: Oxford University Press.

Kymlicka, Will and Wayne J. Norman. 1994. "Return of the Citizen: A Survey of Recent Work on Citizenship Theory," *Ethics* 104: 352–81.

Laird, Ian A. 2004. "Betrayal, Shock and Outrage – Recent Developments in NAFTA Article 1105," in Weiler (ed.), pp. 49–75.

Lajoie, Andrée. 1971. *Expropriation et Fédéralisme au Canada*. Montréal: Les Presses de l'Université de Montréal.

Lamont, Lansing. 1988. "A Singular U.S.-Canada Achievement," *The New York Times* (January 19), p. A27.

Lapham, Lewis. 2001. "Mirror, Mirror on the Wall," *Harper's Magazine* (April), pp. 12–15.

Lash, Scott and John Urry. 1994. *Economies of Sign and Space*. London: Sage.

Laski, Harold. 1919. *Authority in the Modern State*. New Haven, CT: Yale University Press.

   1938. *A Grammar of Politics*, 4th edn. London: George Allen & Unwin.

Laslett, Peter, ed. 1988. *Two Treatises of Government*. Cambridge: Cambridge University Press.

Lauterpacht, Elihu. 1997. "International Law and Private Foreign Investment," *Indiana Journal of Global Legal Studies* 4: 259–76.

Lauterpacht H. 1929. "Decisions of Municipal Courts as a Source of International Law," *British Yearbook of International Law* 10: 65.

Laxer, Gordon. 2001 "The Movement that Dare Not Speak Its Name: The Return of Left Nationalism/Internationalism." *Alternatives* 26(1): pp. 1–32.

Lefort, Claude. *Democracy and Political Theory*. Minneapolis: University of Minnesota Press.

Léger, Marie (ed.) 1994. *Aboriginal Peoples: Toward Self-Government*. Montreal: Black Rose Books.

Lehning, Percy B. 1997. "Pluralism, Contractarianism and European Union," in Percy B. Lehning and Albert Weale (eds), *Citizenship, Democracy and Justice in the New Europe*. London: Routledge, pp. 107–24.

Lester, Kevin. 2007. "The Regulatory Framework of Black Economic Empowerment," in Xolela Mangcu, Gill Marcus, Khehla Shubane, and Adrian Hadland (eds), *Visions of Black Economic Empowerment*. Auckland Park: Jacana Media, pp. 118–31.

Le Sueur, Andrew, Javan Herberg, and Rosalind English. 1999. *Principles of Public Law*, 2nd edn. London: Cavendish.

Levine, Judith. 2006. "Dealing with Arbitrator 'Issue Conflicts' in International Arbitration," *Dispute Resolution Journal* (February/April 2006): 60–7.

Levinson, Daryl J. 2000. "Making Government Pay: Markets, Politics, and the Allocation of Constitutional Costs," *University of Chicago Law Review* 67: 345–420.

Levmore, Saul. 1990. "Just Compensation and Just Politics," *Connecticut Law Review* 22: 285–322.

Levy, Leonard W. 1957. *The Law of the Commonwealth and Chief Justice Shaw.* New York: Oxford University Press.

Linares, Alejandro and Maristella Aldana. 1997. "Colombia: Privatization Laws: Latin Law" *LatinFinance* (January 11), p. 23.

Lindsaens, Birgit and Lone Lindholt. 1999. "National Human Rights Institutions: Standard-Setting and Achievements," in Hugo Stokke and Arne Tostensen (eds), *Human Rights in Development Yearbook 1998.* The Hague and Oslo: Kluwer Law International and Nordic Human Rights Publications, pp. 1–33.

Lipsey, Richard G., Daniel Schwanen, and Ronald J. Wonnacott. 1993. "Inside or Outside the NAFTA? The Consequences of Canada's Choice," *C.D. Howe Institute Commentary* (No. 4).

Lipson, Charles. 1985. *Standing Guard: Protecting Foreign Capital in the Nineteenth and Twentieth Centuries.* Berkeley: University of California Press.

Liptak, Adam. 2006. "Case Won on Appeal (To Public)," *The New York Times* (July 30), p. WK 3.

Locke, John. 1988. "The Second Treatise of Government," in Laslett (ed.), pp. 265–427.

Loranger, Sylvain and Joseph Zayed. 1997. "Environmental Contamination and Human Exposure to Airborne Total and Respirable Manganese in Montreal," *Journal of Air and Waste Management Association* 47: 983–9.

Lowe, Vaughan. 2002. "Regulation or Expropriation," *Current Legal Problems* 55: 447.

Lusztig, Michael. 1996. *Risking Free Trade.* Pittsburgh: University of Pittsburgh Press.

Lutz, Donald S. 1995. "Toward a Theory of Constitutional Amendment," in Sanford Levinson (ed.), *Responding to Imperfection: The Theory and Practice of Constitutional Amendment.* Princeton, NJ: Princeton University Press, pp. 237–74.

Lynam D. R., J. W. Roos, G. D. Pfeifer, B. F. Fort, and T. G. Pullin. 1999. "Environmental Effects and Exposures from Use of Methylcyclopentadienyl Manganese Tricarbonyl (MMT) in Gasoline," *NeuroToxicology* 20(2–3): 145–50.

Lyznicki, James M., Mitchell S. Karlan, Mohamed Khaleem Khan for the Council on Scientific Affairs, American Medical Association. 1999. "Manganese in Gasoline," *Journal of Occupational and Environmental Medicine* 41(3): 140–3.

Mabey, Nick. 1999. "Defending the Legacy of Rio: The Civil Society Campaign against the MAI," in Picciotto and Mayne (eds), pp. 60–81.

MacDonald, Michael. 2004. "The Political Economy of Identity Politics," *The South Atlantic Quarterly* 103(4): 629–56.

MacDonald, Roderick A. 1998. "Metaphors of Multiplicity: Civil Society, Regimes and Legal Pluralism," *Arizona Journal of International Law* 15: 69–91.

Machipisa, Lewis. 1998. "Trade Rules Must Also Help Africa, Warns Mandela," *Electronic Mail & Guardian* (May), pp. 2–20.

Maine, Sir Henry Sumner. 1909. *Popular Government*. London: John Murray.

Maluleke, Eddie. 2004. "Finding a balance between the rights of the few and the many," *Business Day* (May 10) at www.businessday.co.za (accessed February 10, 2006).

Mann F. A. 1959. "Outlines of a History of Expropriation," *The Law Quarterly Review* 75: 188–219.

1981. "British Treaties for the Promotion and Protection of Investors," *British Yearbook of International Law* 52: 241.

1990. *Further Studies in International Law*. Oxford: Clarendon Press.

Mann, Howard and Conrad Von Moltke. 1999. *NAFTA's Chapter 11 and the Environment: Addressing the Impacts of the Investor-State Process on the Environment*. Winnipeg: International Institute for Sustainable Development.

2005. *A Southern Agenda on Investment?* Winnipeg: International Institute for Sustainable Development, online at www.iisd.org/publications/pub. aspx?id=687

Mann, Howard, Conrad Von Moltke, Aaron Cosbey, and Luke Eric Peterson. 2005. *IISD Model International Agreement on Investment for Sustainable Development*. Winnipeg: International Institute for Sustainable Development, online at www.iisd.org/publications/pub.aspx?id=685

Mapp, Wayne. 1993. *The Iran-United States Claims Tribunal: The First Ten Years*. Manchester: Manchester University Press.

Marais, Hein. 1998. *South Africa: Limits to Change: The Political Economy of Transformation*. London and Cape Town: Zed Books and UCT Press.

Marshall, Don D. 1996. "National Development and the Globalisation Discourse: Confronting 'Imperative' and 'Convergence' Notions," *Third World Quarterly* 17: 875–901.

Marshall, Fiona and Howard Mann. 2006. "Good Governance and the Rule of Law: Express Rules for Investor-State Arbitration Required" (IISD Submission re Revision of UNCITRAL Arbitration Rules) (September), online at www.iisd.org/pdf/2006/investment_uncitral_rules_rrevision.pdf

Marshall, T. H. 1965. "Citizenship and Social Class," in T. H. Marshall (ed.), *Class, Citizenship, and Social Development*. Garden City, NY: Anchor Books, pp. 71–134.

Martin, Roger and Gordon Nixon. 2007. "Whoa Canada: More Must be done to Protect Companies from Foreign Takeovers," *The Globe and Mail* (July 2) B1.

Maslin, Janet. 1998. "At Sundance, Talk of Life Imitating Art," *The New York Times* (January 24), p. B7.

Massing, Michael. 2001. "From Protest to Program," *American Prospect* (July 2) 12(12): S2.

Matthews, Charolotte. 2007. "Anglo Coal in R7bn BEE Transaction," *Business Day* (February 9).

Maus, Ingeborg. 2006. "From Nation-State to Global State, or the Decline of Democracy," *Constellations* 13: 465–84.

Maxfield, Sylvia. 1997. *Gatekeepers of Growth: The International Political Economy of Central Banking in Developing Countries*. Princeton, NJ: Princeton University Press.

Maxwell. 1896. *On the Interpretation of Statutes*, 3rd edn, ed. A. B. Kempe. London: Sweet & Maxwell.

Mayne, Ruth. 2005. "Regionalism, Bilateralism, and 'TRIPS-Plus' Agreements: The Threat to Developing Countries," United Nations Human Development Report Office Occasional Paper 2005/18, online at: http://hdr.undp.org/docs/publications/background_papers/2005/ HDR2005_Mayne_Ruth_18.pdf

McCarthy, Shawn. 1998a. "Threat of NAFTA Case Kills Canada's MMT Ban," *The Globe and Mail* (July 20), pp. A1, A5.

1998b. "Failed Ban Becomes Selling Point for MMT," *The Globe and Mail* (July 21), p. A3.

2000. "Ottawa Wins Round in Lumber Suit," *The Globe and Mail* (June 28) p. B3.

McCarthy, Thomas. 1991. "Complexity and Democracy: The Seducement of Systems Theory," in Thomas McCarthy (ed.), *Ideals and Illusions: On Reconstruction and Deconstruction in Contemporary Critical Theory*. Cambridge, MA: MIT Press.

McCarthy Tétrault. 2003. "Memorandum to Ed Cramm, Secretary, The Council of Atlantic Premiers," online at http://www.cap-cpma.ca/ images/worddocuments/Memo%20re%20International%20Trade.doc

McCrudden, Christopher. 1999. "International Economic Law and the Pursuit of Human Rights: A Framework for Discussion of 'Selective Purchasing' Laws under the WTO Government Procurement Agreement," *Journal of International Economic Law* 3: 8.

McGinnis, John P. and Mark L. Movsevian. 2000. "The World Trade Constitution," *Harvard Law Review* 114: 511–605.

McGregor, Glen. 2004. "Generic Drugmakers Balk at Third World Exports," *Ottawa Citizen* (February 21, 2004), p. A11.

McIlroy, James. 2004. "Canada's New Foreign Investment Protection and Promotion Agreement: Two Steps Forward, One Step Back?" *Journal of World Investment and Trade* 5: 621–46.

McIlwain, Charles Howard. 1966. *Constitutionalism Ancient and Modern.* Ithaca, NY: Cornell University Press.

McKinnon, Mark. 2000. "Canada Seeks Review of NAFTA's Chapter 11," *The Globe and Mail* (December 13), p. B1.

McLennan, Gregor. 2004. "Travelling with Vehicular Ideas: The Case of the Third Way," *Economy and Society* 33: 484–99.

McRobbie, Angela. 1991. "New Times in Cultural Studies," *New Formations* 13: 1–17.

McUsic, Molly. 1996. "The Ghost of *Lochner*: Modern Takings Doctrine and its Impact on Economic Legislation," *Boston University Law Review* 76: 605–67.

Mendelson M. H. 1985. "Compensation for Expropriation: The Case Law," *American Journal of International Law* 79: 414–20.

Mergler, Donna., Baldwin, M., Bélanger, S., Laribbe, F., Beuter, A., Bowler, R., Panniset, M., Edwards, R., De Geoffray, A., Sassine, M.P., and Hudnell, K. 1999. "Manganese Neurotoxicity, a Continuum of Dysfunction: Results from a Community Based Study," *NeuroToxicology* 20(2–3): 327–42.

Merrill, Thomas W. 2000. "The Landscape of Constitutional Property," *Virginia Law Review* 86: 885–998.

Michelman, Frank. 1967. "Property, Utility, and Fairness: Comments on the Ethical Foundations of 'Just Compensation' Law," *Harvard Law Review* 80: 1165–258.

1988a. "Takings, 1987," *Columbia Law Review* 88: 1600.

1988b. "Law's Republic," *Yale Law Journal* 97: 1493.

Milanovic, Branko. 2005. *Worlds Apart: Measuring International and Global Inequality.* Princeton, NJ: Princeton University Press.

Minor, Michael S. 1994. "The Demise of Expropriation as an Instrument of LDC Policy," *International Business Studies* 25: 177.

Monahan, Patrick. 1994, in Canada, Senate, *Proceedings of the Standing Senate Committee on Legal and Constitutional Affairs*, No.12 (October 27, 1994), pp. 12.6–12.44.

Moore, Mike. 2003. *A World without Walls: Freedom, Development, Free Trade and Global Governance.* Cambridge: Cambridge University Press.

Moran, Theodore H. ed. 1998. *Managing International Political Risk.* Oxford, UK: Blackwell.

Mortensen, Jon. 2006. "WTO v. BEE: Why Trace Liberalisation May Block Black South African's Access to Wealth, Prosperity, or Just a White Collar Job," Danish Institute for International Studies Paper

No. 2006/30, online at www.diis.dk/graphics/Publications/WP2006/WP%202006-30.final.pdf

Mostert, Hanri. 2003. "The Distinction between Deprivations and Expropriations and the Future of the 'Doctrine' of Constructive Expropriation in South Africa," *South African Journal on Human Rights* 19: 563–92.

Mouffe, Chantal. 1993. *The Return of the Political*. London: Verso.

ed. 1999. *The Challenge of Carl Schmitt*. London: Verso.

Mountfield, Helen. 2002. "Regulatory Expropriations in Europe: The Approach of the European Court of Human Rights," *New York University Environmental Law Journal* 11: 136–47.

Mouri, Allahayar. 1994. *The International Law of Expropriation as Reflected in the Work of the Iran-U.S. Claims Tribunal*. Dordrecht: Martinus Nijhoff.

Mulchinski, Peter. 1995. *Multinational Enterprises and the Law*. Oxford: Blackwell.

1997. "'Global Bukowina' Examined: Viewing the Multinational Enterprise as a Transnational Law-Making Community," in Teubner (ed.), pp. 79–108.

Multilateral Investment Guarantee Agency (MIGA). 2001. *Annual Report*. Washington: MIGA, online at www.miga.org

2006. *Annual Report*. Washington: MIGA, online at www.miga.org

Murphy Jr., Ewell E. 1995. "Access and Protection of Foreign Investment in Mexico Under Mexico's New Foreign Investment Law and the North American Free Trade Agreement," *ISCID Review – Foreign Investment Law Journal* 10: 54–97.

Murphy, John. 1995. "Property Rights and Judicial Restraint: A Reply to Chaskalson," *South African Journal of Human Rights* 9: 385–98.

NAFTA Free Trade Commission. 2001. "Notes of Interpretation of Certain Chapter 11 Provisions" (July 31), *World Trade and Arbitration Materials* 13: 139–40.

2003. "NAFTA at 10 Free Trade Commission Joint Statement," online at http://www.ustr.gov/assets/Trade_Agreements/Regional/NAFTA/asset_upload_file50_3598.pdf

NAFTA Secretariat. 2004. "Overview of Dispute Settlement Provisions of the North American Free Trade Agreement (NAFTA)," online at http://www.nafta-sec-alena.org/DefaultSite/index_e.aspx?DetailID'8

National Public Radio (NPR). 2001. "All Things Considered" (broadcast August 14), on www.westlaw.com

National Security Council. 2002. *The National Security Strategy of the United States of America* (September), online at www.whitehouse.gov/nsc/nss/2002/nss.pdf

National Trade Data Bank. 1996. "Colombia: Investment Climate," *International Market Insight* (August 13).

Nava, Mica. 1987. "Consumerism and Its Contradictions," *Cultural Studies* 1: 204–10.

1991. "Consumerism Reconsidered: Buying and Power," *Cultural Studies* 5: 157–73.

Nedelsky, Jennifer.1990. *Private Property and the Limits of American Constitutionalism*. Chicago: University of Chicago Press.

Neumann, Franz. 1930. "The Social Significance of the Basic Laws in the Weimar Constitution," in Tribe (ed.), pp. 27–43.

1931. "On the Preconditions and Legal Concept of an Economic Constitution," in Tribe (ed.), pp. 44–65.

1934. "Rechtsstaat, the Division of Powers and Socialism," in Tribe (ed.), pp. 66–74.

1937. "The Change in the Function of Law in Modern Society," in Scheuerman (ed.), pp. 101–41.

1953. "The Concept of Political Freedom," in Scheuerman (ed.), pp. 195–230.

1986. *The Rule of Law: Political Theory and the Legal System in Modern Society*. Leamington Spa: Berg.

Neumayer, Eric and Laura Spess. 2005. "Do Bilateral Investment Treaties Increase Foreign Direct Investment to Developing Countries?" *World Development* 33: 1567–85.

New Brunswick. 2004a. Select Committee on Public Automobile Insurance. *Final Report on Public Automobile Insurance in Ontario*, online at http://www.gnb.ca/legis/business/committees/reports/2004 auto/report-e.asp

2004b. News Release. "Auto Insurance Reforms to Lower Rates, Increase Choice, Help First-Time Drivers (04/06/29)," online at http://www.gnb. ca/cnb/news/jus/2004e0750ju.htm

*New York Times* (NYT). 2000. "Thinkers on the Left Get a Hearing Everywhere But at Home," *The New York Times* (November 11), p. A17.

2001a. "South Africa's AIDS Victory," *The New York Times* (April 20), p. A18.

2001b. "Mexico: Waste Settlement," *The New York Times* (June 15), p. W1.

2006. "Energy Firms Bow to Demands Set by Bolivia" (October 30).

Newcombe, Andrew. 2005. "The Boundaries of Regulatory Expropriation in International Law," *ICSID Review – Foreign Investment Law Journal* 20: 1–57.

Nexus. 1998. "The Third Way: Summary of the NEXUS On-Line Discussion," ed. David Halpern with David Mikosz, online at http://www.netnexus.org/library/papers/3way.html#clashes

Niosi, Jorge. 1994. "Foreign Direct Investment in Canada," in Lorraine Eden (ed.), *Multinationals in North America*. Calgary: University of Calgary Press, pp. 367–88.

Noam, Eli. 2003. "The Internet Still Wide Open and Competitive?" online at http://tprc.org/papers/2003/200/noam_TPRC2003.pdf

Noel, Alain, Gerard Boismenu, and Lizette Jalbert. 1993. "The Political Foundations of State Regulation in Canada," in Jane Jenson, Riane Mahon, and Manfred Bienfeld (eds), *Production, Space, Identity: Political Economy Faces the 21st Century*. Toronto: Canadian Scholars Press, pp. 171–94.

Non-Smokers' Rights Association (NSRA). 2006. "Tobacco Related Litigation in Canada" (March), online at www.nsra-adnf.ca/cms/index.cfm

North, Douglass C. 1990. *Institutions, Institutional Change and Economic Performance*. NY: Cambridge University Press.

Note. (1994) "Takings 1992: Scalia's Jurisprudence and a Fifth Amendment Doctrine to Avoid a *Lochner Redivivus*," *Valpraiso University Law Review* 28: 743.

Notes from Nowhere. 2003. "Networks: The Ecology of Movements," in Notes from Nowhere (ed.), *We Are Everywhere: The Irresistible Rise of Global Anticapitalism*. London: Verso, pp. 63–73.

Novack, William J. *The People's Welfare: Law and Regulation in Nineteenth Century America*. Chapel Hill: University of North Carolina Press.

Ocampo, José Antonio. 1987. "Crisis and Economic Policy in Colombia, 1980–5," in Rosemary Thorp and Laurence Whitehead (eds), *Latin American Debt and the Adjustment Crisis*. Pittsburgh: University of Pittsburgh Press, pp. 239–70.

OECD. 1992. *OECD Declaration and Decisions on International Investment and Multinational Enterprises, 1991 Review*. Paris: OECD.

1996. "Main Features of the Multilateral Agreement on Investment," at www.oecd.org/daf/mail/pdf/ng/ng984e.pdf

OECD Documents. 1996. *Towards Multilateral Investment Rules*. Paris: OECD.

Offe, Claus. 1996. *Modernity and the State: East, West*. Cambridge, MA: MIT Press.

Ohmae, Kenichi. 1995. *The End of the Nation State: The Rise of Regional Economies*. New York: The Free Press.

Olson, Mancur. 1965. *The Logic of Collective Action*. Cambridge, MA: Harvard University Press.

Oppenheim L. 1949. *International Law: A Treatise*, vol. 1, 8th edn, ed. H. Lauterpacht. London: Longman's Green.

O'Rourke K. 2000. "Tariffs and Growth in the Late 19th Century," *Economic Journal* 110: 465–83

Ostry, Sylvia and Julie Soloway. 1998. "The MMT Case Ended Too Soon," *The Globe and Mail* (July 25), p. A21.

O'Sullivan R. C. 2005. "Learning from OPIC's Experience with Claims and Arbitration," in Theodore Moran and Gerald West (eds), *International*

*Political Risk Management: Looking to the Future.* Washington: The World Bank.

Pacuzzi, David J. 1994. "International Trade and Foreign Investment in Colombia: A Sound Economic Policy Amidst Crisis," *Florida Journal of International Law* 9: 443–77.

Palacios, Marco. 2006. *Between Legitimacy and Violence: A History of Colombia, 1875–2002.* Durham, NC: Duke University Press.

Panitch, Leo. 1996a. "Globalization, States, and Left Strategies," *Social Justice* 23: 79–90.

1996b. "Rethinking the Role of the State," in James Mittelman (ed.), *Globalization: Critical Reflections.* International Political Economy Yearbook, vol. 9. Boulder, CO: Lynne Reiner.

Parker, Richard W. 1999. "The Use and Abuse of Trade Leverage to Protect the Global Commons: What Can We Learn from the Tuna-Dolphin Conflict," *Georgetown International Environmental Law Review* 12: 1.

Parra, Antonio R. 1996. "The Scope of New Investment Laws and International Instruments," in Pritchard (ed.), pp. 27–44.

Paterson, Robert K., Martine M. N. Brand, with Jock A. Finlayson and Jeffrey S. Thomas. 1994. *International Trade and Investment Law in Canada*, 2nd edn. Scarborough: Carswell.

Paulsson, Jan and Zachary Douglas. 2004. "Indirect Expropriations in Investment Treaty Arbitrations," in Horn and Kröll (eds), pp. 145–58.

Perezcano, Hugo. 2003. "Investment Protection Agreements: Should a Multilateral Approach Be Reconsidered?" *Journal of World Investment* 4: 929–39.

Petersen, Melody. 2001. "Lifting the Curtain on the Real Costs of Making AIDS Drugs," *The New York Times* (April 24), p. A1.

Petersmann, Ernst-Ulrich. 1991a. *Constitutional Functions and Constitutional Problems of International Economic Law.* Fribourg: University Press.

1991b. "Constitutionalism, Constitutional Law and European Integration," *Aussenwirtschaft* 46: 247–80.

1992. "National Constitutions, Foreign Trade Policy and European Community Law," *European Journal of International Law* 3: 1–35.

1996–7. "Constitutionalism and International Organizations," *Northwestern Journal of International Law and Business* 17: 398–469.

2000. "The WTO Constitution and Human Rights," *Journal of International Economic Law* 3(1): 19–25.

Peterson, Luke Eric. 2004. "International Treaty Implications Color Canadian Province's Debate over Public Auto Insurance," *INVEST-SD Bulletin* (May 11), online at www.iisd.org/pdf/2004/investment_investsd_may11_2004.pdf

2006a. "UK Farm Group Settles BIT Claim Over Venezuelan Land Seizures and Invasions," *Investment Treaty News* (April 11), online at http://www.iisd.org/pdf/2006/itn_april11_2006.pdf

2006b. "Analysis: Foreign Investors Still in the Dark as to Terms of Bolivian Nationalization," *Investment Treaty News* (May 16), online at http://www.iisd.org/pdf/2006/itn_may16_2006.pdf

2006c. "South Africa's Bilateral Investment Treaties: Implications for Development and Human Rights," *Dialogue on Globalization Occasional Paper No. 26* (November). Geneva: Friedrich-Ebert-Stiftung, online at http://www.fes-globalization.org/publications/FES_OCP26_Peterson_SA_BITs.pdf

2007. "Analysis: Arbitrator Challenges Raising Tough Questions as to Who Resolves BIT Cases," *Investment Treaty News* (January 17), online at http://www.iisd.org/pdf/2007/itn_jan17_2007.pdf

Peterson, Luke Eric and Kevin R. Gray. 2003. "International Human Rights in Bilateral Investment Treaties and in Investment Treaty Arbitration" (April). Winnipeg: International Institute for Sustainable Development, online at http://www.iisd.org/pdf/2003/investment_int_human_rights_bits.pdf

Petras, James. 1977. "State Capitalism and the Third World," *Development and Change* 8: 1–18.

Pettigrew, Pierre S. 2000. "We're Minding the Store," *National Post* (May 8).

2001. "We Need to 'Clarify' NAFTA to Fix Tribunal 'Errors,'" *Financial Post* (March 23), p. C15.

Pharmaceutical Manufacturers' Association (PMA). 1998. "Notice of Motion," in *PMA v Republic of South Africa*, online at http://www.cptech.org/ip/health/sa/pharmasuit.html

Phasiwe, Khulu. 2004. "Foreign Miners Warn They May Sue Government," *Business Day* (January 11), online at www.businessday.co.za

Phillip Morris. 2002. "Submission by Phillip Morris International Inc. in Response to the Center for Standards and Certification Information" [Unpublished].

Picciotto, Sol. 1998. "Linkages in International Investment Regulation: The Antinomies of the Draft Agreement of Investment," *University of Pennsylvania Journal of International Economic Law* 19(3): 731–68.

1999. "A Critical Assessment of the MAI," in Picciotto and Mayne (eds), pp. 82–102.

Picciotto, Sol and Ruth Mayne. eds. 1999. *Regulating International Business: Beyond Liberalization*. Houndsmills: Macmillan and Oxfam.

Poirier, Marc R. 2002. "The Virtue of Vagueness in Takings Doctrine," *Cardozo Law Review* 24: 93–191.

Polanyi, Karl. 1957. *The Great Transformation*. Boston: Beacon Press.

Pollack, Andrew. 2001. "Defensive Drug Industry: Fueling Clash over Patents," *The New York Times* (April 20), p. A6.

Ponte, Stefano, Simon Roberts, and Lance van Sittert. 2006. *To BEE or Not To BEE? South Africa's 'Black Economic Empowerment' (BEE), Corporate Governance and the State in the South* (Danish Institute for International Studies Working Paper no. 2006/27) online at http://www.diis.dk/graphics/Publications/WP2006/WP%202006-27.final.pdf

Posadas, Alejandro. 2001. "Metalclad Corporation v. The United Mexican States, Background Information Relevant to Presentation by Prof. Alejandro Posadas, Counsel for Mexico," online at www.law.duke.edu/curricu.PDF (accessed September 21, 2007)

Posner, Richard. 1987. "The Constitution as Economic Document," *George Washington Law Review* 56: 4.

Powers, Linda F. 1998. "New Forms of Protection for International Infrastructure Investors," in Moran (ed.), pp. 125–38.

Preuss, Ulrich K. 1999. "Political Order and Democracy: Carl Schmitt and His Influence," in Mouffe (ed.), pp. 155–79.

Pritchard, Robert, ed. 1996. *Economic Development, Foreign Investment and the Law*. London: Kluwer and IBA.

Pross, A. Paul and Iain S. Stewart. 1994. "Breaking the Habit: Attentive Publics and Tobacco Regulation," in Susan D. Phillips (ed.), *How Ottawa Spends 1994–95: Making Change*. Ottawa: Carleton University Press.

PRS Group. 1996. "Climate for Business," *Political Risk Service* (November 1).

Przeworski, Adam. 1991. *Democracy and the Market: Political and Economic Reforms in Eastern Europe and Latin America*. NY: Cambridge University Press.

1999. "A Better Democracy, a Better Economy," *The Boston Review* 21: 2.

Przeworski, Adam and Fernando Limongi. 1993. "Political Regimes and Economic Growth," *Journal of Economic Perspectives* 7: 51–69.

Radin, Margaret Jane. 1993. *Reinterpreting Property*. Chicago: University of Chicago Press.

Rawls, John. 1993. *Political Liberalism*. New York. Columbia University Press.

Raz, Joseph. 1979. "The Rule of Law and Its Virtue," in Robert L. Cunningham (ed.), *Liberty and the Rule of Law*. College Station: Texas A&M University Press, pp. 3–21.

Reed J. 2005a. "Sasol Sells Stake in Unit to Black Investors," *Financial Times* (September 23): 30.

2005b. "A Race to Meet Black Empowerment Rules," *Financial Times* (September 26): 16.

Regan, Donald H. "The Supreme Court and State Protectionism: Making Sense of the Dormant Commerce Clause," *Michigan Law Review* 84: 1091–287.

Reich, Robert. 1991. *The Work of Nations*. New York: Random House.

Reinisch, A. 2006. "Necessity in International Investment Arbitration – An Unnecessary Split of Opinions in Recent ICSID Cases? Comments on CMS v. *Argentina* and *LG&E* v. *Argentina*," transnational-dispute-management.com 3(5) (December).

Rheingold, Howard. 1993. "A Slice of Life in My Virtual Community," in Linda Harasim (ed.), *Global Networks: Computers and International Communication*. Cambridge, MA: MIT Press.

Riddell, William Renwick. 1912. "The Constitution of the United States and Canada," *Canada Law Times* 32: 849.

Rittich, Kerry. 2002 *Recharacterizing Restructuring: Law, Distribution and Gender in Market Reform*. The Hague: Kluwer Law International.

2006. "The Future of Law and Development: Second-Generation Reforms and the Incorporation of the Social," in Trubek and Santos (eds), 2006, pp. 203–52.

Robert, Maryse. 2000. *Negotiating NAFTA: Explaining the Outcome in Culture, Textiles, Autos, and Pharmaceuticals*. Toronto: University of Toronto Press.

Robertson, Roland. 1992. *Globalization: Social Theory and Global Culture*. London: Sage.

Robertson, Roland and Frank Lechner. 1985. "Modernization, Globalization and the Problem of Culture in World Systems Theory," *Theory Culture and Society* 2: 103.

Robinson, Ian. 1993. "Neo-Conservative Trade Policy and Canadian Federalism: Constitutional Reform by Other Means," in D. M. Brown (ed.), *Canada: The State of the Federation 1993*. Kingston: Institute for Intergovernmental Relations.

Robinson, William I. 2001. "Social Theory and Globalization: The Rise of the Transnational State," *Theory and Society* 30: 157–200.

Rodgers, Daniel T. 1992. "Republicanism: The Career of a Concept," *Journal of American History* 79: 11.

Rodríguez, César. 2001. "Globalization, Judicial Reform and the Rule of Law in Latin America: The Return of Law and Development," *Beyond Law: Más Allá Del Derecho* 7 (#23): 13–42.

Rodrik, Dani. 1997. *Has Globalization Gone Too Far?* Washington DC: Institute for International Economics.

1999. "Governing the Global Economy: Does One Architectural Style Fit All?" in Susan M. Collins and Robert Z. Lawrence (eds), *Brookings Trade Forum 1999*. Washington, DC: Brookings Institution Press.

2001. "Development Strategies for the 21st Century" *Annual World Bank Conference on Development Economics 2000*. Washington: The International bank for Reconstruction and Development/The World Bank, pp. 85–108.

2002. "Feasible Globalizations" [mimeo], at http://ksghome.harvard.edu/~drodrik/papers.html

Root, Elihu. 1910. "The Basis of Protection to Citizen's Residing Abroad," *Proceedings of the American Society of International Law* 7: 16–27.

1913. *Experiments in Government and the Essentials of the Constitution.* Princeton: Princeton University Press.

1916. *Addresses on Government and Citizenship.* Cambridge, MA: Harvard University Press.

Rose, Carol. 1998. "Canons of Property Talk, or Blackstone's Anxiety," *Yale Law Journal* 108: 601.

2000. "Property and Expropriation," *Utah Law Review* 4: 1–41.

Rose, Rob. 2004. "US Groups in SA Say Empowerment Deters Investment," *Business Day* (December 14) at www.businessday.co.za (accessed February 20, 2005).

Rosenau, James. 1998. "Governance and Democracy in a Globalizing World," in Daniele Archibugi, David Held, and Martin Köhler (eds), *Re-Imagining Political Community: Studies in Cosmopolitan Democracy.* Stanford, CA: Stanford University Press, pp. 28–57.

Rosenberg, Tina. 2001. Look at Brazil. *The New York Times Magazine* (January 28), pp. 26–31, 52, 58, 62–3.

Roth, Andreas H. 1949. *The Minimum Standard of International Law Applied to Aliens.* Leiden: A. W. Sijthoff's Uitgeversmaatschappij N.V.

Rotstein, Abraham. 1972. "Development and Dependence," in Abraham Rotstein and Gary Lax (eds), *Independence: The Canadian Challenge.* Toronto: Committee for an Independent Canada, pp. 29–39.

Roux, Theunis. 2003. "Property," in Woolman et al. (eds), chapter 46.

Rubins, Noah and N. Stephan Kinsella. 2005. *International Investment, Political Risk and Dispute Resolution: A Practitioner's Guide.* Dobbs Ferry, NY: Oceana.

Ruggie, John Gerald. 1998. *Constructing the World Polity: Essays on International Institutionalization.* London and New York: Routledge.

Ruggiero, Renato. 1996. "Foreign Direct Investment and the Multilateral Trading System," *Transnational Corporations* 5: 1–8.

Ruigrock, Winfried and Rob van Tulder. 1995. *The Logic of International Restructuring.* London: Routledge.

Rumney, Reg. 2006. "SA's Lesson in Humiltity," *Mail & Guardian Online* (June 26) online at http://www.mg.co.za/insight/insight_economy_ business/&article.

Ryan, Brendan. 2007. "Mining Law: Big Test of Rights," Financial Mail (February 23), online at http://secure.financialmail.co.za/07/0223/ features/efeat.htm

Sáchica, Luis Carlos. 1989. *Constitucionalismo Colombiano.* Bogota: Temis.

Salacuse, Jeswald W. 2004. "Towards a Global Treaty on Foreign Investment: The Search for the Grand Bargain," in Horn and Kröll (eds), pp. 51–88.

Salacuse, Jeswald W. and Nicholas P. Sullivan. 2005. "Do BITs Really Work? An Evaluation of Bilateral Investment Treaties and Their Grand Bargain," *Harvard International Law Journal* 46: 67–130.

Sally, Razeen. 1994. "Multinational Enterprises, Political Economy and Institutional Theory: Domestic Embeddedness in the Context of Internationalisation," *Review of International Political Economy* 1: 161.

Sandrino, Gloria. 1994. "The NAFTA Investment Chapter and Foreign Direct Investment in Mexico: A Third World Perspective," *Vanderbilt Journal of Transnational Law* 27: 259–327.

Sands, Phillipe. 2005. *Lawless World: America and the Making and Breaking of Global Rules.* London: Allen Lane.

Sanín, Francisco Gutiérrez and Ana María Jaramillo. 2005. "Paradoxical Pacts," in Boaventura de Sousa Santos (ed.), pp. 193–219.

Santos, Alvaros. 2006. "The World Bank's Uses of the 'Rule of Law' Promise in Economic Development," in Trubek and Santos (eds), pp. 253–300.

Santos, Boaventura de Sousa. 1995. *Toward a New Common Sense: Law, Science and Politics in the Paradigmatic Transition.* New York: Routledge.

2002. *Toward a New Legal Common Sense: Law, Globalization, and Emancipation,* 2nd edn. London: Butterworths.

ed. 2005. *Democratizing Democracy: Beyond the Liberal Canon.* London: Verso.

Santos, Boaventura de Sousa and Leonardo Avritzer. 2005. "Introduction: Opening Up the Canon of Democracy," in Boaventura de Sousa Santos (ed.), pp. xxxiv–lxxiv.

Santos, Boaventura de Sousa and César A. Rodríguez-Garavito, eds. 2005. *Law and Globalization from Below: Toward a Cosmopolitan Legality.* Cambridge: Cambridge University Press.

Sassen, Saskia. 1997. *Losing Control? Sovereignty in an Age of Globalization.* New York: Columbia University Press

2003. "Globalization or Denationalization?" *Review of International Political Economy* 10: 1–22.

2006. *Territory, Authority, Rights: From Medieval to Global Assemblages.* Princeton, NJ: Princeton University Press.

Sauvé, Pierre. 1996. "Market Access through Market Presence: New Directions in Investment Rulemaking," in Sauvé and Schwanen (eds), pp. 26–35.

Sauvé, Pierre and Daniel Schwanen, eds. 1996. *Investment Rules for the Global Economy: Enhancing and Access to Markets.* Toronto: C. D. Howe Institute.

Sax, Joseph L. 1964. "Takings and the Police Power," *Yale Law Journal* 74: 36–76.

Scheiber, Harry N. 1971. "The Road to *Munn*: Eminent Domain and the Concept of Public Purpose in the State Courts," in Donald Fleming and

Bernard Bailyn (eds), *Perspectives in American History*, vol. V. Cambridge: Charles Warren Centre for Studies in American History.

1973. "Property Law, Expropriation, and Resource Allocation by Government: The United States, 1789–1910," *Journal of Economic History* 33: 232–51.

1989. "The Jurisprudence – and Mythology – of Eminent Domain in American Legal History," in Ellen Frankel Paul and Howard Dickman (eds), *Liberty, Property and Government: Constitutional Interpretation before the New Deal*. Albany: State University of New York Press, pp. 217–238.

ed. 1964. *United States Economic History: Selected Readings*. New York: Alfred A. Knopf.

Scheppele, Kim Lane. 2004. "A Realpolitik Defense of Social Rights," *Texas Law Review* 82: 1921–62.

2005. "Democracy by Judiciary. Or, Why Courts Can be More Democratic than Parliaments," in Adam Czarnota, Martin Krygier, and Wojiech Sadurski (eds), *Rethinking the Rule of Law after Communism*. Budapest: Central European University Press, pp. 25–60.

Scheuerman, William E. 1994. *Between the Norm and the Exception: The Frankfurt School and the Rule of Law*. Cambridge, MA: MIT Press.

1999a. "Economic Globalization and the Rule of Law," *Constellations* 6: 3–25.

1999b. *Carl Schmitt: The End of Law*. Lanham, MD: Rowman & Littlefield.

2002. "Between Radicalism and Resignation: Democratic Theory in Habermas' between Facts and Norms," in René Von Schomberg and Kenneth Baynes (eds), *Discourse and Democracy: Essays on Habermas' between Facts and Norms*. Albany: State University Press of New York, pp. 61–85.

ed. 1996. *The Rule of Law under Siege: Selected Essays of Franz L. Neumann and Otto Kircheimer*. Berkeley: University of California Press.

Schill, Stephan. 2006. "From Calvo to CMS: Burying an International Law Legacy? Argentina's Currency Reform in the Face of Investor Protection: The ICSID Case CMS v. Argentina," transnational-dispute-management.com (April) 3(2).

Schmitt, Carl. 1922 [1985]. *Political Theology: Four Chapters on the Concept of Sovereignty*, 1st edn., trans. George Schwab. Cambridge, MA: MIT Press.

1923 [1988]. *The Crisis of Parliamentary Democracy*, trans. Ellen Kennedy. Cambridge, MA: MIT Press.

1926. *Unabhängigkeit der Richter, Gleichheit vor dem Gesetz und Gewährleistung des Privateigentums nach der Weimarer Verfassung* [Judicial Independence, Equality Before the Law, and the Protection of Private Property According to the Weimar Constitution: A Report on Proposed

Legislation in Regards to the Property Disputes Surrounding the Estates of the Former Landed Aristocracy]. Berlin: Walter de Gruyter.

1932 [1996]. *The Concept of the Political*, 1st edn. trans. George Schwab. Chicago: University of Chicago Press.

1993. *Théorie de la Constitution*, trans. L. Deroche [trans. of *Die Verfassungslehre*, 1928]. Paris: Presses Universitaires de France.

Schneiderman, David. 1996. "NAFTA's Takings Rule: American Constitutionalism Comes to Canada," *University of Toronto Law Journal* 46: 499–537.

1998. "A.V. Dicey, Lord Watson, and the Law of the Constitution of the Late Nineteenth Century," *Law and History Review* 16: 495–526.

1999a. "MMT Promises: How the Ethyl Corporation Beat the Federal Ban," *Encompass Magazine* (February) 3(3): 12–13.

1999b. "The Constitutional Strictures of the Multilateral Agreement on Investment," *The Good Society* 9(2): 90–5.

1999c. "Implementing Human Rights Commitments: The Difficulties of Divided Jurisdiction," online at www.hri.ca/doccentre/docs/schneiderman.shtml

2000. "Constitutional Approaches to Privatization: An Inquiry into the Magnitude of Neo-Liberal Constitutionalism," *Law and Contemporary Problems* 63: 83–109.

2004. "Habermas, Market-Friendly Human Rights, and the Revisibility of Economic Globalization," *Citizenship Studies* 8: 419–36.

2006. "Property Rights, Investor Rights, and Regulatory Innovation: Comparing Constitutional Cultures in Transition," *International Journal of Constitutional Law* 4: 371–91.

2007. "Constitution or Model Treaty? Struggling over the Interpretive Authority of NAFTA," in Sujit Choudhry (ed.), *The Migration of Constitutional Ideas*. Cambridge: Cambridge University Press, pp. 294–315.

Schønberg, Søren J. 2000. *Legitimate Expectations in Administrative Law*. Oxford: Oxford University Press.

Schreuer, Christoph H. 2001. *The ICSID Convention: A Commentary*. Cambridge: Cambridge University Press.

2005. "Fair and Equitable Treatment in Arbitral Practice," *Journal of World Investment and Trade* 6: 357–86.

Schreuer, Christoph H. 2006. "Diversity and Harmonization of Treaty Interpretation in Investment Arbitration," transnational-dispute-management.com (April) 3(2).

Schumpeter, Joseph A. 1947. *Capitalism, Socialism, and Democracy*, 3rd edn. New York: Harper & Brothers.

Schwanen, Daniel. 1996. "Investment and the Global Economy: Key Issues in Rulemaking," in Sauvé and Schwanen (eds), pp. 1–25.

Schwebel, Stephen M. 2006. "The United States 2004 Model Bilateral Investment Treaty: An Exercise in the Regressive Development of International Law," *Transnational-Dispute-Management* 3(2) April.

Scoffield, Heather. 1998a. "U.S. Firm Hits Ottawa with NAFTA Suit," *The Globe and Mail* (August 21), p. B1.

1998a. "U.S. Firm Hits Ottawa with NAFTA Suit," *The Globe and Mail* (August 21), p. B1.

1998b. "PCB Export Ban Breached NAFTA, Firm Says," *The Globe and Mail* (September 1), p. B2.

1998c. "Time Says Copps Misses Boat on Magazine Bill," *The Globe and Mail* (November 18), p. B9.

1999. "Methanex Set to Sue Uncle Sam under NAFTA over Gas Additive," *The Globe and Mail* (November 3).

2000. "Mexico Holds Firm on NAFTA Investment Rules," *The Globe and Mail* (September 2), p. B3.

Seidman, Gay W. 2007. *Beyond the Boycott: Labour Rights, Human Rights, and Transnational Activism*. New York: Russell Sage Foundation.

Sell, Susan K. 2003. *Private Power, Public Law: The Globalization of Intellectual Property Rights*. Cambridge: Cambridge University Press.

Senate of Canada. 1995. *Report of the Special Committee on the Pearson Airport Agreements*. Ottawa: Supply and Services Canada.

Shea, Donald R. 1955. *The Calvo Clause: A Problem of Inter-American and International Law And Diplomacy*. Minneapolis: University of Minnesota Press.

Shihata, Ibrahim F. I. 1988. *MIGA and Foreign Investment*. Dordrecht: Martinus Nijhoff.

1993. *Legal Treatment of Foreign Investment: The World Bank Guidelines*. Dordrecht: Martinus Nijhoff.

1994. "Recent Trends Relating to Entry of Foreign Direct Investment," *ISCID Review – Foreign Investment Law Journal* 9: 47–70.

Shklar, Judith. 1991. *American Citizenship: The Quest for Inclusion*. Cambridge, MA: Harvard University Press.

Shrybman, Steven and Scott Sinclair. 2004. "Public Auto Insurance and Trade Treaties," 5: 1 Briefing Papers, online at www.citizen-org/documents/newbrunswick-auto.pdf

Siegel, Reva. 1997. "Why Equal Protection No Longer Protects: The Evolving Forms of Status-Enforcing State Action," *Stanford Law Review* 49: 1111–48.

Silbey, Susan S. 2005. "After Legal Consciousness" *Annual Review of Law and Social Science* 1: 323–68.

Singer, Joseph William. 2000. *Entitlement: The Paradoxes of Property*. Cambridge, MA: Harvard University Press.

Singer, Joseph William and Jack M. Beermann. 1993. "The Social Origins of Property," *Canadian Journal of Law and Jurisprudence* 6: 217–48.

Siqueiros, Jose Luis. 1994. "Bilateral Treaties on the Reciprocal Protection of Foreign Investment," *California Western International Law Journal* 24: 255–75.

Sklair, Leslie. 1996. "Conceptualizing and Researching the Transnational Capitalist Class in Australia," *Australia and New Zealand Journal of Sociology* 32: 1–19.

1998 "Social Movements and Capitalism," in Frederic Jameson and Masao Miyoshi (eds), *The Cultures of Globalization*. Durham, NC, and London: Duke University Press.

2001. *The Transnational Capitalist Class*. Oxford: Blackwell.

Skocpol, Theda. 1985. "Bringing the State Back In: Strategies of Analysis in Current Research," in Peter B. Evans, Dietrich Rueschemeyer, and Theda Skocpol (eds), *Bringing the State Back In*. Cambridge: Cambridge University Press.

1992. *Protecting Soldiers and Mothers: The Political Origins of Social Policy in the United States*. Cambridge, MA: Harvard University Press.

Smith, Peter J. and Elizabeth Smythe. 1999. "Globalization, Citizenship and Technology: The MAI Meets the Internet," *Canadian Foreign Policy* 7 (2): 83–105.

Smith, T. Lynn. 1967. *Colombia: Social Structure and the Process of Development*. Gainesville: University of Florida Press.

Smith, Welsley R. 1992. "Salinas Prepares Mexican Agriculture for Free Trade," *Mexico Trade & Law Reporter* 10: 7.

Sohn, Louis B. and R. R. Baxter. 1961. "Responsibility of States for Injuries to the Economic Interests of Aliens," *American Journal of International Law* 55: 545–84.

Soloway, Julie. 1999. "Environmental Trade Barriers under NAFTA: The MMT Fuel Additives Controversy," *Minnesota Journal of Global Trade* 8: 55–95.

*Some Opinions, Articles and Reports Bearing upon the Treaty of Trianon and the Claims of the Hungarian Nationals with Regard to Their Lands in Transylvania*, vol. 1, 1929. London: W. P. Griffith.

Sornarajah, M. 1997. "Power and Justice in Foreign Investment Arbitration," *Journal of International Arbitration* 14: 103–40.

2000. *The Settlement of Foreign Investment Disputes*. The Hague: Kluwer Law International.

2004. *The International Law on Foreign Investment*, 2nd edn. Cambridge: Cambridge University Press.

Spitz, Richard with Matthew Chaskalson. 2000. *The Politics of Transition: The Hidden History of South Africa's Negotiated Settlement*. Oxford: Hart.

Spivak, Giyatri Chakravorty. 1988. "Can the Subaltern Speak?" in Cary Nelson and Lawrence Grosberg (eds), *Marxism and the Interpretation of Culture*. Urbana: University of Illinois Press.

1993. *Outside in the Teaching Machine*. London: Routledge.

Statistics Canada. 1997. *Canada's International Investment Position, 1992 to 1996*. Ottawa: Minister of Industry.

Stiglitz, Joseph E. 1994. *Whither Socialism?* Cambridge, MA: MIT Press.

2002. *Globalization and Its Discontents*. New York: W.W. Norton.

2006. *Making Globalization Work*. New York: W.W. Norton & Company.

Stiglitz, Joseph E. and Andrew Charlton. 2005. *Fair Trade for All: How Trade Can Promote Development*. New York: Oxford University Press.

Stoller, Richard. 1995. "Alfonso López Pumarejo and Liberal Radicalism in 1930s Colombia," *Journal of Latin American Studies* 27: 367–97.

Stokes, Bruce. 2007. "Black Economic Empowerment," *The National Journal* (February 3), p. 30.

Stone, Alec. 1994. "What Is a Supranational Constitution? An Essay in International Relations Theory," *The Review of Politics* 56: 441–74.

Stone Sweet, Alec. 2000. *Governing with Judges: Constitutional Politics in Europe*. Oxford: Oxford University Press.

2004. *The Judicial Construction of Europe*. Oxford: Oxford University Press.

Stopford, John and Susan Strange. 1991. *Rival States, Rival Firms: Competition for World Market Shares*. Cambridge: Cambridge University Press.

Strange, Susan. 1994. "The Defective State," *Daedalus* 124: 55–75.

Streeck, Wolfgang. 1995. "From Market-Making to State-Building? Reflections on the Political Economy of European Social Policy," in Stephan Leibfried and Paul Pierson (eds), *European Social Policy: Between Fragmentation and Integration*. Washington DC: The Brookings Institution, pp. 389–431.

Strupp, Karl. 1927. "The Roumano-Hungarian Dispute Concerning the Hungarian Optants in Roumania Terrritory," in *Agrarian Reform in Roumania*, pp. 289–99.

Strydom, Hennie and Kevin Hopkins. 2005. "International Law," in Woolman et al. (eds) (2004).

Stumberg, Robert. 1998. "Sovereignty by Subtraction: The Multilateral Agreement on Investment," *Cornell International Law Journal* 31: 491–598.

2000. "Preemption and Human Rights: Local Options after *Crosby* v. *NFTC*," *Law & Policy in International Business* 32: 110–96.

Subramanian, Arvind. 2000. "The AIDS Crisis, Differential Pricing of Drugs, and the TRIPS Agreement," *The Journal of World Intellectual Property* 4: 323–36.

Sugarman, David. 1983. "The Legal Boundaries of Liberty: Dicey, Liberalism, and Legal Science," *Modern Law Review* 46: 102–11.

  1991. "'A Hatred of Disorder': Legal Science, Liberalism and Imperialism," in Peter Fitzpatrick (ed.), *Dangerous Supplements: Resistance and Renewal in Jurisprudence*. Durham, NC: Duke University Press, pp. 34–67.

Sunstein, Cass. 1993. *The Partial Constitution*. Cambridge, MA: Harvard University Press.

  1991. "Constitutionalism and Secession," *University of Chicago Law Review* 58: 633–70.

  1994. "On Property and Constitutionalism," in Michel Rosenfeld (ed.), *Constitutionalism, Identity, Difference, and Legitimacy*. Durham, NC: Duke University Press.

Swafford, David. March 1999. "Halo of Hope," LatinFinance, p. 45.

Sylla, Richard. 2000. "Experimental Federalism: The Economics of American Government, 1789–1914," in Engerman and Gallman (eds), pp. 483–541.

Sypnowich, Christine. 1999. "Utopia and the Rule of Law," in Dyzenhaus (ed.), pp. 178–95.

Taggart, Michael. 1998. "Expropriation, Public Purpose and the Constitution," in Christopher Forsythe and Ivan Hare (eds), *The Golden Metawand and the Crooked Cord: Essays in Public Law in Honour of Sir William Wade QC*. Oxford: Clarendon Press, pp. 91–112.

Tamanaha, Brian Z. 2004. *On the Rule of Law: History, Politics, Theory*. Cambridge: Cambridge University Press.

Tamayo, Arturo Boja. 2001. "The New Federalism in Mexico and Foreign Economic Policy: An Alternative Two-Level Game Analysis of the Metalclad Case," *Latin American Politics and Society* 43: 67–90.

Tamburini, Francesco. 2002. "Historia Y Destino De La "Doctrina Calvo": ¿Actualidad U Obsolescencia Del Pensamiento De Carlos Calvo? " *Rev. estud. hist.-juríd.* 24: 81–101, online at http://www.scielo.cl/scielo.php?script=sci_arttext&pid=S0716-54552002002400005&lng=en&nrm=iso

Tarrow, Sydney. 2005. *The New Transnational Activism*. Cambridge: Cambridge University Press.

Tarullo, Daniel K. 1987. "Beyond Normalcy in the Regulation of International Trade," *Harvard Law Review* 100: 547–628.

Taylor, Charles. 1993. "Alternative Futures: Legitimacy, Identity, and Alienation in Late Twentieth-Century Canada," in Guy Laforest (ed.), *Reconciling the Solitudes: Essays on Canadian Federalism and Nationalism*. Montreal: McGill-Queen's University Press.

Taylor, Peter J. 2000. "Izations of the World: Americanization, Modernization and Globalization," in Hay and Marsh (eds), pp. 49–70.

Tempkin, Sanchia. 2007. "Charter Fails to Address the Vital Issues Facing Lawyers," *Business Day* (May 29), p. 20.

Teubner, Gunther. 1997. "'Global Bukowina': Legal Pluralism in the World Society," in Teubner (ed.), *Global Law Without a State*. Aldershot: Dartmouth, pp. 3–28.

Text. 1999. "Canadian Memo on Investor-State Provisions," *Inside US Trade* (February 12).

Third World Network (TWN). 2001. "TWN Report on the WTO Discussion on TRIPS and Public Health" (June 20), online at www. twnside.org.sg/title/drugs1.htm

Thompson, E. P. 1975. *Whigs and Hunters: The Origin of the Black Act*. New York: Pantheon.

Tilly, Charles and Sidney Tarrow. 2007. *Contentious Politics*. Boulder, CO: Paradigm.

Tobey, Pam. 2006. "Digital Divide," *The Washington Post* (September 19), p. A2.

Tobin, Jennifer and Susan Rose-Ackerman. 2004. "Foreign Direct Investment and the Business Environment in Developing Countries: The Impact of Bilateral Investment Treaties," Center for Law, Economics and Public Policy Research Paper No. 293, Yale Law School, online at http://ssrn.com

2006. "Bilateral Investment Treaties: Do They Stimulate Foreign Direct Investment?" online at http://ssrn.com

Tomlins, Christopher L. 1993. *Law, Labour, and Ideology in the Early American Republic*. Cambridge: Cambridge University Press.

2003. "In a Wilderness of Tigers: Violence, the Discourse of English Colonizing, and the Refusals of American History," *Theoretical Inquiries in Law* 4: 451–89, online at http://www.bepress.com/til/default/vol4/iss2/art4

Tocqueville, Alexis de. 2000. *Democracy in America*, trans. Harvey C. Mansfield and Delba Winthrop. Chicago: University of Chicago Press.

Todd, Eric C. E. 1992. *The Law of Expropriation in Canada*, 2nd edn. Scarborough: Carswell.

Trade Law Centre for Southern Africa (TRALAC). 2004. "Investment Project: South African Case Study" (prepared by TRALAC for IISD) (May).

"Trade – Mexico Must Do More to Protect Foreign Investors." 2000. 1(10) LatinAdvisory.com (December), online at www.imakenews.com/texec/e_article000010599.cfm (accessed September 21, 2007).

Treanor, William Michael. 1995. "The Original Understanding of the Takings Clause and the Political Process," *Columbia Law Review* 95: 782–887.

Trebilcock, Michael J. and Robert Howse. 1995. *The Regulation of International Trade*, 2nd edn. London: Routledge.

2005. *The Regulation of International Trade*, 3rd edn. London: Routledge.

Tribe, Keith, ed. 1987. *Social Democracy and the Rule of Law: Otto Kirchheimer and Franz Neumann*. London: Allen & Unwin.

Tribe, Laurence H. 1988. *American Constitutional Law*, 2nd edn. Mineola: Foundation Press.

2001. "*Gore* v. *Bush* and Its Disguises: Freeing *Bush* v. *Gore* from Its Hall of Mirrors," *Harvard Law Review* 115: 170–304.

Triepel, Heinrich. 1924. *Goldbilanzenverordnung und Vorzugsaktien*. Berlin: Walter de Gruyter.

Trubek, David M. and Alvaros Santos, eds. 2006. *The New Law and Economic Development: A Critical Appraisal*. Cambridge: Cambridge University Press.

Tullock, Gordon. 1976. *The Vote Motive: An Essay in the Economics of Politics with Applications to the British Economy*. London: Institute for Economic Affairs.

Tully, James. 1995. *Strange Multiplicity: Constitutionalism in an Age of Diversity*. Cambridge: Cambridge University Press.

2002. "The Unfreedom of the Moderns in Comparison to Their Ideals of Constitutional Democracy," *Modern Law Review* 65: 204–28.

Tushnet, Mark. 1979. "Rethinking the Dormant Commerce Clause," *Wisconsin Law Review* 1979: 125–65.

1999. "Foreword: The New Constitutional Order and the Chastening of Constitutional Aspiration," *Harvard Law Review* 113: 26–109.

2000. "Globalization and Federalism in a Post-*Printz* World," *Tulsa Law Journal* 36: 11–41.

U.N. Centre on Transnational Corporations. 1988. *Bilateral Investment Treaties*. London: U.N. and Graham & Trotman.

U.N. Conference on Trade and Development. 1996. *World Investment Report 1996: Investment, Trade and International Policy Arrangements*. New York and Geneva: United Nations.

1997a. *World Investment Report 1997: Transnational Corporations, Market Structure and Competition Policy*. New York and London: United Nations.

1997b. *Trade and Development Report, 1997*. New York and London: United Nations.

1998a. *World Investment Report 1998: Trends and Determinants*. New York and London: United Nations.

1998b. *Bilateral Investment Treaties in the Mid-1990s*. New York and London: United Nations.

1999. *World Investment Report 1999: Foreign Direct Investment and the Challenges of Development*. New York and London: United Nations.

2000. *Bilateral Investment Treaties, 1959–1999*. New York and London: United Nations.

2002. *International Investment Instruments: A Compendium*, vol. VII. New York and Geneva: United Nations.

2003. *World Investment Report 2003: FDI Policies for Development: National and International Perspectives*. New York and Geneva: United Nations.

2004a. *World Investment Report 2004: The Shift toward Services*. New York and Geneva: United Nations.

2004b. *International Investment Agreements: Key Issues*, vol. 1. New York and Geneva: United Nations.

2004c. *The REIO Exception in MFN Treatment Clauses*. New York and Geneva: United Nations.

2005a. *World Investment Report 2005: Transnational Corporations and the Internationalization of R&D*. New York and Geneva: United Nations.

2005b. *Investor–State Disputes Arising from Investment Treaties: A Review*. New York and Geneva: United Nations.

2005c. "Investment Brief" (No. 4), online at http://www.unctad.org/en/docs/webiteiia200511_en.pdf

2006a. *International Investment Arrangements: Trends and Emerging Issues*. New York and Geneva: United Nations.

2006b. *World Investment Report 2006: FDI from Developing and Transition Economies: Implications for Development*. New York and Geneva: United Nations.

2006c. *Preserving Flexibility in IIAs: The Use of Reservations*. New York and Geneva: UNCTAD online at www.unctad.org/en/docs/iteiit20058_en.pdf

2007. *World Investment Report 2007: Transnational Corporations, Extractive Industries and Development*. New York and Geneva: United Nations.

Underkuffler, Laura S. 2003. *The Idea of Property: Its Meaning and Power*. Oxford: Oxford University Press.

2004. "Tahoe's Requiem: The Death of the Scalian View of Property and Justice," *Constitutional Commentary* 21: 727–55.

Unger, Roberto Mangabeira. 1987. *False Necessity: Anti-Necessitarian Social Theory in the Service of Radical Democracy*. Cambridge: Cambridge University Press.

1996. *What Should Legal Analysis Become?* London: Verso.

1998. *Democracy Realized*. London: Verso.

United Nations Development Programme (UNDP). 1997. *Human Development Report 1997*. New York: Oxford University Press.

1998. *Human Development Report 1998*. New York: Oxford University Press.

2002. *Human Development Report 2002*. New York: Oxford University Press.

2005. *Human Development Report 2005: International Cooperation at a Crossroads: Aid, Trade and Security in an Unequal World*. New York: United Nations Development Programme.

United Mexican States. 2001. "Petitioner's Outline of Argument," Filed February 5, 2001, in *United Mexican States v. Metalclad Corporation* in the Supreme Court of British Columbia, No. L002904, Vancouver Registry, online at www.gwv.edu/~nsarchiv/NSAEBB/NSAEBB65/ metmexa.pdf

United States, Department of Commerce (USDC). 1953. *Investment in Colombia: Conditions and Outlook for United States Investors.* Washington: U.S. Government Printing Office.

United States, Department of State. 2005. "2005 Investment Climate Statement – South Africa," online at http://www.state.gov/e/eeb/ifd/2005/42112.htm

United States Trade Representative (USTR). 2001. "Press Release" (June 25), online at www.ustr.gov

2002. "Paragraph 6 of the Doha Declaration on the TRIPS Agreement and Public Health: Second Communication from the United States," IP/C/358 (July 9), online at www.ustr.gov

2004a. "U.S. and Morocco Conclude Free Trade Agreement," online at www.ustr.gov/Document_Library/Press_Releases/2004/March/US_Morocco_Conclude_Free_Trade_Agreement.html

2004b. "U.S. Model Bilateral Investment Treaty," online at http://www.ustr.gov/assets/Trade_Sectors/Investment/Model_BIT/asset_upload_file847_6897.pdf

Upriminy, Rodrigo and Mauricio García-Villegas. 2005. "The Constitutional Court and Social Emancipation in Colombia," in Santos (ed.), pp. 66–100.

Vallely, Paul. 1999. "How the Web Saved the World," *The Independent on Sunday* (January 10), Culture, p. 2.

Van Aelst, Peter and Stefaan Walgrave. 2005. "New Media, New Movements? The Role of the Internet in Shaping the 'Anti-Globalization' Movement," in Van de Donk et al. (eds), pp. 97–122.

Van de Donk, Wim, Brian D. Loader, Paul G. Nixon, and Dieter Rucht, eds. 2005. *Cyberprotest: New Media, Citizens and Social Movements.* London: Routledge.

Van der Walt, André. 1994. "Property Rights, Land Rights, and Environmental Rights," in David van Wyk, John Dugard, Bertus de Villiers, and Dennis Davis (eds), *Rights and Constitutionalism: The New South African Legal Order.* Kenwyn: Juta, pp. 455–501.

1997. *The Constitutional Property Clause.* Kenwyn: Juta.

2002. "Moving towards Recognition of Constructive Expropriation? *Steinberg v South Peninsula Municipality 2001 4 SA 1243 (SCA),*" *Tydskrif vir Hedendaagse Romeins-Hollandse Reg* 65: 459–73.

2004. "Striving for the Better Interpretation – A Critical Reflection on the Constitutional Court's *Harksen* and *FNB* Decisions on the Property Clause," *The South African Law Journal* 121: 854–78.

2005a. "Retreating from the *FNB* Arbitrariness Test Already? *Mkontwana v Nelson Mandela Metropolitan Municipality; Bissett v Buffalo City Municipality; Transfer Rights Action Campaign v MEC for Local Government and Housing, Gauteng,*" *The South African Law Journal* 122: 75–89.

2005b. "The State's Duty to Pay 'Just and Equitable' Compensation for Expropriation: Reflections on the *DuToit* Case," *The South African Law Journal* 122: 765–78.

Vandevelde, Keneth J. 1992a. *United States Investment Treaties: Policy and Practice.* Deventer: Kluwer.

1992b. "The BIT Program: A Fifteen-Year Appraisal," *American Society of International Law, Proceedings of the 86th Annual Meeting.* Washington: ASIL pp. 532–40.

1998. "The Political Economy of a Bilateral Investment Treaty," *American Journal of International Law.* 92: 621–41.

2000. "The Economics of Bilateral Investment Treaties," *Harvard International Law Journal* 41(2): 469–502.

Vargas, Jorge A. 1994. "NAFTA, the Chiapas Rebellion, and the Emergence of Mexican Ethnic Law," *California Western International Law Journal* 25: 1–79.

Vickers, Brendan. 2003. *Investment Climate Reform in South Africa,* A Case Study Commissioned by the Department of International Development, U.K. (November) available at http://siteresources.worldbank.org/ INTWDR2005/Resources/477407-1096581040435/dfid_vickers_7.pdf

Vilas, Carlos. 1995. "Forward Back: Capitalist Restructuring, the State and the Working Class in Latin America," in Bernd Magnus and Stephen Cullenberg (eds), *Whither Marxism? Global Crises in International Perspective.* New York: Routledge, pp. 123–51.

Vogel, Thomas. 1999. "Colombia Woos Foreign Investors in Bid to End Economic Slump," *The Globe and Mail* (May 31, 1999), p. A11.

Wachman, Richard. 2005. "South Africa's Balancing Act," *The Observer* (February 13, 2005) at http://www.guardian.co.uk/southafrica/story/ 0,1411726,00.html

Wade, Sir William and Christopher Forsyth. 2004. *Administrative Law,* 9th edn. Oxford: Oxford University Press.

Wadula, Patrick. 2005. "Stake in Proudfoot's Africa arm sold to black investors," *Business Day* (February 17, 2005), p. 15.

Wagner, J. Martin. 1999. "International Investment, Expropriation and Environmental Protection," *Golden Gate University Law Review* 29: 465–527.

Wai, Robert. 2003. "Countering, Branding, Dealing: Using Economic and Social Rights in and around the International Trade Regime," *European Journal of International Law* 14: 35–84.

Wälde, Thomas. 2003. "Introductory Note to SVEA Court of Appeals: Czech Republic v. CME Czech Republic B.V.," *International Legal Materials* 42: 915–18.

2005. "Remedies and Compensation in International and Investment Law," transnational-dispute-management.com (November) 2(5).

Wälde, Thomas and Stephen Dow. 2000. "Treaties and Regulatory Risk in Infrastructure Investment," *Journal of World Trade* 34(2): 1–61.

Wälde, Thomas and Abba Kolo. 2001. "Environmental Regulation, Investment Protection and 'Regulatory Taking' in International Law," *International and Comparative Law Quarterly* 50: 811–48.

Waldron, Jeremy. "Precommitment and Disagreement," in Larry Alexander (ed.) *Constitutionalism: Philosophical Foundation*. Cambridge: Cambridge University Press, pp. 271–99.

Walker, Neil. 2001. "The EU and the WTO: Constitutionalism in a New Key," in Gráinne de Búrca and Joanne Scott (eds), *The EU and the WTO: Legal and Constitutional Issues*. Oxford: Hart, pp. 31–57.

2002. "The Idea of Constitutional Pluralism," *Modern Law Review* 65: 317.

Walker, R. B. J. 1993. *Inside/Outside: International Relations as Political Theory*. Cambridge: Cambridge University Press.

Wallace, Cynthia Day. 1983. *Legal Control of the Multinational Enterprise*. The Hague: Martinus Nijhoff.

Wallach, Lori and Michelle Sforza. 1999. *Whose Trade Organization? Corporate Globalization and the Erosion of Democracy*. Washington: Public Citizen.

Wayne, Leslie. 2001. "For Trade Protestors, 'Slower, Sadder Songs,'" *The New York Times* (October 28), p. B1.

Webb, William H. 1994. "Letter from President of Phillip Morris Inc. to Standing Committee on Health" (May 5) [Unpublished].

Webb-Vidal, Andy. 2006. "Colombia Sell-Off a 'Win–Win Situation,'" *Financial Times* (July 27), p. 10.

Weekes, John M. 1999. "Why Canada Needs the WTO," *Time* (Cndn. ed.) (November 29), pp. 32–3.

Weiler, J. H. H. 1994. "A Quiet Revolution: The European Court of Justice and Its Interlocutors," *Comparative Political Studies* 26: 510–34.

1996. "European Neo-Constitutionalism: In Search of Foundations for the European Constitutional Order," *Political Studies* 64: 517–83.

1999. *The Constitution of Europe: "Do the Clothes Have an Emperor?" and Other Essays on European Integration*. Cambridge: Cambridge University Press.

Weiler, Todd J. 2000. "'The Minimum Standard of Treatment' in International Law: Some Old Cases, Some New," *Canadian International Lawyer* 3: 207–11.

2005a. "Methanex Corp. v. U.S.A.: Turning the Page on NAFTA Chapter Eleven?" *Journal of World Investment and Trade* 6: 903–21.

2005b. "Good Faith and Regulatory Transparency: The Story of *Metalclad v. Mexico*," in Weiler (ed.), pp. 701–45.

ed. 2004. *NAFTA Investment Law and Arbitration: Pats Issues, Current Practice, Future Prospects*. Ardsley, NY: Transnational.

ed. 2005. *International Investment Law and Arbitration: Leading Cases from the ICSID, NAFTA, Bilateral Treaties and Customary International Law*. London: Cameron May.

Weiss, Linda. 1998. *The Myth of the Powerless State*. Ithaca, NY: Cornell University Press.

2005. "Global Governance, National Strategies: How Industrialized States Make Room to Move under the WTO," *Review of International Political Economy* 12: 723–49.

Weitzman, Hal. 2006. "Morales Pledges to Nationalise Mining Industry in Bolivia," *Financial Times* (May 9), p. A8.

Weizman, Leif. 1998. "Colombia: Model Bilateral Investment Treaty of 1993," *Inter-American Legal Materials* 8: 113–25.

Wells, Jr., Louis T. (1998) "God and Fair Competition: Does the Foreign Direct Investor Face Still Other Risks in Emerging Markets," in Moran (ed.), pp. 15–43.

Wells, Louis T. and Rafiq Ahmed. 2007. *Making Foreign Investment Safe: Property Rights and International Sovereignty*. Oxford: Oxford University Press.

West, Gerald and Ethel Tarazona. 2001. *Investment Insurance and Developmental Impact*. Washington, DC: World Bank.

Weston, Burns H. 1975. "'Constructive Takings' under International Law: A Modest Foray into the Problem of 'Creeping Expropriation,'" *Virginia Journal of International Law* 16: 103–75.

Wheat, Andrew. 1995. "Toxic Shock in a Mexican Village," *Multinational Monitor* (October) 16(10), online at www.essential.org/monitor/hyper/mm1095.07.html

White, G. Edward. 1993. *Justice Oliver Wendell Holmes: Law and the Inner Self*. New York: Oxford University Press.

Wiesner, Eduardo A. 1993. "ANCOM: A New Attitude toward Foreign Investment?" *University of Miami Inter-American Law Review* 24: 435–65.

Wild, Jr. Payson S. 1939. "International Law and Mexican Oil," *The Quarterly Journal of Inter-American Relations* 1: 5–21.

Williams, Raymond. 1961. *The Long Revolution*. Harmondsworth: Penguin Books.

Williams, Sir John Fischer. 1928. "International Law and the Property of Aliens," *British Yearbook of International Law* 9: 1–30.

Wilson, Timothy Ross. 2000. "Trade Rules: Ethyl Corporation v. Canada (NAFTA Chapter 11)," *NAFTA: Law and Business Review of the Americas* 52: 205–41.

Wines, Michael. 2006. "AIDS Cited in the Climb in South Africa's Death Rate" *The New York Times* (September 8), p. A6.

Winham, Gilbert R. 1994. "NAFTA and the Trade Policy Revolution of the 1980s: A Canadian Perspective," *International Journal* 49: 472–508.

Winston, Morton. 1998. "U.S. Litigation with regard to Corporate Responsibility for Human Rights" Conference on Companies and Human Rights, University of Antwerp, Institute of Development Policy and Management, Antwerp Belgium (November 13, 1998).

Witherell, William H. 1995. "The OECD Multilateral Agreement on Investment," *Transnational Corporations* 4(2): 1–14.

Woellert, Lorraine. 2006. "Tobacco May Be Partying Too Soon," *Business Week* (July 24), pp. 26–9.

Wolin, Sheldon. 1989. *The Presence of the Past: Essays on the State and the Constitution.* Baltimore, MD: Johns Hopkins University Press.

1996. "Fugitive Democracy," in Benhabib (ed.), pp. 31–45.

Wood, Grace and Maria Egyed. 1994. *Risk Assessment for the Combustion Products of Methylcyclopentadienyl Manganese Tricarbonyl (MMT) in Gasoline.* Ottawa: Environmental Health Directorate, Health Canada (December 6), online at http://www.hc-sc.gc.ca/ewh-semt/pubs/air/combustion-e.html

Woolman, Stuart, Theunix Roux, Jonathan Klaaren, Anthony Stein, Matthew Chaskalson, and Michael Bishop, eds. 2004. *Constitutional Law of South Africa*, 2nd edn. Kenwyn: Juta.

Workers Rights Consortium (WRC). 2001. "WRC Investigation Re: Complaint against Kukdong (Mexico) Report and Recommendations" (June 20), online at http://www.workersrights.org/Freports/Report_Kukdong_2.pdf

World Bank. 1993. *The East Asian Miracle: Economic Growth and Public Policy.* New York: Oxford University Press.

1997. *World Development Report 1997: The State in a Changing World.* New York Oxford University Press.

2007. *Global Economic Prospects: Managing the Next Wave of Globalization.* Washington, DC: IBRD/The World Bank.

World Health Organization (WHO). 2006. Public Health: Innovation and Intellectual Property Rights (Report of the Commission on Intellectual Property Rights, Innovation and Public Health), online at http://www.who.int/intellectualproperty/documents/thereport/CIPIHReport23032006.pdf

World Trade Organization (WTO). 1996. *Trade Policy Review: Colombia.* Geneva: World Trade Organization (February 1997).

World Trade Organization Secretariat. 1996. "Trade and Foreign Direct Investment," *World Trade and Arbitration Materials* 8: 37–100.

Wyatt, Derek and Alan Dashwood. 1993. *European Community Law*. London: Sweet & Maxwell.

Yackee, Jason W. 2006. "Sacrificing Sovereignty: Bilateral Investment Treaties, International Arbitration, and the Quest for Capital," USC Center in Law, Economics and Organization Research Paper No. C06–15, online at http://law.usc.edu/academics/assets/docs/C06_15_paper.pdf

Young, Iris Marion Young. 1990. *Justice and the Politics of Difference*. Princeton, NJ: Princeton University Press.

Young, Oran R. 1999. *Governance in World Affairs*. Ithaca, NY: Cornell University Press.

Zasloff, Jonathan. 2003. "Law and the Shaping of American Foreign Policy: From the Gilded Age to the New Era," *New York University Law Review* 78: 239–320.

Zayed, Joseph, Morad Mikhail, Sylvain Loranger, Greg Kennedy, and Gilles L'Esparance. 1996. "Exposure of Taxi Drivers and Office Workers to Total and Respirable Manganese in an Urban Environment," *American Industrial Hygiene Association Journal* 57(4): 376–81.

Zayed, Joseph, Christiane Thibault, Lise Gareau, and Greg Kennedy. 1999. "Airborne Manganese Particulates and Methylcyclopentadienyl Manganese Tricarbonyl (MMT) at Selected Outdoor Sites in Montreal," *NeuroToxicology* 20(2–3): 151–8.

Ziff, Bruce. 2005. "Taking' Liberties: Protections for Private Property in Canada," in Elizabeth Cooke (ed.), *Modern Studies in Property Law*, vol. 3. Oxford: Hart, pp. 341–60.

Zimmerman, Jill. 2005. "Property on the Line: Is an Expropriation-Centred Land Reform Constitutionally Permissible?" *The South African Law Journal* 122: 378–418.

Zoellick, Robert B. 2001. "Countering Terror with Trade," *Washington Post* (September 20), p. A35.

Zumbansen, Peer. 2002. "Piercing the Legal Veil: Commercial Arbitration and Transnational Law," *European Law Journal* 8: 400–32.

2006. "Transnational Law," in Jan M. Smits (ed.), *Elgar Encyclopedia of Comparative Law*. Cheltenham: Edward Elgar, pp. 738–54.

## CASES

### Canada

*Attorney General of Canada* v. *S. D. Myers* [2004] FC 38 (T.D.).

*Canada (A.G.)* v. *JTI-Macdonald Corp.* [2007] SCC 30.

*Council of Canadians* v. *Canada (Attorney General* [2006] Ontario Court of Appeal Docket No. C43995 (November 30).

*Council of Canadians* v. *Canada (Attorney General)* [2005] OJ No. 3422 (Ont. Sup. Ct.).

*Delgamuukw* v. *British Columbia* [1997] 3 SCR 1010 (SCC).
*Friends of the Oldman River Society* v. *Canada* (1992) 88 DLR (4th) 1 at 7 (SCC).
*Irwin Toy* v. *Quebec (Attorney-General)*, [1989] 1 SCR 927.
*Manitoba Fisheries Ltd.* v. *The Queen* (1978) 88 D.L.R. (3d) 462 (SCC).
*Mariner Real Estate Ltd.* v. *Nova Scotia* (Attorney General) 68 LCR 1 (NSCA 1999).
*R.* v. *Appleby* (No. 2) (1976) 76 D.L.R. (3d) 110 (NBAD).
*R.* v. *Edwards Books and Art Ltd.* [1986] 2 SCR 713.
*R.* v. *Tener* [1985] 1 SCR 533.
*Reference re section 94(2) of the Motor Vehicle Act (B.C.)*, [1970] 2 SCR 486.
*RJR-MacDonald Inc.* v. *Canada* (1995) 127 D.L.R (4th) 1.
*Sparrow* v. *R.* [1990] 1 SCR 1075 (SCC).
*United Mexican States* v. *Metalclad*, 2001 BCSC 664 (BCSC).

## Colombia
C-037/94
C-452/95
C-358/96

## Europe
*Brunner et al.* v. *The European Union Treaty* [1994] 1 CMLR 57.
*Commission* v. *Belgium* [1983] ECR 531.
*E.C. Commission* v. *France* [1981] CMLR 743.
*Generalitat de Cataluna* [1994] 1 CMLR 887 (ECJ).
*James* v. *The United Kingdom* (1986) 98 Eur. Ct. H. R. (ser. A) 9.
*Sporrong & Lönnroth* v. *Sweden* (1982) 52 Eur. Ct. H.R. (ser. A).

## GATT/WTO
*Asbestos*. 2001. WTO Appellate Body Report, *European Communities – Measures Affecting Asbestos and Asbestos-Containing Products* (WT/DS135/AB/R) (March 12) (adopted).
*Reformulated Gasoline*. 1996. WTO Appellate Body Report, *United States – Standards for Reformulated and Conventional Gasoline* (WT/DS2/AB/R) (April 29) (adopted).
*Shrimp/Turtle*. 1998. WTO Appellate Body Report, *United States – Import Prohibition of Certain Shrimp and Shrimp Products* (WT/DS58/AB/R) (October 12) (adopted).
2001. WTO Appellate Body Report, *United States – Import Prohibition of Certain Shrimp and Shrimp Products, Recourse to Article 21.5 of the DSU by Malaysia* (WT/DS58/AB/RW) (October 22) (adopted).
*Thai Cigarette*. 1990. GATT Panel Report, *Thailand – Restrictions on Importation of and Internal Taxes on Cigarettes*. DS10/R-37S/200 (November 7) (adopted).

*Tuna/Dolphin I*. 1991. GATT Panel Report, *United States – Restrictions on Import of Tuna* (DS21/R-39S/155) (September 3) (unadopted).
*Tuna/Dolphin II*. 1994. GATT Panel Report, *United States – Restrictions on Import of Tuna* (DS29/R) (June 16) (unadopted).

## Hungary
*Hungarian Benefits Case*, Decision 43/1995 (30 June), in Vicki C. Jackson and Mark Tushnet, *Comparative Constitutional Law*, 2nd edn. New York: Foundation Press, pp. 1709–20.

## International
*Amoco International Finance Corp.* v. *Iran* (1990) 83 International Law Reports 501
*Aragonesa de Publicidad Exterior SA and Publivia SAE v. Departmento de Sanidad y Seguridad Social de la Case Concerning the Factory at Chorzów (Claim for Indemnity)*. 1928. P.C.I.J. (ser. A) No. 17 (September 13)
*Compañía del Desarrollo de Santa Elena, S.A. and the Republic of Costa Rica* (2000) ICSID Case No. ARB/96/1.
*L. F. H. Neer and Pauline E. Neer* v. *Mexico*. 1926. Journal of the American Society of International Law 21 (1927): 555.
*Norwegian Shipowner's Claims (Norway* v. *USA)*. 1922. Reports of International Arbitral Awards 309–346 (October 13).
*Oscar Chinn Case (U.K.* v. *Belgium)*. 1934. P.C.I.J. (ser. A/B) No. 63 (December 12).
*Revere Copper* v. *OPIC* (1980) 56 International Law Reports 258.
*Southern Pacific Properties (Middle East) Limited* v. *Arab Republic of Egypt* (1993) 32 International Legal Materials 933.

## International Investment Arbitration
*ADF Group Inc.* v. *United States*. 2003. ICSID Reports 6: 470.
*Aguas del Tunari, S. A.* v. *Republic of Bolivia*, 2005. Decision on Respondent's Objections to Jurisdiction. [October 21], World Trade and Arbitration Materials 18 (2006): 271–376. (ICSID Case No. ARB/03/3)
*Azurix* v. *Argentine Republic*. 2006. ICSID Case No. ARB/01/12 [July 14]
*CME Czech Republic BV* v. *Czech Republic*. 2001 (Partial Award). ICSID Reports 9(2006): 121–264.
*CMS Gas Transmission Company* c. *República Argentina*. 2005. Case No. ARB/01/08.
*Compañia de Aguas del Aconquija* v. *Argentina*. 2001. International Legal Materials (2001) 40: 425–53.
*El Paso Energy International Company* v. *The Argentine Republic*. 2006. ICSID Case No. ARB/03/15 (April 27)

*Feldman* v. *Mexico*. 2002. International Legal Materials 42 (2003): 625–82.

*GAMI* v. *Mexico*. 2004. International Legal Materials 44 (2005): 545–68.

*Genin* v. *Estonia*, 2001. ICSID Case No. ARB/99/2 (June 25)

*International Thunderbird Gaming Corporation* v. *Mexico*. 2006. Arbitral Award [January 26] World Trade and Arbitration Materials 18 (2006): 59–268.

*Lanco International Inc.* v. *Argentina*. 2004. International Legal Materials (2001) 40: 457–73.

*Lauder* v. *Czech Republic*. 2001. ICSID Reports 9 (2006): 62–112.

*LG&E Energy Corp.* v. *Argentine Republic*. 2006. ICSID Case No. ARB/02/01 (October 3)

*Loewen* v. *United States*. 2003. International Legal Materials 42 (2003): 811–51.

*Metalclad Corporation and the United Mexican States*. 2000. World Trade and Arbitration Materials 13 (2001): 47–80.

*Methanex* v. *U.S.A.*. 2002. First Partial Award [August 7], online at www. state.gov/documents/organization/12613.pdf

*Methanex* v. *U.S.A.* 2005. Final Award of the Trbunal on Jurisdiction and Merits [August 3] International Legal Materials 44: 1345–464.

*Methanex* v. *U.S.A.* 2005. Final Award of the Tribunal on Jurisdiction and Merits [August 3] International Legal Materials 44: 1345–1464.

*Mondev International Ltd.* v. *United States*. 2002. International Legal Materials (2003) 42: 85–120.

*Occcidental Exploration and Production Company* v. *Ecuador*. 2004. 43 International Legal Materials 43 (2004): 1248.

*Pope & Talbot and Government of Canada*. 2001. Award on Merits Phase 2 [April 10]. World Trade and Arbitration Materials (2001) 13(4): 61–155.

*Pope & Talbot and Government of Canada*. 2002. Award in Respect of Damages. [May 31] International Legal Materials (2002) 14: 1347.

*Pope & Talbot Inc and the Government of Canada*, 2000a. Interim Award. [June 26]. World Trade and Arbitration Materials 13 (2001): 19–59.

*Pope & Talbot Inc and the Government of Canada*. 2000b. Motion for Interim Measures. [August 7] online at http://www.international.gc.ca/tna-nac/documents/pubdoc6.pdf

*Pope & Talbot Inc and the Government of Canada*. 2000c. Decision [September 6] online at http://www.international.gc.ca/tna-nac/documents/pubdoc8.pdf

*S. D. Myers, Inc.* v. *Government of Canada*. 2001. International Legal Materials (2001) 40:1408.

*Saluka Investments BV* v. *The Czech Republic*. 2006. Partial Award [17 March] Permanent Court of Arbitration under UNCITRAL Rules 1976 online at http://www.pca-cpa.org/upload/files/SAL-CZ%20Partial%20Award%2020170306.pdf

*Tecnicas Medioambientales TECMED S. A.* v. *Mexico*. 2003. International Legal Materials (2004) 43: 133.

*United Parcel Service of America Inc.* v. *Government of Canada.* 2007. Award on the Merits (May 24) online at http://www.naftaclaims.com/Disputes/Canada/UPS/UPS-Canada-Final_Award_and_Dissent.pdf
*Waste Management* v. *Mexico.* 2004. International Legal Materials 43 (2004): 967–1008.

## Philippines
*Tanada* v. *Angara* 272 SCRA 18 (1997), online at www.supremecourt.gov.ph/jurisprudence/1997/may1997/118295.htm

## South Africa
*Certification of the Amended Text of the Constitution of the Republic of South Africa (Second Certification Decision).* 1996. (2) SA 97 (CC).
*Du Toit* v. *Minister of Transport.* 2005. Case CCT 22/04.
*First National Bank of South Africa Ltd t/a Westbank* v. *Commissioner, South African Revenue Services* (FNB). 2002. (4) SA 768 (CC).
*Government of Republic of South Africa* v. *Grootboom.* 2000. (1) SA 46 (CC)
*Harksen* v. *Lane.* 1998. (1) SA 300 (CC).
*Mkontwana* v. *Nelson Mandela Metropolitan Municipality.* 2004. Case CCT 57/03.
*Port Elizabeth Municipality* v. *Various Occupiers.* 2005. (1) SA 217 (CC).
*Steinberg* v. *South Peninsula Municipality.* 2001. (4) SA 1243 (SCA).

## United Kingdom
*Secretary of State for Defence* v. *Guardian Newspapers Ltd* [1985] AC 339.

## United States
*Baker* v. *Boston,* 12 Pick. 183 (1831).
*Berman* v. *Parker* 348 U.S. 26 (1954).
*Brown* v. *Washington Legal Foundation,* 538 U.S. 216 (2003)
*Bush* v. *Gore,* 531 U.S. 98 (2000).
*Charles River Bridge* v. *Warren Bridge,* 36 US (11 Pet.) 420 (1837).
*Commonwealth* v. *Alger,* 7 Cush. 53 (1851).
*Crosby* v. *National Foreign Trade Council,* 530 U.S. 363 (2000).
*Dolan* v. *City of Tigard,* 129 L. Ed. 2d 304 (1994).
*Eastern Enterprises* v. *Apfel,* 524 U.S. 498 (1997).
*Hawaii Housing Authority* v. *Midkiff,* 467 U.S. 228 (1984).
*Kaiser Aetna* v. *United States,* 444 U.S. 164, 175 (1979).
*Kelo* v. *City of New London,* 545 U.S. 469 (2005).
*Lingle* v. *Chevron U.S.A. Inc.,* 544 U.S. 528 (2005).
*Lochner* v. *New York,* 198 U.S. 45 (1904).
*Loretto* v. *Teleprompter Manhattan CATV Corp.,*458 U.S. 419 (1982).

*Lucas v. South Carolina Coastal Council*, 112 S.Ct. 2886 (1992).

*McCulloch v. Maryland*, 17 U.S. (4 Wheat.) 316 (1819).

*New York Times v. Sullivan*, 376 U.S. 254 (1964).

*Nollan v. California Coastal Commission*, 483 U.S. 825 (1986).

*Palazzolo v. Rhode Island*, 522 U.S. 606.

*Parratt v. Taylor*, 451 US 527 (1981).

*Penn Central Transportation Co. v. New York City*, 438 U.S. 104 (1977).

*Pennsylvania Coal v. Mahon*, 438 U.S. 393 at 1569 (1922).

*Petition of Mt. Washington Road Co.*, 35 N.H. 134 (1857).

*Phillips v. Washington Legal Foundation*, 524 U.S. 156 (1998).

*San Diego Gas & Electricity Co. v. San Diego*, 450 U.S. 621 (1981).

*Sierra Club v. USEPA*, 118 F. 3d 1324 (9th Cir. 1997).

*Tahoe-Sierra Preservation Council, Inc. v. Tahoe Regional Planning Agency*, 535 U.S. 302 (2002).

*Trustees of Dartmouth College v. Woodward*, 17 US (4 Wheat.) 517 (1819).

*United States v. Carolene Products Co.*, 304 U.S. 144 (1938).

*Virginia State Board of Pharmacy v. Virginia Citizens Consumer Council*, 425 U.S. 748 (1976).

*Williamson v. Lee Optical Inc.*, 348 U.S. 483 (1955).

# INDEX